I0868909

Principles and Practices of Small-Scale Sport Event Management

Anestis Fotiadis
Zayed University, UAE

Chris Vassiliadis
University of Macedonia, Greece

A volume in the Advances in Business Strategy and Competitive Advantage (ABSCA) Book Series

IGI Global
PUBLISHER of TIMELY KNOWLEDGE

Published in the United States of America by
IGI Global
Business Science Reference (an imprint of IGI Global)
701 E. Chocolate Avenue
Hershey PA, USA 17033
Tel: 717-533-8845
Fax: 717-533-8661
E-mail: cust@igi-global.com
Web site: http://www.igi-global.com

Library of Congress Cataloging-in-Publication Data

Names: Fotiadis, Anestis, 1976- editor. | Vassiliadis, Chris, 1968- editor.

Title: Principles and practices of small-scale sport event management / Anestis Fotiadis and Chris Vassiliadis, editors.
Description: Hershey, PA : Business Science Reference, 2020. | Includes bibliographical references and index. | Summary: "This book examines the successful organization and planning of small-scale sporting events"-- Provided by publisher.
Identifiers: LCCN 2019058349 (print) | LCCN 2019058350 (ebook) | ISBN 9781799847571 (hardcover) | ISBN 9781799850526 (paperback) | ISBN 9781799847588 (ebook)
Subjects: LCSH: Hosting of sporting events.
Classification: LCC GV712 .P75 2020 (print) | LCC GV712 (ebook) | DDC 796.04--dc23
LC record available at https://lccn.loc.gov/2019058349
LC ebook record available at https://lccn.loc.gov/2019058350

This book is published in the IGI Global book series Advances in Business Strategy and Competitive Advantage (ABSCA) (ISSN: 2327-3429; eISSN: 2327-3437)

British Cataloguing in Publication Data
A Cataloguing in Publication record for this book is available from the British Library.

Advances in Business Strategy and Competitive Advantage (ABSCA) Book Series

ISSN:2327-3429
EISSN:2327-3437

Editor-in-Chief: Patricia Ordóñez de Pablos, Universidad de Oviedo, Spain

MISSION

Business entities are constantly seeking new ways through which to gain advantage over their competitors and strengthen their position within the business environment. With competition at an all-time high due to technological advancements allowing for competition on a global scale, firms continue to seek new ways through which to improve and strengthen their business processes, procedures, and profitability.

The **Advances in Business Strategy and Competitive Advantage (ABSCA) Book Series** is a timely series responding to the high demand for state-of-the-art research on how business strategies are created, implemented and re-designed to meet the demands of globalized competitive markets. With a focus on local and global challenges, business opportunities and the needs of society, the **ABSCA** encourages scientific discourse on doing business and managing information technologies for the creation of sustainable competitive advantage.

COVERAGE

- Strategy Performance Management
- Tacit Knowledge
- Adaptive Enterprise
- Entrepreneurship & Innovation
- International Business Strategy
- Core Competencies
- Customer-Orientation Strategy
- Innovation Strategy
- Outsourcing
- Balanced Scorecard

IGI Global is currently accepting manuscripts for publication within this series. To submit a proposal for a volume in this series, please contact our Acquisition Editors at Acquisitions@igi-global.com or visit: http://www.igi-global.com/publish/.

The Advances in Business Strategy and Competitive Advantage (ABSCA) Book Series (ISSN 2327-3429) is published by IGI Global, 701 E. Chocolate Avenue, Hershey, PA 17033-1240, USA, www.igi-global.com. This series is composed of titles available for purchase individually; each title is edited to be contextually exclusive from any other title within the series. For pricing and ordering information please visit http://www.igi-global.com/book-series/advances-business-strategy-competitive-advantage/73672. Postmaster: Send all address changes to above address.

Titles in this Series

For a list of additional titles in this series, please visit:
http://www.igi-global.com/book-series/advances-business-strategy-competitive-advantage/73672

Entrepreneurial Innovation for Securing Long-Term Growth in a Short-Term Economy
Jorge Gamez-Gutierrez (Universitaria Agustiniana, Colombia) and Jose Manuel Saiz-Alvarez (Tecnologico de Monterrey, Spain)
Business Science Reference • © 2020 • 300pp • H/C (ISBN: 9781799835684) • US $215.00

Handbook of Research on Transmedia Storytelling, Audience Engagement, and Business Strategies
Víctor Hernández-Santaolalla (University of Seville, Spain) and Mónica Barrientos-Bueno (University of Seville, Spain)
Business Science Reference • © 2020 • 457pp • H/C (ISBN: 9781799831198) • US $265.00

Developing Creative Economy Through Disruptive Leadership Emerging Research and Opportunities
Kristin Joyce Tardif (University of Arkansas – Fort Smith, USA)
Business Science Reference • © 2020 • 226pp • H/C (ISBN: 9781799834168) • US $185.00

Knowledge Management, Innovation, and Entrepreneurship in a Changing World
Murray Eugene Jennex (San Diego State University, USA)
Business Science Reference • © 2020 • 463pp • H/C (ISBN: 9781799823551) • US $215.00

Developing Entrepreneurial Competencies for Start-Ups and Small Business
Jarmila Šebestová (Silesian University in Opava, Czech Republic)
Business Science Reference • © 2020 • 316pp • H/C (ISBN: 9781799827146) • US $225.00

Leadership and Followership in an Organizational Change Context
Sajjad Nawaz Khan (University Malaysia Sarawak, Malaysia) and Abdul Halim Busari (University Malaysia Sarawak, Malaysia)
Business Science Reference • © 2020 • 300pp • H/C (ISBN: 9781799828075) • US $225.00

For an entire list of titles in this series, please visit:
http://www.igi-global.com/book-series/advances-business-strategy-competitive-advantage/73672

IGI Global
PUBLISHER of TIMELY KNOWLEDGE

701 East Chocolate Avenue, Hershey, PA 17033, USA
Tel: 717-533-8845 x100 • Fax: 717-533-8661
E-Mail: cust@igi-global.com • www.igi-global.com

Table of Contents

Detailed Table of Contents

The chapter shows the variety of sporting events and hints at the potential of developing these alternative activities. In order to pursue the above objective of the chapter, the various criteria for categorizing sporting events are presented first. The chapter then focuses on providing relevant examples to inform the reader about the practices and trends of sporting events that are prevalent internationally. The reality of the emergence of a variety of sporting events and activities locally and internationally is an element of interpretation of modern lifestyles. At the same time, a careful study and analysis of the varieties and types of sports, facilitates managers, and designers of sports activities and sports programs at a visitor destination is presented to identify easily opportunities for their development and exploitation.

This work aims to investigate the key role of local community through volunteerism experience in small-scale sport events and the impact that the community engagement in small sport events can have on the local destination in terms of sustainable tourism. To do this analysis, the authors take into consideration the triple bottom line approach. Given the interdisciplinary character of sustainability, the chapter investigates the relation between small sport events and community, underlining two main aspects: the strategic role of volunteers in terms of community capabilities and the impact that small sport events have on local community in terms of social cohesion and local identity. Small-scale sport events, indeed, strengthen the sense of community and tradition, thus attracting visitors. In the last section of the chapter, an interesting case study and a series of sustainable tourism indicators are illustrated.

With issues related to overtourism and, more specifically, tourismphobia, the impacts of any tourism-related activities are being scrutinised. Events falling under this category are therefore being scrutinised. Community events having been hailed to contribute to bridge the gap between locals and visitors, this chapter is going to look at small scale events and, more specifically, community sport event in Winchester (UK). Research carried by Seraphin et al. provided evidence that locals are overall very supportive of events going on in the city. That said, the research did not look at types of events, but events overall. This chapter is therefore going to provide a

Foreword

This textbook is the perfect introduction to be informed about the essentials of the *Principles and Practices of Small-Scale Sport Event Management* and related aspects whether you are a practitioner, a student or a researcher interested in this knowledge field.

The structure of this book is user friendly oriented and formatted. The content of each chapter is based on the scope to give to the readership a well description and contemporary literature but also future trends that can affect positively or negatively the small- scaled sport events market (S-SSEM). The authors of each chapter are researchers that contribute to the knowledge field bringing "fresh" ideas to the readers of this book. The book gives with the contribution of diagrams, tables and figures, data sets, e and web Links, case studies and paradigms and useful statistical information, a wide range of alternative sources to build a good knowledge background about the topic of S-SSEM. I can define some basic sections of this book that are useful for the readership that is interested in organizing small scaled sport events, namely the following parts:

- S-SSEM consumer behavior with case studies from different countries e.g., motor sport events, and non-motor sport events
- CSR (corporate social responsibility) aspects
- Volunteerism and social aspects with emphasis to the local communities
- Organizational and managerial methodologies, resource planning functional aspects, strategies and planning procedures
- Typological categorization(s) and the effective management of sport events
- Financial and sponsorship related aspects
- Event marketing and management aspects
- Proposals for managerial applications

I think finally for the above reasons that this book can contribute to enforce, the lacking literature review for S-SSEM and the related research and practice of this knowledge area. This book highlights the importance of creating sustainable small-scaled sport events but also the effective management, finance and marketing strategies, the volunteer and consumer behavior, the business environmental effects through the prism of ethical considerations and community engagement, the data & successful event business information source management in sport activities and data analytics.

Tzung-Cheng (T. C.) Huan
Tainan University of Technology, Taiwan

Tzung-Cheng (T. C.) Huan *is President of Tainan University of Technology, Taiwan.*

Preface

THE SMALL-SCALE EVENT PROBLEMATIC

Due to the ease of participation, small sporting events are a good opportunity to improve the quality of life for groups of people who do not belong to the category of professional athletes. Careful planning of sports that could be developed strategically by the administrative authority of an area in order to attract visitors, strengthen the health of residents and residents in the area are important milestones in a sustainable development plan for a sports event. In this effort, small-scale sporting events contribute positively to the economic and social balance caused by the effects they have, especially on sports and participation teams of non-professional athletes, e.g. such as quality of life, income for professionals, liveliness and human activity in outdoor areas or areas with reduced or aging population, creating shared empathy for the need for exercise in wider population groups and volunteering, employment opportunities and health and lifelong support members of society. Small-scale sport events can be part of the whole strategic destination-planning program. They can contribute to the local financial and social aspects of such kind of planning programs. Small-scale sport events can have an important impact on local host communities.

In many cases, small sporting events can and do support the effort to reduce seasonal demand fluctuations for visits to spring or winter destinations. Careful study of the characteristics of an area that can, along with attractions, appropriate infrastructure and services, contribute to this effort would enhance the prospects and potential for the implementation of a portfolio of selections suitable for a variety of small-scale sports that could help strengthen visitors. in a geographical area. Studying the relevant literature, one realizes that there is a significant gap in the research and analysis of the usefulness of the application of management workshops in small-scale sporting events. In fact, the literature is limited even to the issues of detecting the positive and / or negative effects caused by the organization of small-scale sports events. In difficult times, the smallest events in the field of sports are easier to adapt their strategies to the new conditions. Small-scale events do not present the high risk of failure experienced by large-scale or mega events, they also need fewer human, financial and infrastructure/ facility resources. Larger-scale sporting events should address the high risks of failure and the high adverse effects on participants like the companies and organizations contracted to the event. Small-scale events can meet the particular interests of groups of athletes who would not be interested in wider groups of professional athletes. For example, the emergence of some historical sports activities in a geographical unit may not be of interest to professional athletes but to non-professionals who are motivated by, among other things, leisure, socializing and having fun opportunities.

THE NEED FOR ORGANIZING SMALL-SCALE SPORT EVENTS

In the final writing and publishing process of this book, we all realized that the need to support sports and strengthen our physical condition remains a biological requirement that during the covi19 epidemic seemed to be a major priority in the quarantine's bizarre daily life. Thus, this book has made another important contribution to the development of this primary commodity, which is in line with our biological nature. The need for exercise and group approach in common areas has been replaced by the pandemic in several countries by limited and geographically defined physical activity control and the need for protection. The sport has remained active even in the face of restrictions imposed by governments on a need that has evolved into home sports activities with or without the support of new technologies. There are organizations today such as the *VR Institute of Health and Exercise* that highlight the importance and contribution of new technologies in the development of physical movement in individuals and between groups. We therefore believe that changes in the environment of societies and businesses can affect in the near future, our needs and perceptions for more participation in sports services, for volunteering in the promotion of sports and positive changes in our lifestyle. We also believe that after returning from the epidemic crisis, people will appreciate the physical need for exercise, communication, and body motion even more.

THE CHAPTERS AND THEIR CONTENT

To support the readership to understand the wide range of this knowledge area we present at next the content of this book based on the involved book-chapters.

Sports Management, Project Management, and Sports Event Management

In this chapter the readership can be informed about the planning procedures and the similarities and the differences between Sport Event Management, Project Management and Sports Management. The scope of this chapter is to enforce the point of view that the small-scale sport events are related significantly on project management as they have a specific budget, a specific timeframe, and specific performance criteria. The difference is that they focus on customer perspective and local society contribution.

Different Types of Sport Events

This chapter sets out the variety of sporting events and hint at the potential of developing these alternative activities. In order to pursue the above objective of the chapter, the various criteria for categorizing sporting events are presented first. The chapter then focuses on providing relevant examples to inform the reader about the practices and trends of sporting events that are prevalent internationally. The reality of the emergence of a variety of sporting events and activities locally and internationally is an element of interpretation of modern lifestyles. At the same time, a careful study and analysis of the varieties and types of sports, facilitates managers and such as designers of sports activities and sports programs at a visitor destination, to identify easily and identify opportunities for their development and exploitation.

The Engagement of Community and Volunteers in a Small-Scale Sport Events and the Impact on Sustainable Tourism

The aim of the chapter is to define the characteristics of sport community and volunteering network, taking in consideration the previous literature studies on the subject and the reasons that push people to volunteer. The key role of the community and volunteers in the organization of small-scale sport event is illustrated, and the impact of event organization on local community has been explained through the triple bottom line approach (social, economic and environmental pillars). This work provides a list of indicators to measure the sustainable impact of the event on the local community. Best practices in community engagement and volunteer management in an event organization are described, focusing the attention on the recruiting and selection stage, training, and development. A study case is illustrated at the end of the chapter as evidence of the community and volunteer engagement in a small-scale sport event.

Small-Scale Sport Events and Local Community Perception

This chapter is an adoption of simultaneously connected two approaches namely the inductive and deductive approaches. From a methodological point of view, the study is going to be based on data collected from a previous study by the lead author. That said, for this study, only the data collected on sport events are analyzed and discussed. The findings of this study (focused on small scale events in Winchester), has been compared to the perception that locals have of other types of events. This comparison helps the authors to draw some conclusion regarding the position that small-scale events are holding within communities. As a destination, Winchester is not well researched. The same could be said for small-scale event. This chapter is therefore going to fill some gaps. Additionally, this chapter is to some extent offering a connection with over-tourism and tourism phobia, which are at the moment 'hot topics'.

Small-Scale Event Volunteering: Insights From Three Greek Running Events

This chapter evaluates the contribution of the volunteerism to small-scale sport events. More specifically it presents a study that was implemented to identify the volunteer motivations and intentions and to compare them with those of two small-scale events, organized annually. Through this study it also explores whether volunteer participation increases the sense of community. Insights from three small scale sport events are provided with a view to helping the reader comprehend the working areas where volunteers may offer their services and the package that they gain after their contribution.

Basic Marketing Strategies and Marketing Mix in Small-Scale Sports Events

This chapter covers all the step-by-step procedure for planning any small-scale sports event. The following procedures are analytically presented: 1. Developing small-scale sport event ideas, 2. Knowing and understanding your target audience, 3. Planning small-scale sport events, 4. Roles and Responsibilities of the team, 5. Choice of the venue, 6. Third-Party service providers, 7. Event timelines, and 8. Contingency Planning processes.

Organizing Small-Scale Sports Events: Issues and Challenges

This chapter addresses the issues and challenges in organizing small-scale sports event. Existing study on sporting events tends to focus on mega-sporting events compared to small-scale sports events. This is due to mega-sporting events gives more benefits in terms of economic to the destinations besides attract more visitors'. To ensure the continuity of the growth of tourism products for a local destination, small-scale sports events is one of the good choices for a destination to diversify their local tourism products. Besides, this event also special due to the uniqueness of the activities that have been offered. However, besides the uniqueness of this small-scale event, there are also issues and challenges facing by the organizer and also the local community. Consequently, the aim of this chapter is to provide an overview of the issues and challenges that have been facing by the organizer and also the local community. Understanding the key issues in organizing this small-scale sports event will help this event to become as one of the tourism attractions for a local destination.

Basic Marketing Strategies and Marketing Mix in Small-Scale Sports Events

According to the literature study of this chapter, the following aims are made in the section that is titled "Small-Scale Sports Event Marketing". Firstly, the concept of event marketing has been discussed, the differences between large-scale and small-scale sports events are examined by considering the marketing factor according to the distinction made considering the size of each event, questions in the process of small-scale sports event marketing has been answered, also a detailed marketing process has been offered for the small-scale sports events. Finally the elements of the event marketing mix are discussed in detail in the light of the above discussion.

Small-Scale Sports Event Marketing Using New Marketing Concepts and Communication Tools

This chapter analyses the marketing planning stages to be more effective. The basic concept is that although small-scale sports event marketers may be constrained by limited resources – budgets, time and people – creative planning is achievable for everyone. Setting out a coordinated marketing plan at the beginning can at least improve the odds for delivering a successful event, reflected in a positive experience enjoyed among all attendees. Concentrating limited efforts into critical marketing activities is the key to delivering a positive experience. The author supports that following this marketing framework is one way to improve the odds.

Small-Scale Sports Event Sponsorship

The readers of this chapter are expected to understand, through the description of the basic sponsorship operation procedures, the importance of supporting sport event-based business operations. To this end, following a brief introduction including a description of the international situation in the Sports Sponsorship Market, as well as the necessary concepts, types of sponsorships, and developments, the structure of the book chapter focuses also on the key elements of the content of a sponsorship management plan for Small Scale Sporting Events. Additionally, important is the contribution of this chapter in clarifying how sponsors of a sporting event can be attracted.

When Ethical Values Drive the Creation and Development of Sport Events

In this chapter the authors analyze a case study of ColleMarathon. More specifically this chapter aims to describe how local volunteers were able to transform a very small-scale sport event into a successful happening that merges sport with ethical values and generates positive outcome for the local communities. Members of local sport associations and volunteers are the inventors, managers and workers of a marathon that wants to communicate the spirit of care and authentic values as its title suggests "the Marathon of Values". Ongoing growth (from 350 to more than 1000 athletes) and participation of new businesses and entities did not transformed the governance and the aim of the race: after 17 years ColleMarathon is still managed by an Organizing Committee made by representatives of the sport associations and volunteers, who are triggered by the values they want to disseminate with the event. Values are the glue that binds all actors and still attract participants that have to run through villages, hills, old castles and meet the local people and their cultural traditions.

Analyzing Spectators' Behavior at a Motor Sport: The World Rally Championship Case Study

This chapter provides useful information about segmentation practices based on consumer behavior differences. The authors use empirical data from a primary data analysis study with the scope to compare first and repeat sports event tourists in terms of their spending behaviors, satisfaction, and intention to return and to recommend others for visit the same event. Finally, solutions, recommendations, future research directions, and a conclusion are presented.

SUMMARY

The book, which has been completed as a single project, as you can see from the above chapter abstract presentations, contains sections that illuminate the reader on important applications and related theoretical directions of sports events. After a thorough research of the literature review process and after the results of relevant research conducted and published by the responsible book editors and authors of this publication, they considered that there was a significant scientific literature gap in the coverage and research related with the management of small-scale sporting events. So, following the suggestion of the IGI publishing house, we came up with this publication that we think can be a helpful contribution as a textbook that could support the interested reader e.g., student, postgraduate student, doctoral candidate and professional in the field of sports management and the administration of small scaled sports event problematic. Our collaboration with, the authors, the reviewers, the IGI publisher and his support-team, have been very productive and we thank them in particular for this unique collaborative experience. Each chapter of the book was reviewed by anonymous reviewers (blind review process), and after the chapter proposal and final chapter acceptance, we are happy that the result for the readers is this present book structure. More specifically, the chapter based structure follows the thematic sections dealing with the next ten important scientific topics in the knowledge field of Small Scaled Sports Event Management, namely the:

- Sports, Project & Event, Management
- Types of Sport Events
- Sports Event Planning
- Sports Event Marketing
- Sports Event Sponsorship
- Community engagement and volunteer, sport event management
- Local community perception analysis
- Motor sport events & Visitor behavior and satisfaction aspects
- Organizational small event management tools and practices
- Ethical issues related to the development of small-scale sport event practices

Given that in the modern environment of internationalized economies and societies, the administration of events and more specifically of small scaled sport events can make a significant contribution to the development and destination management of outdoor and urban area small scale sport events, we hope that the present material of this volume is considered to satisfy various readers interested in destination management, event management and visitor management topics of this volume.

Acknowledgment

We would like to acknowledge and express our thank to all book chapter reviewers who worked closely with us to provide invaluable insights. More of that we would like to thank each author for their valuable contributions, as this book couldn't be achieved without their help.

Section 1

Introduction to Small-Scale Sport Event Management

This section introduces readers to the basics of small-scale management in sports while exploring the importance and the engagement for different stakeholders on event development procedure.

Chapter 1
Sports Management, Project Management, and Sports Event Management

Anestis Fotiadis
https://orcid.org/0000-0001-8806-7987
Zayed University, UAE

ABSTRACT

Event management requires the use of project management and organizational skills to envision, plan, and execute social and business events. It involves studying the brand, identifying its target audience, devising the event concept, and coordinating the technical aspects before actually launching the event. Individuals who develop expertise in event management work in principle with budgets, schedules, and vendors and third-party service providers, and community stakeholders guaranty that they create successful events that meet the needs of their organization or the expectations of their client.

INTRODUCTION

Event management requires the use of project management and organizational skills to envision, plan and execute social and business events. It involves studying the brand, identifying its target audience, devising the event concept, and coordinating the technical aspects before actually launching the event. Individuals who develop expertise in event management work in principle with budgets, schedules, and vendors and third-party service providers, and community stakeholders guaranty that they create successful events that meet the needs of their organization or the

DOI: 10.4018/978-1-7998-4757-1.ch001

expectations of their clients. The events industry encompasses events of all sizes and types. In terms of size, events are categorized as large scale events (e.g., Olympic games, world cup), mid-scale events (e.g., a wedding), and small scale events (e.g., a birthday party). In terms of type, events are categorized as corporate events when organized by a for-profit organization and social events when organized by a not-for-profit organization. Events of any size require a certain level of planning and coordination, which often referred to as 'event planning'. The larger is an event, the more complex is its level of planning. An event must be seen as a service type project which means that each event is different in its nature and the socio-economic context it is expected to be hosted. Therefore, the planning and execution process of each event will differ on the basis of size and type as well as the socio-economic context.

A sporting event is one of the world's most fascinate event tickets (here we refer to event tickets as any forms of events where the event organization engages in the process of buying tickets to participants). Sporting events are athletic activities that require physical prowess and skills. Sporting events are typically known for their competitive nature and their entertainment level and are also governed by a set of rules that vary from one sport to another (see: https://www.lawinsider.com/dictionary/sporting-event). Sports event legacy is a complex and contested phenomenon(Thomson et al., 2019). Sports are played and watched by most of the world's population and have changed from being an amateur pastime to a massive industry that employs millions of people (Nicholson, Smith, Stewart, & Hoye, 2018). In principle, sports turn out to be a vital social activity as it helps improve physical and mental well-being; creates a sense of sharing and belonging that also provide entertainment and escapism besides being an employment generator both at local and national levels. Many people practice their most favorite sport because doing so helps them define their personal identity, whereas many others either practice actively or involve in sporting activity as a means to make their living. Sports have always played an important role in society on a variety of levels before transforming into a global industry. The sports industry is reported to be one of the fastest-growing sectors for brands that outpace the GDP growth of most countries with its market estimate that falls between $480 billion to $620 billion (QARA, 2019). Most people around the world, regardless of their age and social status, are passionate about some sports or the others. They either pursue it as a hobby or leisurely activity or are involved in it as participants at competitions of varying levels; then they are mere spectators at sports events. Keeping this in mind, since eras together, events in the arena of sports have been an integral part of society, at large.

Event Management

Event management is the process that encompasses the planning, preparation, and production of an event as an outcome that meets certain objectives. Similar to another form of project management, event management includes a range of managerial process (e.g., assessment, planning, direction, control, allocation of time and resources), development of infrastructure, resources (e.g., manpower, money), acquisition of services and products from third-party, and stakeholder management allocation to achieve well-defined objectives. A person who oversees an event is called an event manager. Thus, the event manager is expected to use the management principles and process (e.g., planning, control, and evaluation) to guaranty event success(Fotiadis, Xie, Li, & Huan, 2016). The event management market is divided into different market segments called "event tickets". According to a recent estimate, the Event Tickets market segment is expected to generate US$63,895m in 2020 and expected to hit the threshold of US$87,531m by 2024 with an estimated annual growth rate of 8.2%. Compared to the rest of the world, the US represents the top geographic event tickets segment with its estimate of US$22,811m in 2020. And the world's largest event ticket segment is 'Music Events' which is estimated to generate US$24,837m in 2020.

Classification and Outlook of the Events Industry

Events are often classified by their type into the following types: corporate events, cause-related & fundraising events, exhibitions, expositions & fairs, entertainment & leisure events, government & civic events, marketing events, meeting & convention events, social/life-cycle events, and sports events. Below we present a description of each type of event commonly found in the literature.

- **Corporate Events.** Corporate events are any type of events that are organized to support a range of organizational and business objectives that cannot take place within the confinement of the employees' office, which may include corporate communication, management functions, training, incentives, employee relations, marketing, and customer relations.
- **Cause-Related & Fundraising Events.** Cause-Related & Fundraising Events particularly type of events organized by or for a charitable or cause-related group. These kinds of events are designed either to attract revenue, support certain causes (e.g., environmental protection), and/or awareness. These kinds of events may be scheduled alone or in conjunction with other events.

- **Exhibitions, Expositions & Fairs.** Exhibitions, Expositions & Fairs are the types of events that are organized by business organizations to demonstrate and showcase their products and services to potential buyers and the general public. These kinds of events may be scheduled alone or in conjunction with other events.
- **Entertainment & Leisure Events.** Entertainment and Leisure Events are sorts of events that are organized for entertainment or leisure purposes (e.g., electronic music, casino, classical theater, movies). Entertainment and leisure events may just once in a lifetime. In most cases, entertainment and leisure events are organized periodically and may free or ticketed events that are scheduled alone or in conjunction with other events.
- **Government & Civic Events.** Government and Civic Events are types of events that are organized by government entities, political parties, municipalities or communities. Government and civic events may have different purposes. This may include and not limited to promote certain ideologies or political campaigns, encourage a change in certain social behaviors aiming at facing some social and environmental challenges. Government and civic events may be crafted along with other types of events.
- **Marketing Events**. Marketing Events are the sorts of commerce-oriented events that are organized to promote and increase the awareness of a new product or service, or business. Such events may be scheduled to happen alone or along with other events.
- **Meeting & Convention Events**. Meeting & Convention Events the kinds of events that are organized for the purpose of exchanging information, debate or discussion over a range of subject matters, education, and networking. Seminars, conferences, galas, business dinners, and banquets fall into the category of meeting and convention events. These kinds of events may be scheduled alone or along with other events.
- **Social/Life-Cycle Events.** Social or Life-Cycle Events are most of the time organized privately, meaning one can only attend by invitation. These kinds of events are often organized to commemorate or celebrate certain occasions ranging from religious or cultural aspects, or a change of social status, or some special events like weddings, Baby Naming, and communions.
- **Sports Events.** Sports events are the types of competitive contests or recreational activities that involve physical efforts and skills and are also governed by a set of rules. Sports events usually involve direct participants (teams/players, referees) and indirect participants (spectators). A sporting event can be scheduled to take place alone or along with events. In terms of size, sports events are categorized as large scale events (e.g., Olympic games, world cup), mid-scale events (e.g., a wedding), and small scale events (e.g., a

birthday party). Over the past decades, sports events have been transformed into a contested phenomenon and complex (Thomson et al., 2019) and have also become a multi-billion dollars industry. According to a report by Statista, the sports events market segment is expected to yield nearly US$23,674m in revenue for the year 2020 with an annual growth rate of 7.3% which expected to yield US$31,349m in revenue by 2024. Currently, the average revenue per visitor is estimated to be US$81.63. compared to the rest of the world, the US occupies the largest market share of the sports events with an estimate of US$10,921m in 2020.

Sports tourism denotes travel which encompasses either direct participation or indirect participation (meaning observing) sporting event. With many regards, sports tourism remains the fastest-growing and the greatest segment of the tourism industry (UNWTO). According to a recent forecast, the global Sports Tourism market is expected to register a compound annual growth rate (CAGR) of about 36% during the period spanning from 2019 to 2023 (Absolute Report, 2019). Regardless of the purpose of the journey, more tourists seem to attracted by sports activities during their journeys. Eventually, sports events of different sizes and kinds are often scheduled as part of the agenda of many tourists. As tourists are often excited to learn about local culture, destinations are getting more inclined to add local flavors to any sporting events as a means to differentiate themselves from the competition by providing tourists authentic local experiences.

Mega-sporting events provide professional athletes the opportunity to represent their country and showcase their talents and also provide host countries the opportunity to promote and present their cultures and national identities on a global scale (Dolles & Söderman, 2008). More importantly, Mega sports events such as World Cups and Olympics represent a catalyst for tourism development particularly if these events successfully leveraged in terms of infrastructure and development destination branding and also leveraged in terms of their social and economic benefits.

Sports tourism includes all forms of active and passive involvement in sporting activity, participated in casually or in an organized way for non-commercial or business/commercial reasons, that necessitate travel away from home and work locality. Countries and cities across the globe are constantly bidding for sporting events and thereby building facilities to attract sports tourism in order to benefit from the potential economic growth associated with this kind of tourism(Vassiliadis & Fotiadis, 2014). Though sports tourism generally attracts tourists from different cultural and economic backgrounds, individual sports tend to attract more tourists from specific demographic profiles. Having specific demographic profiles of tourists for individual sports makes it far easier for marketing departments to better segment the market, build compelling promotional campaigns, and identify the suitable promotional channels to communicate with a specific tourism market segment.

Mega sports events have the potential to offer substantial benefits to a country while at the same time entail enormous risk due to the massive resource utilization (Emery, 2002). The US was the most successful bidding nation for a sporting event in 2018, prevailing over France, the bidding winner of 2017. The US counts a portfolio of five (5) major events worth 12,027 points based on the GSI Bidding Nations Index. Given the economic impact of mega sporting events, the US along with its neighboring North American countries Mexico and Canada have submitted a joint bid to co-host the 2026 FIFA World Cup on Monday, with three-quarters of the games are expected to be played in the U.S (Carlisle, 2017).

In principle, sports tourists are enthusiastic individuals with strong willingness to go out for long journeys, ready to spend a large amount of money one can imagine acquiring equipment and materials needed in order to fully enjoy their favorite sport. He looks for special places to be able to tell them when he returns from vacation, for his "businesses", he informs himself by reading specialized magazines and has as a reference the champions of his sport.

There are different kinds of tourist-related to the sport. This includes:

- All the individuals who decide to visit a destination that is scheduled to host a sporting event regardless of their ability to play the sport are scheduled or not;
- Practitioners who play at an amateur level who decide to participate in training sessions, competitions, tournaments, etc.
- Professionals who attend sporting events either for business or professional reasons (e.g., physiotherapists, medical staff, nutritionists, trainers).
- Staff, employees, and management of both amateur and professional sports clubs.
- Juries and referees who prepared for the checks and evaluations of regular conduct of the events and also ensure that rules of the game are duly respected.
- Journalists, radio and television crews whose role is to comment, broadcast, and resume sporting event competitions.
- The "sportsman" who travels to watch sporting events and/or support their favorite team (e.g., individual sports enthusiasts, organized fan clubs).
- Individuals who travel to watch a sport either for the purpose of learning it or because it goes "in fashion".
- For this we must "unite" the opportunity to practice or attend a sporting event the opportunity to spend a holiday of wellness and fun, expand the offer, in order to involve the group or the family that accompanies the tourist sports.

Sport Event Management

Sports event management requires, in general, many planning activities regardless it is about large scale level, inter-collegiate level or the inter-school, although there might be certain variation in the level of planning. The planning process of sports event management encompasses the pre-sports or qualifying rounds and leading up to the final day of the event. In fact, mega-scale and mid-scale sporting events require planning and implementation well in advance. This particularly the case of Olympic games and international sports competitions such as tennis, basketball, cricket, and football to name just a few. Sports events remain an essential part of any recreation and leisure program. They can engage a whole community, increase awareness and help put an organization or an activity on the map. Some sports events are programmed to attract top-class performers, whereas others are programmed beginners to display their talents. Also, some sporting events are programmed to provide fun and adventure, novelty, entertainment, and glamor. Sports events can help destinations to influence visitors to come back and create visibility when they are well organized. On the contrary, badly organized sports events can reduce the capability of destinations to influence visitors to come back. Importantly, sports events can help destinations sustainable substantial promotional advantages when they are carried out of the ordinary.

Events generally need a large number of qualified individuals in order to guaranty their success. Most of the time, organizations or entities that are responsible to the organization the event do not have enough resources to recruit competent staff. Therefore, organizations rely heavily on volunteer staff to guarantee successful events. This also holds true in the case of sports events. However, the successful sports events from mega-scale to small scale require hard-working, dedicating, and sometimes highly competent volunteers. While volunteering at sporting events often expect to have free access in exchange for their donation of time. To some extent, having free access to an event venue seems to be the primary reason that most people are willing to volunteer. Consequently, event committees may attract people with a good intention of volunteering but with different attitudes that determine whether they are a good fit or not for the organization that is undertaking sports events. Sometimes, some people will embark on volunteering at a sporting event with the intention of organizing their own little event and often at the expense of the event. Some people will eventually take on too much and others disappear when their present is mostly needed. Therefore, a successful sports event quality recruitment process, retention strategy, and relationship building (Reamon, 2016) which necessitate a highly competent coordinator.

The preparations for events like the world cup and the Olympics begin several years preceding the event. And this is not only including the preparation of various locations but ensuring that the infrastructure in the host country is ready to lodge participants and spectators. Managing sporting events often require a large number of people, meaning that a team of ten to twelve people. In mega and mid-scale sport event settings, hundreds of people are involved in putting together international events. Also, sport event management requires a large sum of money. During sports events like the World Cups, a number of sponsors are prepared to lend their full support, knowing that, the event will attract hundreds of thousands of visitors and spectators. In addition to the ground sponsorships, there are organizations and industries that have a stake in participating or supporting sports events. Thus, the sources of income for such events are many and varied widely.

Prior to planning and implement sports events, organizations have to go through a bidding process. Bidding for sports events is highly competitive as many organizations/institutions are eager to reap the economic benefit of hosting these kinds of events. To win a sports event bid, organizations generally need to provide supporting evidence that they can put on the best event. As a primary step that determines which organization will host an event, bidding thus falls under the responsibility of the event manager and is, therefore, part of event management. In practice, there is a representative body having the mandate to select which organization or country will host a prospective sport event. Thereby, every competing organization has to submit a bidding proposal that duly explains how they organize and stage the event. The main objective of the bid process for sports events is to:

- Prove that the bidding organization has the competence and resources to stage the event;
- Provide further details on why the bidding organization should be chosen over other rival bidders. These further details may include, for example, the evidence that the sporting event will draw more finance and support with bidder A compared to its rival. Bidder A can provide better facilities to host the event. Public support is more guaranty with bitter A.

Some of the most important steps in sport event management are the following:

- Bidding for sport events
- Working with key stakeholders to outline project timelines for event
- Providing hospitality to sponsors and other “clients” of the sporting event
- Communicating with broadcasters and members of the press
- Recruiting, selecting, and managing volunteers
- Identifying the most suitable venue and joining forces with staff on preparations

- Arranging for accommodation and transportation to the event location for participants
- Applying safety measures for spectators and athletes
- Making parking accessible to attendees
- Engaging community leaders to support the event;
- Negotiating contracts with vendors and sponsors
- Building a contingency plan to mitigate any factors that can negatively influence the success of the sporting event (e.g., change in weather conditions).

Mission Statements

A mission statement is a short writing statement that explains the purpose, the overall goal of organizations of any kind, including sports events management organizations. This statement may also include the type of product or service the organization produces, its primary customers or market, and its geographical district of operation. By having a clearly writing mission statement, sport event organizations may avoid the risk of strategic confusion. For instance, members, players, spectators, coaches, staff, sponsors, media, and government authorities may have different explanations for the purpose of a sports organization. Simply put, a well-defined mission statement is beneficial since it helps to prevent an organization from diverting from its mission.

Vision Statements

It is obvious that behind the intention of defining a clear strategic direction for any organization is the necessity to be visionary, which supposes that all the members have a clear and the same mental image of what an organization could become or look like in the future. this way of thinking suggests that the organization has the capability to collect information and conduct a meaningful analysis of this information in order to discover the opportunities they present. A vision statement denotes the culmination of this sort of rationale. It is also a statement that shapes the medium- to long-range objectives of any organization.

It goes without saying that organizations that have well-defined, comprehensible, and meaningful mission statements and vision are more likely to gain substantial competitive advantages over their competitors, meaning they are more capable of developing long-term relationships with their customers, suppliers, and other groups of stakeholders.

Objectives

Successful sports events are the end result of achieving a set of organizational objectives. It should be noted that achieving successful sports events largely depends on the objectives are defined and communicated. More importantly, the objectives of any sports events should be in synch with both the vision and mission of the organization that is implementing the event. As a rule of thumb, the objectives of sports events must be clearly defined and follow the SMART principle, meaning they need to be Specific, Measurable, Achievable, Relevant and Time-bound:

- Specific meanings that sport event managers need to be explicit about what objectives should be achieved.
- Measurable means having a method and appropriate unit measures that facilitate the monitoring and progress towards achieving the proposed objectives. This could be done through visitor research and/or ticket data capture for example.
- Achievable means that the sporting event objectives are attainable and should, therefore, reflect the capability of the organizations in terms of competence and resources. It is always tempted to overstate the objectives of an event in order to attract sponsors. This is a trap that all sport event managers need to wisely avoid.
- Relevant means that the objectives of the sports events must be connected with the bigger picture of what is expected to achieve (the main objective). If, for example, a sporting event is scheduled to encourage sustainable consumption of tourism products or services (the main objective) in line with this main objective.
- Time-bound means a start and finish date must be attached to each objective.

Sport Management

Managing sports organizations at the start of the twenty-first century involve the application of techniques and strategies evident in the majority of modern business, government and nonprofit organizations. The sporting industry often uses sports management and sports administration are often used interchangeably. Nevertheless, sports management emphasizes on the entire sport and team from a business standpoint, whereas sports administration emphasizes more on the management and development of players, particularly those who play at the professional level. Trained, and high skilled or experienced individuals in sports administration and sports management often call sports managers. They are in charge of overseeing

Figure 1.

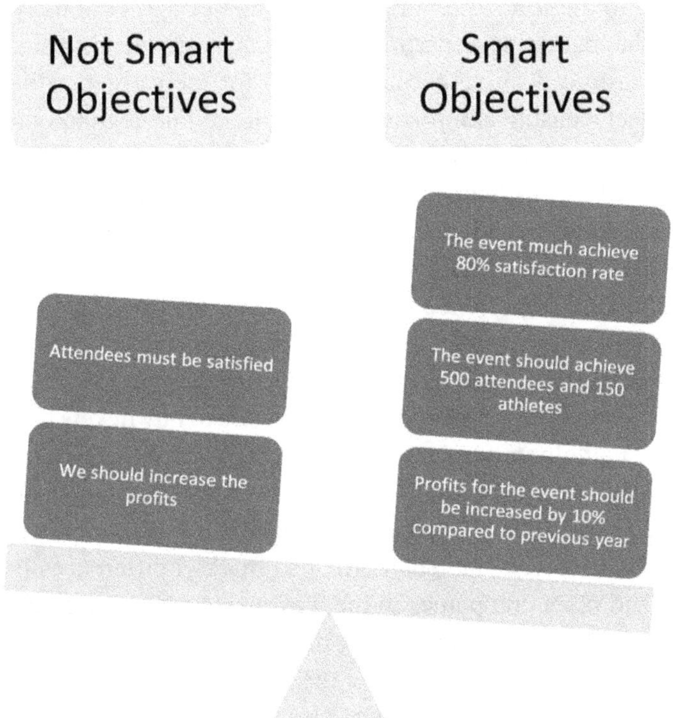

sports teams or businesses that deal with athletes (Priporas, Vassiliadis, Stylos, & Fotiadis, 2018). The responsibilities of sports managers vary in accordance with their clientele. For instance, a sports manager can work amateur leagues level, high school level, professional team level, even for an individual athlete. Some sports managers who work for an individual athlete is mainly in charge of ensuring that their athlete client(s) are in good physical health and mental conditions. They can also be in charge of hiring personal trainers and manage differences between their client athlete and the team. A sports manager may serve as a spokesperson for their client athlete, meaning that they need to work with the media to warrant their client a good image and credit they deserve. Additionally, a sports manager who works for an individual athlete often oversees that every aspect of the athlete's life is well-organized.

The responsibility of sports managers who work for a team or organization is relatively different. While working for an entire organization, sports managers need to make sure that every element of the network that is required to run the operation is well-organized and works properly. Sports managers working in an organization setting are responsible for managing the inner mechanisms of their organization and smoothing out any conflicts between departments. They may also be responsible for and not limited to the following: promote clients through various types of media, working with the marketing department the organization/team maintain a positive public image, sustain positive public relations for their organization, handle and negotiate contracts, ensure compliance with policies and regulations.

Smith and Stewart (2007) provide a list of ten unique features of sport that can help us understand why the management of sports organizations necessitates the use of specific management techniques. A unique feature of the sport is the phenomenon of people who develop irrational passions for sports athletes, teams, or competitions. Sport is of symbolic importance in relation to performance results, success and celebration of achievements that do not occur in other areas of economic and social activity. Therefore, sport managers need to learn how to tap into the irrational passions of sports lovers by appealing to their desire to buy tickets for events, donate their time to run a voluntary association, become a member of a fan club, or buy sporting merchandise. They must also learn how to apply strong business logic and management techniques to sustain traditions and links with nostalgic aspects of sports consumption and involvement. There are also marked differences between sports organizations and other companies in the way they assess performance.

Generally speaking, private or publicly listed companies are more profit-oriented, meaning that their priority is to increase the wealth of shareholders. In the context of sports business, sports organizations there are many other imperatives that may rule over making a profit. These imperatives may include and not limited to provide services members and stakeholders, winning championships, meet community stakeholders' expectations. It is, therefore, important that sport managers are aware of these imperatives. However, they need to ensure that the organization has enough financial resources to support its strategic objectives. In the traditional business ecosystems, the main goal of every company is to secure the largest market share possible or even secure full market control by crushing all competitors. However, in the context of the sports business ecosystem, ensuring a competitive balance is detrimental to the existence and viability of every sports organization within the league, which determines the interdependent nature of the relationships between sports organizations. The competitive balance remains exceptional and unique amid sports organizations. While they seem to be harsh competitors in the field, outside the field still cooperate to guarantee the long-term viability of clubs and thus their leagues.

In sports leagues, teams and clubs need their opponents to stay in business. Therefore, they must collaborate to play talent and share revenue, and regulate themselves in order to maximize the level of in the outcome of games between them and reduce the level of uncertainty. By doing so, they maintain the interest of both the interest their fans and ensure their own viability. While such behavior could be considered as anti-competitive, governments support such actions for the unique characteristics of sport.

The sports products may fluctuate in quality when they take the form of contests and games. In any sports, the outcomes of the games are generally uncertain and the level of attraction and excitement, which are determined by the level of challenge, are the key factors that spectators are looking for. Therefore, if one team dominates totally the game, that will eventually reduce the attractiveness of the game and spectators' perceptions about the quality of the game particularly if their team loses. It should be noted that spectators' perceptions regarding the quality of a game are determined when there is a tit of tap challenge between two players or teams. The variable quality within the sport settings, therefore, makes it hard to ensure quality in the marketplace comparative to any other service industry or consumer products such as cars mobile phones, or other general household goods. Sport also enjoys a high degree of brand loyalty or product. This thus suggests that fans are unlikely to switch team or club or change sporting codes for a poor standard of officiating and/or match result. In the context of consumers of household products, they have a range of competing products to choose from and will readily switch brands for reasons of price or quality. In the case of sporting competitions, however, it is hard to find a substitute. While this seems to be a relative advantage, it also has a negative implication. For example, sporting codes are difficult to be used to expand market share and attract new fans from other codes owing to familiarity of the fans with the traditions and customs of their existing sports affiliation. Sport stimulates unique behaviors in people, such as wearing the uniform of their favorite player, emulating their sporting heroes in play, or buying the products endorsed by sporting celebrities.

This indirect identification with the abilities, skills, and lifestyles of athletes can be used by sports managers and related industries to influence the purchasing decisions of sport service consumers. Sports fans also display a high degree of optimism. They often stress that their team, despite a series of bad losses, is only a game or a week away from winning the next championship. Similarly, owners and managers of sports franchises show a high level of optimism. They often see the recruitment of a star or new coach as the means to succeed in the field.

According to Smith and Stewart (2010), sports organizations are reluctant to adopt new technologies unless they are linked to the science of sport, where performance on the ground can be improved. In this sense, sports organizations can be considered as more conservative and connected to traditions and behavior compared to other organizations. The last unique aspect of the sport is its limited availability. In other sectors, organizations can increase their production to meet demand, but in sport, clubs are limited by the length of the season and the number of games that are scheduled. This thus limits their ability to maximize revenues through ticket sales and other sources of revenues. This suggests that sports managers need to understand the nature of their business, the level of demand for their services and products (in whatever form) and the suitable time to deliver them. Jointly, these unique characteristics of sport create significant challenges for managers of sports events and organizations. It is important to understand the effects of these characteristics on the management approaches and tactics used by sport managers.

Project Management

Project management may be defined as the use of knowledge, skills, tools, and techniques to project activities to meet the project requirements.

A project is said to be **temporary** because it has, in principle, a defined beginning and end in time, and therefore defined scope and resources.

And a project is **unique** in that it is different from any routine operations. It is a specific set of operations that are designed to accomplish a specific goal. So a project team often includes people who do not generally work together; therefore, they may from different organizations and across multiple geographies.

Project management processes fall into five groups:

Initiating

According to PMI, the process of Initiating helps to build a vision of what is to be accomplished. At this stage, the initial scope of the project is defined and the project sponsors give the authorization to undertake the project. Stakeholder identification is also vital at this stage because, in principle, key or influence groups of stakeholders may influence project success. In most cases, they can prevent the project from being implemented particularly if they were not a priori informed.

Planning

A key element of planning is writing up the total scope of the project. Though the total scope of the project may appear to be completed at the Initiating stage, scope (along with risks, milestones, summary and budget) was well-defined there at a high level. At this point, an iterative and more detailed planning process called progressive elaboration, project documents are developed at a much more detailed level.

Executing

In principle, the execution phase comes just after the planning of the project; that is work real work is started by implementing what tasks described in the project management plan. The project management plan not only helps to execute the tasks related to the project but also helps to keep track of each task. At this stage, the project team starts doing the work of creating the deliverables, whereas the project manager coordinates and controls the relevant resources.

Monitoring and Controlling

While the other process groups occur sequentially, Controlling and Monitoring, however, happen throughout the project cycle and do not follow a linear sequence. Some areas that often attract tight control include scope, cost, and schedule. All of these areas will certainly vary depending on the tools and techniques used to control them. But what each has in common is that they have baselines that have been defined in the planning.

Closing

The close phase is the process where all the project, phase or contract activities are terminated. The key benefits of this process are the project or phase information is archived and also the planned deliverables are completed leading to the release of all organizational team resources. Thereby, the project team becomes free to pursue new activities.

Project management knowledge areas:

1. Project Integration Management

Project integration management is an umbrella that covers all other areas of project management knowledge. It combines all its individual processes and tasks in a single project with defined objectives and outcomes.

2. Project Scope Management

Project scope management is the process of ensuring that a particular project includes all relevant work needed to achieve the objectives of the project. Its main objective is to control what is and is not involved in the project. Scope management techniques thereby allow project leaders and supervisors to allocate the right amount of resources to complete the project.

3. Project Time Management

The first step in developing a project schedule is to define the specific activities that need to be done to complete the project. Scheduling is the simplest way of managing the time frame attributed to each task or deliverable. At this stage, the activities of the project are estimated and the time intervals are determined based on the resources needed to complete each activity. In addition to the estimate and resource allocation, cost constantly plays a significant role in time management because scheduling over-runs are quite expensive. This is done, in principle using the work breakdown structure (WBS) technique developed during the project scope management phase. The WBS lists all of the work packages that are needed to be done in order to complete all the project deliverables. For each work package, project managers need to define activities that need to be done in order to complete the work package.

4. Project Cost Management

The cost management process starts with the project planning phase, where costs are approved by management prior to implementation. Second, when the project is implemented, expenditures are carefully monitored and recorded to ensure that they are aligned with the cost management plan. At the end of the project, the actual costs that were collected and documented are compared to the estimated costs determined at the start of the project. This actual comparison with that expected is valuable information for forecasting future project costs.

5. Project Quality Management

Project quality management includes the processes and activities that are used to identify and achieve the quality of project outcomes. Quality is simply what the client or stakeholder needs from the project deliverables.

6. Project Human Resource Management

Project human resources management includes organizing and managing a project team. The team is usually constituted of people with specific skills and responsibilities. The project team, also known as Project staff, must be involved in the plans and decision-making process from the outset of the project. Project Human Resources Management describes the processes that allow the project leader to organize and lead the project team.

7. Project Communications Management

Project communications management comprises the procedures necessary to ensure timely and proper generation, collection, storage, distribution, and final disposition of project information. Effective communication is very important to create a bridge between diverse groups of stakeholders and project team members.

8. Project Risk Management

Project risk management involves risk identification, risk management planning, risk assessments and risk control. This knowledge area consists of six processes. The area focuses on the identification, analysis, and planning of responses to "threat risks" and "opportunity risks".

9. Project Procurement Management

This knowledge area deals with the processes that project managers typically follow to obtain the materials required for the successful completion of the project. In this area of Knowledge, project managers prepare the procurement implementation plan, monitor the procurement and close the procurement.

10. Project Stakeholder Management:

The project stakeholder management area includes all processes that a project manager uses to identify and satisfy those affected by the project. The affected parties may be internal or external in nature. Project managers need to pay particular attention to interested parties who can have a positive or negative impact on the project.

Figure 2.

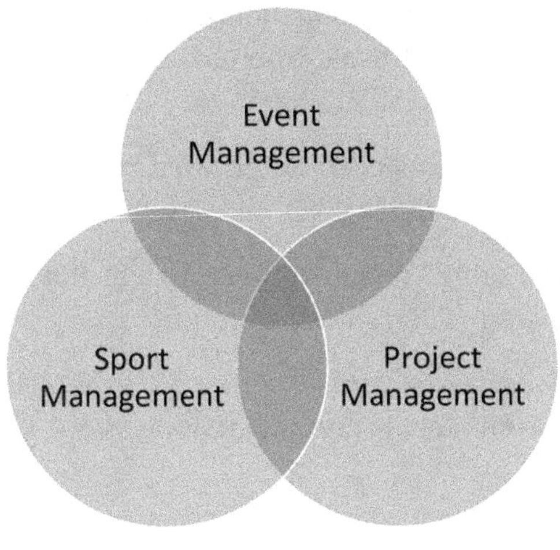

While events and projects share close similarities, it does not necessarily mean that a project is an event. We can consider event management as project management, but most projects have little to do with events. Of course, sports events management is linked to the management of sports, but the management of sports is usually part of the sports event management.

REFERENCES

Carlisle, J. (2017). *U.S., Mexico and Canada officially launch bid to co-host 2026 World Cup*. Retrieved from https://www.espn.co.uk/football/fifa-world-cup/story/3100808/usmexico-and-canada-officially-launch-bid-to-co-host-2026-world-cup

Dolles, H., & Söderman, S. (2008). Mega-Sporting Events in Asia — Impacts on Society, Business and Management: An Introduction. *Asian Business & Management, 7*(2), 147–162. doi:10.1057/abm.2008.7

Emery, P. R. (2002). Bidding to host a major sports event: The local organising committee perspective. *International Journal of Public Sector Management, 15*(4), 316–335. doi:10.1108/09513550210430255

Fotiadis, A., Xie, L., Li, Y., & Huan, T.-C. T. C. (2016). Attracting athletes to small-scale sports events using motivational decision-making factors. *Journal of Business Research, 69*(11), 5467–5472. doi:10.1016/j.jbusres.2016.04.157

Nicholson, M., Smith, A. C., Stewart, B., & Hoye, R. (2018). *Sport management: Principles and applications*. Routledge.

Priporas, C.-V., Vassiliadis, C. A., Stylos, N., & Fotiadis, A. K. (2018). The Effect of Sport Tourists' Travel Style, Destination and Event Choices, and Motivation on Their Involvement in Small-Scale Sports Events. *Event Management, 22*(5), 745–765. doi:10.3727/152599518X15299559637707

QARA. (2019). *Sports Industry Insights*. Retrieved from https://medium.com/qara/sports-industry-report-3244bd253b8

Reamon, S. (2016). Managing Volunteers: Recruitment, Retention, and Relationship Building. *SPNHA Review, 12*(1), 74–95.

Report, A. (2019). *Global sports tourism market 2019-2023*. Retrieved from https://www.absolutereports.com/global-sports-tourism-market-13792981

Smith, A., & Stewart, B. (2007). The travelling fan: Understanding the mechanisms of sport fan consumption in a sport tourism setting. *Journal of Sport & Tourism, 12*(3), 155–181. doi:10.1080/14775080701736924

Thomson, A., Cuskelly, G., Toohey, K., Kennelly, M., Burton, P., & Fredline, L. (2019). Sport event legacy: A systematic quantitative review of literature. *Sport Management Review, 22*(3), 295–321. doi:10.1016/j.smr.2018.06.011

Vassiliadis, C., & Fotiadis, A. (2014). *Conjoint analysis of sporting events: the case of Taiwan*. Paper presented at the 2nd International Conference on Contemporary Marketing Issues, Athens, Greece.

Chapter 2
Different Types of Sport Events

Chris A. Vassiliadis
https://orcid.org/0000-0001-8814-1518
University of Macedonia, Greece

Anestis Fotiadis
Zayed University, UAE

ABSTRACT

The chapter shows the variety of sporting events and hints at the potential of developing these alternative activities. In order to pursue the above objective of the chapter, the various criteria for categorizing sporting events are presented first. The chapter then focuses on providing relevant examples to inform the reader about the practices and trends of sporting events that are prevalent internationally. The reality of the emergence of a variety of sporting events and activities locally and internationally is an element of interpretation of modern lifestyles. At the same time, a careful study and analysis of the varieties and types of sports, facilitates managers, and designers of sports activities and sports programs at a visitor destination is presented to identify easily opportunities for their development and exploitation.

INTRODUCTION

The modern reality in the development of sports activities is characterized by the international reputation and recognition of large-scale sports events. Indeed, this tendency is often linked to the large investment interest of players and sponsors who support the above sports activities. However, the attraction of local and regional sporting events from the larger ones does not hinder the emergence of more and more smaller sporting events that can be considered important for the economic and

DOI: 10.4018/978-1-7998-4757-1.ch002

social development of local communities. In this chapter, the reader is expected to learn about possible categorizations of sporting events with examples concerning sporting events subsections, as well as developments that could support their planning and development process. Particular emphasis is placed on small-scale sports events where there is a relative need in the literature for their categorization and management. This chapter defines how to approach the Small-Scale Sporting Events and to highlight also the specific characteristics of these sport events in destination and event management decisions.

For the above purpose a literature review will be made initially. The importance of sports typologies in business practice is initially defined, emphasizing its link to strategic decision-making tools for designing viable product categories in a tourist destination. A comprehensive presentation of the typology criteria for sporting events will follow and examples of business practice will be compared. Finally, a summary of trends and developments is provided and useful business strategies for developing small scale sports events are outlined.

Emergencies, such as the global covi-19 epidemic that we are experiencing in 2020, are creating new problems for how one could still be in a physical state through the use of digital applications. YouTube is proving useful for creating live presentations of various coaches to maintain our fitness. However, the combination of physical activity and digital media is a new necessary reality that is used by various members of a household and can include both amateur and professional athletes or otherwise inexperienced and experienced users. Companies that do not belong to the field of electronic game but to the construction of electronic systems to support physical exercise eg Peloton and Ergatta create products such as bicycles and sports equipment for sports and support them with digital platforms in digital environments that simulate their home space or the professional space in electronic sports and competition areas. These new trends are a prelude and affect the way future events and events unfold, and therefore the formation of new types of sporting events that will take place in the coming decades. At the same time, the possibility of exercising at home or in the professional field, regardless of weather conditions, is a new perspective for sports that show seasonal dependence on weather conditions. The following text focuses on the traditional sporting process that requires the presence of the user in the natural conventional sports space and activation and therefore concerns the typology of events and activities that are activated in the natural environment.

THE PROBLEMATIC OF CATEGORIZING (SPORTING) EVENTS

The existing literature review can lead the reader to a difficult situation where he or she has to deal with a confusion of concept categorizations and varieties (see Table 1 & Fig. 1). Unfortunately, this situation cannot easily highlight to the reader an easy way of sport event classification(s) that is expected of him. An important problem is also that the standardization of criteria often concerns categories of events, such cultural, political, private oriented events, and not just sports and especially small-scale sport events. Gammon (2012, p.105) stated this problem. According to him "Unsurprisingly numerous sports events have ben situated within the special event category (which is a term often used as an umbrella term for all planned events) [...] ". Small-Scale Sport Events in relation to Large-Scale Sport Events also have a more beneficial impact on the local community, affecting positively the "three pillars" of its development (economy, society, natural environment) (Gibson, Kaplanidou & Kang, 2012; Ziakas, 2010).

If we remove from the above world cloud (see Figure 1) the words Sport, sports, sporting, and events the most common word constructs to describe sport events in the related literature are the words: "Tourism", "International", "Spectator", "Mega", "Major", "One-Off", "Irregular" and "Competitor-competitions". The words that are mainly related with the small scaled sport events like the "Minor", "Festivals", "Local", "Annually", "Regional" aren't expressed as categorization criteria. This gives as a general view of the main focus of the basic literature review that is the famous and major tourism international competitive sport events.

However, despite the above categorization of events, reflection on the distinction between small-scale, mid-scale and long-scale sport events can be an additional problem in the process of classifying, comparing, planning and evaluating events by the researcher concerned. Non-discrimination of sporting events can cause problems in identifying the factors that affect their performance in practice, both economically and environmentally and socially. Some sport categories that are in the frame of multisport activities can be the following, National, Regional, Sub-regional, Political, Historical-Heritage and Ethno-cultural based, Occupational, Special (disability and sexual oriented) and gender or age based categorizations (see also Houlihan & Green, 2011). Higham (1999) explain that a Small-Scale Events: a. can contribute to reduce the seasonality of business activities in the destinations, b. are more manageable, c. usually uses the local infrastructure, and low levels of extra budgets i.e., from public income sources, in contrast to a larger-scaled sport event (e.g., Mega or Hallmark event). He also defines Small-Scale Sport Events as "regular season sporting competitions, international sporting fixtures, domestic competitions, Masters or disabled sports, and the like" (p. 87) (see above in table 1: "source" No. 5). A concise classification of sports can be supported from a destination manager,

Different Types of Sport Events

Table 1. Sport & event categorization literature

	Source	Categorization Criteria
1	Gratton, Dobson & Shibli, (2000)	• Mega events • Major annually organized spectator sports events • Irregular major sporting competitions • Major competitor driven events
2	Wilson (2006) Gibson, Kaplanidou & Kang (2012)	• Mega events • Major annually organized spectator sports events • Irregular major sporting competitions • Major competitor driven events • Minor events (for small and medium sized communities)
3	Gammon (2012)	• Mega sport events • Hallmark sport events • Special sport events • Sports heritage, parades & festivals • Small-scale/ community sports events
4	Bladen, Kennell, Abson & Wilde (2018)	• Global event (mega-event) • International • National • Regional • Local
5	Higham (1999)	• Regular season sporting competitions • International sporting fixtures • Domestic competitions • Masters or disabled sports and the like
6	Kurtzman (2005)	• Sport tourism attractions • Sport tourism resorts • Sport tourism cruises • Sport tourism tours • Sport adventure tourism • Sport events tourism
7	Bowdin, Allen, O'Tool, Harris & McDonnell (2011); Reic (2017, p.7-8)	• Events by sector • Events by size • Events by geographical reach • Events by content • Events by format
8	UK Sport (2004); Bowdin, Allen, O'Tool, Harris & McDonnell (2011, p.24)	• Mega Events • Calendar Events • "One-off" events • Showcase events
9	Gratton,Dobson, Shibli (2000); Duglio & Beltramo (2017)	• Irregular, one-off, major international spectators • Major spectator events • Irregular, one-off, major international competitor/ spectator event • Major competitor events • Minor competitor/ spectator events
10	Getz (2007)	• Professional or amateur • Indoor or outdoor • Regularly scheduled • Local, regional, national or international in scope • For participants, for spectators, or both • Sport festivals/ single or multi-sport events
11	Getz & Page (2016)	• Professional leagues • Participatory • Recreational / fun • One-day excursions and tournaments

Note: Self-created table

Figure 1. Word cloud; Result of the categorization analysis criteria
Note: Wordle word cloud application result

a researcher and an analyst by considering the list of approximately 3,000 sports presented in the 2003 World Sports Encyclopedia, a resume of the world wide sports and their categorizations presented from the Professor Liponski (Liponski, 2003). The main categories include the Physical Sports, Mind Sports, Competitive model sports another classification scheme can be the typology of 13 sport categories, those are namely the following, Air sports, Athletics (track and field), Electronic sports, Endurance sports, Goal sports, Skating sports, Snowsports, Strength sports, Table sports, Target sports, Team sports, Windsports and Fictional sports. In addition Olympic sports can be classified into spring and winter sports according to the categorization proposed by the International Olympic Committee (see table 2).

The stage of relocating and renewing product offerings to a destination through an appropriate mix of sporting events and -as mentioned above- infrastructures and innovations should be an important point of reference in managing the sustainability of destinations.

BACKGROUND

Why is it important to know the types of sports activities that need to be developed? The use of standardized categories by categories of sports services such as the

Table 2. The Time Period-Sports Matrix; Indicative presentation of matching sports and their season of activity

Sport Events	Time Periods of the Year SS		Sport Events	Time Periods of the Year WS	
	Spring	**Summer**		**Autumn**	**Winter**
Archery			Alpine Skiing		
Artistic swimming			Biathlon		
Athletics -Running -			Bobsleigh		
Badminton			Cross Country Skiing		
Basketball			Curling		
Beach Volleyball			Figure Skating		
Boxing			Freestyle Skiing		
Canoe Slalom			Ice Hockey		
Canoe Sprint			Luge		
Cycling BMX			Nordic Combined		
Cycling Mountain Bike			Short Track		
Cycling Road			Skeleton		
Cycling Track			Ski Jumping		
Diving			Snowboard		
Equestrian/ Dressage			Speed Skating		
Equestrian Eventing					
Equestrian Jumping					
Fencing					
Football					
Golf					
Gymnastics artistic					
Gymnastics Rhythmic					
Handball					
Hockey					
Judo					
Marathon swimming					
Modern Pentathlon					
Rowing					
Rugby					
Sailing					

continued on following page

Table 2. Continued

Sport Events	Time Periods of the Year SS		Sport Events	Time Periods of the Year WS	
	Spring	Summer		Autumn	Winter
Shooting					
Swimming					
Table Tennis					
Taekwondo					
Tennis					
Trampoline					
Triathlon					
Volleyball					
Water Polo					
Weightlifting					
Wrestling Freestyle					
Wrestling Greco-Roman					

Note: Sports categorization based on the International Olympic Committee; IOC Self construction after adoption.from the source: https://www.olympic.org/sports.

category of small-scale sporting events can and does support the planning and development of tourism and hospitality business activities in a geographical area e.g., reduce seasonality, increase sales of local business etc., that can be defined locally, regionally or even nationally. Management tools can be supported and relied upon when analyzing the typical categories of sporting goods and services. More specifically the sports event categorizations can support the product – market analysis of business strategic planning tools e.g. Strategic product portfolio planning tools, such as BCG, McKinsey GA Matrix, Ansoff, as useful business tools that help them identify and explore their growth options (Fig.2).

Categorization helps identify the key stages that follow a sporting event that "goes through a lifetime" in the Product Life Cycle Management (PLC, PLM or PLCM concept) (Levitt, 1965). Managers of sporting events interested in the development of tourism destinations, and in particular tourism destination managers, can identify the potential of developing these alternative products (sporting events) through the analysis of the PLCMs and their sports event product portfolios, thus enhancing the supply of activities in their destination. Similar to the PLCM concept is also the TALC proposal of Butler (1980) that explains the evolution of a tourist area life cycle.

The theories of PLCs are based on the evolution of destinations /products /brands, that follow a successive time sequence from basic time periods or levels of evolution of their sales and returns. These time periods of sales and profit development (dependent variable) can also be combined with the features of the competition in each time period situation (independent variable) and also with the strategic management applications of the MKT tools (4Ps, 7Ps) (Clifford, 1965; Kotler, 2000).

Small events can be defined as products in the PLCM process. Thus, any relevant sporting event can be defined in terms of its performance prospects by activating a framework for timely control of the related product specific strategic decisions. Based on Butler's Tourism Area Cycle (TAC or else TALC), (Butler 1980, p.6), "[..] the pattern which is put forward here is based upon the product cycle concept, whereby sales of a product proceed slowly at first, experience a rapid rate of growth, stabilize, and subsequently decline; in other words, a basic asymptotic curve is followed. [..]". Sport event categorizations per type of small-scale sport event, can be very useful for event tourism destination management purposes (Fig.2, 3).

By changing the above initial theoretical model of TALC scheme and adapting the PLCM to small-scale sporting events, we come up with a centralized PLCM that

Figure 2. An indicative destination Management Ansoff's Matrix example of possible collaboration between small-scale sport events i.e., product(s) and market categorization(s) (product-market analysis).

Note: Self-created table; Self creation based on the adoption of Ansoff's theory, see also Ansoff, I. (1957). Strategies for Diversification. Harvard Business Review, 35(5), p.113-114.

Product(s)/service(s) line
New, Present [Sumer semester =SS, WS= Winter semester, sports]

*Football school festival, e.g., Summer festival for sport academies (SS)
*Marathons e.g., Half- countryside marathon (SS)
*Triathlon races (WS), e.g., Summer, Winter sports
*Skiing e.g., langlauf marathons, [..]

Market(s) New, Present		
• Local • Regional • National • International • Adult people • Young people • Children	[NEW/NEW] Region X Diversification Strategy	[PRESENT/ NEW] Region X Market Development
• Individual • Schools • Sport organizations • B2C sport markets • B2B sport markets	[NEW/PRESENT] Region X Product Development	[PRESENT/PRESENT] Region X Market Penetration

relates to a tourist destination that would like to highlight his brand image through different combinations of small-scale sports in its area. (Fig. 3)

In particular, the steps in the development of the Life Cycle of alternative types of small sporting events could hypothetically follow the following series of discrete time periods (stages) between them.

First period: The stage of Exploration. Sporadic and fragmentary short-range sporting events are organized at the site of the visit. The number of visitors is not able to make a significant contribution to the consumption of local economy products. Small-scaled sport events aren't related for the tourists with the brand image of the destination. Athletes and spectators from other distant regions have identified some small-scale sport event(s) and organized on their own their trip in the area in order to visit the destination and the sporting event. Curiosity and personal interest are important motivational factors for the visitors. The regional and national media coverage is very low in this stage. For the most of the small-scale sport events it isn't easy in this first period to attract stakeholders and other investors e.g., the business sponsors, funding from the regional office of tourism development office, communication and transportation sponsors. Their business situation to negotiate with other investors and stakeholders is very weak because they have to prove and persuade about the potential of the small-scale event to bring benefits to each partner involved. The destination officers treat sporting events as occasional events that do not yield over time and have little impact on the sustainability of the tourist destination. Partnerships between local professionals, support for government, regional and local government, volunteering - community relations, and supplier relationships as well as coordination of actions in the area between organizers and stakeholders are usually under-planned procedure and not notably operational. At this stage, individuals or organizations that serve their own goals and objectives mainly make the first investments in small sporting events.

Second period: The Involvement stage. The vigor and success of the actions of the individual organizers who invest their money and resources because of their own interest in the development of small-scale sport events also motivates other investors and stakeholders. These small-scale sport events start and attract visitors from e.g., other large urban areas, and gain a reputation on a regional and national level. Visiting athletes and spectators are no longer just ordinary travelers, they stay in the area and consume i.e., during their short stay they taste the local dishes offered by the professionals. They also get in touch with local professionals who plan to support sports events in their area e.g. equipment, catering, tech support, athlete care, lodging, hire, and tours. The local network of volunteers and partnerships with organizations and agencies is strengthened e.g., by coordinating actions with the Red Cross, working with a nearby hospital in the area for first aid, coordinating with local or regional voluntary crisis management teams etc. Regional executives are keen to see local investors and stakeholders try to highlight their area by investing in short-range small-scale sports events but are pressured by investment developments and are considering incentives from their region area's investors, about potential support, and facilities for those sport events in their region area. The successful presence of each sporting event and the depreciation of the initial invested funds lead these small-scale sporting events to their timeless presence. These events attract year by year more athletes and spectators and of course tickets, entries and income for the event organisers, sponsors, & local business investors.

Third period: The Development stage. Recognizing the name of the place as a tourist sport destination is a prerequisite for establishing the event brand name and for the corresponding events in the region. Often, and after the involvement stage, an event or a group of different type of sport events initially succeed with a dynamic presence in the media or in the social media networks, and dominate and highlight a destination through small-scale sports events, e.g., some brand name(s) of places of Saronic and Cyclades islands in Greece are related with specific type(s) of local small-scale sport events like the Spetsathlon-a Triathlon sprint in May, and the Mykonos Run in September, while other places associate their name with the same type of sports but with different characteristics and properties such as the Thessaloniki night-time semi-marathon and the Thessaloniki Alexander the Great International Marathon during the April race, which includes also dynamic hiking events and Schoolchildren running races. Cultural, Natural attractions and man-made attractions and facilities are included in the event and tourism destination communication strategy. Businesses (sponsors) are more likely to invest their budgets in recognized events with reputed brands for consumers and the public. National and regional administrations are now more interested in recognizing their efforts to develop the place. The evaluation and financing of sporting events and the creation of modern infrastructure and promotions are an important step in tackling the seasonality of tourism activities, and to enforce the business activities and the employment in their tourism destinations. They often even incorporate activities into funding programs to achieve the above objectives. The number of tourists, of sport events, registrations, and tickets is growing up year by year in the geographical region.

A striking example is the long-standing effort of the Region of Eastern Macedonia and Thrace as the last region of the European Union to become a destination for sporting activities. The Region has invested resources since the late 1990s in promoting and presenting it at tourist exhibitions abroad. Today the region is enjoying the result of its efforts. Regional development programs have strengthened infrastructure by creating, for example, bicycle lanes in the Rhodope area (Macedonia-Thrace Operational Program 2007-2013, Municipality of Komotini Single Renewal Program), funding programs supports professionals who are activated in urban, extreme and rural area sports (i.e., climbing, crossing canyons, flying fox, rafting, canoeing, trekking, climbing, archery, mountain biking, urban biking, horseback riding) in Xanthi Prefecture, Motorcycle racing and 4x4 trail raid meetings & off-road racing sports such as the Motocross event of the Athletic Motorcycle Federation of Greece that has been organized in Kastanies in Evros Sub-Region prefecture and the Evros 4x4 car club meetings and tour and travel activities in the country. Another famous sport event the last years i.e., after the 2016 first running race is the Via Egnatia Run International road race that includes also a mixed type of sports namely, a Half-marathon run, a Public race-power walking, a Race for people with disabilities and a Kids race. This sporting event is also organized and supported by the regional unit of Evros-Region of Eastern Macedonia and Thrace and it attracts 300 and more volunteers. It is also evident that the performance of the destination is not only judged by the region's "officially" sponsored sporting events. In the case of Eastern Macedonia Thrace, local authorities and private investors are also active, attracting a large number of athletes and spectators to their sporting events. Some successful examples are the Football Academy Events in the sports center of Xanthi FC is located in Pigadia area (a December –Christmas and April-Easter Football Tournament event for Football academies of Children's Tournament, Pre-school Tournament and Junior Tournament, est., from 1999-2000; Organizer: The Organizing Committee of Xanthi FC), the Wave Running event in Avdira Municipality rural area (a July, August or September running coastal route event of 28, 10, 5 and 1 Km running routs, est., from 2014 under the auspices of UNESCO and the GNTO; Organizer two private investors), Virgin Forest Trail in Paranesti Municipality rural area (a October mountain trail running event of 162, 110, 46 and 10 km running routs, est., from 2007; Organizer: The Organizing Committee of Municipality of Paranesti) and the Democritus Half Marathon running event in Xanthi Municipality urban area (a November running urban event of 21, 5, and 1 Km running routs, est., from 2014 under the auspices of the Hellenic Athletic Federation - SEGAS; Organizers: Xanthi's Runners Team and Diomides Athletic Society).

Fourth period: The Consolidation stage. During this phase of the Small Scaled sporting events that took place in the tourist destination at a high annual rate during the four seasons of the last year(s), they now appear to have a lower growth rate. The growth in visitor numbers is slowing, while various sporting events in the geographic area are stepping up their efforts to attract visitors in order to stabilize their number of tickets and revenues to previous high levels of performance. Destination managers now emphasize not only the promotion of sports activities but also how to deal with seasonality and increase the capacity of the sports events market. Some residents are skeptical of the growing number of visiting athletes and attendants in their area of residence. The number of visitors and employees of sporting events organized per year in an area can be greater than the number of residents in that area per year, especially in the case of outdoor destinations.

Fifth period: The Stagnation stage. The large mass of visitors has also a negative impact on social and environmental issues. Destination due to noise, crowds, difficulties in finding suitable facilities, services, and amenities in and around the place of the sporting events tend to create unpleasant situations and experiences for the sport event visitors. Tickets will be available, entries and registrations for participation; will be lower than previous years. Elaborate “Servicescapes” (Booms and Bitner, 1981; Bitner, 1992) remains no longer attractive; it creates a negative impression about the services of sporting event visitors and the destinations that host it. Sport event visitors tend mostly to provide neutral and negative recommendations, they write in the social media environment not favorable reviews or they didn’t give any more positive word-of-mouth referrals to their social surroundings. Due to modern infrastructure, the original reception area changes its identity, losing its traditional texture and heritage. Also many local professionals do not view the development of the events positively and do not support sporting events such as sponsorships both in kind and in cash, which also do not support them in promoting their company and their local products. The image and the related positioning of the Destination Brand, the Event Brand, the Product Characteristics of the Event aren’t for the visitors any more “in fashion” (Butler 1980, p.8). The authentic visitor space due to modern infrastructure changes its identity while losing its traditional texture and heritage. Many residents who associate their memories and lives with past experiences and experiences of life, reminisce of space before it evolves and disintegrate thereby disagreeing with the subversive change due to the development of their space and their area of residence. Visitors do not find any authenticity, e.g., cultural, physical, social response and culture, to the elements of the environment and the competitive advantage of a destination’s diversity is weakened.

Sixth period: The Decline stage. The potential of the destination to be highlighted by the intensive organization of sporting events is limited. The number of sporting events is shrinking both geographically and numerically. Sporting events in the area are no longer an important attraction for visitors. Athletes are primarily amateurs from the area or neighboring areas and do not return to any subsequent sporting event at the destination. The geographical units in which the sporting events were organized are given to other investors or users for use. The event facilities and spaces are used from other investors for non-sport purposes. Prior event camping, parks, and infrastructures change ownership and are maybe reused as student sports & cultural venues, special social services for example disabled people, refugees, pupils, elderly people, army camps, Business purposes like MICE places (i.e., for Meetings, Incentives, Conferences and Other Events) etc., or even for absolutely no investment or business activity.

Seventh period: The Rejuvenation stage. Destination and the related recurring sporting events in it, co-ordinate their efforts to renew and adopt innovations that are

Figure 3. An indicative destination Management TALC example using Small Scale Event paradigms

Note: Self-created figure adopted from the source Butler, R.W. (1980). The concept of tourism area cycle of evolution: implications for management of resources, Canadian Geographer 24(1), p.7. Where: The goal is to enforce the small-scale sport activities per SS and WS [Sumer semester =SS, WS= Winter semester, sports]. More events=More tourists and income for the local economy.

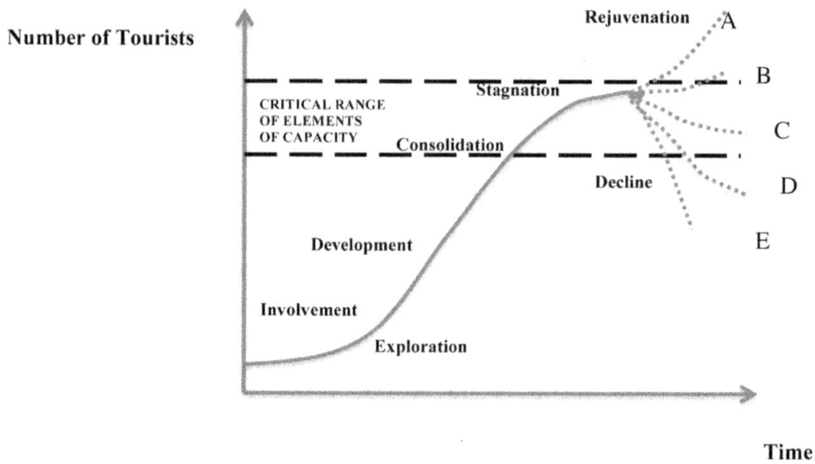

[1] The initial theoretical model

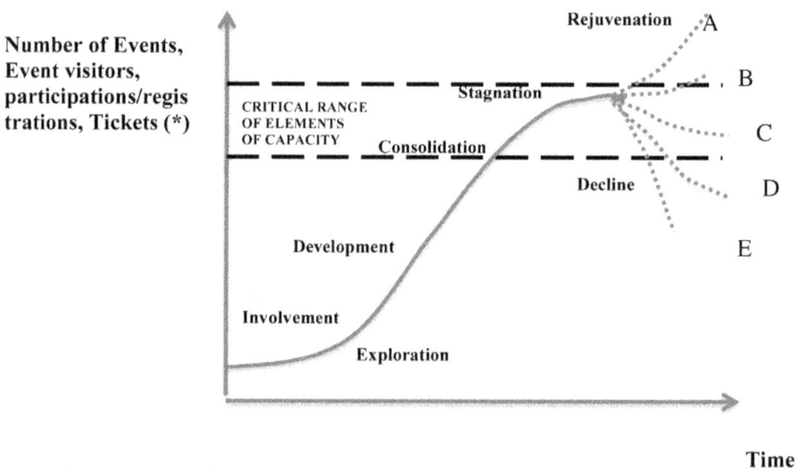

[2] The adapted proposed conceptual model

expected to contribute through attractive infrastructures, facilities and unique features to the repositioning of the destination as a destination of special and unique mix of interesting for the participants small-scale events (Dimanche, 2003; Kaplanidou and Vogt, 2007). Servitization can be the tool of the sport event organizations and destination authorities for selling Product Service Sport Event Service Systems i.e., integrated small-scaled sport event offer by delivering Value in use. By utilizing new and smart innovative materials in sports equipment and infrastructure, destination managers and organizers can and do innovate, making them more competitive in the sports events market and appealing to visitor segments, i.e., using nanomaterial for different sports events or 3D printing techniques to produce new designed sport equipment materials e.g., seats for spectators new designed titanium cycles. The use also of smart visitor and user friendly Internet of Things technologies can help the athletes and internet users to plan and analyze their sport activities, performance measures and effectiveness i.e., without the risk of injury (Bichi, Wijlens and Wallace, 2017). Smart urban and rural event destination areas can differentiate their service offer system ("servitization" process) thru the investment on Technological, Institutional, and Human, development factors e.g., thru smart transportation, health care, safety, education, environment, energy services, (Nam and Pardo, 2011).

Figure 4. An indicative destination Management section elevation diagram with winter and summer season mixed events per geographical area
Note: Self-created figure

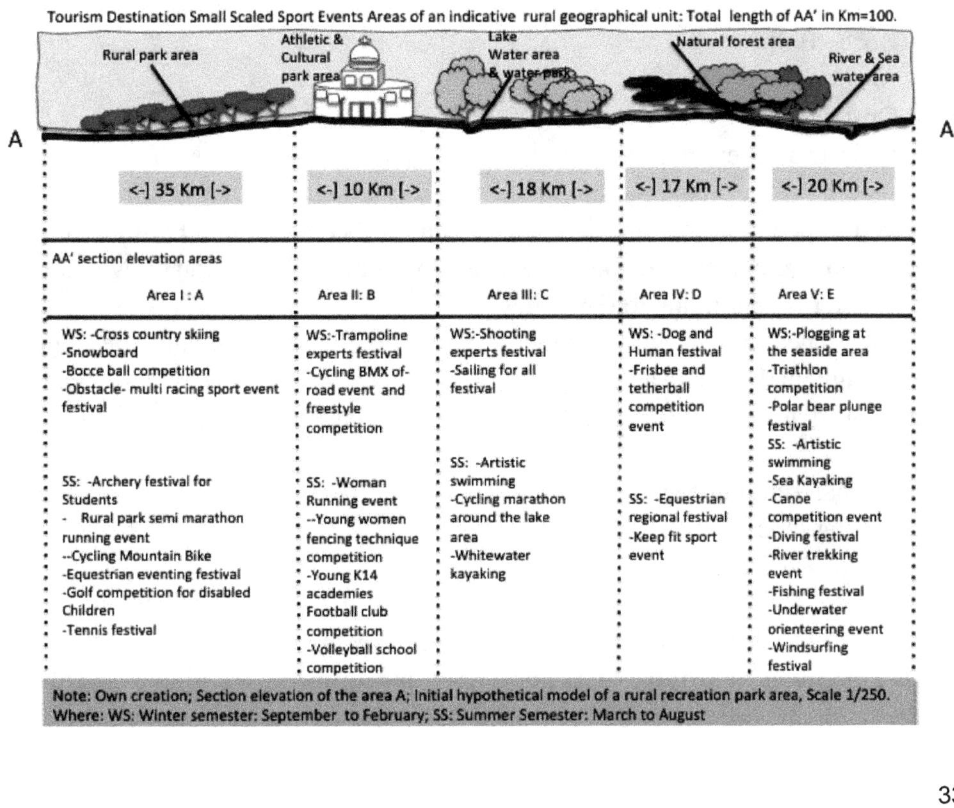

Product Portfolio Analysis for Tourism Destination Event Product Categories

If we want to gather multiple data from small-scale sporting events and then form a more complete picture of these Life Cycles, then the ability to use Boston Consulting Group's Growth-Share Matrix as a strategic consulting tool for analyzing sport event product portfolios would help administrative decisions concerning concerns about the right mix of sporting events. In the next section of this chapter we define through an example the procedure of developing the wright small-scaled event product portfolios with the use of section elevation diagrams and sport event categories. This information is important for the sport event based developing and analysis of the related BCG Growth-Share Matrix (Reeves, Moose and Venema, 2014). We present in figure 4, the AA' section elevation area of a hypothetical case study. In this section elevation we identify the five areas with different geographical and topological characteristics, with the scope to define the most attractive event mix product portfolio investments. Each event is related with on of the two time periods (seasons) of the year, namely the, "SS": March to August and "WS": September to February.

If we analyze based on the BCG Event Product Portfolio Matrix (see figure 5), the event mix of this tourist destination we recognize that the events:

- Bocce Ball
- Artistic swimming
- Obstacle racing
- Equestrian eventing,

have the potential to gain market share and to become Stars. Destination and Event managers can invest to these event categories because they can growth rapidly if the market is continuing to Growth.

Small-scaled sport event stars generate large amount of cash because they enjoy a relative high market share and they bring also in the future cash flows and financial sustainability for the destination. In our case the event stars are, the:

- Woman running event
- Sailing for all
- Whitewater kayaking.

Market growth for some of the sport events seems to be to low when many competitors organize year-by-year same type of sport events in near regions and places for the same categories of target visitors. Many "sport event stars" are transformed

Figure 5. The BCG Product Portfolio Matrix in the case of small-scaled sport events
Note: Self-created figure

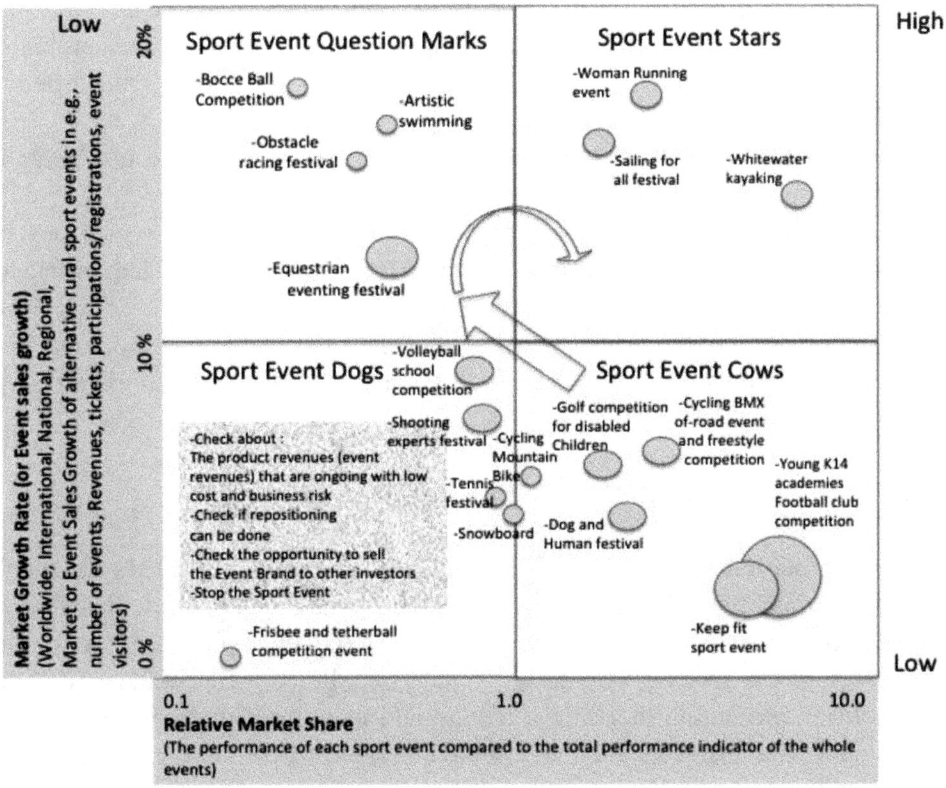

into "cash cows" (i.e., "sport event cows"). In this mature market situation these event product categories have still a large relative market share and they contribute with a high volume of cash flows e.g., revenues from tickets, participations/registrations, to the whole destination event product portfolio investment policy. In the above case the event mix of Golf competition for disabled children, Dog and Human festival, Cycling BMX of road event and freestyle competition, Young K14 academies football club competition and keep fit sport event are "event cows" and must be managed and supported to compete for long-term periods the other events of the competitors.

Sport Event, "Stars" and "Question marks" can be supported from cash flows of the "Sport Event Cows".

Sport event "Stars" and "Cows", through their success, are more likely to promote also the image and brand name of each event and in the same time the image of the venue place or else the tourist destination. The final category of "Sport event dogs" consists of events that are activated in a declining market with small relative market share opportunities. These categories are not attractive for the investors, but they have the ability to create revenues to help the organizers to overcome problems from the seasonality or other problematic situations that came up e.g., from different crisis situational factors.

Based on the above, it appears that event categorization significantly helps in the strategic planning of both events and destinations.

The decisions made for each category and type of sporting event service must be based on an analysis of the three important characteristics of the services provided. These elements are the, tangible, & intangible features of the sport event services, and the component of the service type based on the analyses of service product mix and services product line(s) of the whole product offer provided. In detail these features are presented below.

Tangible features as design elements of a sporting event.

Visitors, participants and the audience (attendees) of the small scaled sport events can through tangible information more easily understand i.e., through their senses, the level of service provided and the anticipated experience provided through the experience of the service. The design should be tailored to the standards of the stakeholders, presenting the values, culture and identity of the organizers in the space, relevant to the event and the host environment. (Brown, 2020; Bitner, 1992; Kotler, 1973; Nelson, 2009). The visual appeal of the event's website, the ease of use of search tools with smart website redirection tools, the visual information and design of its appearance, the ability to easily identify processes with symbols, information, site-space usage eg transaction capability, are essential features for an effective e-servicescape or e-atmospherics design. Also in the online environment ambient conditions, design aspects, search aids & slogans, functional aspects, and perceived quality, are basic tangible aspects of the whole e-servicescape design offer (Hopkins, Grove, Raymond and LaForge, 2009; Richards, Marques and Mein, 2014).

Intangible features as design elements of a sporting event.

Brand awareness, servicescapes and brandscapes can contribute to the positive perception forming procedure that takes places in the mind of, event visitors, participants and attendees (Hall, 2008). The intangible nature of the services is interpreted subjectively and as a tendency through the experiences of experiences that express the inner world of spectators and participants in a sporting event. The emotional state of the athletes, attendants, spectators, and their co-producers of support staff and event organizers is a productive mix of emotional situations and social contacts. These factors create unique pleasures when a sporting event is successfully designed (Nelson, 2009).

The sport event services product mix and product line(s) components.

Alternative event "products" and "product-lines" to which they belong can help the event analyst and manager to decide, about:

- the contribution of each event to the product group to which it belongs e.g. group of spring / summer activities
- the performance, improvement, maintenance, merger or even the elimination (i.e., "pruning") of the event
- the efficient operation of teams from sporting events and markets serving e.g. a group of spring / summer events for adults
- on investment and financing of new events that will likely be developed to enrich the event's product lines

In our case the geographical space (AA') comprise five elements of sub-units namely, the: A-"Rural park area", B-"Athletic cultural park area", C-"Lake water area & water park", D-"Natural forest area", and E-"River & Sea water area". Those sub-regions are divided for event seasonal observation purposes in two groups. As we can see in our example in Figure 6, there are two sets of events in the AA 'geographic area of interest, that are Spring and Summer ([Summer Semester; SS]) and Fall and Winter ([Winter Semester; WS]) sport event group Activities. For example, the "A" sub-unit of the geographical area comprises six elements of spring and summer events (SS: A1-A6) and four elements of autumn and winter events (WS: A1-A4). By monitoring the event's Life Cycle and the overall event portfolio of the area (see also Figures 3 and 5), the event planner - manager evaluates the sustainability of sport events and can remove (pruning), combine, improve, and change their venue-date categorization or even their seasonal service offer. These categories and the standardization of event-by-market specify, to the event planner and manager, in the process of analyzing the overall event portfolio, the target markets that serve or even aim to activate and develop them e.g. in our example (see Figure 7), the sport-event(s):

1. "question marks" with regard to the sport-event group of potential new sport-event entrants that may developed in the future into "star" sport-events, are related with the Mature Markets (Rural park area, Season WS; WS.A.3>"Older People Market"), the Markets for Athletes (Lake water area and water park,

Season SS; SS.C.1-Artistic swimming & Rural park area, Season WS; WS.A.4-Obstacle multi racing sport event festival >both events the Professionals and the Amateur markets), the Markets "for All" (Rural park area, Season SS; SS.A.4>"For All"-equestrian, families markets), and the Business Markets for the Professionals, investors and sponsors (Rural park area, Season SS; SS.A.4 & Season WS; WS.A.4>Business market –local enterprises, investors, sponsors, staff motivation opportunities markets etc.). These events should be supported by financial resources e.g. self-financing from local authorities and resources and revenues generated by the local "sport event cows" organizing activities or from other resources (professionals with a common fund for activities in the area, region and e.g, National & EU funding programs, investors and sponsors).

2. "event dogs", here the "WS.D.2" ("Frisbee and tetherball competition event") sporting event does not appear to be performing in the product line as it has been transferred to the area of sporting events dogs (se Figure 5) where it appears that his performance relative to other events is particularly low in terms of its relative market-share and market growth rate in which it operates. Repositioning and season change alternatives but also merging it in to another sport-event can be some strategic product portfolio decisions to change his position and it viability prospects in to the whole event portfolio matrix of the tourist and visitor destination. If this feature and support requires more support resources than the revenue it generates, it might also be worth considering the stopping of the sport-event.

SUMMARY

Often the concern of a manager in the event selection process is related to the ability to present and adopt appropriate and attractive visitor categories of sporting events. Often, both an individual business manager and a destination manager need information on a possible event categorization(s) that will enhance their product portfolio from small-scales sport events. The rationale for enriching the visitors' experiences is supported by detailed mapping e.g. section elevation diagrams, defining seasonal opportunities for developing appropriate sporting events by region or geographical area of interest. In this way, the designer can and does prepare the appropriate mix of events to target categories of visitors who prefer this kind of seasonal activity. This record also facilitates intermediate partners and promoters of events e.g., sport tour operators, e-tour operators, NTO regional offices etc., by enriching their offerings based on seasonal and visitor activity programs per visiting place. This chapter contributes to the understanding of the importance of

Figure 6. Indicative product lines and the relevant Marketing mix in the previous case study

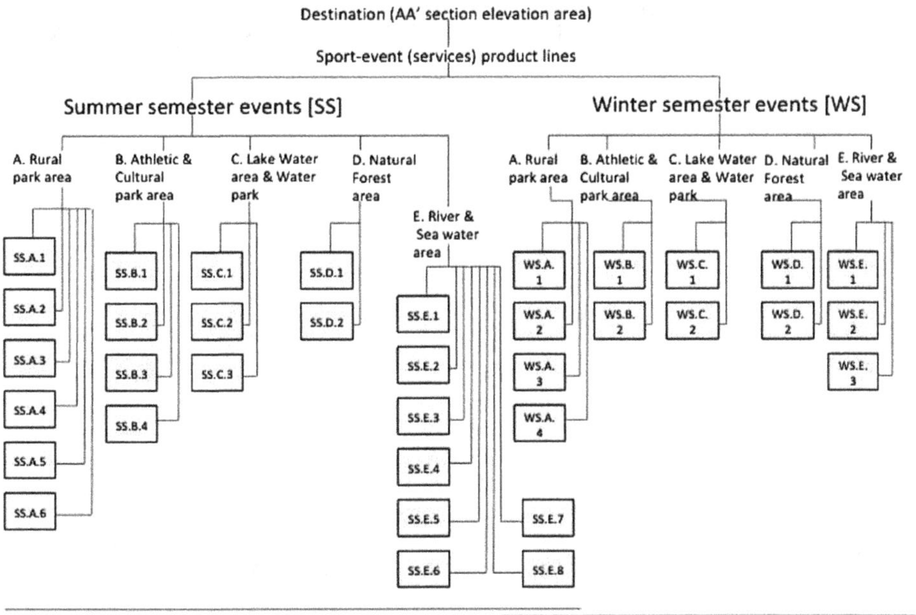

Note: Where,			
SS.A.1	: Archery festival for students	WS.A.1	: Cross country skiing
SS.A.2	: Rural park semi marathon running event	WS.A.2	: Snowboard
SS.A.3	: Cycling mountain bike festival	WS.A.3	: Bocce ball competition
SS.A.4	: Equestrian Eventing festival	WS.A.4	: Obstacle- multi racing sport event festival
SS.A.5	: Golf competition for disabled children	WS.B.1	: Trampoline experts festival
SS.A.6	: Tennis festival	WS.B.2	: Cycling BMX of-road event and freestyle competition
SS.B.1	: Woman Running event	WS.C.1	: Shooting experts festival
SS.B.2	: Young women fencing technique competition	WS.C.2	: Sailing for all festival
SS.B.3	: Young K14 academies Football club competition	WS.D.1	: Dog and Human festival
SS.B.4	: Volleyball school competition	WS.D.2	: Frisbee and tetherball competition event
SS.C.1	: Artistic swimming	WS.E.1	: Plogging at the seaside area
SS.C.2	: Cycling marathon around the lake area	WS.E.2	: Triathlon competition
SS.C.3	: Whitewater kayaking festival	WS.E.3	: Polar bear plunge festival
SS.D.1	: Equestrian regional festival		
SS.D.2	: "Keep fit" sport event		
SS.E.1	: Artistic swimming		
SS.E.2	: Sea Kayaking		
SS.E.3	: Canoe competition event		
SS.E.4	: Diving festival		
SS.E.5	: River trekking event		
SS.E.6	: Fishing festival		
SS.E.7	: Underwater orienteering event		
SS.E.8	: Windsurfing festival		

categorizing events at the level of strategic product portfolio analysis on an annual basis. At the same time, it proposes a combination of various tools such as Product Life Cycle/ Tourist Area Life Cycle, Ansoff Product – Market strategy Matrix,

Figure 7. Product – Market matrix of the small sports event offer in the tourist destination (geographical area AA')

Products / Markets	A. Rural park area		B. Athletic & cultural park area		C. Lake water area & water park		D. Natural forest area		E. River & sea water area	
	[SS]	[WS]	[SS]	[WS]	[SS]	[WS]	[SS]	[WS]	[SS]	[WS]
Young people		WS.A.2	SS.B.3	WS.B.:1,2				WS.D.:1		
Students/pupils	SS.A.1	WS.A.:1,2	SS.B.4							
Disable children	SS.A.5							WS.D.:1		
Older people		WS.A.3						WS.D.:1		
Women			SS.B.:1,2							
Men			SS.B.3							
Athletes (professional, non-professional)	SS.A.: 2,3,6	WS.A.4	SS.B.: 1,2,3		SS.C.1,2,3	WS.C.1			SS.E.: 1,2,3,4,5, 7,8	WS.E.2
"For all" (equestrian, families)	SS.A.:4,5			WS.B.1		WS.C.2	SS.D.:1,2	WS.D.:1,2	SS.E.6	WS.E.:1,3
Business (local enterprises, investors, sponsors, staff motivation etc.)	SS.A.:4,5	WS.A.4		WS.B.1		WS.C.2	SS.D.:1,2	WS.D.:1,2	SS.E.6	WS.E.:1,3

Note: Where,

SS.A.1 : Archery festival for students
SS.A.2 : Rural park semi marathon running event
SS.A.3 : Cycling mountain bike festival
SS.A.4 : Equestrian Eventing festival
SS.A.5 : Golf competition for disabled children
SS.A.6 : Tennis festival

SS.B.1 : Woman Running event
SS.B.2 : Young women fencing technique competition
SS.B.3 : Young K14 academies Football club competition
SS.B.4 : Volleyball school competition

SS.C.1 : Artistic swimming
SS.C.2 : Cycling marathon around the lake area
SS.C.3 : Whitewater kayaking festival
SS.D.1 : Equestrian regional festival
SS.D.2 : "Keep fit" sport event
SS.E.1 : Artistic swimming
SS.E.2 : Sea Kayaking
SS.E.3 : Canoe competition event
SS.E.4 : Diving festival
SS.E.5 : River trekking event
SS.E.6 : Fishing festival
SS.E.7 : Underwater orienteering event
SS.E.8 : Windsurfing festival

WS.A.1 : Cross country skiing
WS.A.2 : Snowboard
WS.A.3 : Bocce ball competition
WS.A.4 : Obstacle- multi racing sport event festival
WS.B.1 : Trampoline experts festival
WS.B.2 : Cycling BMX of-road event and freestyle competition
WS.C.1 : Shooting experts festival
WS.C.2 : Sailing for all festival
WS.D.1 : Dog and Human festival
WS.D.2 : Frisbee and tetherball competition event
WS.E.1 : Plogging at the seaside area
WS.E.2 : Triathlon competition
WS.E.3 : Polar bear plunge festival

Boston Consulting Group Product Portfolio Matrix and finally the use of section elevation diagrams to facilitate to the management decisions about the distribution of events over the seasons of a year.

REVIEW QUESTIONS

1. What is the major problem in categorizing sporting events and especially small scaled events?
2. How to manage an event portfolio through sharing or combining categories of event types and strategic product portfolios?
3. How can one determine the position of a small event per season and phase of the Product Life Cycle in the case of a Tourism Destination? Discuss the answer and propose some own ideas.
4. What kind of small-scale sporting event categorization would best support administrative decisions in the case of strategic product analysis and selection by:
   a. Ansoff (Ansoff's Matrix Theory)?
   b. TALC ?
   c. BCG Product Portfolio Matrix incorporated with section elevation diagrams?

   Discuss your answer and give some examples too.
5. What is a Section elevation Diagram and how can we use it for small scales sport events?

REFERENCES

Ansoff, I. (1957). Strategies for Diversification. *Harvard Business Review*, *35*(5), 113–124.

Bichi, A., Wijlens, R., & Wallace, E. (2017). *Strategic research and Innovation Agenda 2016-2021*. EPSI.

Bitner, M. J. (1992). Servicescapes: The Impact of Physical Surroundings on Customers and Employees. *Journal of Marketing*, *56*(2), 57–71. doi:10.1177/002224299205600205

Bladen, C., Kennell, J., Abson, E., & Wilde, N. (2018). *Events management: an introduction* (2nd ed.). Routledge.

Booms, B. H., & Bitner, M. J. (1981). Marketing strategies and organisation structures for service firms. In J. Donnelly & W. R. George (Eds.), *Marketing of Services*. American Marketing Association.

Bowdin, G. A. J., Allen, J., O'Toole, W., Harris, R., & McDonnell, I. (2011). *Events Management* (3rd ed.). Butterworth-Heinemann, Elsevier.

Brown, G. (2020). *Eventscapes-Transforming Place, Space and Experiences*. Routledge.

Butler, R. W. (1980). The concept of tourism area cycle of evolution: Implications for management of resources. *The Canadian Geographer. Geographe Canadien, 24*(1), 5–12. doi:10.1111/j.1541-0064.1980.tb00970.x

Clifford, D. K. Jr. (1965). Managing the Product Life Cycle. *Management Review, 54*(6), 34–38.

Dimanche, F. (2003). The role of sport events in destination marketing. Aiest 53rd Congress in Sport and Tourism, Athens, Greece.

Duglio, S., & Beltramo, R. (2017). Estimating the economic impacts of a small-scale sport tourism event: The case of the Italo-Swiss mountain trail CollonTrek. *Sustainability, 9*(3), 1–17. doi:10.3390u9030343

Gammon, S. (2012). Sports events: Typologies, people and place. In S. J. Page & J. Connell (Eds.), *The Routledge handbook of events* (pp. 104–118). Routledge.

Getz, D. (2007). *Event studies: Theory, research, and policy for planned events*. Elsevier.

Getz, D., & Page, S. J. (2016). Progress and prospects for event tourism research. *Tourism Management, 52*, 593–631. doi:10.1016/j.tourman.2015.03.007

Gibson, H. J., Kaplanidou, K., & Kang, S. J. (2012). Small-scale event sport tourism: A case study in sustainable tourism. *Sport Management Review, 15*(2), 160–170. doi:10.1016/j.smr.2011.08.013

Gratton, C., Shibili, S., & Dobson, N. (2000). The economic importance of major sports events. *Managing Leisure, 5*(1), 17–28. doi:10.1080/136067100375713

Hall, C. M. (2008). Servicescapes, designscapes, branding, and the creation of place-identity: South of Litchfield, Christchurch. *Journal of Travel & Tourism Marketing, 25*(3-4), 233–250. doi:10.1080/10548400802508101

Higham, J. (1999). Commentary—sport as an avenue of tourism development: An analysis of the positive and negative impacts of sport tourism. *Current Issues in Tourism, 2*(1), 82–90. doi:10.1080/13683509908667845

Hopkins, C. D., Grove, S. J., Raymond, M. A., & LaForge, M. C. (2009). Designing the e-Servicescape: Implications for Online Retailers. *Journal of Internet Commerce, 8*(1-2), 23–43. doi:10.1080/15332860903182487

Houlihan, B., & Green, M. (2011). *Routledge Handbook of Sports Development.* Routledge.

Kaplanidou, K., & Vogt, C. (2007). The interrelationship between sport event and destination image and sport tourists' behaviours. *Journal of Sport & Tourism, 12*(3-4), 183–206. doi:10.1080/14775080701736932

Kotler, P. (1973). Atmospherics as a marketing tool. *Journal of Retailing, 49*(4), 48–64.

Kotler, P. (2000). *Principles of Marketing, Product life cycle: characteristic, strategies and objectives.* Pearson Education.

Kurtzman, J. (2005). Sports tourism categories. *Journal of Sport & Tourism, 10*(1), 15–20. doi:10.1080/14775080500101502

Levitt, T. (1965). EXPLOIT the Product Life Cycle. *Harvard Business Review, 43*(6), 81–94.

Liponski, W. (2003). World Sports Encyclopedia; Worldwide list of traditional games and sports. MIB Publishing Company LLC.

Nam, T., & Pardo, T. A. (2011). Conceptualizing Smart City with Dimensions of Technology, People, and Institutions. *12th Annual International Conference on Digital Government Research.* 10.1145/2037556.2037602

Nelson, K. B. (2009). Enhancing the Attendee's Experience through Creative Design of the Event Environment: Applying Goffman's Dramaturgical Perspective. *Journal of Convention & Event Tourism, 10*(2), 120–133. doi:10.1080/15470140902922023

Reeves, M., Moose, S., & Venema, T. (2014). The Growth Share Matrix. BCG – The Boston Consulting Group.

Reic, I. (2017). *Events Marketing Management; A consumer perspective.* Routledge.

Richards, G., Marques, L., & Mein, K. (2014). Event design: conclusions and future research directions. In G. Richards, L. Marques, & K. Mein (Eds.), *Event Design: Social perspectives and practices* (pp. 198–212). Routledge. doi:10.4324/9780203761908

Sport, U. K. (2004). *Measuring success 2: Thee economic impact of Major Sport Events.* UK Sports.

Wilson, R. (2006). The economic impact of local sport events: Significant, limited or otherwise? A case study of four swimming events. *Managing Leisure, 11*(1), 57–70. doi:10.1080/13606710500445718

Ziakas, V. (2010). Understanding an event portfolio: The uncovering of interrelationships, synergies, and leveraging opportunities. *Journal of Policy Research in Tourism, Leisure & Events*, *2*(2), 144–164. doi:10.1080/19407963.2010.482274

Chapter 3
The Engagement of Community and Volunteers in a Small-Scale Sport Event and the Impact on Sustainable Tourism

Valentina Della Corte
https://orcid.org/0000-0001-7113-3167
University of Naples Federico II, Italy

Giovanna Del Gaudio
University of Naples Federico II, Italy

Giuliana Nevola
University of Naples Federico II, Italy

ABSTRACT

This work aims to investigate the key role of local community through volunteerism experience in small-scale sport events and the impact that the community engagement in small sport events can have on the local destination in terms of sustainable tourism. To do this analysis, the authors take into consideration the triple bottom line approach. Given the interdisciplinary character of sustainability, the chapter investigates the relation between small sport events and community, underlining two main aspects: the strategic role of volunteers in terms of community capabilities and the impact that small sport events have on local community in terms of social cohesion and local identity. Small-scale sport events, indeed, strengthen the sense of community and tradition, thus attracting visitors. In the last section of the chapter, an interesting case study and a series of sustainable tourism indicators are illustrated.

DOI: 10.4018/978-1-7998-4757-1.ch003

INTRODUCTION

Sport can be considered a physical activity organized through the participation of different actors that interact with each other to reach a common objective, such as the victory of a competition. Most of sports are collective activities where different athletes interact. Sport activities are organized through some rules that are commonly shared and roles attributed to each player. Sport is represented by a community of stakeholders such as players, coaches, attendances that share the same mission, objective and rules.

The organization of a sport event is supported by the cooperation of several stakeholders and in the specific case of a small-scale sport event a key role is played by the local community and a network of volunteers that provide own capacities and skills to help managers to organize efficient and successful event organizations.

Today volunteerism is considered a new segment market of the tourism and leisure sectors. Millions of travellers take part to many voluntary programmes around the world visiting developing countries (Guttentag, 2009). According to Save Children (2018), voluntourism is one of the fastest-growing travel trends, with 1.6 million people volunteering overseas each year and an expenditure of $2.6 billion is estimated annually.

Although the voluntourism in developing countries has a strong impact in the tourism sector, volunteerism related to the event industry has also an effect on local community in terms of sustainable tourism, indeed the participation of local volunteers in sport event represent a factor of attractiveness for tourists to visit a destination.

Volunteers represent a relevant resource for the local tourism and for the event organization. A correct management of volunteers is needed to manage a sport event organization in the best efficient way. Especially in small scale sport events (S-SSE) where the event organizers need to interact with local community and to create a strong mutual relationship between event organization and volunteers.

The main scope of this chapter is to underline the relationship between the event organization and the local volunteers as well as to study how a S-SSE can affect the development of local community in terms of sustainable tourism and the contribution of the community to the implementation of the event.

Sport Event Typology And The Planning Process In A Community

Several authors offer an overview regarding the different typology of sport events, most of them pay attention to mega events and only few of them try to give a definition of small events. Previous authors (Gratton, Nigel Dobson & Simon Shibli, 2000) offer a classification identifying four man categories: 1) Mega Events as Olympic and The Fifa World Cup Game, 2) Major spectators' sport events held annually, 3) Irregular major sporting competitions as international level swimming event; 4) Major competitor driven events, 5)Small scale sport events include minor events where competitors are often more than spectators, they occur annually and are not characterized by a large national media interest and a limited economic activity compared to the large-scale events.

There is not a clear distinction about the differences among events but the are many indicators on the which the categorization is based: the economic impact, the local, regional, national and international level, the media interest, the regular or irregular occurrence, the number of spectator and players, the tourism impact and the sport development opportunity.

Through these indicators the chapter provides a typology of sport events (Gammon, 2014)

1. Mega event is a large and great sporting event, large in terms of size and the adjective great is referred to the resonance and level of pleasantness. (Maennig & Zimbalist, 2012). The main indicators to identify a mega-event consist in the numbers of athletes, attendees and viewers; the share of attendees and viewers coming from outside the area where the event takes place, the number of TV transmissions and the number of hours addressed to transmit the event. Another important aspect to take in consideration is represented to the visibility of the events, in terms of audience, it can be measured considering the number of people that follows the event on internet and in printed media or on the radio. On the other hand, an important aspect that helps to define a mega event is its economic impact in term of revenues that it produces the, attendee's expenditure, the employment rate that produces.
2. Special events are considered events that are outside the normal routine organization, the specialness of this typology is linked to the organization rather than the perception of spectator and attendances. It is hard to distinguish this kind of the event from the others, especially from mega events that are often considered special. The meaning of the character "special" is subjective, different authors offer different point of views. (Van Niekerk, 2017).
3. Hall Mark Events represent all those that have a closed link with the place where they take place that have a huge impact on the local community and tourism (Allen, O'toole, Harris, & McDonnell,2008). This typology of event is considered a major event that occurrences annually or periodically and belongs to the tradition of the place and community. It's not unsurprising that many sport events are considered all mark events because of their closed connection with the land where they take place. Sport often is expression of a community, a tradition. Hall Mark events have a so strong impact on the place

where they take place that people will associate a destination for that event. The impact of the event will also persist after the end of the event. Sport teams often assume a hallmark status with the cities or place where they compete, as example football teams as Manchester United that take place of the city and attract visitors that maybe will stay for more than one day.

4. Festivals and parades include events and sport events linked to festivals, parades and heritage. Also, in this case it's difficult to explain the main characteristics of this typology. They are considered minor events; indeed, the organizers usually prefer to undervalue the competitive character of the event as smaller youth-based event. Due to the closed link with the heritage they are characterized by the role of the spectators that often are involved in the organization. Finally, a sport parade can consist in celebrations in the streets where fans and spectators wait their favourite team after witnessing their competition and victory.
5. Small scale sport events are all those events of small size where the local community is involved in the organization through volunteerism activities. They don't have a media interest at national or international level, they are local or at the best regional events.

Their costs and risks are inferiors than those of mega or major events. Community-based events could range from simple school competitions to regional games. (Watt, 1998; Shone & Parry, 2004). These events have a strong impact on the community in terms of identity, civic pride. The Shrovetide Royal Festival, in Derbyshire UK is certainly the most important event of the city and one of most famous in UK. It is not an even organized for tourism proposes, it is really part of the life and emotion of the Ashbourne population. The competition has ancient origins, which goes back to the XVI century, and it has never interrupted. The whole territory of the city is considered a football field divided in two parts by the river. Each part of the city is connected to the games, in local pub there are relics, trophies of victories, costumes of the Historical game and flags.

Taking in consideration the definitions and indicators proposed by authors illustrated above, a simple event planning process will be illustrated taking in consideration the support of community.

The planning process can be divided in three phases: The preparation phase, a detailed planning and the post event phase.

Each phase consists in a set of tasks and in the preparation phase the main task is the definition of event concept. Most of organizers define the event concept using the 5w's model that favours an easy identification of the main aspects of an event. The organizer has to answer the following questions:

Figure 1. Planning process
Source from: Dowson and Basset (2015)

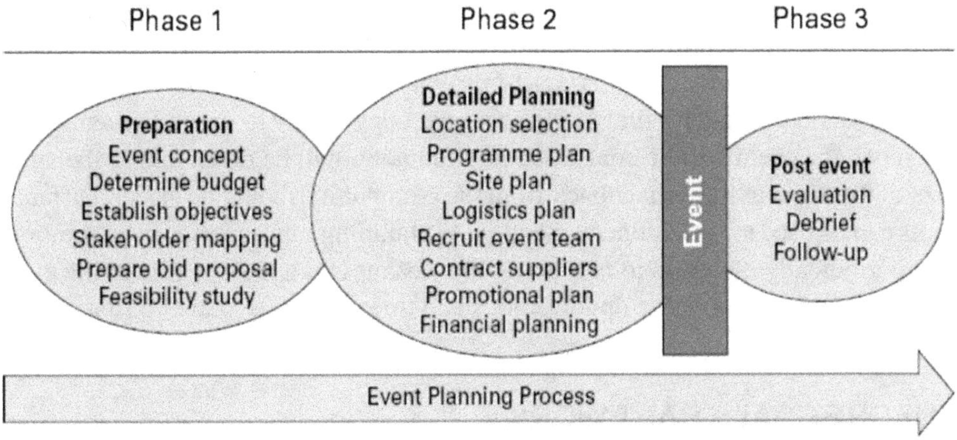

- **Why?** Identifying the reason because the events take place, the motivations and the objectives;
- **Where?** To identifying the venues, the location where the event will take place;
- **Who?** To identifying the target audience, the customer profile and attendee numbers;
- **When?** Planning the time, all the phases of the process, and identify the task for each phase, define the timing of each phase and task;
- **What?** Writing a detailed programme, the activities and format.

In the case of SSSEs that are linked to the community is important to define a valid concept, a reason that can be attractive for the local audience, in this case most of the concept ideas are linked to the tradition, the custom of local people.

After defining the concept It's necessary to determine the budget. When the event organizer determines the budget, he starts to prepare a detailed planning interacting with his stakeholders.

This is the second phase of the planning process that consists to interact with suppliers, to find the venues, to prepare a promotional plan and financial plan, recruiting a team and volunteers. It is necessary to understand the financial feasibility for the event. In this phase that can be considered and operational phase the organizer will interact with suppliers to find advantageous commercial agreements. A small-scale event supports less costs and risks than a big event and of course the community can be a source in this case, informal agreements favour the use of venues at competitive prices. An event organized at local level favours interpersonal relations that favour advantageous commercial agreements.

In order to find financial resources, small scale events look for sponsorship contracts, an event always offers the opportunity for the sponsor to have great visibility, during a local event many firms, start-ups, youth organizations are well willing to be sponsors because they find in the event the opportunity to promote themselves.

When the event will be concluded an evaluation will be done, due to the small size of the event to have a feedback from the community should be easier. Different tools can be used as: questioners, meeting, the building of a community institutions that periodically meets up to talk about the weaknesses and strengths of the event and to analysis the possible opportunities and threats for the future editions.

THEORETICAL FRAMEWORK

Sport is the expression of a community organized in roles and rules. The community represents a strategic resource of a sport event, especially in case of a sport event at local level. Sport and community have a strong mutual relation. Coalter (2010), provides a theoretical framework to explain how sport events support community development through three main dimensions: Traditional Sport, Sport Plus and Plus Sport.

- Traditional sport: sporting activities that favour the community development;
- Sport Plus: sporting practices aimed to maximize development goals;
- Plus Sport: the popularity of a sport to attract participants and involve them in development program.

According to these three main functions, a theoretical model is proposed to put in evidence the impact of a S-SSE on local communities in terms of capabilities and sustainable tourism.

Sport and Volunteerism

Previous authors (Laverie & McDonald, 2007; Green & Chalip 2004) define volunteerism as a series of leisure activities made with non-profit objectives and volunteers can be considered leisure participants motivated for a common cause and involved in collective activities supported by social contacts.

Different motivations push volunteers to join sport events, such as the willing to support their favourite sport or team as well as their community (Hamm, MacLean & Misener, 2008). Individuals prefer volunteer activities to satisfy social needs,

Figure 2. Theoretical model
Source: our elaboration from Kim et, al. (2018), Wendel et al. (2009), O' Brien & Chalip (2007), Getz et al. (2012)

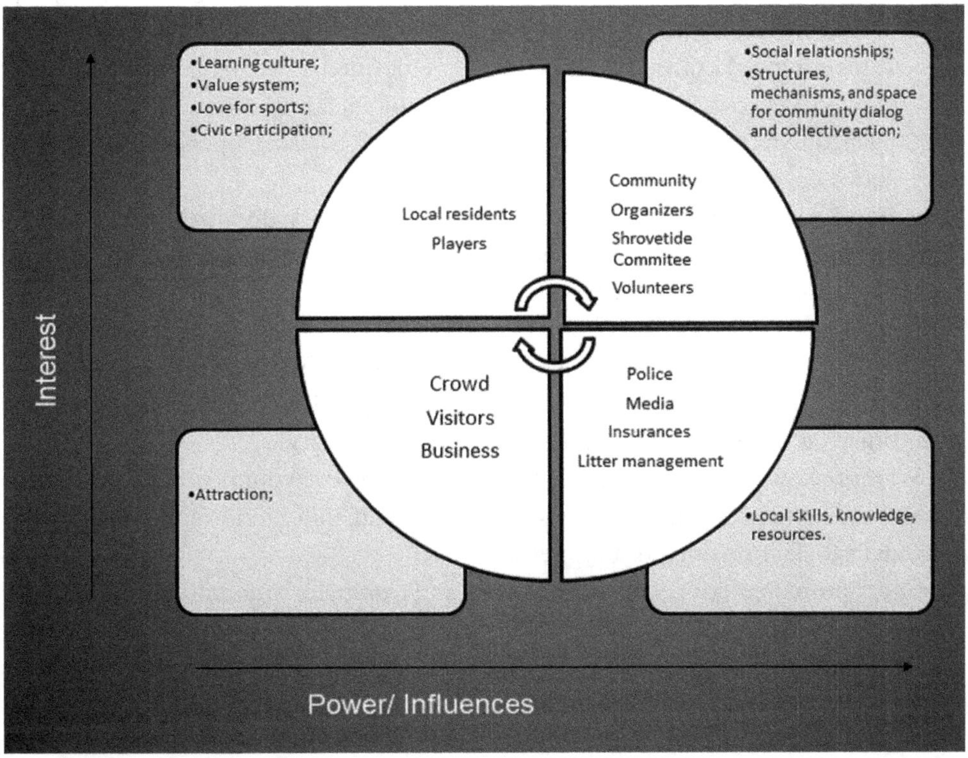

such as socializing and interacting with other volunteers to share common interests in sport activities or to meet new friends.

Kim, Fredline, & Cuskelly, (2018) define six main motivations to join volunteerism in S-SSE.

1. **Expression of value:** The main value that is expressed in volunteerism is "altruism" that is shared across many volunteers during their participation in volunteerism activities. In 2011 The International Labor Organization defines volunteerism as an unpaid non-compulsory work through the which an individual offers their time for free to satisfy social needs.
2. **Career orientation:** It is defined an instrumentalist factor. In this segment the volunteers are identified as youngers that have not started to work yet, and they find in volunteer activities the opportunity to acquire and develop skills and to interact with company managers.

3. **Love for sport:** The motivation is the pure sport interest. Individuals interested in a specific sport express their interest participating to voluntary activities.
4. **Community involvement:** Volunteers want to express their community proud to host the event taking part in voluntary activities.
5. **Interpersonal contacts:** Individuals are defined as social animals that seek new social contacts in order to create new social relations. Individuals are pushed to participate in voluntary activities to satisfice a personal need, their social needs.
6. **Extrinsic rewards:** It is an instrumental factor. Individuals participate in voluntary activities to receive some material and tangible benefits such as: conditions of work and services.

This last motivation category belongs to a set of external factors that don't affect the personal sphere of participants, instead of the previous motivations belonging to intrinsic factors of the human being and its community.

Warner, Newland and Green (2011) state that sport volunteerism strengthens a sense of community that impacts relevant social individual outcomes such as personal satisfaction and commitment.

Sport promotes collective experiences and volunteerism can be considered a social capital outcome (Putnam, 2000; Warner 2012). McCole, Jacobs, Lindley and McAvoy (2012) state that the community sense among volunteers represents a strategic role to retain seasonal employees. Green and Chalip (2004) affirm that belonging to a community means to believe in the same mission and related purposes and therefore to have a common identity. S-SSE volunteer experiences offer the opportunity to strengthen the sense of community and consequently to produce social impact outcome encouraging pro-citizenship and pro-social behaviours.

Sport and Community Capabilities

Wendel et. al (2009) identify seven dimensions of community capabilities developed through volunteer activities in S-SSE: skills, knowledge, and resources; social relationships; structures and mechanisms for community dialog; quality leadership; civic participation; value system; and learning culture.

Edward (2015), examines some sport event practices to identify the elements that may enhance these seven dimensions of community capability.

- **Local skills, knowledge and resources:** They represent the main factors to develop and strengthen a community. The sport event management contributes to develop these elements, sport events represent one of the most relevant links between sport and community building.

Community members involved in voluntary activities in S-SSE usually receive training and experiences and develop new skills related to the capacity building such as planning, administration, fundraising and communication. (Kay, & Bradbury, 2009).

- **Social relationships** represent another key factor of building community capacity, sport events strengthen the social cohesion and social capital.

Most of the sport practices have the objective to put people together, they often provide social inclusion opportunities more than voluntary organizations. Leares and Peachey (2011), argue that a strong social cohesion between volunteers occurs in sport events when an equal status co-exists among group members, common goals, intergroup cooperation and supporting structures. Some sport events can be organized to improve social relations and to break down ethnic, religious barriers. In sport events, volunteers can develop friendship crossing different social classes, religions and other barriers. In many cases, sport is considered to provide social connections in communities, in rural areas and between natives and immigrants (Mata-Codesal, Peperkamp, & Tiesler, 2015).

An example of social cohesion in sport activity at local level is the soccer team in Belfast, Northern Ireland, composed of Catholic and Protestant players. In this specific case sport is considered a link of social interconnection. In the past Catholics used to play Gaelic sports, while soccer and rugby were played by Protestants in the south of the Island.

Football was considered an English game and until 1971 the Gaelic Athletic Association (GGA) banned Catholics to play or attending "foreign" sporting events. When the GAA ban was broken down, soccer became more popular in the south, and more Catholics played in the Northern Ireland Team. Today the Republic of Ireland's nationality law allows anyone from the island to play for the Northern Ireland team (Collins, 2018; Walker, 2019).

The Northern Ireland team represents a community identity that goes beyond religion aspects and it's an expression of social and political changes.

- Structures, mechanisms, and space for community dialog and collective action

The organizational structure is the main pillar on which a community is built. Community capacity requires inter-organizational networks, organization and communication systems, "safe" community space for dialog and problem-solving, and mechanism for empowerment and collective actions (Wender et. al, 2009). Sport events at community level often favour multi- sectoral (government, no-profit, business and media) partnerships at different levels.

Interorganizational partnerships favour an easier access to different resources and competencies and favour a maximization of their exploitation. Sport events are considered communication strategies to disseminate messages at local, national and international level. In this sense, sport events can attract people and encourage a proactive citizen behaviour, break down group barriers and change individual attitudes.

- **Quality of leadership:** for a community building it is important to have some leader figures that can communicate goals, motivate community members, acquire resources, take initiatives to implement strategic decisions. In a sport event volunteers are engaged in some activities and some of them are engaged to be responsible of these activities and to coordinate other volunteers, in this way volunteers develop leadership skills. In sport events, leadership is developed and shared through a participatory approach rather than an autocratic approach, in other words leaders share their knowledge and use their communication and decision taking capabilities in order to satisfice community needs and to engage the rest of the community in the activities in order to achieve common objectives.

In sport events, there are also pivotal actors that held leadership position such as champions, athletes, coaches that have a high level of symbolic power, trust community and credibility. (Burnett, 2006)

- **Civic participation** is a behaviour that is often adopted by volunteers in their activities in sport events. S-SSEs encourage an increasing community identity that equips and empowers volunteers to participate in community activities. Sport often represents an input to civic participation in local cultural, political and economic relations.

S-SSEs are often organized from the bottom up with the auxilium of citizens that have and share different ideas. When community members feel involved in the event organization, they become more empowered and develop a civic participation approach.

- **Value system:** It consists of a set of values on the which the community development is based. The community capacity is often built on this following set of values: equity, democratic participation, collaboration, inclusion and social responsibility. Sport reflects community values but in some nations sport events are reserved to an elite audience that could be in contrast with values such as inclusion and equity. In some Nations the access to sport events could be limited to an elite audience. Often tickets are too expensive that can preclude the access to people holding a low personal income.

- **Learning Culture:** Community needs to develop a critical way to think about its history, structures, to adopt different points of view on different issues, in order to take different problem solving decisions. Different sport institutions defend and support tradition and culture, and volunteer experiences allow members to focus on issues and try to find different solutions for a common objective. Sharing ideas and different point of views enrich the capability of community stakeholders engaged in the event. As example to manage games and sport events that can be considered dangerous (e.g. Shrovetide Royal Festival, case study of this chapter). This traditional and historical sport event for players and participants represents a challenge, the local community shares all its capabilities and skills to preserve this characteristic of the game and to find alternative solutions to preserve players, attendances form any accidents due to the "lack of rule" of the game.

Small- Scale Sport Event, Community and Sustainable Tourism

As the chapter has already analysed the impact of community has a key role to preserve a S-SSE from social changes and from tourism industry development. According to Wendel (2009) and Edward (2015) event organizations contribute to the community development affecting factors as cultural learning, civic participation and so on.

In this section the focus is on the impact of S-SSE on local community in terms of sustainable tourism.

Higham (1999) makes an analysis focused on negative and positive effects of sport on tourism, making a comparison between the sustainable impact of large-scale events and S-SSE.

According to his studies, the main sustainable issues related to large scale sport events consist in financial burdens, the utility of the facilities after the event, the environmental impact and negative social impact as resident displacement.

Higham (1999) argues that S-SSEs tend to generate a relevant visitor flow, to use facilities already existing, to be appropriate for community size, and to require very little financial resources. Taking in consideration community needs and infrastructure building Doshi, Schumacher and Snyder (2001) affirm that an infrastructure built for a sporting event has to meet the needs of the local community and not only the needs of visitors and tournaments. The building of event facilities must be planned to be useful for resident in the long run.

Higham's analysis confirms the interdisciplinary character of sustainability, considering some development issues produced by S-SSEs such as financial burdens, resident dissatisfaction and negative environmental impact) that are tightly related to the three pillars of sustainability (social, economic and environmental).

In 1993 UNWTO argues that the tourism sustainable meets the needs of present tourists and host regions while protecting and enhancing opportunities for the future. Furthermore Catter (1993) adds customer satisfaction as key dimension in sustainable tourism and Liu (2013) affirms that the tourist demand has always to be taken in consideration in any sustainable tourism plan. Policymakers and destination managers have always to take in consideration the carrying capacity of a destination. The sustainable tourism must meet needs of tourists, tourist business, host communities and environmental protection.

O' Brien and Chalip (2007) identify S-SSEs as features of sustainable tourism and suggest that triple bottom line should provide S-SSES with guidelines to implement strategies to achieve sustainable objectives: economic, social and environmental.

Economic Impact

Wilson, (2006) defines S-SSEs as minor events that occur annually, where the number of competitors could be greater than number of spectators, with a limited national media interest and limited economic impact compared to large scale events. These events take place in small size community and provide more economic benefits than if they were hold in large cities. This is since in S-SSEs revenues exceed the costs. Most of the revenues come from accommodation and food, and other business as petrol station and retailer, while the cost reduction is due to the fact that most facilities already exist. In terms of tourist flows, S-SSE attracts. To measure the economic impact Gibson et al. (2012) introduce some indicators that take in account both day trippers and overnight visitors. They consider the patterns of their time spent in community and type of accommodation used and their expenditures

Social Impact

S-SSEs have a positive effect on the quality life of residents and increase the community pride and spirit. The use of volunteers and already existing facilities maximise social, physic and economic impacts. To measure the social impact the researchers' attention is focused on the visitor satisfaction and on the revisit decision of participants, taking in consideration the following factors as the event organization, event administration and quality of facilities.

Environmental Impact

S-SSEs affect the environment negatively lesser than large scale sporting event. This is due to different factors, such as the local dimension of the event, the engagement of local community and the utility of facilities already existing. Local community feels part of the event and is motivated to preserve its home town from any kind of pollution forms.

The utility of facilities already existing favours the environmental equilibrium of the hosting destination, avoiding the ecological footprint reduction. The ecological footprint measures the amount of biologically productive land and water area required to produce the resources that an individual, population or activity consumes and to absorb the waste it generates, given prevailing technology and resource management.

In the small scale event industry, the carbon footprint represents an important measure to study the environmental impact of an event organization on a destination. It represents the amount of carbon dioxide released into the atmosphere as a result of the activities of a particular individual, organization, or community. In this case the carbon footprint results to be lower than large scale events as most visitors are local or they come from close regions, and they don't consume much fuel to reach the hosting destination.

Hall Mark Tourist Events and Community

Taking in consideration the sustainable dimensions of a destination, despite the small size, S-SSE sometimes can be considered Hall Mark event attracting several tourists that otherwise would not come to visit the destinations.

Hall Mark events offer the opportunity local community to guarantee in the tourism market a good visibility at national and international level for a short term (Hall & Selwood, 1987).

The main definition is provided by Ritichie (1984), who argues that hall mark event is a major one time or a recurring event aimed at enhancing the awareness, appeal and profitability of a tourism destination in the short term. Hall Mark event organization is a strategic marketing choice to face seasonal problems of a destinations.

Getz, Svensson, Peterssen, & Gunnervall, (2012) define Hall Market event as short-term events such as festivals, carnivals in small town and villages that have a relevant economic and social impact. They define three main functions of Hall Market Events:

- Benefit tourism and host community attracting tourist, creating and promoting a positive image that is co-branded with the destination, and providing residents with benefits.
- Strengthen the sense of community and the place identity.
- Facilitate identity building.

These events have a strong attractiveness in terms of visitors and tourists, the geographic spread and its appeal compared to competitive events. The attractiveness is strictly connected with the marketing notion of a Unique Selling Proposition. The attractiveness degree can be measured through the willing of people living far away from the host location to travel to experience the event (Mill and Morrison, 1985). Without any doubt sport attracts more tourists than other events and some sport events have reached iconic and hallmark status. Their reputation rooted in the local tradition has a strong impact in terms of visitors and the local support is a prerequisite for its strong appeal. Moreover, reputation attracts a huge number of fund raiser, making the host community a grant taker.

The reputation favours a positive image for the destination and community, the destination is identified in the event and in the community. The event can shape the host community image. Small events strictly connected to the local community can provide a destination with a huge media coverage. A co-branding relation subsist among the event, destination and community.

The community gets several benefits as economic gains deriving from the tourism industry first.

Events can provide residents with sustainable local jobs, and the increasing of local businesses. Periodical local events, often, favour the infrastructural improvement of a community such the building of transport and leisure facilities. As example during sport events as bike tours, roads are completely restructured and the cycle paths will persist after the event. Community is often called to build new infrastructures and a participatory approach is well developed.

Considering the triple bottom line approach Hall mark events answer sustainability criteria. Indeed, they favour the local economy, the social cohesion and they must be green in environmental terms (waste, energy, water, recycling, traffic, carbon emissions).

As already told, they are often subjected to the local and government support, and in order to get some financial benefits they must fit sustainable requirements.

THE CASE STUDY

Ashbourne Shrovetide Royal Festival

Ashbourne Royal Shrovetide Football is a sporting event that occurs annually on the Shrove Tuesday and Ash Wednesday in the market town of Ashbourne in the Derbyshire in United Kingdom. It can be considered a fully immersive event whose venue is the town and main actor is represented by the community. The event is becoming a tourist attraction and favours the promotion of the small town that already has a strategic geographical position.

Ashbourne is a small market town located in the National Peak District in England, the first National Park to be mentioned in UK and the second most visited National Park in the world. It counts between 20 thousand and 26 thousand visitors per year (McCabe and Stockoe, 2004). Ashbourne has a very strategic position, located only 2 miles from Dovedale, a local beauty spot. The town provides visitors with shopping facilities, amenities and leisure shopping, and it offers accommodation to Park National's visitors. Because its strategic geographical location that makes it a tourist destination rich of natural and historical and art resources, the town has experienced structural changes from its traditional industry to tourism service industry. For example, the cattle market, recently has closed and it has been replaced from hotels and the secondary school was split in two sites, and one of these was designated for housing.

The Royal Ashbourne Shrovetide Football Game is an historic mass football game that takes place every year on Shrove Tuesday and Hash Wednesday. This form of game was very popular in UK, It was considered a leisure activity that represented the bases of traditional football and rugby game but there are no evidences of mass nature of the game. It is named Royal because the event received the royal asset two times: once in 1928 by King Edward VIII and again in 2003 by Prince Charles.

The origins of this festival are unknown,and most sources are provided by the publication of an old journal Ashbourne News Telegraph, a weekly newspaper. Porter (1992) argues that this kind of game was popular in England in 1175. Robertson (1967) tries to trace the event chronology taking in consideration the handball created and painted for each edition. The tradition wants that for each edition the handball must be created and painted by a local artisan. Robertson defines the beginning of the game on a Shrove Tuesday in Chester in 1533. Chaudary (2004) identifies the origin of this game in 1526, when the King Henry VIII commissioned a pair of football boots to take part to the game.

Today the game is not anymore widespread on national territory, because it's considered dangerous. This game has virtually no rules, no limits for those who can play and so from the visitor and outsider point of view It can look like a riot, tumultuous sport event. This S-SSE belongs to the tradition of a community and the community supports the event to preserve this tradition. This sport event is a clear example how a traditional event that belongs to community is surviving to modern era and cultural changes. A sport event that can be considered dangerous because of its lack of rules and It is supported by the local community that offers its service to make the event more comfortable and more secure. A network of stakeholders belonging to the community as policemen, volunteers, merchants, artists, players are at the service of the event.

The Royal Ashbourne Festival is an evidence how the key role and the willing of community represent a strategic resource to guarantee the survival of an event threatened by social- institutional changes.

The game takes place every year during the Shrove Tuesday and Ash Wednesday to provide amusement before the Lent. The game consists in two teams, and there are no rules, uniforms, dress code and colours. The entire community is divided in two teams, who was born on the northern of the river Henmore belongs to Upwards' team and who was born on the southern of the river belongs to 'Downwards' team. The launch of the ball in to the crowd takes place from a podium in the main car park of the town centre. The custom wants that on Tuesday the ball is thrown by anyone not born in the town while on Wednesday the launch has done by a local dignitary. The goals are three miles apart, 1.5 miles equidistant from the centre of the town in the site of two oldest mills "Clifton and Sturtson". The goals are represented by the mill wheels that are positioned in the river in order to make the competition harder. The goal has achieved when the ball is thrown for three times in the centre of the mill wheel. There are no specific rules regarding the launch of the ball that can be kicked, carried and thrown and all the game takes place in the crowd.

The game starts at two P.M with the launch of the ball in to the huge of the crowd. The large mass is entirely engaged in to the game. If the goal is scored the ball becomes property of the player that strikes it, while if the goal is unscored the ball becomes property of who keeps it. The ball is different from the traditional football, it is larger and made with a cork interior and leather exterior and painted by local artisans and the paint represents the person engaged into the first launch from the podium. The handball is considered an artwork that takes a couple of weeks to be painted.

Despite the cold temperatures, most of the game is played in the river, the players are so excited to take part to this traditional sport event, they feel part of the game and the event, they are aware that their participation is necessary for the event survival, the local community represents the soul of the event.

The Strategic Role of the Community in the Event and Sense of Belonging

The Royal Ashbourne Shrovetide Festival belongs to the tradition of the local community, indeed if there was not the support of the community the event would not survive.

There are two main sources that guarantee the survival of the event, they are represented by friendliness and hospitality of Ashbourne community and its long historic tradition. These two elements represent the main attractive factors for national and international visitors. The involvement of the community makes this sport event unique, and its uniqueness represent a competitive advantage that encourage visitors to attend the Ashbourne event rather than visiting another place.

The stakeholder community consists in players, attendants, spectators, policemen, volunteers, Shrovetide Committee, local business owners, residents and the visitors. (Wiltshier, Azara & Greatorex, 2018).

The event is organized by a collective through some formal and informal agreements among all stakeholders involve in the community . Most of them are engaged to guarantee the security of the event and attendance.

Wiltshier, Azara, Greatorex, (2018) provide a very extensive community stakeholder analysis. They use a very interesting double approach putting in evidence on a hand the contribution that the community offers to guarantee the implementation and survival of the event and on the other hand they analyse how the event strengthens the sense of belonging.

All community is taken in consideration from children to seniors, local authorities, associations. Stakeholders are divided in two main groups: Internal stakeholders such as community, players, organizers, local businesses and volunteers, and external stakeholders such as local visitors and no local visitors, national and international media, tourists, sponsors, insurances and political groups.

The local players being fully involved in the game support the Shrovetide committee with information about potential hazards in the which the residents can be involved, in order to implement policies to preserve the safety of citizens.

The district council collaborates with the Shrovetide committee in different activities, one of these is the litter management.

The local radio has a key role in the communication that consists to transmit and to tell the historical game all locals cannot join the event for any reasons. It provides community with an overview of the event through a radio service. Also, in this case it's underlined the main scope of the event to preserve the authenticity and the traditional character rather than the tourism promotion of the town and the event.

A group of retain players offers their free time and their previous experiences to help to manage safety risks among the participants, vehicles and property. They differ traffic in case of congestion and they can stop the game if a vehicle is involved in the crowd.

Local primary and secondary schools align holidays with the days in which the event takes place in order to allow their children to enjoy the event. Many children that enjoy the event as spectators in the adult age they could become players.

Local businesses protect their shop windows by wood barriers. This security measure is part of the event image. Newspapers and magazines show images of shops completely cordoned.

All local community is involved in a volunteer network providing their skills and time to preserve the game from social changes and safe restrictions.

The community is engaged and mainly interested to transmit the tradition to the next generation and to preserve the event from social changes.

Figure 3. Community Stakeholder Map and Community Capabilities
Source: our elaboration

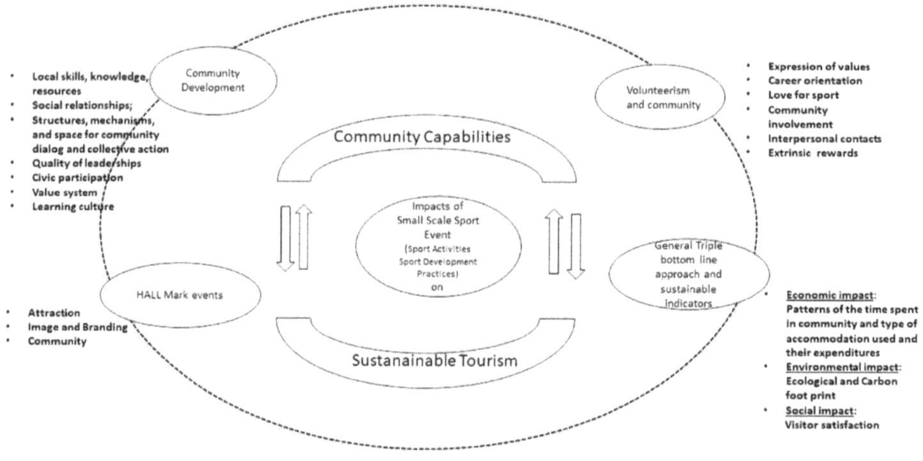

Volunteer Motivation

- **Expression of value:** Most of the Volunteers/ Marshalls were players before, a few are living in Ashbourne, they have a strong desire to maintain the organisation combined with a strong belief in the organisation 's goals and values_(Mowday et al., 1982).
- **Community involvement:** Visitors and players attend the event out of a family/ town tradition. Many state that it brings a sense of community to town; some come to socialize; some have never been before.

- **Interpersonal contacts:** Factors for attendance are escapism, event novelty, excitement, socialization/ family togetherness/ known- group socialisation, relaxation, historical/ cultural exploration/ intellectual growth.
- **External rewards:** Volunteers are provided with free lunch, and they are hosted for free to attend the event and offer their help.
- **Career orientation:** Local artists find in the event the opportunities to promote their skills and ability as artisans. The festival balls are considered real works of art. Younger volunteers can discover their interest in some business sector as event industry and interact with company managers. Finally, they develop first aid skills always required in the job.
- **Love for sport:** Most of volunteers participate to the events because interested to the old sport game, many players have been local children that had attended the event as spectators.

Sport Event and Community Development Analysis

- **Local skills, knowledge and resources:** Players are involved in volunteering programme before the event, they are trained to preserve players and attendances from accidents. They are mentioned as Marshalls. The event favours the storytelling ability of the community about previous edition of the ASRF and develop a community knowledge that is passed down from a generation to another generation. (McCabe, 2006)
- **Social relationship:** The event strengthens the social cohesion, local people share the same mission and they are called to develop strategies aimed to favour the survival of the event facing social changes.
- **Structures, mechanisms, and space for community dialog and collective action:** This traditional football game provides a particularly effective bonding mechanism. Its collaborative, communal structure reflects the social and economic organisation of the market town. Strong community ties appear to be a factor for the continued success (Harrison, 2017).
- **Quality of leadership:** Marshalls and Shrovetide Committee held a leadership role in the events. Anyone who comes to Ashbourne to attend the game must pay full attention to everything that marshals tell them. The committee that is engaged to manage the game in a set of guidelines to ensure the safety of participants (Butterfield, 2019).
- **Civic Participation:** Players join the Shrovetide Player Committee that was set up in 2001 consisting of an equal number of Upards and Downards members. The mission of this community organization consists in prolonging the future and the tradition of community of this old special game. The

Committee endeavours to represent the "Players" of the game in playing matters and raising funds for ongoing costs.

- **Value system:** ASFE is supported by different values such as: media value, historical value, existence value. Identity is the main value taken in consideration during the event, this value represents the community effort to support the event survival. Community is seriously jealous of their history and tradition. Indeed, during volunteer recruitment phase, local players are preferred because they already know the game and they belong to the community.
- **Learning Culture:** Local community becomes more aware of its tradition and social changes. Local people involved in volunteer activities focus their attention to adapt their local event to the new social needs. They develop management strategies to preserve the Ashbourne Shrovetide Royal Festival from social changes and commodification process that threat the sporting event.

Ashbourne Shrovetide Royal Festival and Sustainable Tourism

The friendliness, hospitality and community involvement represent an attractive factor for visitors to attend the events. The folkloristic character has a relevant impact on the destination image and position. Indeed, most of the security measures have become a characteristic image of the event and of the town. Looking for the market town on Internet, the web users will find images of the window shops completely protected by wood barriers.

The event is often attended by reporters and documentary makers from several European countries and from USA and Japan. In 2006 the game was object of a documentary produced by a Los Angeles Film Company and distributed on online and on-demand. Many attendants are local visitors that are used to returning for the Saint Week bringing with them friends. Despite the huge media coverage, the community is jealous of its tradition, local people consider the event a private game. "*It's nice for Ashbourne to be on the front pages but it is really own private game. We must keep the right balance. Enough publicity to satisfy curiosity and little enough so it goes unnoticed by the general population of the country. It is a private game really, although it is played by anyone. (ANT, 2002: 18)*"

The ASRF can be considered a Hallmark Tourist Event, the event is able to provide the host community with an opportunity to be known at local, national and international level. Given the strong influence of community, the market town of Ashbourne could be identified in the event that is able to create tourism demand independently.

The ASRF does not only influence the number of visitors, but it also affects the destination in economic social and environmental terms.

- **Economic Impact:** Every year a number between 3,000 and 5,000 attendees is estimated, most of them are visitors and tourists that discover the market town for the first time or tourists that come to visit friends and relatives (Azara, Wiltshier, Greatorex, 2018).Guest houses and Bed and Breakfasts are booked, but there are not many overnight visitors, most of visitors live in villages not far from the market town. Most of revenues are recorded by the food and beverage sectors, especially pubs and crowded beer houses.
- **Social Impact:** The ASRF occurs annually and has the main objective to reinforce local community identity although it is addressed to a mass segment. McCabe (2006) reports that mounting pressures for social change from the communities. The development of tourism industry is affecting the market town and the football event. Chalip's (2006) affirms that community is rooted in the tradition and the crowd of the annual game strengthens the sense of the place, community identity. Chalip (2001), Weed and Bull (2004) argue the need for stakeholders in events, sport and tourism to become more proactive in institutionalizing the linkages among sport, tourism and economic development. The collaboration among Shrovetide Player Committee, the district council, and volunteers/ marshals is a clear evidence of this institutionalization.
- **Environmental Impact:** In ecological terms the event attracts local visitors and visitors from closes regions that don't take time driving so they don't consume much fuel to reach the market town.

No new facility is needed to be built for the event implementation. The football field takes shape along the market town.

Negative impacts on the environment are due to the litter production, but the Shrovetide committee is engaged to manage it.

CONCLUSION

The community engagement in a S-SSE has a key role in the implementation and survival of a traditional event that is threatened by social changes. A networking of volunteers represents the soul of the event.

Volunteers are motivated by intrinsic factors as love for sport, socialization need, career opportunities, and external factors as volunteer benefits. Volunteers are moved by personal needs, altruism represents the first value on the which volunteerism is based, but the push factors that influence community to participate to voluntary are represented by individual needs, this underlines the theory that a man is a social animal that needs to collaborate with other individuals to satisfy his personal need to socialize.

Sport activities are closed connected to the community, especially to small communities that see in sport their tradition. Sport favours the community development in terms of capabilities, strengthening the local knowledge, personal skills, and leveraging on local resources. Traditional sports encourage volunteers to develop a critical way to think, to focus their attention on issues, and to take alternative problem-solving decisions. S-SSEs require collaboration between event organization and local organization, association and institutions. Sport events favour the development of an interorganizational networking that encourages the sharing of skills and knowledge.

In the planning process the role of community is strategic to obtain advantageous commercial agreement in terms of venue and promotion costs and to find financial resources through sponsorships.

The comparison between S-SSEs and large-scale events evidence that S-SSE represent a sustainable tourism tool. Indeed, they have a larger economic impact than mega sport event in large cities, have an inferior negative environmental impact, and increase the social cohesion.

REFERENCES

Allen, J., O'toole, W., Harris, R., & McDonnell, I. (2008). *Festival and special event management*. John Wiley & Sons Incorporated.

Azara, I., Wiltshier, P., & Greatorex, J. (2018). Against all odds: Embedding new knowledge for event continuity and community well-being. *Event Management, 22*(1), 25–36. doi:10.3727/152599517X15111988553964

Burnett, C. (2006). Building social capital through an 'active community club'. *International Review for the Sociology of Sport, 41*(3/4), 283–294. doi:10.1177/1012690207078381

Buterfield, G. (2019). *Everything you need to know about Ashbourne Royal Festival 2019*. Retrieved February 28, 2019 from: https://www.derbytelegraph.co.uk/news/ashbourne-royal-shrovetide-2019-2570247

Cater, E. (1993). Ecotourism in the third world: Problems for sustainable tourism development. *Tourism Management, 14*(2), 85–90. doi:10.1016/0261-5177(93)90040-R

Chalip, L. (2001). Sport and tourism: Capitalising on the linkage. *The Business of Sport*, 77-89.

Collins, C. (2018). *Ireland's soccer team manager denies targeting Catholic players in Northern Ireland.* Retrieved Mar 3, 2018 from https://cruxnow.com/church-in-uk-and-ireland/2018/03/09/irelands-soccer-team-manager-denies-targeting-catholic-players-northern-ireland/

Doshi, K., Schumacher, D., & Snyder, K. (2001). *Report on economic impact*. NASC.

Dowson, R., & Bassett, D. (2015). *Event planning and Management: A practical handbook for pr and events professionals*. Kogan Page Publishers.

Edwards, M. B. (2015). The role of sport in community capacity building: An examination of sport for development research and practice. *Sport Management Review, 18*(1), 6–19. doi:10.1016/j.smr.2013.08.008

Gammon, S. (2014). Sports events: Typologies, people and place. In *The Routledge handbook of events* (pp. 120–134). Routledge.

Getz, D., Svensson, B., Peterssen, R., & Gunnervall, A. (2012). Hallmark events: Definition and planning process. *International Journal of Event Management Research, 7*(1/2), 47–67.

Gibson, H. J., Kaplanidou, K., & Kang, S. J. (2012). Small-scale event sport tourism: A case study in sustainable tourism. *Sport Management Review, 15*(2), 160–170. doi:10.1016/j.smr.2011.08.013

Gratton, C., Dobson, N., & Shibli, S. (2000). The economic importance of major sports events: a case-study of six events. *Managing leisure, 5*(1), 17-28.

Green, B. C., & Chalip, L. (2004). Paths to volunteer commitment: Lessons from the Sydney Olympic Games. *Volunteering as leisure/leisure as volunteering: An international assessment*, 49-67.

Guttentag, D. A. (2009). The possible negative impacts of volunteer tourism. *International Journal of Tourism Research, 11*(6), 537–551. doi:10.1002/jtr.727

Hall, C. M., & Selwood, H. J. (1987). Cup gained, paradise lost? A case study of the 1987 America's Cup as a hallmark event. Geography and Society in a Global Context, 267-274.

Hamm, S. M., MacLean, J. C., & Misener, K. E. (2008). Understanding the commitment and motivation of episodic volunteers for a large sporting event. *Int J Volunt Adm*, *25*(3), 26–38.

Harrison, S. (2017). The popularity paradox: issues of safeguarding mob football games in the East Midlands of England. In *Sharing Cultures 2017–Proceedings of the 5th International Conference on Intangible Heritage*. Green Line Institute for Sustainable Development.

Higham, J. (1999). Commentary-sport as an avenue of tourism development: An analysis of the positive and negative impacts of sport tourism. *Current Issues in Tourism*, *2*(1), 82–90. doi:10.1080/13683509908667845

Kay, T., & Bradbury, S. (2009). Youth sport volunteering: Developing social capital? *Sport Education and Society*, *14*(1), 121–140. doi:10.1080/13573320802615288

Kim, E., Fredline, L., & Cuskelly, G. (2018). Heterogeneity of sport event volunteer motivations: A segmentation approach. *Tourism Management*, *68*, 375–386. doi:10.1016/j.tourman.2018.04.004

Laverie, D. A., & McDonald, R. E. (2007). Volunteer dedication: Understanding the role of identity importance on participation frequency. *Journal of Macromarketing*, *27*(3), 274–288. doi:10.1177/0276146707302837

Liu, Z. (2003). Sustainable tourism development: A critique. *Journal of Sustainable Tourism*, *11*(6), 459–475. doi:10.1080/09669580308667216

Lyras, A., & Peachey, J. W. (2011). Integrating sport-for-development theory and praxis. *Sport Management Review*, *14*(4), 311–326. doi:10.1016/j.smr.2011.05.006

Maennig, W., & Zimbalist, A. (2012). What is a mega sporting event. *International handbook on the economics of mega sporting events*, 9-14.

Mata-Codesal, D., Peperkamp, E., & Tiesler, N. C. (2015). *Migration, migrants and leisure: meaningful leisure?* Academic Press.

McCabe, S. (2006). The making of community identity through historic festive practice: The case of Ashbourne Royal Shrovetide Football. *Festivals, tourism and social change*, 99-118.

McCabe, S., & Stokoe, E. H. (2004). Place and Identity in Tourists' Accounts. *Annals of Tourism Research, 31*(3), 601–622. doi:10.1016/j.annals.2004.01.005

McCole, D., Jacobs, J., Lindley, B., & McAvoy, L. (2012). The relationship between seasonal employee retention and sense of community: The case of summer camp employment. *Journal of Park and Recreation Administration, 30*(2).

Mill, R. M. (1985). *The Tourism System.* Prentice hall International.

Mowday, R. T., Porter, L. W., & Steers, R. (1982). *Organizational linkages: The psychology of commitment, absenteeism, and turnover.* Academic Press.

O'Brien, D., & Chalip, L. (2007). Sport events and strategic leveraging: pushing towards the triple bottom line. *Tourism management: Analysis, behaviour, and strategy*, 318.

Putnam, R. D. (2000). Bowling alone: America's declining social capital. In *Culture and politics* (pp. 223–234). Palgrave Macmillan.

Save The Children. (2017). *The truth about voluntourism.* Retrieved September 20, 2017 from: https://www.savethechildren.org.au/Our-Stories/The-truth-about-voluntourism

Schulenkorf, N. (2012). Sustainable community development through sport and events: A conceptual framework for sport-for-development projects. *Sport Management Review, 15*(1), 1–12.

Shone, A., & Parry, B. (2004). *Successful event management: a practical handbook.* Cengage Learning EMEA.

Van Niekerk, M. (2017). Contemporary issues in events, festivals and destination management. *International Journal of Contemporary Hospitality Management.*

Walker, M. (2018). *Is Northern Ireland a football team or an expression of identity? What does the Northern Ireland team mean to Protestant community?* Retrieved March 30, 2019 from:https://www.irishtimes.com/sport/soccer/international/is-northern-ireland-a-football-team-or-an-expression-of-identity-1.3843260

Warner, S. (2012). Sport and community. *Sociology of sport and physical activity*, 237-254.

Warner, S., Newland, B. L., & Green, B. C. (2011). More than motivation: Reconsidering volunteer management tools. *Journal of Sport Management*, *25*(5), 391–407. doi:10.1123/jsm.25.5.391

Weed, M., & Bull, C. (2004). Sports Tourism: Participants, Policy and Providers. Elsevier Butterworth, Heinemann.

Wendel, M. L., Burdine, J. N., McLeroy, K. R., Alaniz, A., Norton, B., & Felix, M. R. (2009). Community capacity: theory and application. *Emerging Theories in Health Promotion Practice and Research, 277*, 302.

Wilson, R. (2006). The economic impact of local sport events: significant, limited or otherwise? A case study of four swimming events. *Managing Leisure, 11*(1), 57-70.

Chapter 4
Small-Scale Sport Events and Local Community Perceptions

Hugues Seraphin
University of Winchester, UK

Maximiliano Korstanje
University of Palermo, Argentina

ABSTRACT

With issues related to overtourism and, more specifically, tourismphobia, the impacts of any tourism-related activities are being scrutinised. Events falling under this category are therefore being scrutinised. Community events having been hailed to contribute to bridge the gap between locals and visitors, this chapter is going to look at small scale events and, more specifically, community sport event in Winchester (UK). Research carried by Seraphin et al. provided evidence that locals are overall very supportive of events going on in the city. That said, the research did not look at types of events, but events overall. This chapter is therefore going to provide a close up on a specific type of event in Winchester. The results of the findings of small-scale sport events in Winchester will be compared to the findings of Seraphin et al. that are an overall analysis of the Winchester context with regards to events.

INTRODUCTION

For a very long time, the purpose of the tourism industry has been geared toward growth. The theory of development punctuated on the needs of adopting tourism as a fertile and growing industry. But with the emergence of issues such as overtourism and tourismphobia, practitioners and academia are suggesting degrowth and a

DOI: 10.4018/978-1-7998-4757-1.ch004

better focus on experience (quality) as opposed to quantity (Favre, 2017; Milano, Novelli & Cheer, 2019). With a business view, Visser (2015) to some extent support the current shift of paradigm in the tourism industry when he suggested that sustainability will come from a change of paradigm in management, but also explicitly suggested that size of businesses have an impact of their sustainability. As for the event industry, Seraphin, Gowreesunkar, Zaman and Bourliataux (2019), argued that local community events (which are in general small events) have a strong potential in terms of quality experience, and equally important (as a result of their size), can bridge the gap between locals and visitors. This chapter is going to focus on community sport events, in other terms on small sport events, in order to address the following objectives: (a) Discuss sustainability from an event management point of view (b) identify, engage and discuss current research on children in the tourism, hospitality and event industry (c) and finally, discuss the (non) engagement of children in the sustainability discourse and actions. So doing, this chapter is going to use Winchester (destination) and *Winchester Criterium and Cyclefest* (event) as case studies. From a structural point of view, this chapter is structured around three main sections. The first section is providing a background to the study. The second section is the case study. Finally, section three, discusses the results drawn from the case studies. From a methodological point, this conceptual based chapter is adopting a deductive approach.

INTRODUCTION TO EVENTS AND EVENT TOURISM

The sociological knowledge historically overlooked the importance of sports to enhance the collective legitimacy of the status quo for the society to keep united. In some respect, the founding parents of sociology thought in the anomie and the social ties as the main forces of society. Leisure and play received marginal attention within the constellations of social science. One of the pioneering voices in focusing his attention on this matter was Alfred Weber. From Weber onwards, who primarily focused on leisure as a social force that revitalizes the psychological frustrations, some scholars interrogated furtherly on the role of sports in society (Aitchison 1999). In a landmark book, which is entitled *Quest for Excitement: sports and leisure in the civilizing process,* Eric Dunning & Norbert Elias (1986) not only continued Alfred´s efforts to place "play" in the foreground but explained brilliantly how the civilizing process needs from the alternation of moment of war and conflict with peace-time. The social imaginary believes strongly that warfare is a social malady resulted from dictatorship and the political intolerance. Dunning and Elias amply show how peace and war are inextricably intertwined. Like wars which often mobilize efforts and resources against an external enemy, sports are emotionally based on the needs of confronting with an external 'Otherness'. Hence, the state of conflict revives and transforms social frustration in a deep-seated sentiment of nationalism while social cohesion is enhanced.

Sports seem to be war by other means. The process of bureaucratization brilliantly described by Max Weber led towards a climate of depersonalization and alienation. In normal conditions, lay-citizens are educated to cover their inner-most feelings, or so to speak, are discouraged to express their emotions in public. For the western rationality, emotions are equaled to a sign of inferiority or lack of maturation. The introduction of excitement (risk) delineates the contours between a here-safe and a "there-unsafe". The adrenaline everybody feels when launches to the adventure or a risky situation are conducive to a state of exceptionalism which is emulated through the archetype of the hero. Today, sports are for people something more complex than a form of entertainment. There is much deeper reciprocity between audiences and athletes which straddles the spheres of space and time. The media often packages and disseminates an image of sportsmen as mythical heroes who went through the tragedy to redeem the sins of mankind. As a form of ritualized sacrifice, sportsmen emulate the tribulations ancient heroes faced, as well as remind how important the human soul is. From all the animal kingdom, humans are the only one capable to confront with Gods. Starting from the premise that sports events emulate archetypal battles between the good and evil, Dunning and Elias say overtly that sports alternate the needs of abiding the law (for players not to be seriously harmed) with competition and fight for the local resources. Of course, modern societies are less violent than their predecessors, in which case all appear to indicate the degree of violence is ripe to decline. The brutality that characterized the medieval days has been decreased or domesticated in a form of spectacle, as Dunning and Elias add. The society develops "controlled" risks for their citizens to feel more secure but giving some conditions these risks derive in extreme violence (i.e hooliganism). All we are certainly excited to go beyond the security of our comfortable home we need feelings of excitement to deal with the humdrum routine but in some conditions, it results in a climate of chaos and decontrol. Sports, sociologically speaking, mediate between both, the fear of chaos and contingency and the needs of eternal security (Dunning & Elias 1986).

Over the recent decades, mega-events which oscillate from music festivals to royal weddings or international sport events like the Olympic Games or the FIFA World Cup have captivated the attention of countless colleagues (Kang & Perdue 1994; Roche 1994; Fourie & Santana-Gallego 2011; Gursoy & Kendall 2006). Just after 9/11, these events were suspected to be potentially targeted by radicalized terrorist cells. The meaning of tourism security, as it was applied to event-management, gained a position of credibility in the recent years (Mansfeld & Pizam 2006; Tarlow 2014; Skoll & Korstanje 2014; Korstanje, Tzanelli & Clayton 2014). To the problem of security associates the environmental degradation and pollution these types of spectacles left. It is important not to lose the sight of the fact that these mega-events –far from its economic origin- play a leading role in regulating the legitimacy of the ruling elite. As mere anthropological rituals, media events create a powerful symbolism which tells a history to attendants (a lesson which should be learned). As a sacrificial object, all attendants feel the pride to belong to the same community (Dayan & Katz, 1994). For that reason, sport tourism follows an educational nature which deserves further attention. Having said this, Kotze (2006) laments the impossibilities of scholars to define successfully what sports tourism means. Although there is some consensus to date back tourism from the French Grand tour, sports are practised from immemorial times. To wit, sports can be analyzed from an anthropological insight as a set of rules and rituals aimed at domesticating the contingency. As a leisure-travel activity, sports tourism probably escapes to the classic approaches which affirm the economic-centered paradigm. Small scale event tourism gives some hint to re-discuss the nature of sports beyond the economic-centered paradigm towards a new understanding.

As the previous argument is given, Ritchie & Adair (2004) argue convincingly that sport-related tourism exhibits a prosper and promising sub-industry which annually attract many visitors and investors worldwide. Sports usually follow the use of physical prowess or skills to reach an individual or collective aim. These types of rituals are performed within a constellation of competence and intrinsic rewards. Because of this, modern sports are articulated according to a higher standardization process which imposes bureaucratic rules and norms. Authors differentiate *sports-as-competition* and *sports-as-play*. While the former shapes the activity according to a climate of rivalry, the latter signals to leisure -if not recreational- activities. At a closer look, sports tourism should be understood as an industry dotted of a *demand-side*, which combines not only the tourist´s motivations but also the collective expectances of a complex market, an *impact side* and *an origin-destination approach*. In this respect, the impact-side evaluates –from different models and angles- the effects of tourism on the destination and the environment. Rather, the *origin-destination approach* focuses on the so-called interdependence of generating and receiving sources. Over the recent years, some voices called the attention on the negative effects of mega-sport tourism while emphasizing on the needs of stimulating small-scale sport-related tourism (Ritchie 2004; Weed 2005; Daniels 2007; Kaplanidou & Vogt 2010). As Margaret Daniels (2007) puts it, the limits of sport tourism are given by its negative impact in the territory. Even if it is clear that sports buttress the economic revitalization of some destination, there is a central debate revolving around a sport event co-hosted by two different counties at the same time. To some extent, the fact is that effects of sport tourism vary on context, time and culture, but what is more important, small-scale operations not always are positive for the hosting community. One of the current limitations of applied-research consists in the lack of understanding about the causes behind the economic impact of small-scale sport tourism. Daniels concludes that those destinations dotted of natural attractions but lower infrastructure will experience negative impacts on sport tourism in comparison of urban zones. Hence location factors are of paramount importance to understand the effects of small- scale sport tourism. In this perspective, Kim et al (2015) review the effects of large-scale sport events in some tourist destinations. Some significant economic costs should be evaluated earlier than promoting these types of events. Policy-makers and planners should evaluate and understand the feelings, culture and background of the hosting community. Here two assumptions should be done. The subjective perception –unlike the economic costs- is subject to individual interpretation. Conducting research originally based on hosts feel leads invariably to confusing results. Secondly, the attitude against or in favor of tourists is dependant of resident heterogeneity. The specialized literature punctuates when residents perceive events bring more benefits than risks, they are supportive while –instead- when the costs are greater than the profits, the event is resisted. Kim et al suggest that doubtless, large-scale sport tourism generate psychological and economic impact in the community. The interviewed persons very well dissociate the economic favorable impact from the social negative impact. This means that though the well-being brought by the investment in infrastructure is highlighted, the social costs are mentioned as well. So the theory of sustainability should re-consider the future of large-scale sport events shortly. Locals often perceive that these events generate more insecurity –because of the probabilities to suffer a terrorist attack- adjoined to already-existent traffic problems. Local residents usually agree their opinion was never consulted by the authorities or experts who planned the event. “Being part” seems to be a key factor to develop more sustainable large-scale tourism consumption.

In a seminal paper, Gibson, Willming & Holdnak (2003) distinguish those travelers who move to watch sport games and those who travel to take an active part in a game. Sport tourism represents a fertile ground towards economic prosperity and economic benefits. Although the literature in this direction abounds, no less true is that small event tourism has remained uncovered by the professional fieldworkers and researchers. Basically, these researchers find two important outcomes. On one hand, small-scale sport events generate further incomes for the community than large-scale events. This happens simply because the community receives a direct multiplier effect than other events which are characterized by the presence of large tourist operators and mediators. On another, sport tourists are often engaged in other parallel activities once the event ends.

BACKGROUND OF THE STUDY

Events

Events can be classified into four types, namely family, sport, cultural and business. Events can also be classified according to their size (Bowdin, Allen, O'Toole, Harris & McDonnel, 2010). They are either hallmark; local or community; major or mega (Bowdin et al, 2010). Events also have a strong potential in terms of developing social capitals, and sense of belonging within the member of a community., but also to bridge the gaps between locals and visitors (Seraphin, Gowreesunkar, Zaman & Bourliataux-Lajoinie, 2019). O'Toole (2011, p.18) suggests that a programme of events and festivals are crucial to developing national pride in small developing countries in a post-colonial state of recovery. He goes on to give examples of adaptable DMO led strategies that combine events and tourism objectives and gives examples of how these have been successfully implemented in other countries. These provide both an overview and an insight into the complexities of such strategies and reinforce the notion that both tourism and events are interdependent. As for sport events, they 'have played a significant role in the development of society and that key individuals have managed, sometimes against all odds, to start small beginnings a wide-reaching sport event industry' (Masterman, 2014:15).

Events in the UK

The event industry is a very dynamic sector in the UK (Pulse Report, 2016). Practitioners are very optimistic with the development of the industry. New technology is expected to play a very important role in the development of the industry (Pulse Report, 2016). In 2015, the average budget for an event was £65,943. The cost of programme and content budget; venues being the most important source of expense; followed by food and beverage; etc. (Pulse Report, 2016). The most common types of events organised are class, Training or Workshop; conferences; and networking. Sport events are among the less popular types of events organised (Pulse Report, 2016). Figure 1 provides an exhaustive types of events organised in the UK.

If in 2016, sport events only represented 3% of the overall types of events organised in the UK (Pulse Report, 2016). In 2017, the percentage increased to reach 5.95% (Pulse Report, 2017), as depicted in Figure 2.

The majority of events listed in Figure 1 and 2 are organised in general by some organisations or charities (Figure 3).

Figure 1. Event types
Source: (Pulse Report, 2016)

Figure 2. Event types
Source: (Pulse Report, 2017)

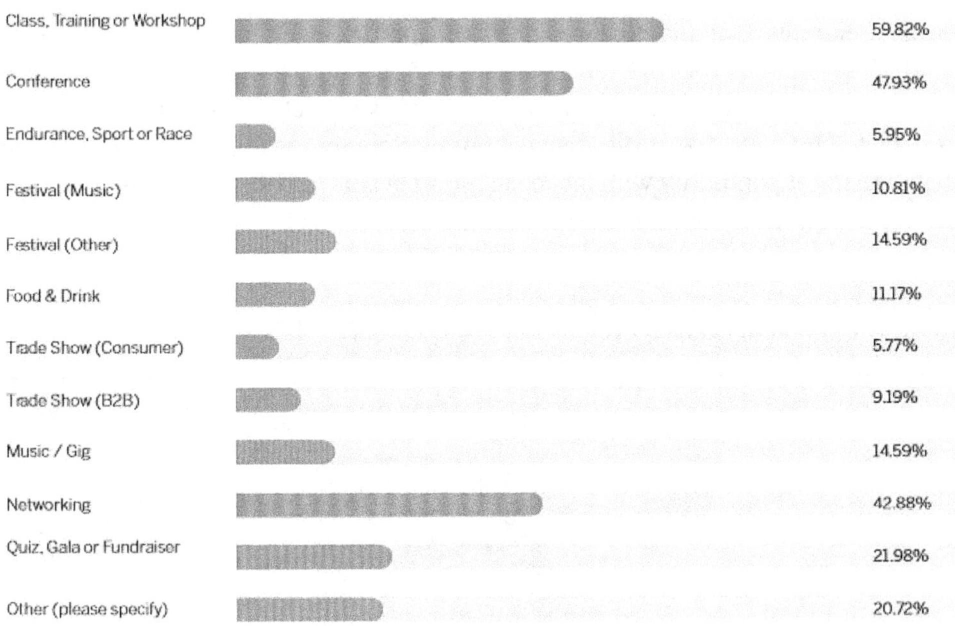

Figure 3. Size of businesses in the event industry (UK)
Source: (Pulse Report, 2018)

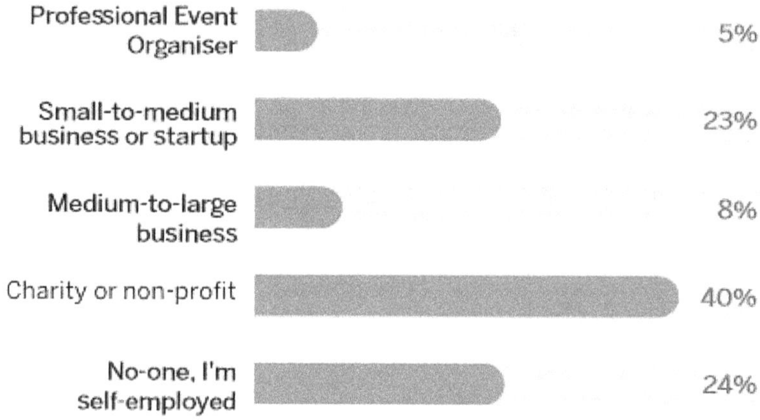

Events in Winchester

Winchester is located in the South of England (UK). As a destination, Winchester is also considered as an eventful destination, which receives the full support of the locals (Seraphin, Platania, Spencer & Modica, 2018). In Winchester, sport events are the less popular types of events in terms of frequency, as opposed to events such as music and comedy events or art and literature events, etc. (Seraphin et al, 2018), as depicted by table 1.A survey carried out by Seraphin et al (2018) also revealed that in terms of popularity with the locals, sport events remain very popular, as they are considered to contribute to level of happiness of locals.

Table 1. Community Based Festivals in Winchester (UK)

Jan	Feb	March	April	May	June	July	Aug	Sept	Oct	Nov	Dec
	Children of Winchester Festival	Winchester Beer Festival	Easter Bunny Hop	Winchester Mayfest	Winchester Speakers Festival	Winchester Festival	Boomtown	SC4M Americana Music Festival	Harvest Weekend	Bonfire	Wooly Hat Fair
			Winchester Fashion Week		Ginchester Fete	Hampshire Food Festival	Cheese & Chilli Festival	Winchester Community Games	Winchester Comedy Festival	Winchester Short Film Festival	
			Winchester Chamber Music Festival		Winchester Criterium and Cyclefest	Southern Cathedrals Festival	Graze Festival	Winchester Jazz Festival	Winchester Poetry Day	Winchester Christmas Light Switch On	
					Winchester Writer's Festival	Winscifest				Christmas Market and Ice Rink	Christmas Market and Ice Rink
					Winchester School of Art Degree Show					Wine Festival Winchester	
					Winchestival						
					Hat Fair						

Fashion events
Science events
Music & comedy events
Children events
Arts & literature events
Food and drink events
Sports events

Source: Seraphin et al (2018)*Sport Events in the UK*

Sport is an integrated part of every society, and is often considered as a social force (Byers, 2016). According to Parents and Smith-Swan (2013), sport events, are classified in seven categories: mega (one-off); hallmark (recurring, tied to a place); major (high attendance, media attention); large-scale (one-off or recurring); festivals (community-based); minor (local/community level with relatively low attendance or media attention) and special events (planned). Sport can also be a form of tourism, known as sport tourism, defined as 'travel to watch or participate in sport such as to visit the Olympic Games' (Page, 2019: 6). Sport tourism has also been a key trend and development in recent years (Page, 2019). In the UK, sport events are the less frequently organised type of events (table 2).

Table 2. Type of events organised in the UK

Ranking	%	Type of Event
1	21.9	Class, training or workshop
2	18.1	Conference
3	15.2	Networking
4	7.5	Quiz, Gala, fund raiser
5	7.2	Others
6	5.6	Festivals
7	5.3	Food and drink
8	5	Music, gig
9	4.1	Music festivals
10	3.6	Trade show (B2B)
11	3.3	Trade show (consumer)
12	3.3.	Endurance, sport, race

Source: (Pulse Report, 2016)

As for in Winchester, sport events are also the less commonly organised type of events (table 3).

Overview of Sport Events

Sport events are an important part of societies. And yet, in the UK (national level), this type of events is the less frequently organised type of events. Even at Winchester level (local level), sport events are less popular type of events. That said, this type of event plays a role in the general happiness of locals in Winchester (table 4). As

Table 3. Type of events organised in Winchester

Ranking	Numbers	Type of Event
1	8	Music and comedy
1	8	Art and literature
2	6	Children events
3	5	Food and drink
4	1	Fashion
5	1	Sport
6	1	Science

Source: (Seraphin et al, 2018)

part of the survey carried by Seraphin et al (2018), the scale went from1 (completely disagree) to 5 (completely agree).

Case Study

Winchester Criterium and Cyclefest

From the website of the event can be read:

*'The Cyclefest takes place in The Broadway as well as the new and improved 'hub' in Abbey Gardens. Abbey Gardens also doubles up as the starting point for our **Family** Cycle Ride which leads out on to the Criterium course before the races get underway. We have a **range of activities** for you to try which are chosen with the whole family in mind. There is the chance to give cycling a go in various forms, opportunities to find out about what is available locally and how to get involved and many more stalls and stands to browse throughout the day. In the lead up to the event and at the CycleFest on the day, we will be offering challenges and competitions with plenty to keep the **younger members of the family** amused'. Source: http://www.winchestercriterium.org/cyclefest/*

*'The Criterium is a 1km circuit race around closed roads in Winchester City Centre which incorporates the South Region Circuit Race Championships within the **U16** and **Senior** races. Riders will start at the top of the High Street, turn left on to St Thomas Street, wind their way past the Cathedral, past the City Council Offices and turn left from Colebrook Street for the long uphill drag to the start/finish line!' Source: http://www.winchestercriterium.org/criterium/*

Table 4. Descriptive analysis of happiness/events in Winchester (UK)

	N	Minimum	Maximum	Mean	Std. Deviation
Arts (e.g. Hat Fair, Winchester Festival, Winchester Mayfest, Winchester School of Art Degree Show, Winchester Speakers Festival, Woolly Hat Fair)	392	1	5	4.02	1.085
Sports (e.g. Winchester Community Games, Winchester Criterium and Cyclefest)	389	1	5	3.59	1.072
Science (e.g. Winchester Science Festival)	387	1	5	3.69	1.021
Music (e.g. Alresford Music Festival, Boomtown, Graze Festival, Winchester Chamber Music Festival, Winchester Jazz Festival)	389	1	5	3.86	1.164
Literature (e.g. Winchester Poetry Festival, Winchester Writers Festival)	390	1	5	3.55	1.083
Food and drink (e.g. Ginchester, Hampshire Food Festival, Harvest Festival, Winchester Beer and Cider Festival, Winchester Cheese and Chilli Festival,, Winchester Cocktail Week, Wine Festival Winchester)	390	1	5	4.02	1.002
Horticulture (e.g. Winchester Cathedral's Festival of Flowers)	390	1	5	3.56	1.051
History (e.g. Heritage Open Days)	386	1	5	3.91	1.020
Film (e.g. Winchester Short Film Festival)	390	1	5	3.33	1.093
Fashion (e.g. Winchester Fashion Week)	391	1	5	3.20	1.136
Comedy (e.g. Winchester Comedy Festival, Winchestival)	392	1	5	3.65	1.072
Christmas (e.g. Winchester Christmas Lights Switch On, Winchester Christmas Lantern Parade, Winchester Christmas Market and Ice Rink,)	392	1	5	4.03	1.079
Children's (e.g. Children of Winchester Festival)	387	1	5	3.53	1.031
Architecture (e.g. Winchester Cathedral's Stonemasonry Festival)	391	1	5	3.61	1.066
Valid N (listwise)	368				

Source: Seraphin et al (2018)

Interim Conclusion Drawn

From the quote it could be argued that *Winchester Criterium and Cyclefest* is a family sport event that contribute to bridge the gap between generations. This event could also be said to overall develop social capital (between different generations of a same family and/or community).

Based on *Winchester Criterium and Cyclefest* (and analysis of the analysis of events in general in Winchester), small (sport) events, in local communities (such as Winchester), contribute to:

1. Locals' happiness
2. Develop social capitals

As opposed to major sport events, which are very complex in terms of organisation and revenue orientated (Byers, 2016; Parent & Smith-Swan, 2019), small scale events, are differently orientated.

From Revenue Management to Social Capital Management

Revenue Management

Revenue Management (RM) is used by a wide range of industries, including the tourism industry (Ivanov & Zhechev, 2012), as part of their marketing and pricing strategies (Byers, 2016; Getz, 2012). Using RM is particularly important when the product or service on offer is perishable, as it helps to cope with demand fluctuation (Getz, 2012), and maximise potential revenue by controlling inventory levels and using price to manipulate customer demand (Bowie, Buttle, Brookes, & Mariussen, 2017). RM has therefore a pricing and non-pricing aspect (Ivanov & Zhechev, 2012), and the latter concerns segmenting customers and forecasting demand (Bowie et al., 2017). The purpose of RM, also called Yield Management (Ivanov & Zhechev, 2012; Lacagnina & Provenzano, 2016) is to create demand by dividing customers into different segments in order to allocate them the right product or service, at the right time and at the right price in a way that maximises the revenue of an organisation (Vives, Jacob, & Aguiló, 2018). With the development of ICT (Information and Communication Technologies) the choice of 'the right distribution channel' has become crucial (Tyrrell, 2017). As a tool, RM is applicable to a wide range of industry including the tourism and hospitality industry (Lacagnina & Provenzano, 2016), and is based on two main tools, namely pricing and non-pricing tools (Ivanov & Zhechev, 2012). The purpose of RM is to maximise the revenue of organisations by offering distinct segments the right products or services at the right time and place

(Ivanov & Zhechev, 2012). RM does not require the organisation to offer different products/services or target different customers (Vives, Jacob, & Payeras, 2018). To improve their revenue, organisations need to innovate, that is, find a way to balance exploitation of existing products/services and customers (present), and exploring new opportunities (future). As far as customers are concerned, at the moment, they are segmented between leisure and business (Ivanov & Zhechev, 2012; Vives, Jacob, & Payeras, 2018).

Heritage, events, etc. are now commodified to entertain visitors (Park, 2014). They are also source of incomes for the private and public sector (Park, 2014). As any other products and services, events need to be profitable, as a results, revenue management strategies are applied to them (Byers, 2016; Parent & Smith-Swan, 2019). As Favre (2017), suggested, small matters. The focus should no longer be on a strategy of growth in terms of size or numbers but, toward providing quality experience. Visser (2015) is suggesting an 8 step strategy toward this.

Unlocking Changes Toward Sustainability

Visser (2015) 8 steps toward sustainability are as follow:

- Unlocking change through transformational leadership
- Unlocking change through enterprise reform
- Unlocking change through technology innovation
- Unlocking change through corporate transparency
- Unlocking change through stakeholders engagement
- Unlocking change through social responsibility
- Unlocking change through integrated value
- Unlocking change through future-fitness

The sustainable changes suggested earlier in the chapter could come from entreprise reform (deep reform only happen the purpose of businesses are changed); social responsibility a new CSR model that would contribute to improve the context in which locals live); and integrated value (introducing policies that reshape capitalism and its relationship to society). Small sport events have this potential due to the fact that sport is an integrated part of society; small events have social potential; finally, in some contexts (such as Winchester) they contribute to the quality and enjoyment of life of locals. Since the issues related to overtourism, there is a change of paradigm in tourism from mass tourism to Special Interest Tourism (Seraphin et al, 2019). Small events can be part of this change of paradigm in the event industry. Instead of talking about Revenue Management, many service industries such as tourism, hospitality, events, etc…should focus on Social Capital Management.

Social Capital

The key features of Social Capital are as follow:

'Collective active, cooperation, networks, relationships, shared norms and values, social interaction and trust' (Moscardo, Konovalov, Murphy & McGehee, 2017: 2)

'Shared norms and values, mutual obligations, and relationships built on trust and reciprocity' (Moscardo et al, 2017: 3)

The benefits of development of Social Capital are as follow:

'Improve health, education, agriculture, business and entrepreneurship, and environmental management' (Moscardo et al, 2017: 3).

Small (sport) events in Winchester has proven to have the ability to gather the local community and family around a common interest, while bridging the gap between the generations (as discussed previously in this chapter). Despite the importance of Social Capital Management, it is also important to think the economic aspect of events, as without sponsors events would not run (Parent & Smith-Swan, 2019), no matter how small or big it is. Hence the importance of finding a balance between Social Capital Management (SCM) and Revenue Management (RM). This balance can be found using Organisational Ambidexterity (OA).

Balancing Social Capital and Revenue Management: An Ambidextrous Management Approach

Organisational ambidexterity (OA) is about putting together opposite, while finding a balance between them (Smith, 2017).

Nature, which could be thought of as all that is alive and original, precedes culture and surrounds people. Nature can also be defined by people's inner essence person or phenomena (Clement & Demonque, 1995). As for culture it is multi faced as it is thought of as agriculture (working the land) and education (intellectual development), and civilisation in a broader sense. As a result, culture can be seen as a transformation, a process, and the outcome of a process (Clement & Demonque, 1995). By questioning its nature, the humanity is questioning its own culture. Taking this reasoning under consideration the question arising is: Are we perceived as advanced or transformed beings? (Clement & Demonque, 1995). The issue of culture vs nature is just a paradigm of the ambiguous and multi faced environment in which humanity is involved. This paradoxical and continuing complexity is depicted in places and processes. Among them being an organisation's long-term or short-term strategy, and/or a centralised or decentralised organisation among others (Jules & Good, 2014). However, it is very challenging to bring awareness about this paradox and manage such a competing demand at the same time (Jules & Good, 2014). Nevertheless, investigating paradoxes is considered as an added value, because balancing conflicting ends contributes not only to transcending paradoxes, but also to developing dual strategies (Heracleous & Wirtz, 2014). For this though to be achieved, a new mind-set is required (Jules & Good, 2014), as paradoxes are "[…] contradictory and yet interrelated opposites that exist simultaneously and persist over time" (Cunha & Putnam, 2019: 95). This mind-set is to be related to the 'Janusian process' or 'Janusian thinking' (Rothenberg, 1996).

Originally called oppositional thinking, 'Janusian thinking' is a reference to Janus, the Roman god with two faces, who faced simultaneously opposite directions, and played also an essential role in the creation of the world (Rothenberg, 1971). As a result, the 'Janusian process' or 'Janusian thinking', is a process that involves conceiving and utilising multiple incompatible opposites or contradictory ideas, concepts, images, or antitheses simultaneously (Rothenberg, 1971, 1996). Rothenberg (1996) argues the prime outcome of this process is creativity, in other words, the development of new and valuable phenomena (Rothenberg, 1996). Similarly, in business, OA, which is in a sense involves two opposites, namely exploitation vs exploration (Smith, 2017), could be considered as a practical application of the 'Janusian thinking/process'. Indeed, Papachroni, Heracleous, and Paroutis (2015) argue that in OA the paradoxical poles (exploration and exploration) and the tension coming out of the oppositions (old/new; capability/rigidity; continuity/change; chaos/inertia; leverage/stretch; efficiency/flexibility) interrelate over time. This interrelation leads to success (Smith, 2017). Rothenberg (1971) states that Aristotle and Poincare were firm supporters of 'Janusian thinking' as it is linked to artistic creation, literature and mathematics among others. The 'Janusian thinking/process' has also influenced many other concepts such as the Yin and Yang in Eastern culture; the Being and Becoming in Western culture; God and the Devil; Eros and Thanatos; among others. All of which convey an integration of opposites (Rothenberg, 1971). That said, it is important to mention "[…] there is a wide variety of types of opposition, ranging from strong opposition containing logical antithesis or contradiction to mild opposition consisting of simple contrast […]. Strong opposition or logical antithesis it has the greatest shock or surprise value; it conveys the greatest sense of novelty and may also convey the greatest truths." (Rothenberg, 1971: 204). This range of opposition is also reflected in OA (Papachroni et al., 2015), where a range of tensions (spatial separation; temporal separation; moving beyond of spatial and temporal separations) are triggered by a variety of approaches to ambidexterity (structural, contextual, temporal ambidexterity; paradox theory). Because "[…] there is a notable lack of empirical evidence on how individuals actually perceive and manage the tensions of exploration and exploitation within everyday business practice" (Papachroni et al., 2015: 84).

CONCLUSION

Framework of the Research

Figure 4 summarises the framework of this study.

Figure 4. Framework of the study
Source: The authors

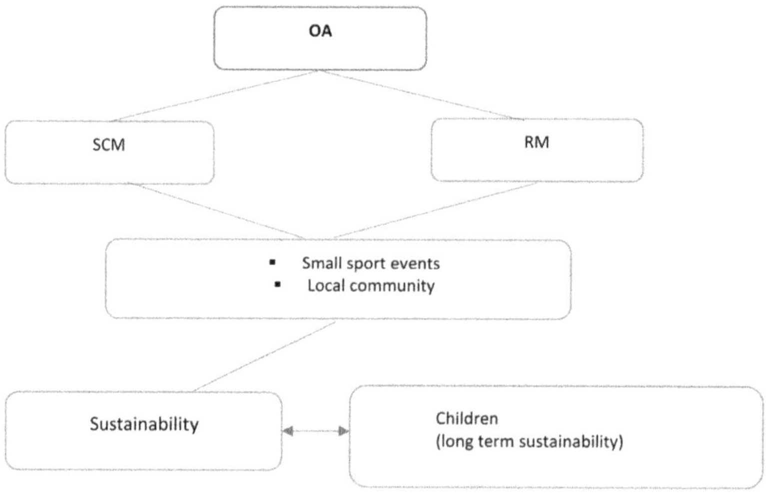

Children and Long Term Sustainability

Because "Sustainability is possibly the most important issue facing the tourism industry in the twenty-first century" (Edgell & Swanson, 2018: 45), and also because "children are the tourists of the future" (Cullingford, 1995: 126), this chapter is arguing that research on sustainable tourism, and responsible tourism initiatives should engage with children. At the moment they are invisible and undermined as community members (Dowse, Powell & Weed, 2018). In order to understand the future of sustainable and responsible tourism, it is necessary to understand at which stage is research on children and their role and importance in the industry, as well as practical initiatives that are done to engage them with regard to "respect the socio-cultural authenticity of host communities, conserve their built and living cultural heritage and traditional values and contribute to inter-cultural understanding and tolerance" (Tribe, 2016: 419). In this chapter, responsible tourism is to be understood as a practice based application of the concept of sustainable tourism, and subsequently sustainable tourism as a conceptual based application of responsible tourism (Burrai, Buda & Stanford, 2019). At the moment there is no existing literature connecting children and sustainable tourism research. That said, there is some research, even if limited on children in the tourism industry (Seraphin & Yallop, 2019). Despite the fact the tourism industry as a whole is recognising the importance of children as customers, because they influence the choice of families' tourist destinations and venues, and also because they have a great interest in travel for holidays (Lugosi, Robinson, Golubovskaya, & Foley, 2016), their role remains under-valued (Poria & Timothy, 2014). Taking into consideration children in the event industry, Dowse, Powell, and Weed (2018) even added that they are invisible and undermine as community members, whereas they should be considered as meaningful stakeholders. This is all the more important as "children may be the best informants about themselves" (Poria & Timothy, 2014: 95). The tourism and hospitality would particularly benefit from educating children because "children are the tourists of the future" (Cullingford, 1995: 126), and as such, it is important to groom them toward this role (Cullingford, 1995).

- Children have an important role to play on the long-term sustainability of the industry (Poria & Timothy, 2014), and are keen to learn while on holidays (Radic, 2019)
- Resort mini-clubs have the potential to educate children, while they are having fun, and can also be turned into a competitive advantage for a resort and a destination (Seraphin & Yallop, 2019)
- Unlocking changes to achieve sustainability can be achieved through stakeholders' engagements; corporate social responsibility; and integrated value (Visser, 2015)

REFERENCES

Aitchison, C. (1999). New cultural geographies: The spatiality of leisure, gender and sexuality. *Leisure Studies*, *18*(1), 19–39. doi:10.1080/026143699375032

Bowdin, G., Allen, J., O'Toole, W., Harris, R., & McDonnell, I. (2010). *Events Management*. Butterworth-Heinemann.

Burrai, E., Buda, D.-M., & Stanford, D. (2019). Rethinking the ideology of responsible tourism. *Journal of Sustainable Tourism*, *1*(16).

Byers, T. (Ed.). (2016). *Contemporary issues in sport management: A critical introduction*. Sage Publications. doi:10.4135/9781473919761

Clement, E., & Demonque, C. (1995). *Philosophie*. Paris: Hatier. Available from: http://www.winchestercriterium.org/criterium/

Cullingford, C. (1995). Children's attitudes to holidays overseas. *Tourism Management*, *16*(2), 121–127. doi:10.1016/0261-5177(94)00022-3

Cunha, M. P., & Putnam, L. L. (2019). Paradox theory and the paradox of success. *Strategic Organization*, *17*(1), 95–106. doi:10.1177/1476127017739536

Cyclefest. (n.d.). Available from: http://www.winchestercriterium.org/cyclefest/

Daniels, M. J. (2007). Central place theory and sport tourism impacts. *Annals of Tourism Research*, *34*(2), 332–347. doi:10.1016/j.annals.2006.09.004

Dayan, D., & Katz, E. (1994). *Media events*. Harvard University Press.

Dowse, S., Powell, S., & Weed, M. (2018). Mega-sporting events and children's rights and interests – towards a better future. *Leisure Studies*, *37*(1), 97–108. doi:10.1080/02614367.2017.1347698

Dunning, E., & Elias, N. (1986). *Quest for excitement: Sport and Leisure in the Civilizing Process*. Basil Blackwell.

Edgell, D. L., & Swanson, J. R. (2018). *Tourism policy and planning: Yesterday, today, and tomorrow* (3rd ed.). Routledge. doi:10.4324/9781351033541

Favre, C. (2017). The Small2Mighty tourism academy: Growing business to grow women as a transformative strategy for emerging destinations. *Worldwide Hospitality and Tourism Themes*, *9*(5), 555–563. doi:10.1108/WHATT-07-2017-0034

Fourie, J., & Santana-Gallego, M. (2011). The impact of mega-sport events on tourist arrivals. *Tourism Management*, *32*(6), 1364–1370. doi:10.1016/j.tourman.2011.01.011

Fredline, E. (2005). Host and guest relations and sport tourism. *Sport in Society*, *8*(2), 263–279. doi:10.1080/17430430500087328

Getz, D. (2012). *Event studies: Theory, research and policy for planned events* (2nd ed.). Routledge.

Gibson, H. J., Kaplanidou, K., & Kang, S. J. (2012). Small-scale event sport tourism: A case study in sustainable tourism. *Sport Management Review*, *15*(2), 160–170. doi:10.1016/j.smr.2011.08.013

Gibson, H. J., Willming, C., & Holdnak, A. (2003). Small-scale event sport tourism: Fans as tourists. *Tourism Management*, *24*(2), 181–190. doi:10.1016/S0261-5177(02)00058-4

Gursoy, D., & Kendall, K. W. (2006). Hosting mega events: Modeling locals' support. *Annals of Tourism Research*, *33*(3), 603–623. doi:10.1016/j.annals.2006.01.005

Heracleous, L., & Wirtz, J. (2014). Singapore Airlines: Achieving sustainable advantage through mastering paradox. *The Journal of Applied Behavioral Science*, *50*(2), 150–170. doi:10.1177/0021886314522323

Ivanov, S., & Zhechev, V. (2012). Hotel revenue management - A critical literature review. *Tourism Review*, *60*(2), 175–197.

Jules, C., & Good, D. (2014). Introduction to special issue on paradox in context: Advances in theory and practice. *The Journal of Applied Behavioral Science*, *50*(2), 123–126. doi:10.1177/0021886314524920

Kang, Y. S., & Perdue, R. (1994). Long-term impact of a mega-event on international tourism to the host country: A conceptual model and the case of the 1988 Seoul Olympics. *Journal of International Consumer Marketing*, *6*(3-4), 205–225. doi:10.1300/J046v06n03_11

Kaplanidou, K., & Gibson, H. J. (2010). Predicting behavioral intentions of active event sport tourists: The case of a small-scale recurring sports event. *Journal of Sport & Tourism*, *15*(2), 163–179. doi:10.1080/14775085.2010.498261

Kaplanidou, K., & Vogt, C. (2010). The meaning and measurement of a sport event experience among active sport tourists. *Journal of Sport Management*, *24*(5), 544–566. doi:10.1123/jsm.24.5.544

Kim, W., Jun, H. M., Walker, M., & Drane, D. (2015). Evaluating the perceived social impacts of hosting large-scale sport tourism events: Scale development and validation. *Tourism Management*, *48*, 21–32. doi:10.1016/j.tourman.2014.10.015

Lugosi, P., Robinson, R. N. S., Golubovskaya, M., & Foley, L. (2016). The hospitality consumption experience of parents and carers with children: A qualitative study of foodservice settings. *International Journal of Hospitality Management, 54*, 84–94. doi:10.1016/j.ijhm.2016.01.012

Mansfeld, Y., & Pizam, A. (Eds.). (2006). *Tourism, security and safety*. Routledge.

Masterman, G. (2014). *Strategic sports event management* (3rd ed.). Routledge. doi:10.4324/9780203114674

Milano, C., Novelli, M., & Cheer, J. (2019). Overtourism and degrowth: A social movements perspective. *Journal of Sustainable Tourism, 27*(12), 1857–1875. Advance online publication. doi:10.1080/09669582.2019.1650054

Moscardo, G., Konovalov, E., Murphy, L., McGehee, N. G., & Schurmann, A. (2017). Linking tourism to social capital in destination communities. *Journal of Destination Marketing & Management, 6*(4), 286–295. doi:10.1016/j.jdmm.2017.10.001

O'Toole, W. (2011). *Events feasibility and development from strategy to operations*. Elsevier.

Page, S. J. (2019). *Tourism management*. Routledge. doi:10.4324/9780429422898

Papachroni, A., Heracleous, L., & Paroutis, S. (2015). Organizational ambidexterity through the lens of paradox theory: Building a novel research agenda. *The Journal of Applied Behavioral Science, 51*(1), 71–93. doi:10.1177/0021886314553101

Parent, M. M., & Smith-Swan, S. (2013). *Managing major sports events. Theory and practice*. Routledge. doi:10.4324/9780203132371

Park, Y. P. (2014). *Heritage Tourism*. Routledge.

Poria, Y., & Timothy, D. J. (2014). Where are the children in tourism research? *Annals of Tourism Research, 47*, 93–95. doi:10.1016/j.annals.2014.03.002

Poris, M. (2006). Understanding what fun means to today's kids. *Young Consumers, 7*(1), 14–22. doi:10.1108/17473610610701358

ReportP. (2016). Available from: www.eventbrite.co.uk/how-it-works/

ReportP. (2017). Available from: www.eventbrite.co.uk/how-it-works/

ReportP. (2018). Available from: www.eventbrite.co.uk/how-it-works/

Ritchie, B. W. (2004). Exploring small-scale sport event tourism: The case of Rugby Union and the Super 12 competition. *Sport tourism: Interrelationships, impacts and issues*, 135-154.

Ritchie, B. W., & Adair, D. (Eds.). (2004). *Sport tourism: Interrelationships, impacts and issues* (Vol. 14). Channel View Publications. doi:10.21832/9781873150672

Roche, M. (1994). Mega-events and urban policy. *Annals of Tourism Research, 21*(1), 1–19. doi:10.1016/0160-7383(94)90002-7

Rothenberg, A. (1971). The process of Janusian thinking in creativity. *Archives of General Psychiatry, 24*(3), 195–205. doi:10.1001/archpsyc.1971.01750090001001 PMID:5542345

Rothenberg, A. (1996). The Janusian process in scientific creativity. *Creativity Research Journal, 9*(2-3), 207–231. doi:10.1080/10400419.1996.9651173

Seraphin, H., Gowreesunkar, V., Zaman, M., & Bourliataux, S. (2019). Community Based Festivals as a tool to tackle tourismphobia and antitourism movements. *Journal of Hospitality and Tourism Management, 39*, 219–223. Advance online publication. doi:10.1016/j.jhtm.2018.12.001

Seraphin, H., Platania, M., Spencer, P., & Modica, G. (2018). Event and tourism development within a local community: The case of Winchester (UK). *Sustainability, 10*(10), 3728. doi:10.3390u10103728

Seraphin, H., & Yallop, A. (2019). Proposed Framework for the Management of Resorts Mini Clubs: An Ambidextrous Approach. *Leisure Studies, 38*(4), 535–547. Advance online publication. doi:10.1080/02614367.2019.1581249

Skoll, G. R., & Korstanje, M. E. (2014). Terrorism, homeland safety and event management. *International Journal of Hospitality and Event Management, 1*(1), 95–110. doi:10.1504/IJHEM.2014.062869

Smith, S. M. (2017). Organisational ambidexterity: Welcome to paradox city. *Human Resource Management International Digest, 25*(1), 1–3. doi:10.1108/HRMID-06-2016-0087

Spivey, N. (2005). *The Ancient Olympics*. Oxford University Press.

Tarlow, P. (2014). *Tourism security: strategies for effectively managing travel risk and safety*. Elsevier.

Tribe, J. (2016). *The economics of recreation, leisure and tourism* (5th ed.). Routledge.

Tyrrell, T. (2017). Revenue management. In L. L. Lowry (Ed.), *The SAGE international encyclopedia of travel and tourism* (pp. 1030–1034). Sage Publications.

Visser, W. (2015). *Sustainable Frontiers. Unlocking Change through Business, Leadership and Innovation*. Greenleaf Publishing.

Vives, A., Jacob, M., & Aguiló, E. (2018). Online hotel demand model and own-price elasticities: An empirical application in a mature resort destination. *Tourism Economics*. Advance online publication. doi:10.1177/1354816618800643

Vives, A., Jacob, M., & Payeras, M. (2018). Revenue management and price optimization techniques in the hotel sector: A critical literature review. *Tourism Economics*, *24*(6), 720–752. doi:10.1177/1354816618777590

Weed, M. (Ed.). (2007). *Sport & tourism: A reader*. Routledge. doi:10.4324/9780203937686

Wertz, S. (1991). *Talking a good game: inquiries into the principle of sports*. Southern Methodist University Press.

Yeoman, I. (2013). A futurist's thoughts on consumer trends shaping future festivals and events. *International Journal of Event and Festival Management*, *4*(3), 249–260. doi:10.1108/IJEFM-06-2013-0017

Chapter 5
Small-Scale Event Volunteering:
Insights From Three Greek Running Events

Sofia K. Gkarane
https://orcid.org/0000-0002-6057-5477
University of Macedonia, Greece

ABSTRACT

Volunteers are the main driving force and absolutely necessary for the smooth organization of small-scale events. Through the description of the volunteering concept regarding the events, the readers are getting deeper into the volunteerism perception. This chapter presents the volunteering motivational factors based on selective bibliographical sources. It also gives emphasis to the volunteerism link with the community. Insights from three small-scale sport events are provided with a view to helping the reader comprehend the working areas where volunteers may offer their services and the package that they gain after their contribution.

INTRODUCTION

Every day volunteers provide their time and services to several organizations and projects around the world, including events; they undertake a wide range of roles in order to carry out very important tasks, they face challenges and gain new experiences. Without them a small scale event is not possible. The organizers highly rely on volunteers to provide their valuable services for the event. If they are carefully

DOI: 10.4018/978-1-7998-4757-1.ch005

managed, they can become a rich resource and an important human support for the event as they usually work at every level to prepare a successful result.

The definition of volunteerism is difficult given the variety of roles and the difference of operations that volunteers may participate (Bussell & Forbes, 2002). According to the International Labor Organization (ILO, 2011, p. 13) volunteer work is defined as "*unpaid non-compulsory work; that is time individuals give without pay to activities either through an organization or directly for others outside their own household*". Stebbins (1996) approaches volunteering as "*an uncoerced helping activity that is engaged in not primarily for financial gain...different in definition from work, slavery or conscription*". Another definition is provided by Monga (2006, p. 47) as following: "*volunteers are the people who offer their labor, knowledge, skills, and experience at no wage cost to the utilizing organization*". Omoto & Packar (2016) define volunteerism as "*an active and intentional process in which individuals and groups seek out opportunities to assist others*". They state that the volunteers' actions are based on freewill and are undertaken by choice.

Volunteerism is assumed as a leisure activity, providing relaxing and/or exercising and learning opportunities (Doherty, 2005; Stebbins, 1996) with little or no particular training to enjoy it (Stebbins, 2009) but not all its forms (like giving blood) are really fun, even if they may be satisfying (Stebbins, 1996).

Regarding events, we can say that volunteering is the contribution of labor, time, skills, energy, efforts and services from the part of the individuals, that enables them to experience several benefits (and costs) and provides to the event managers the opportunity to perform well-organized and successful events (Bang et all, 2009; Doherty, 2009; Kervin et all, 2015).

There is a consensus in the existing academic literature that the contribution of the volunteers to the events is substantial (Bang & Ross, 2009; Hallmann & Zehrer, 2017; Kervin et. Al, 2015; Kim et al., 2018). Their work is regarded as one of the main pillars of special events (Leigh et al., 2013). Their help for the operations of an event is absolutely necessary (Hallmann & Zehrer, 2017; Kerwin et al., 2015) through the important responsibilities that they usually undertake (Lockstone-Binney et al., 2015). Their support is essential not only for mega-events but also for smaller local ones (Kerwin et al., 2015).

Indeed, volunteers have been developed into a valuable aspect of the events (Bang & Ross, 2009; Kim, 2018; Kim & Cuskelly, 2017; Pauline, (2011). As a central part of the event, they play a very important role in its success and they may even become the face of the event (Schlesinger & Gubler, 2016), let alone the fact that they may provide the organizers with very special services including legal advice, financial and marketing support and other (Warner et al., 2011).

Volunteers seem to be an extremely useful resource for any event. Their commitment, the time they will spend and the tasks they will undertake will positively influence its organization. Therefore, understanding their motivations, their interests and aspirations, and connecting their roles with the event structuring, will help the organizers build a successful event. This chapter takes a look into the world of small-scale event volunteering and presents some motivational factors in order to help the reader understand the reasons why people volunteer at events. It also describes community volunteering so as the reader gain insights about the way in which individuals take part in community activities on a voluntary basis. The chapter ends with the description of the volunteers' tasks and packages with respect to their participation in three small-scale running events held in Greece.

BACKGROUND

Volunteerism is a growing phenomenon, found in several areas and having received the researchers' attention (Wang, 2004). To honor those who care for others, European Union pronounced 2011 as the *European Year of Volunteering* with the view of increasing the volunteerism in the community and giving awareness to its added value. During 2011, EU funded hundreds of volunteering projects in different European countries. Besides, every year the International Volunteer Day is celebrated on 05th December as an opportunity for volunteers and stakeholders to make their contribution known to the public.

Volunteering in events differs from other volunteering forms, since it usually involves taking part in actions every year (Treuren, 2014) with organizers being heavily reliant on the support of the volunteers (Warner et al., 2011). Event volunteers are more autonomous compared with paid employees; therefore, their management approach should be different; apart from other expectations they await recognition for their contribution (Nichols & Ojala, 2009). Considering that they are not under an obligation to the event managers for their livelihood, they can bring useful feedback to the organizers (Bang & Chelladurai, 2009); that means that they can be straightforward, give precise information and provide in general a more objective approach as regards the event structure.

They have an active contribution in the event organization, they enjoy unique experiences usually through the teamwork and they often support the participants' efforts. They may provide services not only during the event but also before and after it. We can say that volunteers have a real impact on the success of the event. Their services may include interaction with all kinds of the small scale event tasks, for example contact with the athletes, gate control, event area preparation, equipment control, participation in ceremonies, medal preparation and podium set-up, press and photographs, supply support and management, medical assistance, transport coordination, parking management, IT coordination or volunteer team supervision.

Definitely their tasks may cover multilateral event aspects. In addition, every volunteer has their own unique personality with different level of experience, skills and motivation. It is apparent that managing volunteers may be not only an interesting and rewarding but also a very challenging responsibility for a number of reasons.

Indeed, organizers need to recruit a number of volunteers to help athletes, visitors and spectators (Kim, 2018) but attracting them is actually a challenge given that there is a considerable increase in the number of the events (Costa et al., 2006), volunteers come from all walks of life (Lamb, & Ogle, 2016) and often differ in their background and personal characteristics, like their nationality, gender, age, employment status and previous experience (Kim et al., 2018; Schlesinger & Gubler, 2016). Furthermore, they are active in diverse contexts (Bussell & Forbes, 2002), let alone the fact that volunteerism entails a cost for an individual's family and work life (Treuren, 2014), situations that make the organizers' work more difficult. The latter may also confront problems that regard the nonperformance and nonattendance of volunteers, a condition that is described by Pearce as the reliability problem (Boezeman & Ellemers, 2007; Pearce, 1993) giving rise to several operational troubles (Cuskelly et al., 2004). Volunteers are usually free to quit their job anytime, in contrast to paid staff (Farny et al., 2019) who 'need the money from work to meet their daily needs' (Henderson & Sowa, 2019). Other issues may emerge if organizers recruit more volunteers than necessary (Cuskelly et al., 2004). In addition, event volunteers' managers face challenges because of the different nature of episodic and long-term volunteers (Kim & Cuskelly, 2017). Long-term or continuous volunteers take part in events over a long period of time whereas episodic ones get involved once (Hallmann & Harms, 2012). Managers should recruit, supervise and retain episodic volunteers differently from long-term ones (Fairley et al., 2014). The involvement and commitment between core and peripheral volunteers differ so recruitment strategies should be designed accordingly (Ringuet-Riot et al., 2014).

Volunteers' Motivations

However, the most challenging responsibility for the managers is to distinguish among the reasons why volunteers are willing to provide their time and services. Which their motive to offer is; for example, some may volunteer for developing new skills or gaining experiences, others to offer to their community. Recent studies (Brown et al., 2019) have found that individuals are more willing to donate time and effort (volunteer) rather than to contribute through money.

Volunteerism is an act of giving and taking between the organizer and the volunteer where both parties' requirements have to be satisfied for a mutually productive relationship (Doherty, 2005). Through an environment which changes dynamically and in order to comprehend volunteers' decision to offer to the event, the literature's attention is turned to motivation (Kim et al., 2010; Schlesinger & Gubler, 2016). The research on the motivation of volunteers in events, but also in other sectors, has been continuously increasing (Kim, 2018). According to Reber (1995), motivation is "an internal process or a state of an organism that leads to activation", and an essential construct in an effort to understand the decision to become a volunteer (Wang, 2000). For special events, organizers will have to deal with the *diversity* of the volunteers' motivations; the latter are different from those in the areas of human services (Farrell et al., 1998). Individuals volunteer in order to cover their varied needs or motives (Finkelstien, 2009) and their decision to get or to remain involved is greatly affected by the degree that these needs and expectations are met (Stukas et al., 2016).

Recruitment and Retention

It is crucial for event organizers to keep good relationships with volunteers (Kim et al., 2018) and to understand what motivates them to become involved in certain events (Bang & Ross, 2009; Kim & Cuskelly, 2017). Besides, volunteering pool is decreasing therefore it is important for organizers to recognize not only how individuals are motivated but also how they are retained (Bussell & Forbes, 2002). Volunteering projects based on volunteers' needs and requirements should be adopted (Schlesinger & Gubler, 2016).

The determination of the volunteers' satisfaction from the part of the event managers and how their wants will be accomplished, is important for their recruitment and retention (Warner et al., 2011). Furthermore, and according to the authors, satisfied volunteers may inform their acquaintances for the event and, thus, become a recruitment channel for other volunteers.

Baum et al. (2009) set a list of key strategies for retaining volunteers according to Figure 1 which reveals the tasks of a successful volunteering program based on the identification of the best practices. Among others, the strategies include orientation, training, feedback and reward as the dos and avoidance of underutilization of volunteers' skills and wrong awards as the don'ts.

The organizers that understand the volunteers' motivations may target to those that are suitable for recruitment (Hallmann & Zehrer, 2017; Kim et al., 2010; Kim et al., 2018; Schlesinger & Gubler, 2016; Wang, 2000) and develop the relevant human resource management practices so as to better organize everything that regards their management (Kerwin et al., 2015). If organizers provide volunteers with interesting tasks, it is more possible for the latter to engage, based on their initial motivation (Allen & Bartle, 2014).

Figure 1. Volunteer experience life cycle
Source: Baum, T., Deery, M., & Hanlon, C. (Eds.). (2009). People and work in events and conventions: A research perspective. Cabi.

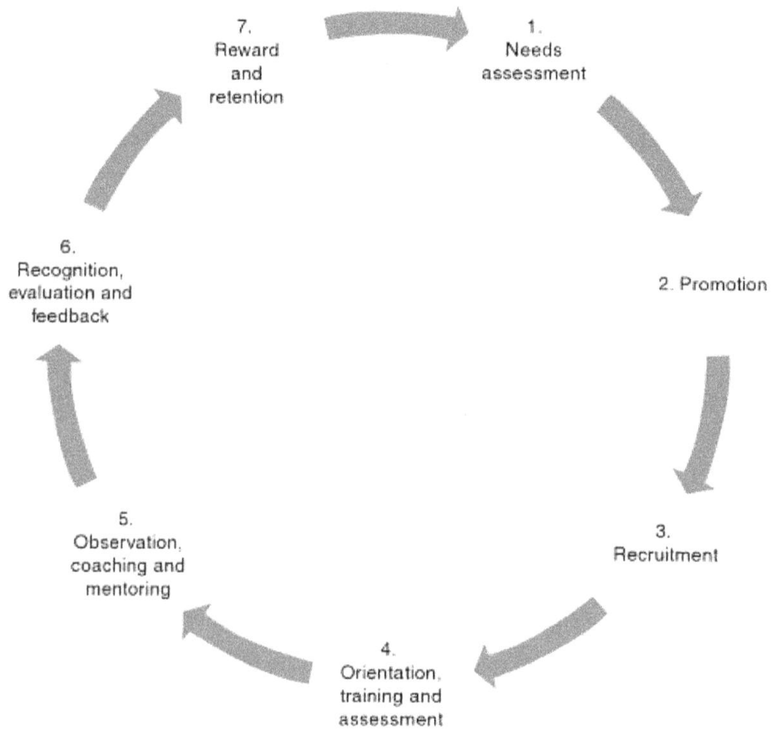

Volunteers are usually recruited through informal social networks instead of formal recruitment methods (Treuren, 2014). Lee et al. (2016) give emphasis on online social interaction ties via social media in order to facilitate team member exchange facilities among volunteers and recommend the creation of a social media website as a good starting point to attract volunteers.

Despite the difficulties they may face, organizers will have to remember that the knowing of the motivation of the volunteers, can lead to the organization of a successful event (Farrell et al., 1998; Hallmann & Harms, 2012). It can also lead to successful promotional opportunities and volunteer positions compliant with the potential volunteers (Yoshioka et al., 2007), adjusted to their different needs (Kim et al., 2018). As long as these needs are fulfilled, it is more likely for volunteers to continue participating in events (Bang & Ross, 2009; Kim et al, 2018).

Undoubtedly, “motivational processes are psychological processes”, dissimilar from one person to another (Kristiansen et al., 2015). Positive experiences during all the event activities along with volunteer communication and recognition increase volunteer satisfaction and should be high in managers' priorities (Farrell et al., 1998). The identification of the volunteers' motivations should be specifically matched with the characteristics of the events, followed by relevant support, directions and feedback, a difficult task for the event managers (Bang & Ross, 2009).

The volunteers' retention or their repeat participation may entail reduction of recruitment costs from the part of the event managers along with the establishment of relationships, like building new friendships (Lee et al., 2016). However, volunteering retention remains a problem (Kristiansen et al., 2015). To avoid difficulties, specific recruitment strategies based on the identification of the volunteers' motivation could be applied, including rewards, recognition, training, and performance management practices (Treuren, 2014). Treuren (2014) highlights the importance of deciding which kind of volunteers the organization prefers to recruit so as to follow then the relevant recruitment strategy. For example, for long-term committed volunteers, the "enthusiasts" would be recruited by emphasizing on the importance of the event. For those who do not have special interest in the event, the direct benefits could be underlined.

Motivational Factors

There may be several *simultaneous* reasons to volunteer (Treuren, 2014) and the literature has identified great many. It has attempted to interpret and understand the different viewpoints of volunteers' motivations and has proposed diverse motivational functions served by volunteerism, which vary according to the attributes and characteristics of the organization (Schlesinger & Gubler, 2016).

A number of papers have already discussed the volunteer motivations in special events, within the domain of psychology, combining volunteers' motives with their attributes. Table 1 presents some selected studies pertinent to several contexts of volunteering motivation with the emphasis being given on events.

Starting from Clary et al. (1998), their scheme increases our understanding in volunteerism through the adoption of the Volunteer Functions Inventory (VFI) Instrument; the VFI identifies six motivational functions, including values, understanding, social, career, protective and enhancement. When the volunteers' initial motivations are fulfilled through their experiences, then it is more possible for them to gain satisfaction from their activities. Volunteers who present high levels of VFI factors will more likely continue volunteering. The VFI motivational functions are applicable to all contexts of volunteer motivations but they will probably differ for sport events volunteers.

Farrel et al. (1998) argue that volunteers' motivations in human services differ from those in special events. Based on data collected through a Canadian women's curling competition, they provide the Special Event Volunteer Motivation Scale

Table 1. Volunteer Motivations in events

Source	Functions	Themes
Clary et al. (1998)	Values	• Altruistic and humanitarian concerns for others • Distinguishes volunteers from non-volunteers
	Understanding	• New learning experiences • Exercise knowledge, skills, abilities • Benefits related to self-development and learning
	Social	• Interaction • Opportunity to be with friends • Networking
	Career	• Prepare for new career • Maintain career relevant skills
	Protective	• Address personal problems • Escape from negative feelings
	Enhancement	• Personal development • Ego's growth
Farrell et al., (1998)	Purposive	• Desire to contribute to the community and the events
	Solidary	• Social interaction, group identification and networking
	External Traditions	• Family Traditions
	Commitments	• Link between external expectations and personal skills with commitment to volunteering
Twynam et al., (2002)	Solidary	• Social Interaction and personal development
	Purposive	• Contribute to the community • Experience Personal benefits
	Commitment	• Fulfil obligations to the event or the community
	External Traditions	• Family/friends also involved
Wang (2004)	Altruistic Value	• Help others • Contribute to society • Express humanitarian concerns
	Personal Development	• Gain new knowledge and experience • Challenge oneself and test skills and abilities • Human capital investment through the enhancement of labor market value
	Community Concern	• An integral part of civil society
	Ego Enhancement	• Pride and self-esteem
	Social Adjustment	• Relationships with others
Monga (2006)	Affiliatory	• Special interest/attachment to the event activity • The event itself is the attractor
	Altruistic	• Help others • A sense of benevolent interest in the welfare of others
	Instrumentalist	• Acquisition of skills, networking or work experience • Material outcomes like souvenirs or appreciation certificates
	Egoistic	• Promotion of own interests
	Solidary	• Social interaction

continued on following page

Table 1. Continued

Source	Functions	Themes
Bang & Chelladurai, (2009)	Values	• Connection with altruism
	Patriotism	• Expression of national pride and sense of belonging
	Interpersonal contacts	• Social interaction
	Career orientation	• Gain practical experience and skills
	Personal growth	• Increase the feelings of self-worth and self-esteem
	Extrinsic rewards	• Free admission, T-shirts, hats, footwear, pins and food
Treuren (2014)	Altruistic	• Help • Make the society better
	Solidary	• Family tradition • Friends participation • Societal culture
	Instrumental	• New career options • Skills development • Gain experience • Collect event material
	Associative	• Become part of the event • Special interest in the event
	Egoistic	• Egoistic intention such as self-esteem or need to feel important
Schlesinger & Gubler, (2016)	Expression of values	• Helping out
	Personal growth	• Gain new perspectives • Feel important
	Interpersonal contacts	• Interact and develop relationships with others
	Career orientation	• Gain experience • Make new contacts
	Extrinsic rewards	• Tickets/free admission, food
	Community involvement	• Express pride • Devotion to the community
	Love of sport	• Enjoying sports
Kim et al., (2018)	Expression of values	• Altruism, freely choose to help others
	Career Orientation	• Gain work-related experience • Make new contacts
	Love of Sport	• Like events related to sport
	Community Involvement	• Express pride in the host community
	Interpersonal Contacts	• Social relationships and network
	Extrinsic Rewards	• Tangible and material benefits

(SEVMS), a 28-item scale which illustrates a number of reasons for event volunteering, grouped into the four presented categories.

Twynam et al. (2002) use the Special Event Volunteer Motivation Scale (SEVMS) as well. The authors identify four motivation factors through the use of an event volunteer sample at the Star Choice World Junior Curling Tournament Event. According to their study, there are many aspects in the motivations of the special event volunteers; volunteerism is considered by some volunteers as a serious leisure experience.

Wang (2004) recognizes the multi-dimensional aspect of volunteering motivation and refers to five principal motivations that are pertinent to Australian sport volunteers through a 20-item scale that measures motivations for sports volunteerism.

Monga (2006) examines the volunteers' motivations through five type of events in Australia; automotive contests, a cultural festival, a public parade, a solar car race and an agricultural show. Her study emphasizes on affiliatory reasons as the strongest ones to volunteer in an event. She adds that the more attached to the event activity the volunteers are, the higher the possibility of participating again is.

To make a comparison with the large events volunteer motivational functions, the study of Bang & Chelladurai (2009) is presented. They develop and validate the volunteer motivation scale for international sporting events (the Asian games volunteers from the 2002 FIFA World Cup) and display a six-factor solution which explains the reason why individuals volunteer at events.

Through the application of cluster analysis on five events (automotive racing, cultural festival, public parade, solar car race, agricultural show), Treuren, (2014) identifies six distinct motivational profiles; three types of enthusiasts who experience differently the volunteerism, two types of conscripts who are unwilling in several ways and are rather forced to volunteer and the instrumentalists who anticipate material benefits. They all have different volunteering experience as well as different desires as regards the benefits; thus, they are recruited in distinct and separate ways.

Schlesinger & Gubler, (2016), through a survey on European Athletics Championships in Zurich in 2014, segment the volunteers based on their mutually exclusive motivational characteristics. They find that there are different motivational processes among sport event volunteers and sometimes volunteers combine different bundles of motives.

Kim et al. (2018) study a sample of volunteers of three separate sport events in Australia, which highly rely on volunteers, that is a golf tournament, a running event and a cycling event. Through the investigation of the distinct features of four volunteer motivational clusters (1. Material-benefit seekers, 2. Sport and community enthusiasts, 3. Altruists, 4. Career and social relationship seekers) in terms of the socio-demographics, the related experiences, and the type of the event, they identify different motivations among the four clusters.

Community

By providing their services, volunteers may not only gain a sense of fulfilment but also create local bonds and benefit their own community. In fact, one of the easiest volunteering forms is the contribution to one's community, the place that one lives and is active. Community support is a common motivational factor (Kerwin et al., 2015) with an important social impact (Pauline, 2011); literature recognizes that volunteers often undertake their jobs in order to improve and contribute to their local community (Farrell et al., 1998; Hallmann & Zehrer, 2017). Nichols (2017) describes community as: "The word community implies the organization exists to serve the needs of a relatively small number of people......in the same geographical area".

The idea of sense of community was initially suggested by Sarason (1974) and included the feeling of being part of a larger well-grounded and steady structure. According to McMillan & Chavis (1986) the sense of community can be defined as "a feeling that members have of belonging, a feeling that members matter to one another and to the group, and a shared faith that members' needs will be met through their commitment to be together".

Warner & Dixon (2011) claim that "the sense of community can be experienced by any individual or member of a geographic or interest group, even one that has little in common with the larger unit of which it is a part". The authors contend that the sense of community is experienced differently between the genders.

The sense of community may be location-based or may have to do with an important issue or leisure activity (Stukas et al., 2016). It increases for small-scale event volunteers (Kerwin et al., 2015) and the higher the volunteerism is, the stronger the sense of community is as well (Stukas et al., 2016).

Regardless of the type of the event, its role in the community's development worth attention (Lamb, & Ogle, 2016). There is a connection between event and community involvement (Hallmann & Zehrer, 2017) and volunteering can add to this involvement (Kim & Cuskelly, 2017; Stebbins, 2009) resulting in social networks, social interaction and building of common interests among the community members (Stebbins, 2009). As regards small scale events, the volunteerism of locals who contribute to events in order to attract tourists to the destination is a well-known and recognized trend (Kim et al, 2018). Contrary to large-scale events which may recruit volunteers outside the host city, small-scale event organizers usually rely on local ones (Kerwin et al., 2015) who are usually selected from the local community, and consequently may serve as a link between the organization and the community (Bang & Chelladurai, 2009). Hence, the perception of the community involvement as a motivation is particularly interesting given that the personal attachment to a region and the volunteering for an event could create a link to community (Bang & Ross, 2009). The promotion of the community involvement and the volunteerism requires attention considering also that the advantages both for the community and for the volunteers are great many, particularly important for democratic societies (Stukas et al., 2016). An illustration will serve to make the above point more comprehensible, namely the organization of an event may lead to intense public-private sector cooperation in the community and become a tool for community development; in case of success, the event can often be the motive for emulation by other communities (Getz, 1984; Getz & Frisby, 1988). What's more, managers should give consideration to the community involvement in order to understand the behavioral intentions of the volunteers (Hallmann & Zehrer, 2017). The authors provide some relevant suggestions, for example, a photo sharing at the social media that will depict the volunteers' relationship with the community, the volunteer of the month award and the creation of a social-media compatible application regarding the volunteers' activities that will provide them with bonus points. These activities may establish a sense of belonging among the volunteers towards the community.

Last but not least, the training of event volunteers could intensify the volunteer commitment and satisfaction through the building of a sense of community among volunteers and staff (Costa et al., 2006). Concluding, when people feel part of a community at its psychological sense, they will more probably adopt prosocial behaviors that will benefit both the community and its members (Omoto & Packar, 2016). Like the saying goes: "Those who can, do. Those who can do more, Volunteer".

CASE STUDY: INSIGHTS FROM SMALL SCALE RUNNING EVENTS

Three successful Greek small-scale running events, SMF, AlmiraMAN and Yedi Kule Conquest, which employ a significant number of volunteers, are shortly described below along with information (Table 2) as regards the working areas and the package per volunteer.

The SMF, Sfendami Mountain Festival (Sfendami.com, 2019), lasts for two days and is organized every April since 2007, in the region of Pieria in North Greece. The aim of the event is to offer to athletes and visitors from Greece and the Balkan an experience of the area.

AlmiraMAN (Almiraman.gr, 2019), a triathlon event race, is held in the Olympic Coast of Katerini (North Greece), near to Thessaloniki, the country's second largest city. It is organized since 2014 and includes open sea swimming, cycling and running. The two-day race event also attracts Greek and Balkan athletes and spectators.

Yedi Kule Conquest (Yedikule.gr, 2019) is a sports and cultural event organized since 2016 and held in the area of Eptapyrgio, Thessaloniki. The historical monuments and the rich cultural heritage of the city are highlighted through the event organization.

All the three events highly depend on the volunteering support and therefore the organizers have prepared the working areas where the volunteer help is essential along with the package that each one will receive. Read the information of Table 2 about the three small-scale sport events and reply to the questions:

Table 2. Three Small Scaled Sport Event Cases from Greece

Small Scale Sport Event	Start Year	Approx No of Volunteers	Working Areas	Volunteers Package
1.SMF **(Sfendami Mountain Festival)-** ***Biathlon sport event*** **~800 Athletes [300 Runners & 500 Bikers (mtb)] *1 or 2 working days**	2007 until today (**)	80	· Registration · Information · Routes preparation · Athletes services · Parking · Food and beverage services · Ceremony · Media · VIP services · Security assistance · Medical assistance · Product exhibition services · Construction/Deconstruction · Volunteer management · Transport	· Experience the event · Make new friends · Refreshments · Volunteer medals · Certificate · Training Session
2. ***AlmiraMAN Triathlon sport event*** **~415 Athletes ~2.500 Visitors *1 or 2 working days**	2014 until today	120	· Accreditation · Registration · Information · Athletes services · Sponsorship · Marketing · Food and beverage services · Ceremony · Media · IT services · VIP services · Product exhibition services · Construction/Deconstruction · Volunteer management · Team hospitality	· Experience the event · Make new friends · AlmiraMAN T-shirt · Certificate · Food and refreshments · Free transportation · Social events and thank-you party · Training Session · Publicize volunteer efforts
3. ***Yedi Kule Conquest*** **-** ***Multi-purpose event*** **~210 Athletes ~1.500 Visitors *1 working day**	2015 until today	100	· Registration · Information · Routes preparation · Athletes services · Ceremony · VIP services · Construction/Deconstruction · Volunteer management	· Experience the event · Make new friends · Yedi Kule Hat · Refreshments · Training Session · Certificate · Pre-event free sightseeing tour · Publicize volunteer efforts

1. Identify the tasks of the training session for the volunteers involved. What would you recommend as mandatory for their training?
2. Consider you are the team leader of each volunteer group per working area. What instructions will you give and how would you organize the shifts?
3. Review on the workings areas and suggest/describe the tasks needed per working area.
4. Imagine you are the event organizer. What is your opinion on the volunteers' package and what would you suggest in order to attract more volunteers the next year?

5. Apart from the tasks on the working areas, what other obligations would be mandatory for the volunteers involved?
6. Suppose the volunteers have high altruistic motivations and want to contribute to their community. How would you organize the volunteers' recruitment and management per event?
7. Imagine you are a member of the local government and you want to create a community volunteer program for each of the three small scale events. Apart from the standard volunteers' package, what else would you offer?

SUMMARY

Volunteers do not just consist an essential part of small scale events; they are the soul of the events. Maintenance of good relationship with volunteers, understanding their motivations and covering their needs based on their requirements and characteristics is a challenge for the event organizers; yet, it is an important step to the building of a successful event. Volunteering is a challenging adventure, which involves stepping out from one's comfort zone. Volunteers can achieve great things if they are well motivated and, in this case, they will probably continue volunteering with even better performance. Community involvement has been considered as a frequent motivational factor.

REFERENCES

Allen, J. B., & Bartle, M. (2014). Sport event volunteers' engagement: Management matters. *Managing Leisure*, *19*(1), 36–50. doi:10.1080/13606719.2013.849502

Almiraman.gr. (2020). *Almira Man - May 2020 Paralia, Katerini, Greece*. Available at: https://www.almiraman.gr/english/almiraman_en.html

Bang, H., & Chelladurai, P. (2009). Development and validation of the volunteer motivations scale for international sporting events (VMS-ISE). *International Journal of Sport Management and Marketing*, *6*(4), 332–350. doi:10.1504/IJSMM.2009.030064

Bang, H., & Ross, S. D. (2009). Volunteer motivation and satisfaction. *Journal of Venue and Event Management*, *1*(1), 61–77.

Baum, T., Deery, M., & Hanlon, C. (Eds.). (2009). *People and work in events and conventions: A research perspective*. Cabi. doi:10.1079/9781845934767.0000

Boezeman, E. J., & Ellemers, N. (2007). Volunteering for charity: Pride, respect, and the commitment of volunteers. *The Journal of Applied Psychology*, *92*(3), 771–785. doi:10.1037/0021-9010.92.3.771 PMID:17484556

Brown, A. L., Meer, J., & Williams, J. F. (2019). Why do people volunteer? An experimental analysis of preferences for time donations. *Management Science*, *65*(4), 1455–1468. doi:10.1287/mnsc.2017.2951

Bussell, H., & Forbes, D. (2002). Understanding the volunteer market: The what, where, who and why of volunteering. *International Journal of Nonprofit and Voluntary Sector Marketing*, *7*(3), 244–257. doi:10.1002/nvsm.183

Clary, E. G., Snyder, M., Ridge, R. D., Copeland, J., Stukas, A. A., Haugen, J., & Miene, P. (1998). Understanding and assessing the motivations of volunteers: A functional approach. *Journal of Personality and Social Psychology*, *74*(6), 1516–1530. doi:10.1037/0022-3514.74.6.1516 PMID:9654757

Costa, C. A., Chalip, L., Green, B. C., & Simes, C. (2006). Reconsidering the role of training in event volunteers' satisfaction. *Sport Management Review*, *9*(2), 165–182. doi:10.1016/S1441-3523(06)70024-9

Cuskelly, G., Auld, C., Harrington, M., & Coleman, D. (2004). Predicting the behavioral dependability of sport event volunteers. *Event Management*, *9*(1-2), 73–89. doi:10.3727/1525995042781011

Doherty, A. (2005). A profile of community sport volunteers. Toronto: Parks and Recreation Ontario and Sport Alliance of Ontario.

Doherty, A. (2009). The volunteer legacy of a major sport event. *Journal of Policy Research in Tourism, Leisure & Events*, *1*(3), 185–207. doi:10.1080/19407960903204356

Fairley, S., Green, B. C., O'Brien, D., & Chalip, L. (2014). Pioneer volunteers: The role identity of continuous volunteers at sport events. *Journal of Sport & Tourism*, *19*(3-4), 233–255. doi:10.1080/14775085.2015.1111774

Farny, S., Kibler, E., Hai, S., & Landoni, P. (2019). Volunteer retention in prosocial venturing: The role of emotional connectivity. *Entrepreneurship Theory and Practice*, *43*(6), 1094–1123. doi:10.1177/1042258718769055

Farrell, J. M., Johnston, M. E., & Twynam, G. D. (1998). Volunteer motivation, satisfaction, and management at an elite sporting competition. *Journal of Sport Management*, *12*(4), 288–300. doi:10.1123/jsm.12.4.288

Finkelstien, M. A. (2009). Intrinsic vs. extrinsic motivational orientations and the volunteer process. *Personality and Individual Differences*, *46*(5-6), 653–658. doi:10.1016/j.paid.2009.01.010

Getz, D. (1984). Tourism, community organization and the social multiplier. *Leisure, Tourism and Social Change*, 85-100.

Getz, D., & Frisby, W. (1988). Evaluating management effectiveness in community-run festivals. *Journal of Travel Research*, *27*(1), 22–27. doi:10.1177/004728758802700105

Hallmann, K., & Harms, G. (2012). Determinants of volunteer motivation and their impact on future voluntary engagement: A comparison of volunteer's motivation at sport events in equestrian and handball. *International Journal of Event and Festival Management, 3*(3), 272-291.

Hallmann, K., & Zehrer, A. (2017). Event and community involvement of sport event volunteers. *International Journal of Event and Festival Management*, *8*(3), 308–323. doi:10.1108/IJEFM-08-2016-0058

Henderson, A. C., & Sowa, J. (2019). Volunteer satisfaction at the boundary of public and nonprofit: Organizational-and individual-level determinants. *Public Performance & Management Review*, *42*(1), 162–189. doi:10.1080/15309576.2018.1471405

International Labour Organization. (2011). *Manual on the measurement of volunteer work*. Retrieved from https://www.ilo.org/wcmsp5/groups/public/---dgreports/---stat/documents/publication/wcms_162119.pdf

Kerwin, S., Warner, S., Walker, M., & Stevens, J. (2015). Exploring sense of community among small-scale sport event volunteers. *European Sport Management Quarterly*, *15*(1), 77–92. doi:10.1080/16184742.2014.996581

Kim, E. (2018). A systematic review of motivation of sport event volunteers. *World Leisure Journal*, *60*(4), 306–329. doi:10.1080/16078055.2017.1373696

Kim, E., & Cuskelly, G. (2017). A systematic quantitative review of volunteer management in events. *Event Management*, *21*(1), 83–100. doi:10.3727/152599517X14809630271195

Kim, E., Fredline, L., & Cuskelly, G. (2018). Heterogeneity of sport event volunteer motivations: A segmentation approach. *Tourism Management*, *68*, 375–386. doi:10.1016/j.tourman.2018.04.004

Kim, M., Zhang, J. J., & Connaughton, D. (2010). Modification of the volunteer functions inventory for application in youth sports. *Sport Management Review*, *13*(1), 25–38. doi:10.1016/j.smr.2009.04.005

Kristiansen, E., Skirstad, B., Parent, M. M., & Waddington, I. (2015). 'We can do it': Community, resistance, social solidarity, and long-term volunteering at a sport event. *Sport Management Review*, *18*(2), 256–267. doi:10.1016/j.smr.2014.06.002

Lamb, D., & Ogle, A. (2016). The Motivations of Event Volunteers at Local Community Events. In *Managing and Developing Communities, Festivals and Events* (pp. 50–68). Palgrave Macmillan. doi:10.1057/9781137508553_4

Lee, Y., Kim, M., & Koo, J. (2016). The impact of social interaction and team member exchange on sport event volunteer management. *Sport Management Review*, *19*(5), 550–562. doi:10.1016/j.smr.2016.04.005

Leigh, J., Lamont, M., & Cairncross, G. (2013). Towards a process model of induction and training for young event volunteers. *International Journal of Event Management Research*, *8*(1), 1–20.

Lockstone-Binney, L., Holmes, K., Smith, K., Baum, T., & Storer, C. (2015). Are all my volunteers here to help out? Clustering event volunteers by their motivations. *Event Management*, *19*(4), 461–477. doi:10.3727/152599515X14465748512605

McMillan, D. W., & Chavis, D. M. (1986). Sense of community: A definition and theory. *Journal of Community Psychology*, *14*(1), 6–23. doi:10.1002/1520-6629(198601)14:1<6::AID-JCOP2290140103>3.0.CO;2-I

Monga, M. (2006). Measuring motivation to volunteer for special events. *Event Management*, *10*(1), 47–61. doi:10.3727/152599506779364633

Nichols, G. (2017). Volunteering in community sports associations: A literature review. *Voluntaristics Review*, *2*(1), 1–75. doi:10.1163/24054933-12340015

Nichols, G., & Ojala, E. (2009). Understanding the management of sports events volunteers through psychological contract theory. *Voluntas*, *20*(4), 369–387. doi:10.100711266-009-9097-9

Omoto, A. M., & Packard, C. D. (2016). The power of connections: Psychological sense of community as a predictor of volunteerism. *The Journal of Social Psychology*, *156*(3), 272–290. doi:10.1080/00224545.2015.1105777 PMID:27064179

Pauline, G. (2011). Volunteer satisfaction and intent to remain: An analysis of contributing factors among professional golf event volunteers. *International Journal of Event Management Research*, 10.

Pearce, J. L. (1993). *Volunteers: The organizational behavior of unpaid workers*. Routledge.

Reber, A. S. (1995). *The Penguin dictionary of psychology*. Penguin Press.

Ringuet-Riot, C., Cuskelly, G., Auld, C., & Zakus, D. H. (2014). Volunteer roles, involvement and commitment in voluntary sport organizations: Evidence of core and peripheral volunteers. *Sport in Society*, *17*(1), 116–133. doi:10.1080/17430437.2013.828902

Sarason, S. B. (1974). *The psychological sense of community: Prospects for a community psychology*. Jossey-Bass.

Schlesinger, T., & Gubler, R. (2016). Motivational profiles of sporting event volunteers. *Sport in Society*, *19*(10), 1419–1439. doi:10.1080/17430437.2015.1133596

Sfendami.com. (2019). *Sfendami*. Available at: http://www.sfendami.com/?lang=en

Stebbins, R. A. (1996). Volunteering: A serious leisure perspective. *Nonprofit and Voluntary Sector Quarterly*, *25*(2), 211–224. doi:10.1177/0899764096252005

Stebbins, R. A. (2009). Would you volunteer? *Society*, *46*(2), 155–159. doi:10.100712115-008-9186-1

Stukas, A. A., Snyder, M., & Clary, E. G. (2016). *Understanding and encouraging volunteerism and community involvement*. Academic Press.

Treuren, G. J. (2014). Enthusiasts, conscripts or instrumentalists? The motivational profiles of event volunteers. *Managing Leisure*, *19*(1), 51–70. doi:10.1080/13606719.2013.849506

Twynam, G. D., Farrell, J. M., & Johnston, M. E. (2002). Leisure and volunteer motivation at a special sporting event. *Leisure/Loisir, 27*(3-4), 363-377.

Wang, P. Z. (2004, January). Assessing motivations for sports volunteerism. In Conference of the Association-for-Consumer-Research (ACR 2003). Assoc Consumer Research.

Warner, S., & Dixon, M. A. (2011). Understanding sense of community from the athlete's perspective. *Journal of Sport Management*, *25*(3), 257–271. doi:10.1123/jsm.25.3.257

Warner, S., Newland, B. L., & Green, B. C. (2011). More than motivation: Reconsidering volunteer management tools. *Journal of Sport Management*, *25*(5), 391–407. doi:10.1123/jsm.25.5.391

Yedikule.gr. (2019). Available at: https://www.yedikule.gr/

Yoshioka, C. F., Brown, W. A., & Ashcraft, R. F. (2007). A functional approach to senior volunteer and non-volunteer motivations. *The International Journal of Volunteer Administration*, *24*(5), 31-43.

Section 2
Small-Scale Event Development and Implementation Phase

In this section, the role of an event facilitator, event structures, and principles in event structures will be discussed along with basic elements of operational planning. Readers will know why quality and authenticity are important elements for successful small-scale sport events. Different methods for event enhancement will be presented.

Chapter 6
Small-Scale Sport Event Planning

Claudel Mombeuil
https://orcid.org/0000-0003-2855-9319
Beijing Institute of Technology, China

ABSTRACT

Event planning remains one of the core elements for the success of small-scale sports events. In the case of for-profit organizations, a small-scale sport event may be planned to increase awareness of a new product or service, whereas a small-scale sport event may be organized by not-for-profit organizations to raise concerns or awareness of social and environmental issues. However, it is important that the sporting event that is being organized is in sync with the mission of the organization and must meet the expectation of the target audience. Therefore, substantial information regarding the target audience is needed. More importantly, the sport event managers must ensure that the objectives and the expected outcomes of the small-scale sporting event are smart. By developing smart small-scale event objectives and outcomes, sport event managers can distribute roles and responsibilities to team members more efficiently. During the planning phase, sport event managers also needs to take into consideration the venue to host the event, the third-party service providers, and a contingency plan.

DOI: 10.4018/978-1-7998-4757-1.ch006

INTRODUCTION

Event planning remains one of the core elements for the success of small-scale sports events. In the case of for-profit organizations, small-scale sports events represent leverage for companies to increase awareness of a new product or service. Similarly, not-for-profit organizations also use small-scale sports events to raise concerns or awareness of social and environmental issues. Particularly, local businesses may obtain substantial benefits using small sports events as leverage (Chalip & Leyns, 2002). However, it is important that the sporting event that is being organized is in sync with the mission of the organization and it must meet the expectation of the target audience. Therefore, substantial information regarding the target audience is needed. More importantly, the event managers must ensure that the objectives and the expected outcomes of the small-scale sporting event are SMART, meaning that the objectives and the outcome must be specific, measurable, achievable, realistic, and time-bound. By developing SMART small-scale event objectives and outcomes, event managers will be to assess the resources, skills, and manpower needed to achieve the underlying objectives. By developing SMART small-scale sports events, event managers may ease track progress of the event and measure eventually the level of success. By assessing the resources, skills, and manpower needed, the event manager can be in the position to build a solid event team. Once the event team is built, the event manager needs to prepare the sports event project plan, and this must be done with full engagement of team members. A small sports event plan is, in principle, a detailed breakdown of the actions or activities needed to reach the objectives along with the due dates and completion status of each activity. With a well-defined sport event plan, event managers can better assign roles and responsibilities to team members and ensure accountability in meeting the objectives.

During the small-scale sport event planning process, the event manager needs to choose an appropriate venue to host the event. It should be noted that a sports event is unique in its sense; therefore, it must guaranty a memorable experience to the participants. In principle, the event manager needs to conduct a field visit with team members in order to assess the appropriateness of the venue where the event will be hosted. It is important to note that no event plan can be successfully implemented without the help of third-party service providers. Consequently, any small sports event planning must carefully monitor and coordinate activities that are under the control of third-party service providers. It is important that the sports event manager has a shortlist of third-party service providers. While the event manager may consider including one particularly third-party service provider for the delivery of a service, he or she must have an arrangement with a second even a third provider in case their selected service provider fails to deliver their promise. Similar to any projects, a small sports event needs a contingency plan. The contingency plan is crucial because of there a number of events that can affect the success of a small sports event. For example, a third-part-service provider may suddenly unable to deliver a crucial service during the sports event that is being planned. Therefore, the event manager should include in the contingency plan contact the details of the second and the third service provider during the planning process. Simply put, the contingency plan should include the most reasonable cost-effective solution to events that can affect the delivery of one activity or the success of the sports event under creation.

This chapter first addresses the development of small-scale sport event ideas with an emphasis on the role of the event team and also the importance of developing SMART sport event objectives. Second, it emphasizes the importance of the event team to fully understand their target audience. Third, it discusses successively planning small-scale sports events, how roles and responsibilities should be assigned to the event team members, and factors that should be taken into account when making the choice of the venue where the event is going to host. This chapter also discusses the importance of third-Party service providers and how they may influence the outcomes of the event. It concludes with the establishment of the event timelines, the role of the contingency planning, and a case study.

DEVELOPING SMALL-SCALE SPORT EVENT IDEAS

There is an increasing trend of using sports events among tourism organizations as a means to build their brand (Chalip & Costa, 2005). Like all events, small-scale sports events start out as an idea. This idea tends to gain momentum as soon as you start to brainstorm it with your team. The brainstorming can be split into different short meetings. As the managers of tourism organizations, it is important that you call out people who are passionate about the type of sports events they want to organize. In most cases, tourism organizations need to select an experienced person that can play the role of the sports event manager. The sports event manager, therefore, need to create a climate that allows people to express their thoughts openly and lets room for constructive criticism regarding the event. During these meetings, you will need to make sure that all the ideas discussed are well-documented with some keynotes regarding the underlying sub-objectives, the audience, and the expected outcomes. Once the team is set up with a common ground agreement regarding how the sporting event in question will look like, you will need to further develop the idea by doing some search on factors that are likely to affect the expected outcome. At this point, it is necessary that you have a clearer understanding of the objectives, expectations of the audience, and the desired outcomes. Consider asking yourself these following questions when setting your objectives and desired outcome on paper: what do we, as a team, want to achieve from this small-sport event? How will we be able to measure the success of this event? What are the key characteristics of this sport-event? In order words, what are the keywords that explicitly describe the sport-event you have in mind? To answer these questions, you need therefore to set SMART objects. That is to say, your objectives must be specific, measurable, achievable, realistic, and time-bound. By developing SMART objectives and outcomes, sport event managers are can easily monitor progress toward process and outcome objectives (Bjerke & Renger, 2017).

Suppose that you have the idea of launching an awareness campaign for a newly eco-tourism business destination that promotes wellbeing, peace of mind, and a sustainable environment in your local area. The main services offered by your eco-tourism business including an open-air restaurant, spa, and massages, visit a green area. Here in this instance, the first question to ask yourself is "what is the most appropriate small-sport event that matches my idea?". We bet you are more likely to choose cycling or running. Let's say you choose cycling as it the most popular sport in your local area. Now that you are clear with the most appropriate small-sport event, the next step is to develop measurable objectives and the desired outcomes. Suppose that you want to increase the visitation rate by 20 percent by the end of December 2020. Remark that we mention the desired outcome first, as it is my ultimate objective. How many people do we need to market our services? Let suppose your search shows that nearly 1 percent of people who participate in small-scale sports events are likely to buy services that were promoted during the event they attended. Consequently, you and your team decide to reach 5000 participants for cycling competing for the event as a sub-objective during summer 2020. This seems reasonable as we assumed earlier that it is the widely practiced sport in your area.

KNOWING AND UNDERSTANDING YOUR TARGET AUDIENCE

There is no way, of course, you can reach the desired outcomes (increase your visitation rate by 20%) if you do not know who will or will likely attend the sporting event you are currently planning. Therefore, you will have to understand the characteristics of your audience so that you can meet their expectation effectively through the provision of suitable activities and effective marketing. The marketing term for this is "targeting". To this end, you will consider searching the following information relative to your target audience: their age group, profession, family status, where they live, and how they will receive the information about your sports event. Suppose your target audience is corporate employees who work companies that truly engage in developing and implementing sustainable business practices. As you are now clear about your target audience, you can start determining the type of programming this group of people might attend, as well as their expectations. Therefore, you need to ask yourself the following questions when marketing your services to this group: 1) what kind of message we (you and your team) want to convey through the cycling event in our example; 2) what is your budget limit for this event and the budget of your target audience for this event? How much time will you need to organize this cycling event? As the success of sports events is in principle depends on volunteer personnel, you also need to consider the needs of your volunteers (*see chapter 11 for more insights*). Eventually, the success of your event will be affected by your employees and local community stakeholders and this will also affect them. Consequently, your investigation should conclude whether these two groups of stakeholders are really in favor of such an event before you start with the planning session.

Planning Small-Scale Sport Events

As you are entering the most crucial stage, planning the small-scale sport event, it is important that you have a clear vision of the event that you are planning. To this end, all the meetings, ideas, and information you have retrieved in stage 1 need to be within your hand to ensure the effectiveness of your planning process. The key elements of your planning must include the following: a well-defined overview of the event; roles and responsibilities of your team members, including volunteers; research on potential venues to host the event; purchasing and renting the necessary equipment; authorization from local authorities; contingency plan. These outlines above are very important in the planning process of any sports events. The importance of these outlines above is not limited to any organizational structure or size. But if you have a small business or humanitarian-based organization, you are more likely to largely depend on sponsors and volunteers to make your event a success; thus, this step will help you to better target your sponsors and recruit volunteer personnel.

Overview of Small-Scale Sport Events

In the overview of your small-scale sport event, you will need to include a title for the event, the date the event is going to happen, time and length of the event, the objectives of the event, a succinct description of the event, your target audience, expected number of attendees, and the programming of the event. Every event bears a title. We shall develop each of these points.

- **Writing up your event title:** There are several aspects that you need to consider when you write your event title. You need to keep in mind that many people will limit their reading to the title of your event. Therefore, the title must be concise, catchy, memorable, easy to remember, and direct to the point in a similar manner as a headline of a newspaper article. In a more explicit term, you will need to determine what kind of information to include and to leave out. The words that you will use for the event title must be appealing and convey a positive emotion and must stand out from the many event titles out there. Due to time constraints and pressure, you might be tempted to copy or replicate some past event titles. One way to make sure that this does not happen to you is to consider highlighting key elements that make your event unique and use them in the event title. Depending on the nature of your event, you might consider tapping into the cultural setting or the popular thinking of your local area. Let us consider these global event titles, like *Dance 4 Life, British Got Talent, Volvo Ocean Race, Ironman Triathlon*. As you can remark, these words taking from the dictionary, but yet short, concise with the names of the events and the target attendees.

- **Date of the Event:** Before you decide on the date of the event, you need to consider several factors. Remember that you are not alone in the business. Many organizations, whatever their nature, may indeed have some events that are being programmed, which will ultimately impact yours. For example, if you program your small-scale sport event the same week with some other organizations in your area, you will need to struggle for sponsorship because every employer has a certain limit when it comes to sponsoring events. Similarly, you will be struggling and competing for attendees! More importantly, you need to schedule your event on a date that is suitable for your target audience. Also, be very mindful of the holidays in your local area. Across culture, holidays mean different things to different people. Some holidays are strictly reserved for family gatherings. You would, therefore, have a low attendance rate. So, you need to do your search appropriately.
- **Time and duration of the event:** Ask yourself this question. What is the best timeframe and length that will suit the audience and the overall planned activities? In particular, the timeframe and duration of the planned event will depend on several factors, such as the nature of the sporting event, the location you choose to host the event and also on the distance between the place your target audience lives and the location where the event is going to be hosted. Thus, you need to choose consciously the time and duration of the event.
- **Event Objectives:** There are three fundamental reasons you need to clearly state your objectives. First, it helps your team to stay focus. Second, it supports your cause for sponsorship. Third and last, it helps you monitor and track the progress of your team towards the ultimate goal (event outcome).

- **Event Outcome:** Here you need to state the desired outcome(s) clearly. As you may expect several outcomes, it is necessary that you point them out using numbers or bullet points.
- **Description of the Event:** at this level, you need to have a short description of your sports event. It will eventually serve people who find interest in your event. It will also be your guide when you want to inform other institutions (e.g., media, sponsors, etc..) about the event.
- **Target Audience:** As we have discussed earlier, you need to have substantial background information about your target audience. Information such as age bracket, gender, professional activities, affiliation, professional network, preferred leisure, family condition, religion, and consumption behavior are important factors that you need to consider. This information is of importance for sponsoring organizations since this will help them to have a good idea of both the social and economic benefits of your sports event, as well as its impact on the hosting community and the benefits that sponsors are likely to gain by supporting the event. Also, it is important that you have an idea about the approximation of the number of people that will attend the event. If your organization has in the past organized sports events, you can base on previous experiences to estimate the number of people that are likely to attend your sports event. If you want to have more attendees to the event, you can think to increase the marketing efforts and strategies or increase a little bit of your marketing budget. If you are new in the business of sports events, you can estimate your attendance based on past events that are similar to what you are planning. Check with your local tourism office or statistics regarding past small-scale sports events that took place in your country. The projection on the number of attendees will also help you determine the suitable location or venue to host the event, amount of food and beverage, restrooms, and garbage cans needed to meet the needs of the attendees.
- **Small-scale sport event programming.** For any sports events, there are those who participate passively and those who participate actively. Those who are on the passive side are composed, in principle, your target audience. The active participants, besides your team members, is composed of those who will play and the referees. The number of active participants can be easily determined based on the regulations of the underlying sport that you choose. The number of active participants can also be determined based on the type of sport and competitors you will invite to join the event. For example, if you want to organize a basketball tournament and the number of teams that will be competing, you can picture out the number of players and referees in advance. This thus will help you determine all the needs of these individuals. Of course, this will help you to determine the amount of beverage, food, etc.

You will also need to look into a sound system or hire the service of a DJ depending on the nature of the sporting event and the venue it is going to be hosted.

Roles and Responsibilities of the Team

Having a solid team is vital for the success of your sports event. These are the individuals that will support you from the moment you start with the idea till the end and the evaluation of the project. Given all the underlying actives surrounding your sports event, you will need to assign roles and responsibilities to the teams. Before doing so, you need to make an assessment of the capacity and the skills of the team members. Skills that are important for a smooth sport event including scheduling and planning, creative design, marketing, promotion, communication, sponsorship and development, and project management. There are several reasons you need to make a succinct assessment of the skills of your team. Among others, it will help you assign roles and define responsibilities based on the skills of each team member. Furthermore, it will help determine whether you have all the necessary skills needed to implement your sports event successfully. As we have mentioned earlier, the success of sports events, be it small or large scale, depends on volunteer personnel. Therefore, assessing the skills of your team will also let you know what skills are needed from the panel of volunteers. The next step is to build job descriptions, goals, as well as the timeline associated with the tasks or sub-objectives that each group is going to be responsible for. As a project leader, you will need to create a healthy team climate conducive to cohesion among team members. A healthy team climate is important because it helps team members feel comfortable being part of the team but also make collaboration and sharing ideas easier. A healthy team climate also creates trust among sport event team members.

Choice of the Venue

Whatever the reason that pushes you to organize a sports event, you need to make sure that the event has an impactful effect on the attendees. The importance of having an impactful effect on them is that you want them to advocate for your service and come back eventually. Therefore, you need to provide your attendees with the opportunity to make a memorable experience with your organization that can, in turn, trigger positive emotional responses. Among others, the venue that you choose to host your sports event will contribute to providing a memorable experience to the participants. The choice of the venue, of course, will depend on the style of the sporting event you have chosen and your target participants. In the context of small-scale sports events, you are less likely to go after expensive venues that you cannot afford. Finding a venue that situates in the exact location you want, that has the size to host the number of participants you target, and that fall within your budget threshold is challenging. While searching for a venue to host your sports event, there are several factors that you need to keep in mind because they will affect the outcomes and level of attendees' satisfaction. Among others, you need to evaluate the accessibility, size, design, and layout, the existing equipment. Having an estimate of the number of participants will tell you whether the size of the venue is suitable or not; whether there are enough parking places; and whether there are enough seats and toilets. This will also help you in considering hiring the services of a third party as discussed later in this chapter). That might be, for example, chairs, portable toilets, and so on.

As you may have a limited operating budget, it is important that you find out some affordable options to host your small-scale sport event. Suppose that you are the manager of a non-profit organization that promotes sustainable behavior and consumption in your community. Let's say your objective for next year is to raise awareness of sustainable consumption among households of your local community and thus you set a target to reach 300 households. So, you decide to organize a swimming competition. Rather than choosing a luxury venue with a swimming pool, you can negotiate a good deal with one of the schools near your area that have swimming, and benefit many of their facilities to host the event. During the negotiation, do not hesitate to ask for special consideration since your sports event aims to serve an important cause and that will also contribute to promoting the image of the school that you choose to host your swimming event.

As you may need sound and music, ask those who are in charge of the school if they have one and negotiate all as a complete package in order to reduce the cost. If it happens that you choose a junior high school to host the swimming competition, you and your team need to make sure that you design a plan for the site. It should be assumed that no attendee knows the site, directions to key areas like the administration, food and drink openings, and the toilets should be provided. Do not shy out asking questions. If the venue has hosted sports events, you can ask questions on the success or failure factors of the previous events. Depending on the scope and nature of your small-scale sport event, you might need to have authorization. Suppose that you decide it will be a marathon. In this case, you will need to consult with local authorities regarding the possibility to block temporary some streets or parameters for the event. In many cases, you will need to obtain a permit to organize your sports event because of safety and security concerns. Therefore, consulting with local authorities about the regulations with this regard is very important.

Third-Party Service Providers

Third-party service providers are very important for the success of most events, not to say all. You can see them as the core organizations that provide the infrastructure that will host your sports event. Your dependence on third-party service providers also depends on the venue that you have chosen to host the event. If, for example, you choose a gymnasium to host a swimming competition, there are chances that they have many of the things you need, with sound system, bar, seats, etc. In many cases, some venues, mostly the indoor ones, have not only of the equipment that you might need but also have contractors that provide them additional services. In order cases, you as the event manager are the ones to search for and contact the service providers that you need. This particularly when you want to host your small sports event outdoor or in the "do-it-yourself indoor venue. Consequently, you need to make a list of all the third-party service providers you might need. Sound system leasing companies, a DJ (some DJs have their own sound system; so that will be helpful to negotiate a complete package), companies that lease portable restrooms, chairs, tables, etc. If you want to host the event indoor, you might also need decoration. So, if your team cannot do this job, you will have to embark on a third-party. Of course, the attendees are expected to have food and drinks within their reach; thus, the need to contact a supplier especially for the drinks. As there will be the consumption of food and drinks, you might consider leasing waste cans or find waste service collectors.

For any sports, there are individuals who master all regulations of the discipline. These are sports officials and referees. While you may not have the budget to contract the service of professional referees for the sporting event you are planning to organize, you can obviously consider contracting with amateurs. Additionally, you need to consider services of third-party like health and safety, and insurance, and of course, transportation. Health and insurance are particularly important because sports events are subject to injury and there may be a high cost for treatment if you are not insured. Depending on your context, you might also consider contracting the service of security guards. Who is going to provide transportation for the players and referees or VIP officials? If you do not have means of transportation, you will, therefore, put a transportation service provider on your list too. There are two other groups of third-parties that are crucial for the success of your sports event: the media (discussed in chapter 8) and sponsors (discussed in chapter 9). Moreover, community stakeholders constitute another group of third-party that can influence the success of a small sports event. Therefore, the event manager should be included community stakeholders in the event planning process because the sports event can affect them and the perception that they have about the tourism organization that organizes the event (Mombeuil, 2018).

Event Timelines

For every activity related you the sporting event you are planning, you should consider linking them to a timeline. The reason for a timeline is many folds. You want to make sure that your team is on schedule with their tasks, which will help you monitor their progress. A timeline you help you avoid being in rush and pay unreasonable service fees that will hurt your budget. The best way to develop an overall timeline is to consider itemizing all your activities and set a starting and finishing date. Itemizing all the activities will also help you prepare your budget as discussed later in chapter 7. Consider asking yourself this question: What should be the sequential and the reasonable timeline that can be attributed to each item? Suppose that you have the following activities: renting a venue, renting sports equipment, recruiting volunteers, contract with security, audio/ DJ, awards, and the list goes on. Of course, you are not going to make any equipment renting three (3) prior to the date of the event. An arrangement for equipment renting can reasonably be done several weeks prior to the date of the event while contacting potential sponsors may require several months upfront. You should remember that third-parties are crucial for the success of your sports event. Therefore, your timeline should include follow-ups and reminders in order to make sure they will be available. This suggests that you need to have contacts (phone numbers, e-mail) of them all. Be friends with your contacts on Facebook, Twitter, Instagram or LinkedIn may be very helpful in case of need.

Contingency Planning

Anything can happen days before and during the event. Some unforeseen circumstances can have a negative impact on your event. For example, an abrupt change in the weather conditions often paralyzes outdoor sports events. The third-party equipment rental you have negotiated with months prior to the event may be hurt by unfortunate circumstances that hurt your planning in turn. To minimize or mitigate these instances you should consider building a contingency plan or alternative solutions. Therefore, during your search, you should consider having contacts of an alternative third-party in case the one you negotiated with is not available.

CASE STUDY

With the growing pressures of environmental activist groups, tourism organizations have embraced ecotourism as a new approach to reduce their impact on the environment. By embracing this approach, tourism destinations seek to meet stakeholders' expectations and gain a competitive advantage at the same time by

Table 1. Sports events common checklist

Venue	Cleaning	Marketing and communication	Decoration	Logo
Seating arrangements	Athletes	Press invitation	Program	Athlete Hospitality
Sponsorship Fulfillment	Airfare	Photography/Video	Ad Sales/ Creation	Practice and warm-up area
Sport Equipment Rental	Site Visits	Website	Expo	Car Rental
Security	Parking	Social Media	Advertising	Printing tickets
Lighting/Acoustics	Portable restrooms		Merchandising	
		Start selling tickets	Catering	Legal aspects
Arrival and departure arrangements	Competition results	Trophies, medals and certificates	Contingency plans	

Source: Kent county Council: Sport event checklist

developing new ecotourism products and services. Thereby, small-scale sports events have been used by several local tourist destinations to promote their ecotourism products and services. Therefore, ECO FUN, a local tourist destination, decides to plan a small sports event to promote its brand and ecotourism services and products. During the group discussion, the event team is challenged to organize an event that engages the local community more effectively and the cost of the event must be as low as possible for ECO FUN and the attendees. Therefore, the team decides to organize a swamp soccer tournament as it seems to engage the local community and likely to bring a memorable experience to the participant as it is a new form of event in the local community.

Description of the Swamp Soccer

Swamp soccer is a highly physically demanding sport that is played in the swamp. The rules for play swamp Soccer are grounded on soccer rules but there are some distinct particularities. Swamp Soccer is played in several series; of which everyone can select a suitable way to experience the atmosphere. Swamp soccer is often played by people who enjoy playing sports and having fun of being with their peers. Besides being a fun sport to play, swap soccer provides direct participants with rich and memorable tourism experience. As a physically demanding sport, swamp soccer needs to be played in a soft field to avoid harm. Normally, a referee is there to ensure that every player respects the rules and guarantee the safety of the players using warning and red card. A swamp soccer team involves six (6) players including the goalkeeper and there is no limit in the number of substitutes. On the field, each team needs to align at least (2) players. The team can be mixed, but it must have at least two (2) females.

Suppose that you are selected as the event manager because of your experience in sport event planning and your knowledge about the local market for tourism destinations. You are required to prepare the planning for the swap soccer tournament during the coming summer vacation 2020. The local destination market is organized as follow:

There exist 10 ecotourism destinations in your county. On a yearly basis, these 10 ecotourism destinations count in the total of 200,000 visitors with 40% of the visits happen during the summer during the past 5 years. Out of 40% of the visits, more than 50% of the visitors are usually couples and young professionals with no kids aged between 25 to 30 years old. In principle, local business often supports sport events that can help them create visibility. Among the 10 ecotourism destinations, ECO FUN currently has a market share of 12% and projects to increase it to up 20% in the next three years on (*visit this the following link for more insights on swamp soccer*: http://suopotkupallo.fi/in-english/).

1. Explain how you are going to build the swamp soccer event and what skills you need for this event.
    a. You should consider how you are going to share responsibilities among team members;
    b. You should also include volunteers among the community where the event is going to be hosted;
    c. Prepare a list of all third-parties that are likely to participate in this event.
2. Prepare a list of all the activities that must be included in the swap soccer tournament by considering the following guidelines.
    a. Description of the event, number of swamp soccer teams, direct participants (players, referee, etc.) the direct participants (the target audience you want to be aware of your ecotourism products/services and who are likely to visit ECO FUN;
    b. Prepare a checklist of activities and associate each activity with a specific timeline: start date, finish date, duration;
3. Prepare a list third-party that can influence the tournament and explain how you are going to embark them in supporting the swamp soccer tournament;
    a. Sponsor, Media, service provider, and local community;
    b. Security, ambulance;
4. Prepare an
5. Prepare a set of activities that are going to take place during the event;
    a. A number of teams and the duration of each game.

6. Prepare a list of factors that can affect the success of the swamp soccer tournament and explain how you and your team will mitigate the impact of each factor (contingency plan).

REFERENCES

Bjerke, M. B., & Renger, R. (2017). Being smart about writing SMART objectives. *Evaluation and Program Planning*, *61*, 125–127. doi:10.1016/j.evalprogplan.2016.12.009 PMID:28056403

Chalip, L., & Costa, C. A. (2005). Sport Event Tourism and the Destination Brand: Towards a General Theory. *Sport in Society*, *8*(2), 218–237. doi:10.1080/17430430500108579

Chalip, L., & Leyns, A. (2002). Local Business Leveraging of a Sport Event: Managing an Event for Economic Benefit. *Journal of Sport Management*, *16*(2), 132–158. doi:10.1123/jsm.16.2.132

Council, K. C. (n.d.). *Sports Events Checklist*. Retrieved from https://www.kentsport.org/wp-content/uploads/2016/06/sports_sheet_sports_events_checklist.pdf

Doherty, A. (2009). The volunteer legacy of a major sport event. *Journal of Policy Research in Tourism, Leisure & Events*, *1*(3), 185–207. doi:10.1080/19407960903204356

Loo, R. (2003). Assessing "Team Climate" in Project Teams. *International Journal of Project Management*, *21*(7), 511–517. doi:10.1016/S0263-7863(02)00058-3

Mombeuil, C. (2018). Interaction from tourism development in Port-au-Prince, Haiti. *Journal of Tourism. Heritage & Services Marketing*, *4*(1), 8–14.

Müller, A., & Bíró, M. (2015). *Organizing sports events*. Retrieved from https://sporttudomany.uni-eszterhazy.hu/public/uploads/organising-sports-events_570f84971d1e4.pdf

Pizam, A. (2010). Creating memorable experiences. *International Journal of Hospitality Management*, *29*(3), 343. doi:10.1016/j.ijhm.2010.04.003

Chapter 7
Organizing Small-Scale Sports Events:
Issues and Challenges

Anisah Abdul Wafi
Faculty of Technical and Vocational, Universiti Pendidikan Sultan Idris, Malaysia

Lim Khong Chiu
School of Tourism, Hospitality, and Event Management, Universiti Utara Malaysia, Malaysia

Johan Afendi Ibrahim
School of Tourism, Hospitality, and Event Management, Universiti Utara Malaysia, Malaysia

ABSTRACT

The purpose of this chapter is to have a further understanding of the issue and challenges of visitors in attending the small-scale sport event (SSSE). Although visitors are interested in mega-events, several SSSE is also organized, as SSSE can be a part of the tourism products. Understanding the issues and challenges will enhance SSSE to become one of the popular attractions for local tourism products. The issues that are being faced by the event organizers are insufficient facilities, the age limit of the participant, safety, the event quality, and the suitability of the location. This understanding will enhance the image of the small-scale sports events. Consequently, the organizer of small-scale sports events should better design the events and ensure that it will become an attraction for the enrichment of the local tourism products.

DOI: 10.4018/978-1-7998-4757-1.ch007

CHAPTER OBJECTIVES

After completing this topic you should be able to:

1. Explain the importance of small-scale sports events as a development stimulus for a tourism destination.
2. Identify the issues and challenges in organizing the small-scale sports event.
3. Discuss what event organizer should do in order to overcome the issues and challenges in organizing the small-scale sports event.

INTRODUCTION

Events tourism has become one of the quick-growing tourism industries. Some of the features that have attracted tourists to participate in events tourism are festivals and special events. Besides that, sport-related travel is a prominent practice in tourism where people travel to a destination to join or attend sports events. Gibson (1998) has stated that events sports tourism consists of several categories such as hallmark events, mega-events, and small-scale sports events (SSSE). SSSE is defined as a normal season or a small unique sports events which provide the residents with more advantage, but there is a small number of difficulties compared to hallmark or mega sporting events (Higham, 1999). The difference between SSSE compared to mega or hallmark events is that small-scale sports events have a slightly lower national impact because the events are organized in a community. Moreover, organizing the SSSE will cost minimal funding, the use of existing infrastructure, and is more feasible in terms of crowding and congestions. Compared to mega-sporting events, SSSE has low coverage of publicity because the organizer of SSSE tends to used social media as a medium of promotion.

Due to the growing interest in SSSE, organizers tend to produce and promote their events to cater to the demands. Most of the events were initiated by the local residents and it had been successfully organized as well as attracted people from other states to participate in the events. However, the argument is that small-scale sporting events can become one of the tourism products for the community. In the attempt to develop and attract visitors to participate in SSSE in order to create economic development for the community, issues and challenges that are faced by this small-scale sports events should be resolved to ensure that small-scale sports events can become one of the tourism attractions. Therefore, the SSSE in the northern area of Malaysia will examine the issues and challenges of organizing this sporting event, and furthermore to discuss the strategic development and directions of this sporting event so that it becomes one of the tourism products in a community.

Sport Tourism

Gibson (1998) has stated that events sports tourism is a trip in which the tourists watch sports events. Meanwhile, sports tourism has been defined as a fundamental component of the physical activity associated with the travel experience (Aicher, Karadakis, & Eddosary, 2015). The sport participation among the visitors' in sporting events is associated with the five factors, which are organizational, environmental, social, physical, and emotional. The organizational aspects of the sporting event include the components of the event within the organizer's control. Besides that, the event's reputation and image are also included in the organizational components. The scenery, new places, new culture, best location in the area, and other factors directly related to the host destination are included in the environmental components. The environmental components which reflect the destination attractiveness become the most important attributes to attract sport participation. More specifically, the five components in sport tourism contribute to the success of organizing this event. Most of the studies have established that sports tourism is one of the fastest-growing sectors within the tourism industry (Swart, George, Cassar, & Sneyd, 2016) which can enhance the image of the county, besides promoting the socio-economic development.

It is noticeable that many big cities tend to focus on events sports tourism in generating their incomes and enhancing their image. There are two ways for the host cities to generate incomes under the events of sports tourism such as organizing the hallmark events and the small-scale sports events. Hallmark events is a huge scale event which happens occasionally and it is associated with a specific location. Hinch and Higham (2001) have further explained sports tourism by dividing it into three domains, i.e. hallmark events, health and fitness, and outdoor recreation. Among the three domains, the profile and scale of the hallmark events attract the attention of the tourist compared to the other two. Hallmark events such as the Olympic Games and FIFA World Cup attract the attention of the tourists and these types of events have their loyal fans. Most of the country tend to organize hallmark events due to the benefits it brings to the country in terms of economics. Whether the cost of organizing the hallmark event is higher compared to other types of events or it brings economic benefits to the host country, this event will generate a better return. Besides hallmark events, another event that can be considered as attracting the attention of tourists' participation is a small-scale sports event. Gibson, Kaplanidou and Kang (2012) have stated that competitors may outnumber the spectators in a small-scale sports event and that the events are often held annually with little national media interest and limited economic activity compared to the large-scale events. Whether SSSE generates the minimum profit for the organizer or otherwise, organizing these events have given benefits in terms of economic and social development to the local community.

Small-Scale Sports Events

Small-scale sports events have the potential to become a tourism attraction. They may also have advantages compared to mega-events, especially for the local community by providing additional incomes and for social development. Higham (1999) has stated that there is a potential for tourism development in small-scale events such as holding regular-season sporting competition, international sporting fixtures, domestic competitions, and Masters Games or disabled sports. Several studies have shown that small-scale sporting events may have more positive consequences for the host community, in terms of economic and social impacts. The impact of organizing small-scale sports events has been proven on tourism development besides improving the image of a tourist destination (Malchrowicz-Mośko & Poczta, 2018). In addition, the value of organizing the small-scale sports events not only provides direct economic impact, but also builds the image of the host city in which the event takes place (Tzetzis, Alexandris, & Kapsampeli, 2014). The positive image of organizing the SSSE helps the host city to develop as one of the tourism destinations.

In the meantime, small-scale events are generally considered to be a more sustainable form of tourism products. The small-scale sports event has been categorized as an event for sustainable development, as this event may cause less serious negative impacts. This is because the event uses the already existing infrastructure, uses minimal budget, and raises the local pride and community spirit (Csobán & Serra, 2014). Organizing the SSSE also creates a more manageable level of crowd congestion, and have high-impact regional effects on the community. It is manageable in terms of congestion due to the selected location being more specific and accessible. Besides that, profiling sports tourists attending the small-scale sporting events have also been suggested by the previous study. Understanding the visitors' profile can give the organizers a point of view into the market segments. Understanding the market segment of the visitors' participation would increase the organizers understanding on the hosting of small-scale sporting events, which is also realized by the host communities (Shonk, Greenwell, Bravo, & Won, 2012). Therefore, organizing small-scale sports events can be a good strategy for the host city or the local tourism authority to develop the SSSE as a tourism local product or attraction. Hence, since these events might result in more positive and sustainable effects for the host organizer and communities, understanding the issue and challenges besides avoiding the negative impacts should be identified by both stakeholders.

Issues and Challenges in Small-Scale Sports Events

Small-scale sports events can attract and provide benefits to the community of that particular area by helping and developing it to become a tourist destination.

Furthermore, with a unique theme, good event management, and beautiful scenery of the rural area, this small-scale sports events can further attract attention from local participants, as well as internationals. These factors have influenced a positive impact on the image of the events. Besides developing a new tourist destination, small-scale sports events can also become a new tourism product. Developing a new tourism product request a lot of financials, hence, using small-scale sports events can help overcome this issue by using a minimal budget and existing facilities. Therefore, by having small-scale sports events at certain local rural areas can become an option to help the local tourism authority in developing their new tourism products. In addition to that, small-scale sports events will likely help the local community to increase their income.

However, despite the great contributions, there is also a number of issues that need to be addressed by the stakeholders, such as a need to design proper planning in organizing this small-scale sports event. Since most events in the rural area have been using the existing infrastructure, thus the impact of organizing the event should also be addressed properly. There are suggestions by the participants that the local community and event organizers should have good management planning to ensure events that are conducted in that area can give good contributions to all stakeholders.

In addition, the issues and challenges in organizing this type of event are different compared to the mega-sporting event. As most of the mega-sporting events have issues in financial, whereas issues on small-scale sports events focus more on the management such as safety, security and environmental impacts which related to the maintenance and conservation of that area. Therefore, organizers and the local community should develop proper planning to overcome issues and challenges in organizing this event. The examples of important issues and challenges that should be managed by the event organizers including:

- The safety and security of participants
- The suitable location of the event (in terms of crowd and traffic)
- The proper planning on environmental impacts such as waste

The Growth of Sporting Events in Malaysia

Over the years, mega sporting events have attracted more tourists compared to small-scale sports events. Although visitors are interested in mega-events, several small-scale sports events are also organized, as they can be a part of the tourism products in Malaysia. Kaplanidou and Vogt (2006) have mentioned that the increasing demands from visitors for more active activities have influenced the growth of events sports tourism. Zarei and Yusof (2014) interpret small-scale sports events as a normal sporting seasonal contest or a domestic competition that involves minimum investment. On the other hand, Li and Vogelsong (2006) affirm that a small-scale event gives better benefits to the communities and managers who have hosted the events. This is because events are indirectly promoting rural destinations to visitors. After all most of the small-scale sports events are organized in rural areas. The natural environment of the destinations influences this event, making it more unique as well as contributing to exciting experiences for the visitors.

This statement is agreed upon by Bertella (2014) who has stated that organizing events in the rural area can become the starting point and the potential to promote the events among tourists who are active in sports. The uniqueness of the rural areas in terms of their cultural and local community can become an attraction for the small-scale sporting event to attract active sports tourists to participate. Correspondingly, most of the SSSE in Malaysia has been organized in rural areas to give additional unique experience to the participants. Besides that, other factors that influence the demands of SSSE is due to the changes in the travelling patterns by the domestic tourist. In 2014, the travelling pattern of domestic tourists in Malaysia has only been focused on shopping and holiday. The changes of the travelling patterns by domestics tourists in Malaysia has been confirmed by the statistics in 2018 which show that besides visiting relatives and friends, 5.2 per cent of domestics tourists travel for the reason of attending a special event or sports (DOSM, 2019).

There are several examples of SSSE in Malaysia, particularly in the northern regions, they are The River Sports Festival, Parit Buntar Kampung Run, SP Half Marathon, The Colourful Run, *Karnival Sukan Bendang dan Permainan Tradisional* and Pelikat Batik Run. Most of the SSSE in Malaysia, especially in the northern regions will mix their event with cultural activities to give excitement to the participants. The different themes and activities that have been created by the event organizer cause sporting events in Malaysia to be unique and fun. Besides the reason to create excitement, the fun in these activities is also due to the Malaysian participants' tendency to use sporting events as an activity for the family. Therefore, the environment and motives of the SSSE in Malaysia are a little different in contrast with other sporting events. The favourable experiences of this sporting event help the event organizers in developing and planning their marketing strategy to attract participants.

As there is a demand for organizing small-scale sporting events, instead of relying on mega-sporting events, Malaysia should offer and have a diversity of events sports tourism to attract more visitors each year. As these types of events become an attraction nowadays, the issues and challenges that are raised by the event organizer and participants should be overcome to ensure that this event becomes attractions as one of the local tourism products.

MAIN FOCUS OF THE CHAPTER

Small-Scale Sports Events in Malaysia: Northern Region

The River Sports Festival and Perlis Eastern Wind Fiesta have been chosen as samples in this study. The River Sports Festival is the largest sports event that has been organized in Tanjung Chali, Kedah. This event has been organized since 1931, in conjunction with the Sultan's birthday. River Sports Festival involves sports activities that focus on the tournament of using longboat and dragon boat. Most of the participants who in this event comes from government agencies and also non-government agencies (NGO). A total of 14 categories has been contested in this sports event. This event has been scheduled for two days in March of each year and includes social activities and entertainment for the participants and visitors. Around 3000 local visitors attended this event. The second event in this study is Perlis Eastern Wind Fiesta. Perlis Eastern Wind Fiesta has been organized in Perlis in March each year. The location of this event is based on rotation, each year one of the rural areas or a village in Perlis will be chosen by the organizer to organize this event.

The Perlis East Wind Festival gets its name from the winter-to-summer cycle brought by the wind from the east to the state of Perlis. Against the backdrop of the village, the program is implemented in the plains and has brought out the unique way of life of the peasant communities in the northern peninsula. The event also highlights farmers' lives after the harvest season is over. Most of the sports activities that have been offered by the event organizers are related to the culture of the peasant community. Among the interesting activities are duck hunting, buffalo racing and many more. One of the activities that attract visitors' is *Bendang Motor* and iron buffalo (racing with a tractor). 100,000 of visitors have attended this event. The small-scale sports event in these two states in the northern area of Malaysia is very unique compared to other small-scale sports event.

These two sports events have been chosen due to their popularity and the chances of them to become local tourism products. The state of Kedah is approximately 9, 425 sq. km and is situated in the northern part of Peninsular Malaysia alongside Perlis and Perak. Kedah shares a common border with Thailand and it is a fairly small state compared to the other 13 states in Malaysia. Population in Kedah is about one million and comprises Malay, Chinese and Indian ethnic groups. Moreover, it is known as the "Rice Bowl of Malaysia" where the main economic activity is the rice plains, likewise with Perlis. Kedah produces more than half of the country's homegrown rice supply. The state capital of Kedah is Alor Setar. Kedah's early history has started from the prehistoric period to the archaeological site of Bujang Valley, in Merbok. This location is known as the early maritime trade. Thus, almost all of the tourist attractions in Kedah is related to its history, its beach and nature.

Moreover, Perlis is also the smallest state in Malaysia. It lies at the northern part of the west coast of Peninsular Malaysia and is the nearest to Satun and Songkhla Provinces of Thailand, which is situated on its northern border. Perlis is bordered by the state of Kedah to the south. The capital of Perlis is known as Kangar, while the royal capital of Perlis is Arau. Padang Besar is the most popular tourist destination for shopping. Besides being known as the "shopping heaven" the tourism attraction in Perlis is also related to nature. This is highlighted as Perlis has a popular snake farm, Perlis State Park and *Gua Kelam*. Thus, the uniqueness of these two states should be addressed in the form of SSSE. Table 1 shows the total number of visitors who have participated in SSSE in these two states.

Table 1. Respondents' Demographic Characteristics

Category		Frequency	Percent %
Gender	Male	247	52.8
	Female	241	47.2
Age	< 20	123	26.3
	21-30	182	38.9
	31-40	82	17.5
	41-50	54	11.5
	Over 51	27	5.8
Attractiveness	Yes	395	84.4
	No	73	15.6

Among a total of 468 respondents, a majority of the respondents was male and 47.2 per cent of them was female. There was 84.4 per cent of the respondents who have agreed that SSES was one of the attractive events that they have attended. The findings have shown that the majority of the visitors who have participated in this SSSE agree that this event is one of the attractive events and should be promoted to become an attraction. This event is gaining attention as an attraction due to the fact that the visitors who have participated in this event are from young people who are age 21 to 30 years old. This shows that younger visitors prefer participating in sporting events for their sport-active experience. Findings have also confirmed that demographic characteristics of the visitors or the participants might influence their destination choice and sporting event selection. This has been agreed by Slak Valek, Shaw and Bednarik (2014) who have stated that the socio-demographics of the sporting visitors have been shown to affect their tourism destination choice.

Furthermore, these two states have been chosen due to the popularity of their events and because the Perlis and Kedah state government have actively promoted their small-scale sports events. The other reason for choosing these two locations and their events are the events' popularity among the local visitors. The popularity of the events is based on the social media account which also gains attention among the local and non-local visitors. Almost all the SSSE uses social media as a medium of promotion to promote their events. The social media platform helps event organizers to minimize their cost as the SSSE does not receive any financial provisions from any party. As we can see sometimes the SSSE gets attention from the non-local visitors who are participants from other states. Participation from non-local visitors has proven that SSSE can become a tourist attraction for the local state government. This is due to the fact that the state government is unable to organize mega-sporting events due to obstacles such as finance and infrastructure. To ensure that tourism in Kedah and Perlis remains as an attraction, new tourism attractions should be offered and promoted. Organizing an event can help tourism development as a destination and this has been agreed by Ziakas and Costa (2011). Events are the driving force for yielding tourism revenues by becoming attractions for tourists. Organizing an event can also be linked to the local attractions, products and services in an attempt to attract nearby visitors. Therefore, organizing SSSE will help a state government to produce tourism products that are related to the sports event, and to indirectly promote the tourism product to the nearest destination.

Issues and Challenges Small-Scale Sports Events in Northern Region

The changes of time have influenced the creation of the local community to provide sports activities which can help them to generate income. For that reason, most of the local communities or event organizers have tried to offer sports activities that include traditional and cultural sports activities to attract visitors. Besides practising a healthy lifestyle, the local community tried to offer unique activities to attract visitors. The uniqueness of the activities has helped the local tourism authority in developing new tourism products. The potential of this local tourism product as tourism attraction should be promoted.

However, there are several issues that should be given attention by the event organizer. The issues that are being faced by the event organizers are insufficient facilities (e.g., restroom, sign and directions), the age limit of the participant, safety, the event quality, and the suitability of the location (e.g., close to public transport, close to the main road). All of these should be given attention by the event organizer. The issues arise from the SSSE should be acknowledged by event organizers to ensure that the event can be sustained and become one of the sporting products for tourism. Table 2 shows that sports visitors have a lower level of satisfaction in terms of the facilities that are provided by the event organizer. The event organizer should ensure that there are enough facilities provided to ensure that sports visitors feel the convenience during their participation in the SSSE. The organizer should know the importance of the facilities during the event. Sufficient facilities provision by the event organizer will enhance the level of satisfaction and moreover influence the loyalty to the event. Most of the SSSE organizers have overlooked to provide facilities such as portable toilets during the event. Almost all of the sporting event visitors' have raised this issue during the event. Whether this issue has been categorized as a small issue or otherwise, the event visitors' portable toilet is one of their necessities.

Besides the portable toilet, the event organizer would still need to address infrastructure issues such as signage and directions. Good signage and directions help the event visitors in terms of road accessibility. The importance of adequate information dissemination becomes clear when event visitors recount the difficulties they have experienced on the signage and directions during the event. Despite the event being organized frequently road signage is still lacking. Hence, the event organizer should also enhance its signage and direction during the event. Signage and directions become one of the guidelines for the event visitors to ensure that they can arrive at the location of the event and visit the entertainment locations. Besides attention to signage, concise visitors' maps are also required to help the sporting event visitors. Failure to provide good signage and directions during the events have caused event visitors to give dissatisfied ratings in terms of organizational aspects. This is due to the organizational aspects contribute to the event as is experienced among the visitors. Kaplanidou and Gibson (2010) further confirmed that disorganization and a lack of signage have been noted as particular dislikes of an event, which could also negatively influence the attitudes toward event participation. Hence, on-site signage and labels are categorized as markers or information which influence the attraction during the event. Actually, the signage and advertising banners across the running route contribute to the development of the service environment dimension (Alexandris, Theodorakis, Kaplanidou, & Papadimitriou, 2017). Thus, a recommendation for all event managers is to pay attention to the details of event organization by providing the event visitors with as much information as required, using good signage and directions to prevent any unfavourable circumstances. The event organizer should understand that the participant of the event comes from different ages and by providing enough facilities will help them, and increase, their level of satisfaction.

Besides facilities, an issue in organizing the SSSE also includes transportation. As the location of the events is sometimes far from the main road, the event organizer should provide transportation service to the event visitors or participants. Event organizers should consider the event visitors' transportation in order to cater to a huge number of event visitors. This is because long-distance of walking to the main

Table 2. Visitors' Satisfaction

Satisfaction Constructs	*M*	*SD*
Attraction of Games	3.93	.79
Facilities	3.41	.91
Promotion	3.76	1.01

attraction of the event can affect the visitors' attendance. For instance, providing accessibility to the event visitors will ease them in reaching the location by using the standard transportation that has been provided by the event organizer. Furthermore, the accessibility of transportation also helps the event participants in their decision making to participate. Sometimes participants are looking at convenient locations and destinations of the event that are nearest to available transportation modes. Nearby locations that have transportation accessibility will reduce the cost of participants as they can use public transportations to arrive at the location or destination.

This has been agreed by Sun, Rodriguez, Wu, and Chuang (2013) who have stated that strategic event location that is nearest to public transport allow the event visitors to bear relatively cheap switching costs in terms of time and monetary expenses. Providing event visitors with good accessibility is one of the pull factors which can influence the decision in participation in an event (Prayag, 2012). Getz (2007) has agreed for event organizers should avoid to planning an event near major transportation routes and centres. Other than that, the strategic location nearest to the available public transportations will avoid congestions. As many of the SSSE has been organized near to the main road, using public transportation will help the event organizer to manage the congestions. Congestions do not only come from the event visitors transportation, but it is also from the road users. If the event organizer of the SSSE avoid this issue by planning the event to be near to public transportation and avoid congestion event visitors or participant are less likely to have negative perceptions about the event, inadvertently influence their decision making to attend the SSSE in the future.

Besides the above issues that have been discussed, the event organizers should focus on event promotion. However, in order to ensure that the SSSE has used the right marketing mix, i.e. the 4P's (product, place, price and promotion) the event organizers should re-arrange the way of their marketing strategies. This has been agreed upon by Yusof and Shah (2007) who state that marketing efforts that target active and passive sport tourists should provide detailed information regarding the event, event location and travel-related amenities to the sport event tourists. Providing enough information to the event visitor' becomes a pull factor in attracting them to join the SSSE. Nowadays, media is widely used for promotion, especially social media. Social media marketing is effective in spreading information on an event. Social media marketing has reshaped the way tourism-related information is distributed, reaches travellers and influences how travellers plan their trips (Roque & Raposo, 2015). In spite of that, a growing trend in recent years has shown that sport mega-events are increasingly delivered through a variety of platforms, such as personal websites, mobile phone communication, and the social media like Twitter, Facebook, Blogs and YouTube (Radikonyana, Heath, Fairer-Wessels, Prinsloo, & Pelser, 2015). As we can see, most of the SSSE has also used social media as the medium of promotion. The reason in choosing social media as a medium of promotion is due to the fact that this medium incurs a minimum budget compared to another marketing medium. In addition, using social media can also help the event organizers to promote their event which can reach the different groups of the event target market. This will assist in the understanding of the sport event visitors in terms of specific segmentation profiles and may contribute to a more targeted approach in terms of marketing and promotional activities.

Considering this, there is no doubt that the use of social media in SSSE as a marketing tool can secure attention on a large scale. Prayag and Grivel (2014) have agreed that recognizing these differences in social media marketing should enable SSSE to better market the event to young sports event visitors. Although using social media marketing has proven that this type of marketing can help to promote an event and to gain traffic or attention but the event organizer should actively promote their page. The sporting event visitors have always claimed that most of the event organizers who promote their event using social media have not actively updated their event information, and are slow to respond to the questions that have been asked by participants. If the event organizers fail to respond to potential event visitors, information that is obtained from different sources can sometimes be given in a negative form. Besides that, the failure to answer encourages event visitors to learn from the experiences of others event visitors and while doing so the event visitors or the participants will make decisions and changes in relation to their own experiences and others' opinion. Therefore, the use of social media marketing needs the event organizers or marketers to actively update their page and to respond to the event visitors or the participants' enquiries. The event organizers and event marketers should understand how social media marketing has been designed. Social media marketing is a powerful medium of promotion which requires interaction. Hence, the event organizers or marketers should make use of social media marketing as a medium of promotion for their SSSE and creatively used outdoor and ambient forms of digital communication to offer an enhanced and innovative experience for the event visitors.

Although there is a need for event organizers to used technology as a marketing strategy, in terms of safety issues the organizing of an event needs to be taken care of by the organizers. In organizing an event, the event organizers should do proper planning, especially regarding safety issue because most of the event visitors or the participants will be personally responsible for their own safety during the event and assume all risks and accept full and complete responsibility for any and all damages and personal injury. Hence, if something happens to them, there is no laws or rights that can be used by them to be insured. Therefore, event organizers should ensure that the planning of the SSSE covers the safety of the event visitors and participants. The location of the events should be strategic, i.e. it is not located at the main road. Event organizers should avoid using the main road as their location to ensure the safety of the event participants, besides using the main road can also disrupt road users. If the event organizers need to use the main road as the main location of the event, the event organizers should secure help from the authorities such as policemen to control the traffic. Moreover, the event organizers should have volunteers to help the authorities to control the traffic and handle minor problems during the event.

Event organizers should also minimize safety problems during the event by requesting participants to declare any health problems related to the event. This action will help event organizers to be prepared before the event and to allocate medical assistance during the event. As there are a lot of event visitors and participants who participate in SSSE, the event organizers should be prepared for any unforeseen circumstances. Besides that, the event organizers also should have guidelines or age limit in terms of the participants. Sometimes, event participants who participate in an SSSE bring their children with them. Whether the main focus of the event is for the togetherness of the family or otherwise, the event organizers should acknowledge that there is also a risk for the younger visitors or participants; most parents bring their younger children in a stroller and are running with the stroller. This tendency poses the risk of the children being injured. Besides that, sometimes the SSSE has been organized at night. Organizing the event at night will provide different experiences to the participants nevertheless the event organizers should be ready with proper planning, as in the case of unforeseen weather. Hence, event organizers should prepare additional equipment for the participants or provide voluntary help to avoid any incidents of injury. This has been agreed by Giampiccoli, Lee, and Nauright (2015) who state that issues on the safety and security of the event participants still remain a serious concern in organizing an event and it should be significantly improved by the event organizers.

Besides issues that are related to the infrastructure, location and safety, as SSSE is gaining popularity with the event organizers, the impact of the SSSE in terms of economic and social aspects also should be discussed. Gibson (1998) has pointed out that it is a good strategy to use sports as an attraction for economic and community development. However, the organization of these events can give positive and negative impacts on the city and its surroundings. Gibson et al. (2012) have stated that organizing small-scale sports events can contribute to economic and social development. However, the organizers also need to consider the negative impacts such as the social and involvement of the community to maximize the potential of tourism development. In order to gain support from the community, event organizers should understand how the community perceives these impacts. Kim, Jun, Walker, and Drane (2015) have agreed that it is essential to investigate the social impacts although the economic impacts have a bigger effect on the community. SSSE has initially been organized by the local community with the reason to fill up their free time after completing their activities. For that reason, there is no economic impact since the activities that have been planned and organized are only for the local residents or the community, to strengthen their relationships among themselves. Moreover, the activities that have been organized are more related to cultural and sports activities. After a few years, the local tourism authorities have seen that this SSSE can become a tourism product for the local state government since organizing mega-sporting events needs a lot of financial support and new infrastructures.

Therefore, the local community event or SSSE have been promoted as one of the products in tourism which is more related to sports and cultural activities. The changes have given positive impacts to the local community in terms of economic benefits. The economic benefits stem from an increase in the number of visitors and in creating additional income for the local community (Kwiatkowski & Könecke, 2017). In spite of the positive economic impact, there are also negative social impacts. Csobán and Serra (2014) have specified that whether there is confirmation on the positive impact on the economy, there has been a growing critique in the negative social impact on the SSSE. Therefore, the event organizer should balance these two impacts to ensure the event's sustainability. Developing a new product for tourism is a must in order to attract visitors, however, the issue that has arisen is how to sustain the product that has been developed. Thus, examining the issues and challenges of the small-scale sports event would be useful for the development of local tourism products. It is therefore important for the researcher, organizer and the sports and tourism agencies to work together closely to ensure that the issues and challenges can be managed through proper planning. This strategy will help the host city and country to gain more positive economic benefits and to avoid any of the negative social impacts due to the popularity of sports as a tourism attraction.

SOLUTIONS AND RECOMMENDATIONS

In this chapter, we present the solutions to the issues and challenges in organizing small-scale sports events in Malaysia, particularly in the northern regions. The solutions to these problems are integrated from the findings of the data collections and are also drawn from the previous research. The solutions are classified and synthesized for better solutions and findings. As most of the previous studies that are related to sports events tend to focus on mega-sporting events, the evidence and solutions on the issues and challenges in small-scale sports events are limited. Understanding the issues and challenges faced by the event organizer will enhance the image of the small-scale sports events to become one of the popular attractions for the local tourism products in a state. Besides, the recommendations from this study will help event organizers to offer better experiences to the visitors. Providing better experiences to the participants and visitors can produce a high rank of satisfaction and influence the visitor's intentions to return (Seo, Yun, & Kim, 2014). According to Getz (2007), the event organizer should know the meaning of events experience and how to plan and design experience. In general, the experience is something that the visitors can interact with such as the environment, facilities, or staff. Event organizers can also plan activities for the children during their parents' participation in the events. As there are risks for younger children, suitable activities for the youngest should be planned. Thus, the SSSE is one of the events which can be participated by the entire family and its members.

The understanding of the events' experiences concept provides highly favourable meanings to the visitors, especially in sports events. It is important to fulfil the visitors' demand as the failure to comply with their request will make them turn to other similar events (Shanka & Taylor, 2004). Furthermore, the event organizer should solve the issues that have arisen when organizing the SSSE. The event organizer should find a better location to avoid any unforeseen tragedy and collaborate with the local authorities to ensure that the safety of the event participants and visitors are guaranteed. Besides, before planning and organizing an event, event organizers should secure permission from the local authorities to ensure that standard operating procedures have been followed. As there is a registration fee that should be paid by the event participants, event organizers should ensure that participants will achieve their satisfaction level during the event. This is a must in order to ensure the sustainability of the event in future.

FUTURE RESEARCH DIRECTIONS

The findings of this study contributed to the tourism development in Malaysia which focused on small-scale sports events. Compared to the mega-sporting events, most of the states in Malaysia be able to organize small-scale events. This is due to the issues and challenges that have been discussed previously. The event organizer should pay attention to the issues and challenges that have been discussed to ensure that this event can become as one of the tourism attraction in a state besides given economic implication to the local community. Moreover, the collaboration between the event organizer and the local community of the event respectively may contribute to the greater meaning in organizing this event, especially towards participants' experience.

With this, it may be valuable for future research to examine other aspects in organizing this small-scale sports event besides issues and challenges. Employing the data will help the event organizer and local tourism authority to enhance this event as well as helping to develop this event to become as an attraction from the perspective of participants (Aicher, Karadakis, & M. Eddosary, 2015). In addition, understanding the needs and demands from the participants will assist event organizer to determine the better solutions from the issues and challenges that have been discussed. Furthermore, to fulfil needs, demands and experience of the participants, it is also interesting for the future study to expanding the SEEV (Sport Event Experiential Value) model by Musa and Kassim (2013). Hopefully, this model can give a better understanding from the perspectives of the participants' as this valuable information will help in developing small-scale sports events as one of the tourism products.

CONCLUSION

This section presents a research plan with an overarching goal to solve the issues and challenges faced by the organizer of a small-scale sports event in Malaysia, particularly in the northern regions. The results of this study will help the event organizers to improve their services to provide better experiences for the participants and visitors besides providing knowledge to the academicians and practitioners. This study will encourage academicians to investigate small-scale sports event besides focusing on mega-sporting events to enrich the knowledge of small-scale sports events. These issues might hinder this small-scale sports event to become one of the local tourism products. The issues and challenges that are faced by the event organizers and community provide a comprehensive perspective of how these findings should be overcome by the event organizers, the community and also by the respective government agencies. Consequently, it is critical to find solutions to the issues and challenges in organizing small-scale sports events to better design the events and ensure that it will become an attraction for the enrichment of the local tourism products.

REFERENCES

Aicher, T. J., Karadakis, K., & Eddosary, M. (2015). Comparison of sport tourists' and locals' motivation to participate in a running event. *International Journal of Event and Festival Management*, *3*(3), 215–234. doi:10.1108/IJEFM-03-2015-0011

Alexandris, K., Theodorakis, N., Kaplanidou, K., & Papadimitriou, D. (2017). Event quality and loyalty among runners with different running involvement levels: The case of "The Alexander the Great" International Marathon. *International Journal of Event and Festival Management*, *8*(3), 292–307. doi:10.1108/IJEFM-08-2016-0057

Bertella, G. (2014). Designing small-scale sport events in the countryside. *International Journal of Event and Festival Management*, *5*(2), 132–145. doi:10.1108/IJEFM-05-2013-0008

Csobán, K. V., & Serra, G. (2014). The role of small-scale sports events in developing sustainable sport tourism – a case study of fencing. *Applied Studies in Agribusiness and Commerce*, *8*(4), 17–22. doi:10.19041/Apstract/2014/4/3

DOSM. (2019). *Domestic Tourism Survey 2018*. Department of Statistics Malaysia.

Getz, D. (2007). *Event studies: theory, research and policy for planned events*. Elsevier. Retrieved from http://books.google.com/books

Giampiccoli, A., Lee, S., & Nauright, J. (2015). Destination South Africa: Comparing global sports mega-events and recurring localised sports events in South Africa for tourism and economic development. *Current Issues in Tourism*, *18*(3), 229–248. doi:10.1080/13683500.2013.787050

Gibson, H. J. (1998). Sport Tourism: A Critical Analysis of Research. *Sport Management Review*, *1*(1), 45–76. doi:10.1016/S1441-3523(98)70099-3

Gibson, H. J., Kaplanidou, K., & Kang, S. J. (2012). Small-scale event sport tourism: A case study in sustainable tourism. *Sport Management Review*, *15*(2), 160–170. doi:10.1016/j.smr.2011.08.013

Higham, J. (1999). Commentary - sport as an avenue of tourism development: An analysis of the positive and negative impacts of sport tourism. *Current Issues in Tourism*, *2*(1), 82–90. doi:10.1080/13683509908667845

Hinch, T. D., & Higham, J. E. S. (2001). Sport Tourism : A framework for research. *International Journal of Tourism Research, 3*(1), 45–58. doi:10.1002/1522-1970(200101/02)3:1<45::AID-JTR243>3.0.CO;2-A

Kaplanidou, K., & Gibson, H. J. (2010). Predicting behavioral intentions of active event sport tourists: The case of a small-scale recurring sports event. *Journal of Sport & Tourism, 15*(2), 163–179. doi:10.1080/14775085.2010.498261

Kaplanidou, K., & Vogt, C. (2006). Studying sport tourism event and destination images on intend to travel: a conceptual theoretical model utilising the theory of planned behaviour. *14th EASM Congress.*

Kim, W., Jun, H. M., Walker, M., & Drane, D. (2015). Evaluating the perceived social impacts of hosting large-scale sport tourism events: SCALE development and validation. *Tourism Management, 48*, 21–32. doi:10.1016/j.tourman.2014.10.015

Kwiatkowski, G., & Könecke, T. (2017). Tourism and recurring sport events: Event tourists' and regular tourists' profiles and expenditures at the Windsurf World Cup on Sylt. *Sport, Business and Management. International Journal (Toronto, Ont.), 7*(5), 464–482.

Li, X., & Vogelsong, H. (2006). Comparing Methods of Measuring Image Change: A Case Study of a Small-Scale Community Festival. *Tourism Analysis, 10*(4), 349–360. doi:10.3727/108354206776162769

Malchrowicz-Mośko, E., & Poczta, J. (2018). A small-scale event and a big impact-Is this relationship possible in theworld of sport? The meaning of heritage sporting events for sustainable development of tourism-experiences from Poland. *Sustainability, 10*(11), 1–19. doi:10.3390u10114289 PMID:30607262

Musa, R., & Kassim, R. M. (2013). Predictors and outcomes of sport event experiential value: Insight from Formula One Petronas Malaysia Grand Prix. *International Journal of Management and Marketing Research, 6*(1), 107–121.

Prayag, G. (2012). Senior travelers' motivations and future behavioral intentions: THE CASE OF NICE. *Journal of Travel & Tourism Marketing, 29*(7), 665–681. doi:10.1080/10548408.2012.720153

Prayag, G., & Grivel, E. (2014). Motivation, satisfaction, and behavioral intentions: Segmenting youth participants at the Interamnia World Cup 2012. *Sport Marketing Quarterly, 23*(3), 148–160.

Radikonyana, P. S., Heath, E., Fairer-Wessels, F., Prinsloo, J., & Pelser, T. G. (2015). A Strategic E-Marketing Framework for sport mega event. *Journal of Applied Business Research, 31*(2), 437–454. doi:10.19030/jabr.v31i2.9127

Roque, V., & Raposo, R. (2015). Social media as a communication and marketing tool in tourism: An analysis of online activities from international key player DMO. *Anatolia, 2917*(October), 1–13.

Seo, S., Yun, N., & Kim, O. Y. (2014). Destination food image and intention to eat destination foods: A view from Korea. *Current Issues in Tourism*, (December), 1–22.

Shanka, T., & Taylor, R. (2004). Discriminating factors of first-time and repeat visitors to wine festivals. *Current Issues in Tourism, 7*(2), 134–145. doi:10.1080/13683500408667976

Shonk, D. J., Greenwell, T. C., Bravo, G., & Won, D. (2012). Site selection, satisfaction, and intent to return: An exploratory study of the perceptions of rights holders of small-scale sporting events. *Journal of Convention & Event Tourism, 13*(1), 1–15. doi:10.1080/15470148.2012.649580

Slak Valek, N., Shaw, M., & Bednarik, J. (2014). Socio-demographic characteristics affecting sport tourism choices: A structural model. *Acta Gymnica, 44*(1), 57–65. doi:10.5507/ag.2014.006

Sun, Y. Y., Rodriguez, A., Wu, J. H., & Chuang, S. T. (2013). Why hotel rooms were not full during a hallmark sporting event: The 2009 World Games experience. *Tourism Management, 36*(June), 469–479. doi:10.1016/j.tourman.2012.09.011 PMID:32287741

Swart, K., George, R., Cassar, J., & Sneyd, C. (2016). The 2014 FIFA World Cup: Tourists' satisfaction levels and likelihood of repeat visitation to Rio de Janeiro. *Journal of Destination Marketing & Management*, (January), 1–12.

Tzetzis, G., Alexandris, K., & Kapsampeli, S. (2014). Predicting visitors' satisfaction and behavioral intentions from service quality in the context of a small-scale outdoor sport event. *International Journal of Event and Festival Management, 5*(1), 4–21. doi:10.1108/IJEFM-04-2013-0006

Yusof, A., & Shah, P. M. (2007). An examination of tourist profiles and travel motivations of sport tourist attending an event in lake Kenyir, Malaysia. *Malaysian Journal of Sport Science and Recreation*, 53–68.

Zarei, A., & Yusof, A. B. I. N. (2014). Informational sources of sport tourists attending ISTAF super series. *Journal of Physical Education and Sport, 14*(4), 554–561.

ADDITIONAL READING

Gibson, H. J., Willming, C., & Holdnak, A. (2003). Small-scale event sport tourism: Fans as tourists. *Tourism Management, 24*(2), 181–190. doi:10.1016/S0261-5177(02)00058-4

Higham, J. (2005). *Sport tourism destination: Issues,opportunities and analysis*. Elsevier Butterworth-Heinemann.

Hinch, T. D., & Higham, J. E. S. (2001). Sport Tourism : A framework for research. *International Journal of Tourism Research, 3*(1), 45–58. doi:10.1002/1522-1970(200101/02)3:1<45::AID-JTR243>3.0.CO;2-A

Kaplanidou, K., & Gibson, H. J. (2010). Predicting behavioral intentions of active event sport tourists: The case of a small-scale recurring sports event. *Journal of Sport & Tourism, 15*(2), 163–179. doi:10.1080/14775085.2010.498261

Perić, M., Durkin, J., & Wise, N. (2016). Leveraging small-scale sport events: Challenges of organising, delivering and managing sustainable outcomes in rural communities, the case of Gorski Kotar, Croatia. *Sustainability, 8*(12), 1–17. doi:10.3390u8121337

Reza, H., Niknezhad, M. R., Mohammad Hossein Razavi, S., & Rostamzadeh, N. (2016). Designing Model of Small Scale Sport Tourism Development. *Research Journal of Sport Sciences, 4*, 25–33.

Weed, M. (2005). Sports tourism theory and method: Concepts, issues and epistemologies. *European Sport Management Quarterly, 5*(3), 229–242. doi:10.1080/16184740500190587

Yusof, A., Omar-Fauzee, M. S., Shah, P. M., & Geok, S. K. (2009). Exploring small-scale sport event tourism in Malaysia. *Research Journal of Internatıonal Studıes*, (9), 47–58.

Yusof, A., Shah, P. M., & Geok, S. K. (2012). Application of Leiper's tourist attraction system to small-scale Sport event tourism in Malaysia. *World Applied Sciences Journal, 18*(7), 896–900.

Chapter 8
Basic Marketing Strategies and Marketing Mix in Small-Scale Sports Events

Pinar Yuruk-Kayapinar
https://orcid.org/0000-0002-7460-6465
Trakya University, Turkey

ABSTRACT

The main purpose of this chapter is to explore how small-scale sports events are marketed and what issues are important when marketing them. For this purpose, literature review was made by considering the issues related to event marketing. The success of events depends largely on their marketing. Especially considering the important effects of these events on the location, it is important that the marketing plan process of small-scale sports events, who the event consumers are, why they want to participate in the event, and how they follow the process participate in the event. In addition, it is an important issue why the 5W's of marketing are important for small-scale sports events. The marketing mix of small-scale sports events, which is created to address these questions, and IMC, which is developed specifically for events, are two of the most important tools in event marketing.

DOI: 10.4018/978-1-7998-4757-1.ch008

OBJECTIVES

The main objective of this chapter is to consider all the steps and activities in the process of marketing a small-scale sports event in detail. For this main objective, the sub-objectives of this chapter are as follows:

- To examine the marketing process of small-scale sports events in detail and to discuss the differences between other marketing processes.
- To examine the individuals, who are expressed as consumers in marketing, within the marketing of events:
    - To mention their basic features in small-scale sports events.
    - To emphasize how they are expressed in event marketing especially in small-scale sports events.
    - To investigate how the market is segmented for them.
- To examine the process and motivation factors of an event consumer to make a decision to participate in the event.
- To investigate the marketing mix, which is created for events, different from traditional marketing.
- To examine the Integrated Marketing Communication (IMC) which is required to create, plan and announce the event to target consumers.

INTRODUCTION

Nowadays, the intensity of people's daily activities emphasizes the importance of the concept of leisure time and increases its value. Therefore, people make more efforts to take time for themselves, to engage in activities that may be beneficial for them, to create leisure time for them, and also to have fun. With this special effort, they want to spend their leisure time actively, gain experience and have fun by gaining experience. For this reason, the first choice of individuals is to participate in small-scale sports events that are more easily accessible than other events. By participating in these events, reaching people, enabling them to experience the event, happily rejoining the event and creating loyalty, is the point where events meet marketing, providing the concept of event marketing and emphasizing the importance of marketing for events. The marketing of small-scale sports events tries to reach participants and / or viewers by entertaining and experiencing them, instead of bombarding messages with traditional communication methods. While the main purpose in traditional marketing is to convince consumers to consume, the main purpose in event marketing is not to convince people to buy, but to participate in the event (Tinnish & Mangal, 2012).

When analyzed in the literature, most of the studies on event marketing focus on large scale events (Sofia & Chris, 2017). Given the challenges involved in event marketing, small-scale sports events are expected to result in faster and more positive contributions to the host community at the local level. Kaplanidou & Kang (2012), small-scale sports events have limited effect, limited media attention and a smaller number of participants. These events not only benefit the management and sports organizers at the venue, but also benefit players, coaches, officials and viewers who come to enjoy and entertainment (Bowdin et al., 2012). An effective management and marketing strategy is required in order to have positive effects and guarantee success such as increasing awareness, being a source of pride for the society and creating a positive image (Hanlon & Jago, 2000; Kaplanidou & Vogt, 2007). The success of small-scale sports event marketing is possible with effective marketing strategies (Fotiadis, Vassiliadis & Satiriadis, 2016).

The success of marketing strategies will bring the success of the small-scale sports event. Event marketing is, therefore, one of the most important topics for small-scale sports events, as with any event. As an important part of event management, the marketing process of the small-scale sports event and a detailed examination of each stage in this process will bring the success of the event with it. In this planning process, unlike traditional consumers, meeting the desires and needs of the event consumer, satisfying them and ensuring their reparticipation in the event is the most important purpose of the small-scale sports event. Therefore, to recognize these consumers, to examine how they are motivated to participate in the event and decision making processes is the most important activity of event marketing. The elaboration of these activities will lead to the formation of a small-scale sports event marketing mix and will also be the answer to the questions consisting of "Why, Who, When, Where, What" named as 5W of marketing (Hoyle, 2002).

Noting the importance of the marketing of small-scale sports events, this chapter is designed as follows. Firstly, the concept of event marketing in small-scale sports events is mentioned, the definitions and main objectives of event marketing are explained and the marketing process of small-scale sports events is discussed. Secondly, the concept of consumer, which is the most important concept in marketing, is refered. And it is explained that the role of consumers in small-scale sports events, how market segmentation activities are performed for event consumers and according to which variables and how the event consumers are motivated to participate in the event after the segmentation stages and how the motivation processes are. Then, how the marketing mix is shaped in small-scale sports events is explained and the event marketing mix is examined. Finally, integrated marketing communication strategies, which constitute an important strategy for reaching the event consumer, have been examined.

BACKGROUND

The Concept of the Small-Scale Sports Events

Events usually vary according to their size and scale. Although there are no definite distinctions between the dimensions of the events, they vary according to the number of participants, the location of the events, the magnitude of the effects, the expenditures made for the events and the total cost of the events. The higher the number of participants, the greater the expenditure, the proportion of those affected by the event increases proportionally, and the benefits and costs increase or decrease accordingly. Therefore, the definition of small-scale sports events, which is expressed 'amateur events' (Fotiadis, Vassiliadis & Satiriadis (2016), differs from other types of events.

Higham (1999, p. 87) defined small-scale sports events as: *"regular season sporting competitions (ice hockey, basketball, soccer, rugby leagues), international sporting fixtures, domestic competitions, Masters or disabled sports, and the like"*.

According to the definitions and the characteristics of the small-scale sports events, which is shown in Type E in the Wilson 's (2006) study that involve minor events with few national media attention and limited economic benefits as opposed to large scale events and they are regularly held annually, the size and process of marketing of these events will be different. Even if the factors, that are considered in their marketing, differ and the scales of the events change, all the steps followed in the marketing of an event will also apply to small-scale sports events. Only the size and process of marketing of large scale sports events will be larger and longer, while the size and process of marketing in small-scale sports events will be small and short. Fotiadis, Vassiliadis & Satiriadis (2016) emphasized that event marketers and planners need to design effective marketing strategies to attract more participants to the small-scale sports events, according to the results of the small-scale sport event 'Bike to Remember' in Taiwan.

Small-Scale Sports Events Marketing

Watt (1998) is defined event marketing as: ... is an event management function that can stay in touch with event participants and visitors (consumers), know their needs and motives, create products that satisfy these needs, and construct a communication program that expresses the purpose and goals of the event.

Event marketing first emerged in the late 1980s as an experiential marketing communication strategy in Germany in response to significant changes in the marketing environment and consumer behavior (Wohlfeil & Whelan, 2006). Event marketing, which has three main objectives known as ***three Es, Entertainment, Excitement and Enterprise*** (Hoyle, 2002), differs from traditional marketing approaches.

- The purpose of the ***entertainment*** factor in event marketing is to take out individuals to give them an experience that they can not find in their homes and to make them enjoy an unforgettable, different, unique and specially designed event for them.
- ***Excitement*** expresses that individuals cannot wait to go to an event and enjoy it while experiencing it.
- ***Enterprise*** defined that *"readiness to take risks or try something untried; energy and initiative"* and it is aimed that individuals to use their imagination and try an experience which they have never experienced before.

Today, with the developing technology, people can easily access some small-scale sports events from their homes. But the purpose of event marketing is to get individuals out and experience them by entertaining. Therefore, while the main purpose of traditional marketing is to ensure that consumers buy and be satisfied with their purchases, the main purpose in event marketing is to convince individuals to participate and to encourage more participation by experiencing the events and making them satisfied (Yürük Kayapınar, 2018).

Therefore, before starting a small-scale event marketing process, it must be ensured that this sport event has 3E of event marketing. A sports event should entertain, excite and encourage people to use their imagination. However, after these conditions are met, the event marketing process of this small-scale sports should be started. The marketing process of a small-scale sports goes through the steps in Figure 1.

In the first stage of the event marketing process, the mission and objectives of the small-scale sports event are determined. The main activities of this stage are to determine the management strategy according to the determined mission and objectives, to put forward the works to be done and to examine the results of the SWOT analysis obtained in the market research. It is necessary to determine the strengths, weaknesses, opportunities and threats of performing a small-scale sports event at this stage with SWOT analysis. In addition, all the needs and characteristics that are about small-scale sports events and need to be satisfied for event marketing, who is the target audience, their understanding, attitudes and behaviors and how the market share is analyzed are examined. With the determination of management strategy and situation analysis, resources are determined and the situation of competitors and competition in the market is analyzed. After SWOT Analysis is performed, the stage of dividing and selecting the event target markets is started. At this stage, the objectives of event marketing are regulated according to the situation in the market and stage of the marketing strategies are started. In the marketing

Figure 1. The Event Marketing Process
Source: Bowdin et al., 2012.

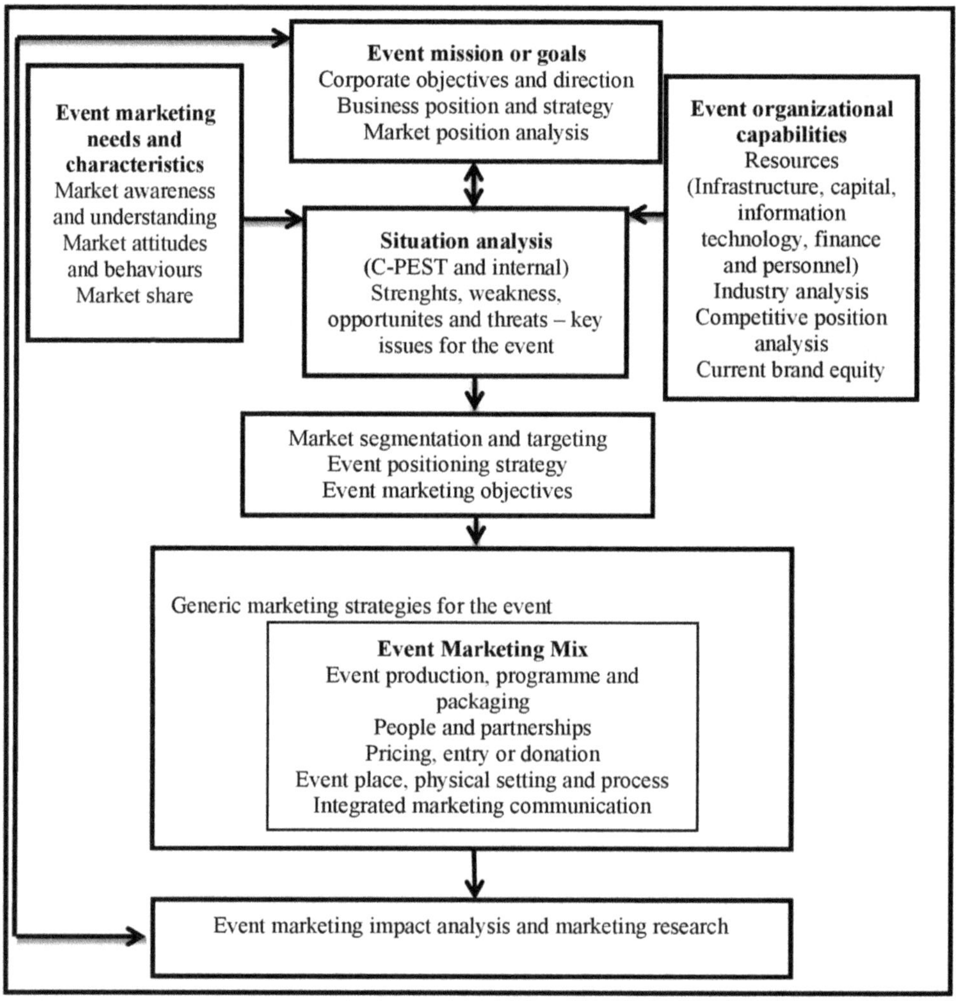

strategies determined for the small-scale sports events, the event marketing mix is formed and communication tools are selected for the event. The final stage of the event marketing process is the analysis of the effects of event marketing, obtaining the results of marketing research, receiving feedback from the participants and measuring the satisfaction levels of the participants of small-scale sports events.

"Consumer" in Small-Scale Sports Event Marketing

An event consumer consists of individuals who have different roles than traditional consumers and adopt different motivational tools, who go to the event to experience, participate in the event and go to see the important places of the event. They are expressed in the small-scale sports event marketing by the names 'participant, attendee, audience, spectator'.

In addition, although these terms differ among different authors, the participants who go to sports events are referred to as a sport tourist and have 3 basic distinctions (Duglio & Beltramo, 2017):

- *First, active-based sport tourism*; individuals traveling to attend in an event.
- *Second, event-based sport tourism*; individuals traveling to attend in an event as audiences. They are called 'fans'.
- *Third, nostalgia-based sport tourism;* individuals travelling to see the most famous sport places. As seen that differentiation of event types requires differentiation of the participants. Some activities are only for private groups, while others are for very large groups.

To better explain the event consumer, market segmentation is essential action. The following factors are important for market segmentation at events (Morrison, 1995).

- Market segmentation must classify the groups most interested in participating and/or traveling to different types of events,
- Determine visitors interested in participating events, pay special attention to existing or potential segments,
- Identify segments by comparison to variables that can be used to improve targeting,
- Determine which communication method to access the segments,
- Recognize the highest "quality" consumer of events,
- Determine the characteristics of segments such as size and quality,
- Identify the distinguishable characteristics for the event after segmenting the market.

As in Figure 2, event marketers or planners must therefore identify the market segments of the participants of the small-scale sports events. They also need to answer segmentation questions to identify these market segments.

- **Where will they come?:** Will the participants of the sports event consist of only the participants in the location where the event will be held or will the participants from the surrounding regions come?,
- **Who exactly are they?:** What are the demographic and psychographic characteristics of these participants? and their socio-economic status?
- **What do they want?:** What do they want from a small-scale sports event? What motivation processes begin in a sports event? Which factors are more powerful to motivate? What benefits will they provide after attending this event?
- **Under what conditions will they attend the event?:** Under what conditions do they want to experience a sports event? If circumstances differ, will the strength of their motivation change?
- **How can we reach them?:** How will the event be announced to the participants? Which method or methods will be used?
- **How often will they visit?:** If the event is held again, will the participants come? Will the number of participants increase in the next event? Or will it be limited to one time only?

Figure 2. Segmentation variables for events.
Source: Getz,2005.

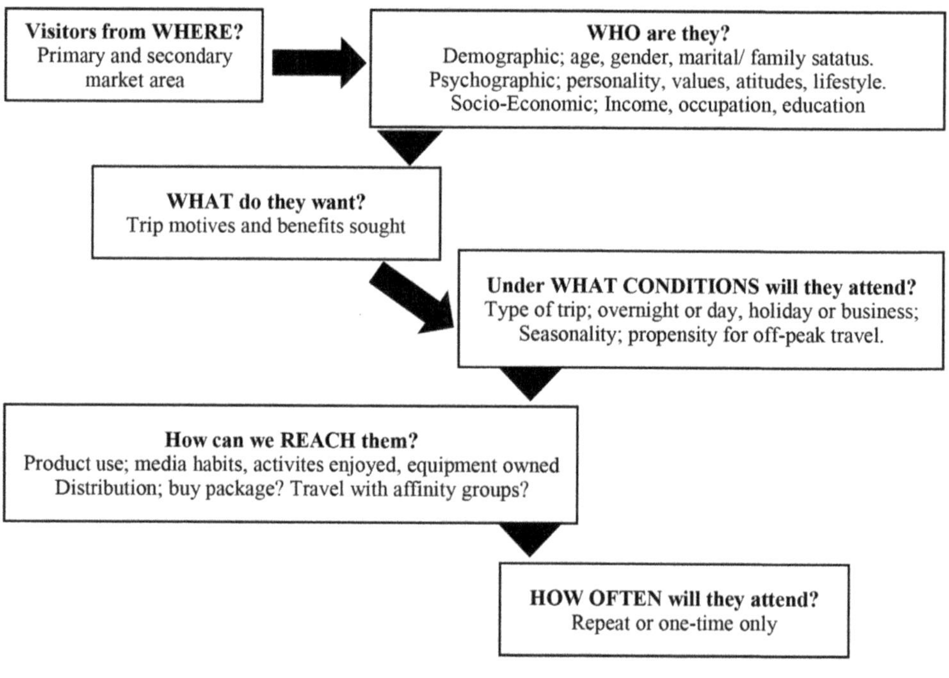

In order to answer the question in step one of Figure 2, the participants of the small-scale sports events must be analyzed very well. In analyzing this, it would be more suitable for event marketers to benefit from approaches to segmenting the market for events such as in the Table 1 (Carmouche, Shukla & Anthonisz, 2010).

Table 1. Approaches to segmenting the market for events

Segment	Type	Value
Geographical	Identifies consumers on the basis of residence: local, regional and / or international markets.	Identifies the catchment area of the market. Includes time and distance the event attendees might travel. Useful for promotion and distribution.
Socio-Economic	Identifies consumer income and often social composition of markets.	Helps to decide pricing strategy of the event, although delegates may not pay themselves for business events.
Demographics	Identifies size, type and structure of the market, including age composition, types of household, families, males and females.	Different events may have different combinations of demegraphics – helps with targeting markets.
Family life-cycle stage	Individuals go through different stages in their life cycles. Markets include, for example, the youth, singles, couples, families with young children, families with teenagers, childless households.	It is useful to understand the types of event that may appeal to individuals in different stages of their life cycles, which is important for promotion and targeting.
Psychographics	Individuals have different values, attitudes, beliefs and lifestyles which can influence buying decisions.	This is useful for developing niche markets for events, for example, the growth of green consumers. Cause-related events may appeal to particular groups.

Source: Carmouche, Shukla & Anthonisz, 2010.

Regardless of the name, being an event consumer requires it to be motivated by one or more factors related to the small-scale sports event. Because attending an this event is a decision that shapes as a results of motivating and stimulating individuals to participate. And this decision is not just a decision that emerged at the time of this event. Motivation and stimulation to participate to the event starts before the start of the event, occurs during the event and continues after the event.

Although there is a change in motivation levels of those who want to participate to the events, the reasons for participation are primarily in the form of celebration of heritage, tradition and interest to the event. In other words, participants need to participate to the events in order to share their experiences and values (Kim, Borges & Chon, 2006), thus becoming consumers of an event. Funk, Toohey & Bruun (2007) state that motivational factors for an event; the main factors are prior participation, feelings toward the host destination, perceived travel opportunities of escape, entertainment, awards, social interaction, prestige, relaxation, culture experience, cultural learning and knowledge exploration. According to Fotiadis, Vassiliadis & Yeh (2016), one of the most important motivation tools to attend the event is *the opportunity to socialize with others*. The motivation process required for an individual to participate in small-scale sports events goes through the process in Figure 3.

Figure 3. Event Consumer Decision Making Process
Source: Getz, 2005.

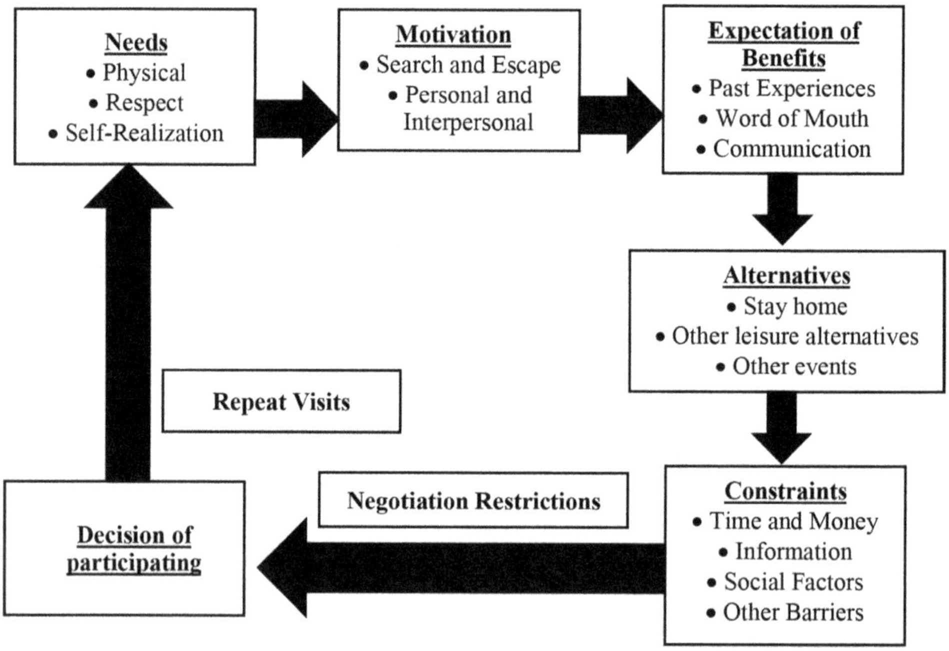

Participation of a individual in a small-scale sports event, that is, becoming an event consumer, begins the aware of his / her physical, respect and self-realization needs. The consumer who becomes aware of these needs, develops motivation to go to the event by thinking that their needs will be met. Event is the motivation for this consumer to escape from daily life and search for different things. Thus, the event consumer will be able to meet his / her personal needs and feel himself / herself belonging to a society by participating in the event. In the third stage, the event consumer expects a benefit from the event. Their past experiences and communication with other consumers related to the event enable the event consumer to benefit from the activity. After this stage, the event consumer considers other alternatives that are at the same time as the activity and can do at home, or go to other activities, After this stage, the event consumer considers other alternatives that are at the same time as the event and can do at home, or go to other events, and reviews the time, money, information and other constraints and decides to participate. When the process is concluded in a positive way, there are repeated visits by the event consumer and this process is re-experienced at each event time.

Successful completion of this motivation process, that is, the motivation and experience of the participant to go to the event depends on the factors that must be in an event for the experience. According to Allen (2009), 5 main factors are needed for a participant to create an experience from the event.

- **Enlightening:** An experience centered around enlightenment bringing harmony between brain, body and spirit, and bringing balance to your home or work life.
- **Engaging:** Experience on the event is achieved by connecting the company/ group as whole.
- **Energizing:** Events focus on personal well-being and active living activities designed to deliver a new energy infusion.
- **Entertaining/Educational:** This experience factor is about teaching the participants while entertaining them. For example, a consumer attending a sports event will have experience by participating in or watching the sport while learning about the sport branch.

Participation in an event is an action triggered by the desire to meet a need. There are three main reasons for investment efforts to better understand the motivation factors that affect participants who come to an event. These are (Crompton & McKay, 1994): *The first reason is* that individuals don't want to buy a marketing product that everyone knows, and they want to buy the expectations of the benefits that satisfy their needs. *The second reason is* the close relationship with satisfaction. Motivation factors appear before experience and after satisfaction. Participants must be satisfied with their previous experience in order to come back to the event. *Finally,* identifying and prioritizing motivating factors is the most important factor in understanding the decision making processes of visitors. Besides, this factor allows other marketing activities to be more effective.

MARKETING MIX OF THE SMALL-SCALE SPORT EVENTS

The marketing mix of small-scale sports events together with the elements in the traditional marketing mix, includes the product of the event, the price of the event, the factors that ensure the announcement of the event, which aim to develop good relations with the society, and the factors that should be considered in the emergence of the event and in short these factors constitute the profile of the event. The event marketing process provides the factors in the event marketing mix. However, before determining the factors in the event marketing mix, some questions about effectiveness should be answered. The "Why, Who, When, Where, What" questions, which are published in the literature as 5 Ws of marketing, are also used in event marketing to determine the applicability, suitability and continuity of a marketing plan. Considering the 5 Ws of marketing, the Table 2 shows 5 Ws of marketing which factors are important in the planning of events and the subsequent the event marketing activities.

Table 2. 5 W's of Marketing

WHY?	• Emphasize Benefits. • Describe Overring Reasons for Events. • Use Personel Approach. • Appeal to Needs.
WHO?	• National, Regional, State, Local Audience. • Disciplines and Interests of Audience. • Audience Awareness of Nature of Event. • Level of Experience (Novice to Expert).
WHEN?	• Market schedules / Patterns. • Time of Day. • Day(s) of Week. • Time of Year (Seasonality).
WHERE?	• Uniqueness of Venue. • Convenience. • Travel Accessibility. • Availability of Local Support.
WHAT?	• Explain Purpose of Events. • Determine and Create Expectations. • Prioritize and Identify Program Features. • Review the 'Who?' Principles.

Source: Hoyle, 2002.

1. **WHY?:** All the factors necessary to promote the small-scale sports event begin with the question of "Why?". Why should someone leave all other alternatives, spend time on your events and spend his / her money if necessary to come to your events? The answer to this question is the first question to be answered by the event planners in small-scale sports event marketing. And the response should be placed as a message on all materials which can be an advertisement, a promotional video, a brochure, or a flyer, used in marketing the event. In these materials, the benefits of the event and whether the event meet the needs of the participants should be stated.
2. **WHO?:** The second important question to be answered is "Who you are doing the small-scale sports event for?". Because the target participants will vary according to the type, size and content of your event. For this reason, it is important to whom you will be doing your event, how you will attract the interest of these potential participants and how you will provide experience to the participants. In addition all these, Allen (2009) also emphasizes that these questions should be answered before marketing the event: What are the age demographics of your participants?, Will children or teenagers be attending?, Is this a corporate event without spouses?...
3. **WHEN?:** The focus of the event is "When a small-scale sports event will be held?". Marketers and planners of the event should determine the time of the event very well. It is an important and difficult decision that whether or not the event coincides with the holidays, in which season of the year, on which day of the week and at what time of day.
4. **WHERE?:** In order to promote an event location can be a major asset. If the events will be *in urban areas,* the factors to be considered are*: the availability of public transportation, valet parking, convenience, and efficiency of travel;* If the events will be *in rural areas,* the factors to be considered are*: a chance to enjoy panoramic views and pastoral scenery;* If the events will be *in shopping malls,* the factors to be considered are*: an opportunity for centralized activities, ease of parking, and ancillary shopping and entertainment features to enjoy;* If the events will be *at resorts,* the factors to be considered are*: the ambiance of pools, golf, upscale shopping, beaches, and gourmet dining;* If the events will be *at airport hotels,* the factors to be considered are*: the inherent efficiency of getting the work done with minimum travel and commuting time because of the fly-in, fly-out design of the location.*
5. **WHAT?**: It should be emphasized by event marketers and planners that the event is unique unto itself, peerless and unmatched. Regardless of what the event is about, it should be presented with a concept that excites and arouses curiosity for the participants. The objectives of the event should be mentioned, the expectations of the participants will be met and created, and the program

should be explained. So, according to Carmouche, Shukla & Anthonisz (2010), the first question to be answered at this stage is *"What is the purpose of the small-scale sports event?"* . Events take place for a variety of purposes, including enjoyment, training and education, releasing and promoting goods and services.

After the answers to the above questions, why, who, when, where and what, the basis of the event marketing mix has emerged. Therefore, at this stage, all questions related to event should be identified and possible answers should be determined. The elements of the event marketing mix are handled by different authors in different ways. As seen in the studies on the event marketing mix, the event marketing mix examined different elements in each study. However, in general dealt with and most commonly used mix are product, price, location (place) positioning and public relations. Therefore, under this heading, product, price, location, positioning and public relations will be mentioned both the common elements in almost all the studies and the most commonly used mixed.

"PRODUCT" in the Small-Scale Sports Events

What is the product, what type, size and purpose of product are, and what will be marketed to the participants will be the first issues to be addressed in the small-scale sports event marketing mix. All planner marketer and organizations which are relation to this event should focus on what the event product is and work around the same purpose.

A major point for the event marketer is the identification of special properties of event product (Carmouche, Shukla & Anthonisz, 2010). To create an event program, each event product forms a whole with the date, quality and value of the event. Every news related to the event is determined by the experiences or past events which is done by the event planners (Goldblatt, 2005). In an event, the product consists of a combination of tangible goods and intangible leisure experiences which are designed to satisfy the needs of the participants. Although the life cycle of an activity product has undergone entry, development and maturity, until it is redesigned in a new form, most events appear in the form of a travel process, and often fluctuations in the lifetime of products or services are unpredictable. Therefore, the life cycle of the event product does not follow a stable course (Bowdin et al., 2012). However, in event marketing, the product has a life cycle, as in the traditional marketing mix. This life cycle consists of the development of a new idea, the start of new services, lunch, growth, maturity and decline stages for the events (Tum, Norton & Wright, 2011) and they are shown in Figure 4.

Figure 4. Life cycle of events
Source: Tum, Norton & Wright, 2011.

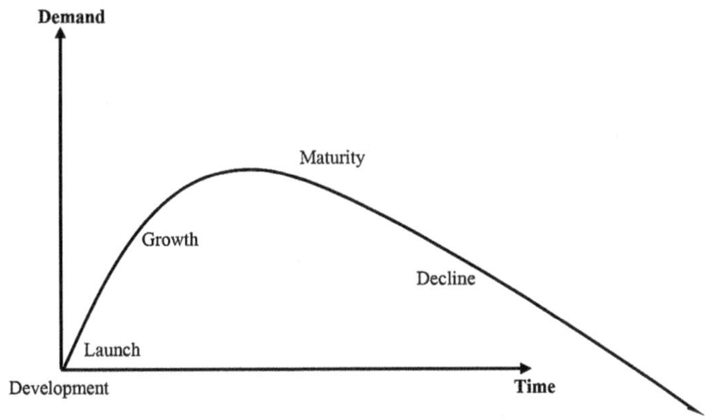

- **Development of a new idea:** This is the stage where research and market tests are conducted, no profit is earned and costs are accrued.
- **Launch of a new service:** This is the stage where costs are met and small returns are made. And this stage is a risky stage which includes pilot studies.
- **Growth:** This is the stage where profits increase. Competitors are emerging and new market segments are emerging. To win share of the market, this is a crucial time.
- **Maturity:** It is the stage in which the revenues become stagnant. The time of this stage varies from event to event. It may take months or even years.
- **Decline:** This is the stage where sales are falling and new products are emerging. Life cycle of event is being updated. People and organizations related to the event should be prepared for new event or have plans for extending the life cycle if it is thought to be possible.

In order to define the concept of product in event marketing, the questions that should be asked are as follows (Hoyle, 2002):

- What is the history of the event?
- What is the value of the product?
- What makes the product unique?

If the small-scale sports event has already been held, the main objective is to increase participation in the this event. However, if this event is being held for the first time, the main purpose is to ensure that the event is long-term and traditional, and to create opportunities to create a history of the event. In small-scale sports event marketing, a behavior that the participants will benefit from should be made important as a message. This message should also indicate the value of the event. The value of the activity can be measured by the satisfaction of the participants. Therefore, the more satisfied the participants are, the more valuable the event will be for them. Event marketers strive to make the event unique by offering participants a unique experience and value, and meeting the needs and desires of the participants. These three basic questions tell us how a small-scale sports event will be as a marketing product. The answers given to these questions are the reasons for the participants to participate in the event.

"PRICE" in the Small-Scale Sports Events

After examining all the factors related to the small-scale sport product in the event marketing, the pricing process of the product starts as the second stage. Questions such as, whether the small-scale sport event will be paid or what will be paid attention to when determining the fee of this event, are the questions that should be answered during the pricing strategy of this event.

It is important to establish a suitable pricing strategy for the event to ensure its success (Shone & Parry, 2004). There are questions to be answered before identifying and developing pricing strategies for a sporting event (Hoyle, 2002):

- What is the corporate financial philosophy?
- What is the cost of doing business?
- What are the financial demographics of the target audience?

Event marketers should first determine what financial philosophies are and how their pricing strategy will be. Some small sports events are aimed at making money and strengthening funding, while others are only for community development. Price represents the cost of goods, services and marketing. Advertising, public relations activities and other basic marketing expenses required to market a small-scale sports event constitute the budget of these events. The market research to be done before starting a small-scale sport event reveals how much the participants are paying or they are willing to pay to this event and constitutes the first stage to form an event plan. The price for this event must be at a price that your participants can pay. Otherwise, participation in the event will be low and the goal will not be achieved. It is therefore important to know how much participants are willing to pay for the event.

In event marketing, the price strategy directly affects the event demand and varies according to the type of event and target markets. The budget for large scale sports events will be larger, while the budget for small-scale sports events will be smaller. In order to fully price the event, it is necessary to develop a strategy according to the social life and financial power of the participants who are likely to participate in the event. High price relative to the target market also represents high value or quality for potential participants (Bowdin et al., 2012).

"LOCATION (PLACE)" in the Small-Scale Sports Events

After determining the pricing strategy in event marketing, the question is asked where the small-scale sports event will be held. Where the event will be held is handled with the introduction of the event at the first stage. However, in the event marketing, which is the third element of event marketing, the concept of place and all the features of the event place are determined in detail.

Place or location expresses the delivery or selling of event products to customers or consumers. This factor facilitates the effectiveness of the events. However, the negative effect of this factor will also affect the effectiveness negatively event (Getz, 2005). The perfect location is much more easily accessible. When location of events is seated exactly right, participants will feel a strong emotional connection (Allen, 2009). For this reason, determining the location of the event takes place in the first stages of event planning. The location of the events varies according to the type and size of the event, but there are factors that need to be considered in each event. These elements (Hoyle, 2002):

- Ease and proximity to travel of potential participants.
- A parking lot where viewers can park their cars.
- The atmosphere and originality of the location of the events.
- Easy logistics support for a special event.
- Infrastructure / space features for special event.
- Existence of audiences and organizations.
- The degree of relevance of the event and the location of event.
- Security for participants.
- Transportation lines are available.
- Availability of sleeping and meeting places.

The location of an event is not only important for participation. In addition, the location of the event shows the character of event and allows the event to be personalized (Carmouche, Shukla & Anthonisz, 2010).

"POSITIONING" in the Small-Scale Sports Events

Positioning is an emerging strategy to determine the fulfillment of expectations of the event through intuition, research and evaluation (Shukla & Nuntsu, 2005) and is an important factor used to create and sustain an image in an event (Getz, 2005). Event marketing is based on where the event is positioning. The success of the marketing plan is based on positioning the product of the event. The positioning strategy determined by intuition, research and evaluation will ensure that the customers' wishes and needs are met effectively. Therefore, there are questions to be answered (Hoyle, 2002):

- What are the niche markets to be met?
- What makes our event different from other events?
- How can we make our event unique?

In order to determine the positioning strategy in event marketing, it is necessary to take into account some factors such as the location of the event that is opposed to competition, the event's unique benefit, and the combination of what customers know and value. (Carmouche, Shukla & Anthonisz, 2010).

"PUBLIC RELATIONS" in the Small-Scale Sports Events

Events especially small-scale events are carried out for the society and the development of the society is aimed. Therefore, the public relations factor in the event marketing mix is more important than the traditional promotion mix.

Public relations defined by Getz (2005) as: *"the actions and communications of the organization that are aimed at fostering awareness, understanding, and positive attitude toward the organization and its operation."* Using the public relations element in event marketing, customers (those who participate or buy tickets for the event), participants (competitors...), sponsors, partners, finance providers (investors…), suppliers (sellers of event tools and equipment, producers…), staff (temporary or permanent staff working in the event) establish relationships with the community and ensure that they are aware of the event. The role of public relations in event marketing also emerges due to their relationship. Public relations element tries to realize these relations or connections with the help of declarations, direct mail, newspapers, special events, sponsorships, personal relations… (Masterman, 2004). This relations are shown in Figure 5.

Figure 5. The role of public relations in the event marketing
Source: Masterman, 2004.

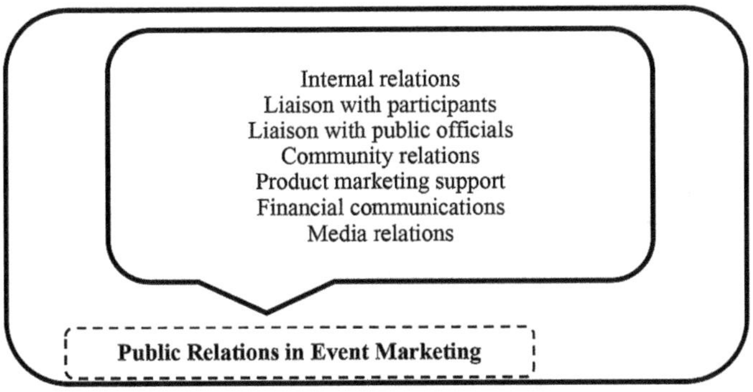

INTEGRATED MARKETING COMMUNICATION (IMC) FOR EVENTS

Shimp (2010 p.10) defined IMC as: *"A communications process that entails the planning, creation, integration and implementation of diverse forms of marcom (advertisements, sales promotions, publicity, releases, events, etc.) that are delivered over time to a brand's targeted customers and prospects."* IMC refers to the communication mix (personal selling, direct mail, sponsorship, word of mouth, exhibitions, etc.) to reach event consumers, communicate with them, and invite to the event and to help them participate by explaining the event and it requires a significant budget spent on planning an event. The factors to be considered in the planning of the IMC, which constitutes an important stage of event marketing, are Figure 6 as follows:

The IMC process in event marketing begins with SWOT analysis. The small-scale sports event marketing process helps at this stage. All databases related to this event are examined and messages are started to be transmitted via IMC media. These messages are made in order to be communicated to all market segments and to all event consumers in these segments and they need to establish a full compliance with the event. These messages can be taken into account in establishing the IMC strategy and positioning the event.

Figure 6. The IMC process in event marketing
Source: Bowdin et al., 2012.

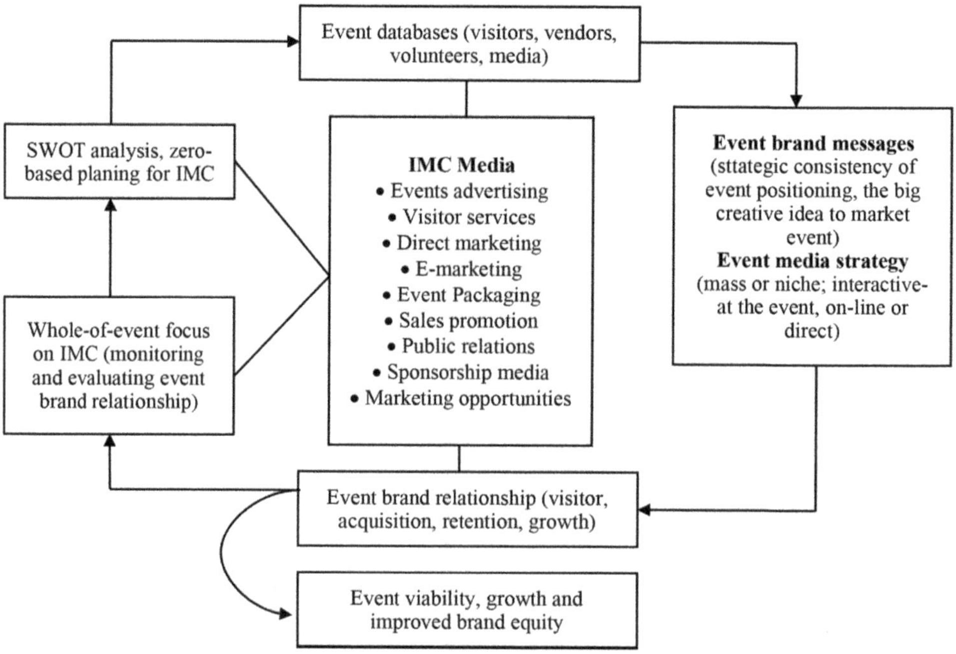

FUTURE RESEARCH DIRECTIONS

This study theoretically describes how to market a small-scale sports events in general. The topics included in the study can be a guide for those planning and managing the organization, which topics should be focused more. In particular, considering the marketing of a small-scale sports events, a research on the subject will provide a more detailed discussion of the topic. And the theoretical framework in this study will ensure that the research on marketing of the event is more robust. This study provides guidance to researchers, marketers and those planning and managing such an event and contributes to the literature. It is hoped that the study will serve as a resource for future studies in addition to the previous ones.

CONCLUSION

Compared to large scale events, small-scale sports activities, that affect a more limited area, are still being performed very often in order to reflect the identity of the society in which the sports activity takes place, to increase its image, to reveal the spirit of the society and to offer a unique experience to the participants. With the marketing of these small-scale sports events, the participants live the entertainment and experience together, establish an interactive communication with the businesses and provide the consumer to meet their brands. Therefore, when planning and marketing a small-scale event, effective and interactive marketing strategies are needed to attract more participants. The time and effort involved in making and marketing large scale events should also be spent, especially for small-scale sports events that affect the location or area. Only then will consumers be more involved in such events, have more impact on the region in which they are made, and will be mentioned for a longer time.

Spreading Entertainment, Excitement and Enterprise to the entire small-scale sport event will differentiate it from other events. All the marketing activities of a small-scale sport events are examined together with the planning process that begins with determining the mission and purpose of the event. Who will participate in the event or the event consumer is determined by the 'market segmentation'. For example, how to make sports tournaments attractive to students at a university and how to convince them to participate in the tournaments is revealed by the market segmentation; and the demographic characteristics of the potential participants, their personalities, what they want, under which conditions they will participate, and how to reach all of them will form the segments of the event. This will result in the decision making process of those university students. The applicability, suitability and continuity of this university event is based on 5 basic questions: 'Why, Who, When, Where, What'. The answers to these questions will be the answer to all the questions about the marketing of the event and the marketing mix of a small-scale sports event will emerge. In the small-scale sports event, what is the 'product', whether it has been done before and what is the main feature that makes it unique will determine the value of the event. Whether this small-scale sport event is paid or not, and whether the participants can easily pay if it is paid, will constitute the 'price' strategy of that event. Where the event will be held, whether the potential participants can be reached easily, the security will be determined with the concept of 'location', and if the event is attractive to these people and if they think that their needs will be met with this event, it will be determined with the concept of 'positioning'. Establishing good relations with the people of the place, where the event will take place and who will be the sponsors, partners and investors will be handled with the concept of 'public relations'. Finally, which the 'IMC' strategy will be selected will enable the communication concept to be planned in the event, while reaching the potential participants who are planning to participate in the small-scale sports event.

Considering all these factors, well planned small-scale sports events and well designed marketing activities will bring success. The businesses, institutions or individuals who accomplish this will achieve a competitive advantage and reach both their corporate and marketing objectives. Considering the marketing activities of small-scale sports events, Kirkpinar Oil Wrestling was examined as a case study.

CASE STUDY: KIRKPINAR OIL WRESTLING

Wrestling, known as one of the world's first and oldest sports, is an indispensable sporting event especially for the Turkish society. The most rooted of the wrestling competitions, which has a very important place in the culture of the Turkish people and keeps a tradition going on for years, is the "Historical Kirkpinar Oil Wrestling" which is held every year (except for the wars in the region) in Sarayiçi in Edirne. The birth of Kirkpinar oil wrestling dates back to the 14th century. And there are many legends about the emergence of Kirkpinar. This event, which is known by the history of Edirne and the cultural identity of the Turkish society, has an important role in the history of sports.

Every year since the birth of Kirkpinar wrestling, it is organized in the last week of June or the first week of July by Edirne Municipality together with various activities in the "Historical Kirkpinar Oil Wrestling and Cultural Activities Week". The dates of Kirkpinar will be determined approximately a year ago and organizing, planning and marketing activities are started in order to realize this. Firstly, announcements are made on the official website of Edirne Municipality, by raising awareness among the stakeholders of the event in the region and negotiations for all the events to be organized within Kirkpinar of that year are started. These events (concerts, competitions, entertainments, food and beverage stands) held in Kirkpinar play an important role in attracting more participants to Kirkpinar every year. In the planning stage of Kirkpinar, additional trips are made by local administrations, parking services are increased and security measures are taken so that everyone can easily reach the venue. Many people are assigned to do all this. These people actively take part from the beginning of the event to the end. In order to reduce the risks that may arise during the event, ambulances and healthcare teams prepare for the task at the time of the event by making their preparations before the event begins. Professional security teams are also assigned to ensure the safety of the event.

In order to promote and announce the event, the event is promoted in the city center, shopping malls, bus stops and billboards in Edirne, brochures are distributed and outdoor advertisements are also made, and announcements are made through social media. Information about Kirkpinar is given wide coverage, especially in the local press.Participants are invited to the Kirkpinar event with a 'Red Bottom Candle'. This traditional method, which has been used since the beginning of Kirkpinar, is one of the most important marketing tools of Kirkpinar.

Kirkpinar reflects the social image, culture and behavior of Edirne, ensures the community spirit and it enables Edirne to become a unique brand. Participation of participants from different places enables local people to know different cultures and that different cultures should know Edirne and its culture more closely. For this reason, the successful realization of the event also increases the reputation of the planners, the image of the place where the event was held and the quality of life of the local people. In particular, it provides the revival of the local economy. Staff actively involved in all planning and marketing activities for the event increase the employment of the city of Edirne, especially during the event. In the process from the event planning to the end, job opportunities are offered to the people of Edirne. The accommodation of the participants in Edirne, the purchase of traditional gifts, food and beverages that reflect the culture of Edirne, constitute a good source of income for the province of Edirne. When the 2019 data of Kirkpinar is analyzed, the total expense of all planning and marketing activities for Kirkpinar is 4 million 272 thousand Turkish Liras, while its total income is 1 million 414 thousand Turkish Liras. These datas reveal how important planning and marketing activities are for the event.

Marketing objectives planned to be given to the participants with Kirkpinar are given by entertaining and the participants are provided with a unique experience. The fact that there are no problems during the event, the participants have an unforgettable experience and leave them pleased, making them satisfied with their experience. Thus, more participants are provided to Kirkpinar, which is planned to be held next.

REFERENCES

Allen, J. (2009). *Event planning: The ultimate guide to successful meetings, corporate events, fundraising galas, conferences, conventions, incentives and other special events*. John Wiley & Sons.

Bowdin, G. A. J., Allen, J., O'Toole, W., Harris, R., & McDonnell, I. (2012). *Events Management*. Taylor & Francis Group.

Carmouche, R., Shukla, N., & Anthonisz, A. (2010). *Events marketing and communication strategy*. JUTA.

Crompton, J. L., & McKay, S. L. (1994). Measuring the economic impact of festivals and events: Some myths, misapplications and ethical dilemmas. *Festival Management & Event Tourism*, *2*(1), 33–43. doi:10.3727/106527094792335782

Duglio, S., & Beltramo, R. (2017). Estimating the economic impacts of a small-scale sport tourism event: The case of the Italo-Swiss mountain trail CollonTrek. *Sustainability*, *9*(3), 343. doi:10.3390u9030343

Fotiadis, A., Vassiliadis, C., & Yeh, S. P. (2016). Participant's preferences for small-scale sporting events: A comparative analysis of a Greek and a Taiwanese cycling event. *EuroMed Journal of Business*, *11*(2), 232–247. doi:10.1108/EMJB-07-2015-0039

Funk, D. C., Toohey, K., & Bruun, T. (2007). International sport event participation: Prior sport involvement; destination image; and travel motives. *European Sport Management Quarterly*, *7*(3), 227–248. doi:10.1080/16184740701511011

Getz, D. (2005). Event management & event tourism. Cognizant Communication Corporation.

Gibson, H., Kaplanidou, K., & Kang, S. J. (2012). Small-scale event sport tourism A case study in sustainable tourism. *Sport Management Review*, *15*(2), 160–170. doi:10.1016/j.smr.2011.08.013

Goldblatt, J. (2005). *Special Events, Event Leadership for a new World*. John Wiley & Sons.

Hanlon, C., & Jago, L. (2000). Pulsating sporting events: An organisational structure to optimise performance. *Events beyond 2000: Setting the agenda*, 93.

Higham, J. (1999). Commentary-sport as an avenue of tourism development: An analysis of the positive and negative impacts of sport tourism. *Current Issues in Tourism*, *2*(1), 82–90. doi:10.1080/13683509908667845

Hoyle, L. H. (2002). *Event Marketing: how to successfully promote events, fesivals, convenions, and expositions*. John Wiley & Sons.

Kaplanidou, K., & Vogt, C. (2007). The interrelationship between sport event and destination image and sport tourists' behaviours. *Journal of Sport & Tourism*, *12*(3-4), 183–206. doi:10.1080/14775080701736932

Kim, H., Borges, M. C., & Chon, J. (2006). Impacts of environmental values on tourism motivation: The case of FICA, Brazil. *Tourism Management*, *27*(5), 957–967. doi:10.1016/j.tourman.2005.09.007 PMID:32287716

Masterman, G. (2014). *Strategic sports event management*. Elsevier. doi:10.4324/9780203114674

Morrison, A. M. (1995). *Hospitality and travel marketing*. Delmar.

Shimp, T. A. (2010). Integrated Marketing Communication in Advertising and Promotion/por Terence A Shimp (No. 658.8 S45.). Academic Press.

Shone, A., & Parry, B. (2004). *Successful event management: a practical handbook*. Cengage Learning EMEA.

Shukla, N., & Nuntsu, N. (2005). Event Marketing. In D. Tassiopoulos (Ed.), *Event Management* (2nd ed.). Juta Academic.

Sofia, G., & Chris, V. (2017). Blueprinting an event and tourist service marketing strategy: the case of the SMF Greek tourism small-scale sport event. In *Strategic Innovative Marketing* (pp. 19–24). Springer. doi:10.1007/978-3-319-33865-1_3

Tinnish, S. M., & Mangal, S. M. (2012, October). Sustainable event marketing in the MICE industry: A theoretical framework. *Journal of Convention & Event Tourism*, *13*(4), 227–249. doi:10.1080/15470148.2012.731850

Tum, J., Norton, P., & Wright, J. N. (2011). *Management of Events Operations*. Elsevier.

Watt, D. C. (1998). *Event management in leisure and tourism*. Addison Wesley Longman Ltd.

Wilson, R. (2006). The economic impact of local sport events: significant, limited or otherwise? A case study of four swimming events. *Managing Leisure, 11*(1), 57-70.

Wohlfeil, M., & Whelan, S. (2006). Consumer motivations to participate in marketing-events: The role of predispositional involvement. *ACR European Advances*, *7*, 125–131.

Yürük Kayapınar, P. (2018). Etkinlik pazarlaması. In N. Altuğ & Ş. Özhan (Eds.), *Pazarlamada güncel gelişmeler* (pp. 261–286). Nobel Akademik.

ADDITIONAL READING

Close, A. G., Finney, R. Z., Lacey, R. Z., & Sneath, J. Z. (2006). Engaging the consumer through event marketing: Linking attendees with the sponsor, community, and brand. *Journal of Advertising Research*, *46*(4), 420–433. doi:10.2501/S0021849906060430

Fotiadis, A., Xie, L., Li, Y., & Huan, T. C. T. (2016). Attracting athletes to small-scale sports events using motivational decision-making factors. *Journal of Business Research*, *69*(11), 5467–5472. doi:10.1016/j.jbusres.2016.04.157

Gibson, H. J., Kaplanidou, K., & Kang, S. J. (2012). Small-scale event sport tourism: A case study in sustainable tourism. *Sport Management Review*, *15*(2), 160–170. doi:10.1016/j.smr.2011.08.013

Gibson, H. J., Willming, C., & Holdnak, A. (2003). Small-scale event sport tourism: Fans as tourists. *Tourism Management*, *24*(2), 181–190. doi:10.1016/S0261-5177(02)00058-4

Hallmann, K., & Breuer, C. (2011). Images of rural destinations hosting small-scale sport events. *International Journal of Event and Festival Management*, *2*(3), 218–244. doi:10.1108/17582951111170290

Hoyle, L. H. (2002). *Event Marketing: how to successfully promote events, fesivals, convenions, and expositions*. John Wiley & Sons.

Kahle, L. R., & Close, A. G. (Eds.). (2011). *Consumer behavior knowledge for effective sports and event marketing*. Routledge. doi:10.4324/9780203844113

Kerwin, S., Warner, S., Walker, M., & Stevens, J. (2015). Exploring sense of community among small-scale sport event volunteers. *European Sport Management Quarterly*, *15*(1), 77–92. doi:10.1080/16184742.2014.996581

Preston, C. (2012). *Event marketing: how to successfully promote events, festivals, conventions, and expositions*. Wiley.

Tzetzis, G., Alexandris, K., & Kapsampeli, S. (2014). Predicting visitors' satisfaction and behavioral intentions from service quality in the context of a small-scale outdoor sport event. *International Journal of Event and Festival Management*, *5*(1), 4–21. doi:10.1108/IJEFM-04-2013-0006

Wohlfeil, M., & Whelan, S. (2006). Consumer motivations to participate in event-marketing strategies. *Journal of Marketing Management*, *22*(5-6), 643–669. doi:10.1362/026725706777978677

KEY TERMS AND DEFINITIONS

Event: Activities organized within the framework of a specific theme or action.

Event Marketing: It is an event management function performed by event planners, which includes activities to produce, price, present an event to potential participants an activity to satisfy the needs of its participants.

IMC for Event: It is a communication method that carry out to inform, remind, and persuade potential participants to participate in an event.

Leisure Time: It is the time that people devote from their daily work to enrich value to themselves.

Marketing Mix of Event: It is the marketing mix of product, price, place, positioning and public relations that enables the marketing of the event.

Participant: Individuals who participate in an event to evaluate their leisure time and gain experience.

W's of Event Marketing: These are the questions (why, who, when, where, what) that need to be answered in order to ensure the feasibility, suitability and sustainability of event marketing.

Chapter 9
Small-Scale Sports Event Marketing Using New Marketing Concepts and Communication Tools

Park Beede
https://orcid.org/0000-0001-7923-4245
Zayed University, UAE

ABSTRACT

Small-scale sporting events are often characterized as local activities limited in size, support, and resources. However, they fulfill an integral social role in the vibrant lives of local communities. Sports events also attract visitors as participants and spectators, benefitting the local economy and supporting tourism activities. To deliver successful events, coordinated marketing activities should be developed in a cohesive marketing plan. Every sports organization can implement effective marketing tools to increase the visibility of their event and enhance satisfaction among a variety of key stakeholders. This chapter outlines a manageable plan of marketing activities that will improve the odds of a successful event.

DOI: 10.4018/978-1-7998-4757-1.ch009

CHAPTER OBJECTIVES

After completing the chapter, the reader should be able to:

- Understand the process of sports marketing applied to small-scale events.
- Adopt a systematic approach to conceptualizing and creating a sports marketing plan.
- Define relevant marketing goals and objectives to be achieved along a timeline.
- Understand the distinction between strategy and tactics, and coordinate an integrated marketing plan designed to achieve event objectives.

INTRODUCTION

When we mention 'sports marketing,' a variety of prominent global sporting identities usually come to mind; the Olympic Games, FIFA World Cup, the NFL Superbowl… depending on your sports of choice. Big sports events also attract big brands. The likes of Nike, Adidas, and Reebok, for example, fuel marketing exposure of sports events with substantial sponsorship support and advertising budgets. Professional sports marketing activities leverage high-profiles players and big brands to attract large audiences (Robinson & France, 2011).

While professional sports benefit from big budgets, amateur sporting events actually attract the majority of participants around the world. In addition, even greater numbers of family, friends, and fans add to the overall audience and exposure of an event. Flow-on effects provide important income opportunities for local businesses, especially in the hospitality and restaurant sectors. Research has indicated that small-scale sports events not only benefit the community, but also support sustainable development of local tourism activities (Gibson, Kaplanidou, & Kang, 2012).

In the overall development and delivery of sports events, the topic of sports marketing is often applied across a wide range of related activities. The principles and tools of sports marketing represent the essential knowledge sports marketers need to successfully promote events, matches and activities to relevant participants and fans. Developing and implementing effective marketing plans requires a framework of marketing tools and techniques focused on 'customer needs' (da Silva & Las Casas, 2017). Key concepts and components under the broad umbrella of sports marketing include:

- attracting participants as competitors,
- creating appeal among fans,
- recruiting administrators and volunteers,
- enticing sponsors in support of the event, and,
- in general, creating positive connections within local communities.

The breadth of these activities reflects two key perspectives; firstly, the marketing *of* sports, and, secondly, marketing *through* sports (Fetchko, Roy, & Clow, 2018). In this context, sports events are promoted for the dual purpose of attracting participants (and associated fans) and marketing benefits attractive to sponsors trying to connect with these people.

While professional sports organizations benefit from substantial budgets funding commercial marketing activities, 'small-scale' sports events generally lack this luxury. Two critical resources are often in short supply – money and manpower. Marketing budgets for small-scale events, in addition to overall funding, are often limited and rely on a lot of goodwill among a network of organizers, sponsors, and participants. Fundraising is often the first phase of small-scale event marketing activities before any expenses can be committed. To do that, of course, requires people. Recruiting key people who can contribute time, expertise, and valuable connections is critical to getting an event off the ground.

Faced with these two key challenges, in particular, marketing activities for small-scale sports events must be manageable to be effective. This chapter presents a practical guide to managing marketing activities, concentrating efforts into the key components of an essential plan. Scaled to a level proportionate with the scope of an event, these four elements are critical for success:

1. Build a brand identity that portrays the event image, is unique, and easy to execute
2. Promote exposure for the event among target audiences and key stakeholders
3. Create engagement opportunities and interaction among all attendees
4. Manage relationships among participants and patrons, reinforcing positive experiences

The adoption of a coordinated marketing plan contributes toward successful event outcomes. Easier said than done, of course, given limited resources. This chapter examines each phase of the process and presents practical recommendations for sports marketers managing these events.

THE STARTING POINT: WHAT IMAGE DO YOU WANT FOR THE EVENT?

Sports events and organizations – large and small – yield a social benefit for the community they engage with. Participants, both competitors and support staff, indulge their passion for the sport. Family, friends, and fans revel in comradery and in supporting their favorite athletes or teams. Sponsors gain commercial benefits while also associating with a favored and fun event. Host venues and local communities benefit from positive exposure and an influx of visitors. Research demonstrates that communities of all sizes can realize a range of short- and long-term benefits derived from hosting sports events (Veltri, Miller, & Harris, 2009).

Central to delivering benefits across all stakeholders is a common event experience, and that starts by building a cohesive image of what to expect. Deciding on and defining what impressions an event should deliver is essentially the brand position. Is the event serious or social? Will it draw people regionally, nationally, or globally? Is it a one-time event, not to be missed, or another staging of a periodic schedule, be it frequent, annual, or even longer? Sports event marketers should clearly define the desired brand image to create interest and deliver a consistent experience across all touchpoints. A strong event brand image builds cumulative strength in associations and will pay dividends over time (Dichter, 1985).

At its core, the branding and promotion of sports events are similar to the marketing activities of any product or, in this case, service. The inherent nature of sport is an experiential activity. Like any service experience, satisfaction is a journey that starts before the event, peaks during participation, and continues to exert influence long after the event. Influencing expectations, in addition to managing the actual experience, is key to success. A strong brand image, as part of the coordinated marketing plan, helps in delivering a positive 'customer experience.'

BUILDING A BRAND IDENTITY

Large or small, professional or amateur, every sports event owns a unique identity; a brand image. Three related qualities are important to consider at the early stage of event creation: identity, image, and reputation (Parent & Foreman, 2007). It is rare for sports marketers to enjoy a relative luxury of creating a new brand from a clean slate. Most often, sports events are established entities in some way, building on a history of associations drawn from past events, an organizing entity, or the broader sport in general. It is natural for people to associate information from anything they already know, forming new impressions based on existing associations held in memory.

Building on existing associations can deliver benefits in creating awareness. At the same time, however, they can also hinder opportunities to create distinct identities.

Occasionally, new event opportunities do arise. While creating new event brands offers exciting potential, it too presents challenges in creating appealing images and building a reputation with limited marketing support (Merrilees, Getz, & O'Brien, 2005). Creative opportunities also present creative challenges!

Another important consideration at the onset is the role of major sponsors. Sports events often leverage commercial sponsorships, which include co-branding with the event owner in identity and marketing materials (Santomier, 2008). Co-branding and dual brand identities can be both a benefit and a constraint. In the short-term, popular business brands add credibility and appeal to an event image. With little knowledge about an actual event or its organizer, a recognized brand (especially if it is relevant to the sport) adds immediate credibility.

On the other hand, a strong brand partner can also dominate the event image. A prominent sponsoring brand is not necessarily a bad aspect, but it does shift a balance in 'brand power' toward the sponsor's advantage. The Red Bull Air Race series, for example, would seem very different if it were sponsored by Lipton Tea! An event marketer in this situation should weigh up the relative benefits associated with co-branding versus limitations in marketing image and management control.

While a fit-for-purpose brand strategy would be ideal, sometimes necessity is the mother of invention, as the saying goes. Sports marketers need to balance overall needs and then set out to develop all three related aspects to create a holistic brand. Determining and defining the core brand identity is typically the first step in this process.

Identifying the event name brand moniker (which is often multiple words) and designing visual logos will give shape to the event image. The actual name may seem obvious, but do consider some options. A few key questions to consider are:

- Is the name descriptive of the sport or distinctive in some unique aspects?
- Is the name common and easily adopted across languages, or is it specific in a local language and associated with cultural aspects?
- Is the name easy to read when printed and easy to pronounce when spoken?
- Is the name generic or unique? Can you protect ownership of it as a registered business name, trademark, or copyright in design? Is the name used as a registered trademark by someone else around the world?

There is no best strategy or solution for any of these issues. Sports marketers should consider overall long-term goals and then ask, 'How does this brand image help or hinder that goal?' In the end, a strong brand name will stand out in memory and evolve into a recognizable event within the community. Over time, it will embody all the associations inherent with the event and assume its own, unique brand personality.

Having established a phonetic name, the brand then comes to life visually through design. It may often be a luxury for small-scale sports event marketers to employ professional design services. These days, however, a laptop computer and readily available clipart can often deliver comparable results. Either way, it is essential to present a cohesive image of the event and differentiate the brand among a cluttered environment competing for attention (Montana, Guzman, & Moll, 2007).

Additionally, professional marketing materials are often available and provided – if not required – by sponsoring partners. With a keen focus on presenting their brands well, sponsors are often a useful resource for support in developing an event identity. Access to their in-house designers and creative agencies can often help produce professional-quality brand resources.

Together, an event name and visual logo form the brand identity. A strong brand builds equity, which in branding means the intangible value built up over time. Like other business assets, brand equity reflects the cumulative value arising from positive feelings about (in this case) an event (Keller, 2001; pp. 3-27). Positive brand equity is valuable in recruiting new participants, growing a fan base, attracting sponsors, and engaging with the community, for example (Vassiliadis & Fotiadis, 2016; pp. 195-215). Given the intangible value of strong event brand identities, organizations need to nurture and protect these intangible assets.

Advice from an attorney specializing in intellectual property (IP) can be worth its weight in gold. Otherwise, a relatively easy option available to organizations is to register an event entity as a business name with a local government service agency. Creating a small business entity under the brand name will generally protect use within that jurisdiction. Sports marketers should be aware, however, of any small business operating requirements that may accompany this action. Local government small business agencies are usually helpful sources of information on this topic.

Another option is to establish copyright protection associated with the brand identity. Often referred to as common law use, copyright protection can be asserted among many countries simply through the commercial application of the brand identity, i.e., unique name and logo used in the business context. However, it is relatively easy and beneficial to register a trademark to ensure protection against infringement. Registering a trademark can often be achieved online. Do keep in mind, though, that trademarks operate in the country of registration. An event attracting interest in multiple countries may warrant registration in more than just a host market. In these cases, the services of a trademark attorney may be prudent.

Having established the brand identity, shaping the broader event brand image then should be aligned with the key strategic objectives (Berry, 2000). Once the desired image is defined, marketing materials and activities should be identified that drive the brand image. Here, the scope is wide, and developing creative ideas should be a collaborative process. More about this aspect will be developed in the next section, but marketers should evaluate early on about how well a brand identity supports the desired image and can be easily executed across a variety of media formats.

In particular, with smaller-scale events, ease of execution is a decisive consideration. For example, does a logo design reproduce well in black-and-white desktop printing or photocopying? Does the design screen print well on clothing and sports equipment, such as water bottles? Does a design 'lock-up' (the total brand identity) integrate well when combined with sponsors' brands and marketing materials? How well does the identity present in digital media, especially mobile devices? It is essential to consider the range of marketing materials and media formats the brand identity will operate most often in and on.

Knowing the operational timeline is also important. For example, is it necessary to build immediate awareness for a new event entity, or should interest build gradually to concentrate the desired response closer to the actual event? Rolling out the event brand campaign across various marketing activities and media coverage will build the brand image and associated interest in the event. Delivering marketing materials to a timeline – and working backwards from required lead times – is solved by applying a project management approach to the marketing plan.

In a broader context, sports marketers also need to be conscious of the reputation that grows over time, influencing the way people think and feel about an event. Not everyone will see it the same way. Different audiences may hold quite different views about an event, the organizers, and associated sponsors. It is critical to recognize public perceptions and manage information to the best of ability in order to influence an event's reputation in the local community and public domain (Parent & Foreman, 2007). Also, amidst the empowered environment of social media, every individual has a voice. While we cannot erase history and change individual experiences, sports marketers can influence future expectations. Consider early on what type of brand personality is best to promote an event and foster through social media. For example, attendees may be much more forgiving of shortcomings encountered in a home-grown, grassroots event image as compared to a slick, professional promise leading to an 'over-promise, under-deliver' experience.

Having built the brand, the next step puts together a marketing and promotion plan to create awareness, build interest, and prompt action.

EXECUTING A PROMOTION PLAN

The emergence of new media has opened immense opportunities for small-scale sports event marketers to achieve large-scale exposure. At the same time, people are bombarded by more information than ever before. A challenge for any event entity is to simply *get noticed...* to stand out from the crowd and attract attention. Whether sports marketers employ new media technologies or generate exposure through traditional media channels – and probably a mix of both – common objectives still apply. While online exposure and social media attract a majority of emphasis these days, do not overlook the benefits of traditional media exposure (Gantz & Lewis, 2014).

One of the drawbacks associated with traditional media channels is a relatively high upfront cost of achieving exposure. Advertising in traditional media choices may be beneficial to build awareness among broad audiences but often carries a high absolute cost as compared to other options. However, community-based media, in particular newspapers, radio, and local television, can be useful in building awareness. Partnering with local media can help leverage cost-effective exposure, creating opportunities for promotional activities, and staging events with media personalities function as free publicity. Live events broadcast on radio, for example, can be useful in building awareness leading up to an event.

In this aspect, traditional media outlets do offer one key competitive advantage: community-based exposure. Local media tend to attract loyal audiences. With the right fit, coordinated publicity activities can deliver big benefits in generating exposure for an event. It is important to allocate efforts toward building media relationships, creating opportunities for joint promotional activities and events, and to make available 'news-friendly' personalities that will attract the media's interests to feature and promote.

Do not overlook the need to create and supply constant newsworthy content to local media as well. Media releases noting interesting stories and significant developments leading up to an event provide local media with potential storylines. It is also important to build some positive support early in the marketing plan. While negative media exposure can be crippling to an event, influencing positive media stories can likewise be a pivotal contributor to success. Build up some image 'credit' early in exposure plan for an event. Establishing early positive impressions can create momentum that benefits an event image over the long-term.

Leveraging sponsor funds with, for example, cooperative advertising opportunities may be another way to stretch limited budgets and add exposure. Local business sponsors, especially retailers, often advertise frequently in local media. Opportunities to run co-sponsored ads offer advertisers an opportunity to say something fresh about their business and get noticed. Leveraging their advertising budgets can expand exposure in the lead up to an event.

Traditional media opportunities such as these, however, are relatively limited to local exposure. They are essential in building community awareness, to be sure, but events that attract participants and patrons from markets outside local media coverage areas need alternative options. Fortunately, the Internet has opened up easy access to a global audience. While sports organizations once needed traditional media outlets to create exposure, they now have direct access to broad audiences through their own digital media (Sherwood, Nicholson, & Marjoribanks, 2017).

Online exposure, in contrast to traditional media advertising, is relatively inexpensive to create. Getting noticed, however, is the challenge. With so much digital media available at our fingertips, creating valued content people notice can be difficult. Consider an online strategy split into two key areas – online marketing and social media (Thompson *et al.,* 2014).

Among an engaged and motivated audience, relevant information should be made easily available through digital channels. Some people will actively seek information about the event. Sports marketers need to support their efforts by providing easy access to valued information. Start with an event website. Be sure the structure and layout are easy to access and navigate, provide relevant information, and is interactive. Video content is essential these days. Keep narrative text limited to essential information and highlight images and video content that will engage viewers. Most of all, make sure the website functions well on mobile devices. People increasingly interact online in their hands – small screens dominate.

Another high priority is search engine optimization (SEO) options. Abundant information is available online to assist in learning about SEO fundamentals and how to maximize an effective strategy. Bear in mind that most people seek information about topics, such as sports events, by typing keywords into search engines. Identifying the key terms associated with an event that people search for and linking an SEO strategy with a website can pay big dividends. In addition to online information about effective strategies, local digital consultants or agencies can often contribute valuable advice accumulated through experience. Do invest time, if not funds, in an effective SEO strategy.

Finally, consider options for online paid advertising exposure. Well-placed banner ads and sponsored links can help drive traffic to an event website. Response rates often appear as small numbers in the overall scheme of marketing activities, but well-targeted campaigns can reach a valuable audience cost-effectively. Most of all, online advertising can reach a global audience. For events attracting international participants and patrons, online advertising may be the best option. Sports marketers should match the advertising budget with potential audience reach in this case.

As compared to paid advertising, social media actively engages individuals through more personalized content. Sports marketers often create engaging content intended to share and spread via social networks as a means of building exposure and promoting direct digital response opportunities. Social media channels offer excellent opportunities to engage interested individuals, and content is viewed as credible. However, in this context, be conscious that control of that content rests in their hands. Positive impressions and experiences shared in social media can be an event's best promotion, but negative sentiments and complaints can also spread like wildfire. Monitoring, and actively addressing, social media is critical for sports event entities in today's environment. Be vigilant, and often get engaged with a conversation if someone shares a negative experience. Showing interest to address disappointment and improve for the future goes a long way in turning negatives into positives.

Toward this end, look to create fresh content continuously that can be shared easily. Social media strategies rely on rapid turnover. Visuals are essential to emphasize. Look to spark new conversations frequently and share visual content promoting the event. Once conversations get started, interest will build, and self-selected 'organic' audiences will grow.

With these tools available, consider the varied information needs and interests among different target audiences. One of the key indicators of success for sporting events is the quantity and quality of competing athletes/participants. As such, relevant information about an event needs to be easily available, if not directed to them. Fotiadis *et al.* (2016), for example, identified that details about seasonal event timing and registration costs were critical factors influencing decisions to attend. Understanding the information needs of your key audiences – especially participating athletes – is essential in building a strong event identity and attracting broader interest. Target participants first, and then expand promotional exposure to build audience interest.

STAGING THE EVENT: AUDIENCE ENGAGEMENT AND INTERACTIVE MEDIA

Obviously, digital media has ushered in an era of interactivity. Research has shown how important social interaction and 'collegiality' is in attracting people to sports events (Xu & Pegg, 2007). In the past, this was achieved in-person with various social activities sponsored throughout an event period. Socializing is still an integral part of any event, to be sure, but we can now expand that experience through social media. Digital discussion boards and social media, combined with actual attendance and participation, all offer opportunities to enhance the personal experience of the event.

At this stage, attendees are actively involved with an event while it is occurring. In addition to daily management, sports marketers should be acutely focused on actively updating online media assets, starting with the event website. Event information, such as daily updates of results, stand-out performances, highlights to look for the next day, and anything else relevant to the event can draw people online and interact with the event website. It can be challenging – in fact, draining – for event marketers to allocate time each day updating website information, but the benefits are notable. The more attendees engage with an event in any way, the stronger their impressions and attitudes grow.

Every online engagement is investing in relationship-building with prime prospects. It is like having a conversation with someone. The more frequent those conversations are, the more familiar the event entity feels. People like to spend time with friends. So, do prioritize an interactive website and social media that can be updated frequently with information during an event. Create and post content daily. Promote discussion forums that connect attendees with others. It is all about buzz.

While digital media platforms may be an obvious emphasis these days, traditional tools and techniques should not be overlooked. Sporting events are, of course, social engagements, especially among participating athletes. Event entertainment and award functions have been identified as one of the most important factors influencing satisfaction among athletes and intention to return again (Fotiadis *et al.,* 2016). Fundamentals of event planning and management are critical elements in delivering a successful event experience; make sure attention is paid to details and activities are adequately resourced. It is also extremely helpful to shape expectations in advance. Promotional content that creates appealing while also realistic expectations are important. Prominent celebrities or an air of intrigue and surprise can be exciting but be careful to somewhat 'under-promise and over-deliver.'

Partnering with sponsors to offer promotional discounts and vouchers can be useful in extending benefits among attendees, and they are easy to execute. The availability of branded products and sports paraphernalia are also important extensions of the event experience. Branded products serve two essential functions; they 'tangiblize' an experience, providing mementos and keepsakes for individuals to reinforces fond memories. They also 'badge' attendees during the event, fostering those tribal alliances core to social bonding. Keep in mind that product supply takes time, so do build in adequate lead times to source products from vendors. Another critical management decision estimates adequate stock levels. Too little or too much can create problems, of course, so it is important to assess realistic volumes accurately. One consideration that can help minimize risk in this area is to avoid customization for one unique event, such as printing a year or annual event number. Branding that can be generalized over time, and perhaps shared with other activities associated with the event organization, can substantially reduce financial burdens on limited marketing budgets.

Beyond the parameters of the actual event itself, in particular, facilities and accommodation, develop a local tourism promotional kit to share with participants and attendees. Research has demonstrated the importance of promoting local entertainment and festivities in attracting athletes to sporting events. As compared to motives among professional athletes, small-scale sporting events are inherently linked with local destination marketing attractions. Participants are often equally motivated, if not more, by the appeal of interesting and novel experiences available among the local host surrounds (Priporas, *et al.,* 2018).

Overall, having built excitement and a sense of anticipation leading up to an event, the experience should peak with a holistically satisfying involvement among everyone – athletes, spectators, and sponsors. That requires much more activity than just the sporting competition itself. The sporting contest is the main event, to be sure, but enhancing the event experience around the competition for everyone involved will be what people talk about for years afterward. Reminiscing rarely focuses on who won.

FOLLOW-UP WITH RELATIONSHIP MARKETING

After all the prizes have been awarded and the gala finale is a memory, it is time to focus on post-event marketing. While relationship marketing efforts start long before the actual event, attendee experiences can be substantially influenced long after the event. Sports marketers need to devote communication efforts during this period, as well (Thompson, *et al.,* 2014). Too often, especially with events reliant on volunteer administrators, marketing activities fall silent afterward.

Among a broad audience, social media is one opportunity to engage attendees again and spark interest among non-attendees for next time. Visuals – images and video – are key to engaging interest and prompting conversations online. Create lots of short content to refresh social media frequently, and bear in mind that the window of interest opportunity is relatively short; a few weeks probably, depending on content. This phase of the marketing plan should reinforce how enjoyable the event was for all involved. Celebrate the great time enjoyed among all.

At a more focused individual level, targeted social media and personalized email campaigns should be used to reinforce loyalty. Reward attendees with personal attention. Share follow-up and ongoing offers available from sponsors. Point ahead to the next event so people can plan and offer reward incentives for early indications and commitments. Too often, in large and small events, the emphasis is directed into attracting new attendees each time. Our best customers are existing customers – reward loyalty. Individual recognition goes a long way.

Another important aspect of post-event marketing is to 'listen' online and take on-board feedback about event experiences. Monitoring social media after an event can provide useful insights about particular strengths and weaknesses in delivery. What specific aspects and activities really resonated with attendees? What issues created particular 'points-of-pain'? People do not hesitate to voice opinions online these days. Do listen, and be objective.

More focused than monitoring social media, attendee experience surveys can be useful to both collect valuable feedback and demonstrate a commitment to improving an event for the future. Even if response rates are low in absolute terms, distributing them does function as a marketing message. The initial introduction should highlight a positive message and, ideally, include a key visual. From there, keep questions short and to the point. The survey purpose should be easily evident to individuals and reflect genuine feedback that can be helpful. Attendees should feel they can make a difference in their experience.

Whatever channel is used to connect with participants and patrons, contact information is a valuable asset… it should be managed as such. All too often, contact data details and lists are managed by volunteer event administrators and databases stored across multiple formats, if at all. Sports marketers value this information, so establish a coordinated strategy for integrating marketing data into a secure database management and marketing information system.

PUTTING THE ENTIRE PLAN TOGETHER

Although limited resources – typically money, people, and time – may constrain small-scale sports event marketers, creative ideas and sound planning are achievable for everyone. Start with a comprehensive plan that breaks down all marketing activities into distinct phases and outcomes. This chapter offers one framework for dividing up key priorities.

First of all, consider the four main phases of event marketing…

- Planning period

Note timelines needed to develop marketing materials, book media partners, and recruit sponsors. Leading up to the desired launch announcement, marketing materials and channel partners need to be in place and available as media deadlines approach.

- Pre-event

Assess how much time is needed to create sufficient awareness, generate interest among target audiences, and spur action among attendees. Too little time, and the event is likely to be under-attended. Too *much* time, and early interest may erode as attention wanes. Often, it is helpful to define a few stages of pre-event marketing objectives. Start with an awareness of key details and build event familiarity. Next, move into marketing opportunities that engage people and foster momentum in the lead up to the actual event dates. Finally, maximize media exposure for a brief period before the event, activating participants, spectators, and supporters to commit.

- Event occasion

All marketing attention should be focused here on delivering the most enjoyable experience possible. Among participants and patrons alike, deliver on a great event experience. Often, attention and emphasis are directed toward showcasing the competition. No doubt, the sporting event is a prime focus and needs to function as required. However, all the ancillary activities will often influence long-term satisfaction. The event experience includes all aspects start-to-finish; the overall experience should seek to 'surprise and delight.'

- Post-event

Be sure to plan for follow-up marketing efforts with media and attendees during the weeks afterward. Mainly, attendees should feel appreciated. Leave them with an impression of 'thanks for coming, and we look forward to seeing you again.'

Next, identify and define the key target audiences for different marketing activities…

- Competitors and contenders – committed

Depending on the nature of a sporting event, there is most likely a core group of committed competitors who will seek to participate. These people are, effectively, loyal customers in every sense of the marketing term. They are also likely to be key influencers and can be valuable allies in promoting positive aspects of the event. Nurture their involvement and support their commitment.

- Participants and entrants – casual

Again, depending on the nature of the event, many participants may be more motivated by the social interaction offered in the event. Completing the event is valued, but enjoying a fun experience is the main motivator. It is vital to cater for social activities and engagements that create a delightful event environment and personal experience.

- Families and friends

A network of invested fans are directly connected to event participants. Consider how well they can be catered for. Support activities such as kids' zones and time-out areas, for example, are often appreciated. Recommendations throughout the local community and discount offers among sponsors add value to the experience. Lots of little 'acts of consideration' can assure a satisfying experience and encourage positive recommendations.

- Fans

One of the visible indicators of event success is often reflected in the total number of spectators attending. A broad range of marketing opportunities and activities can be executed to enhance fans' experiences. While event venue facilities may be relatively fixed, sponsors and the local community can be engaged as partners in many ways to broaden the overall event experience.

- Sponsors

Relationships with event sponsors are a two-way street. Develop various packages of benefits that will be valued by sponsors, either themselves directly, and as perks they can share with their business partners.

Finally, put together a marketing and media plan across options…

- Traditional media

Often, local media channels can be engaged as exclusive media-sponsoring partners. Television, radio, and newspapers, in particular, can be core partners in creating exposure and building awareness throughout the local community. Traditional media channels also maintain an online presence, as well.

- Digital media – event website

A strong website presence is important these days. It is essential to create a dynamic, easy-to-navigate website. A key focus in technical terms is to maximize the user experience (UX). Make it easy, informative, and enjoyable. And remember, more time is now spent on small screens.

- Digital media – online marketing

Start with SEO marketing priorities, look next at key website partners and network marketing opportunities, and then consider paid advertising options.

- Social media

Create event social media profiles in popular platforms. It is critical, though, to create fresh content frequently. Be active, often, on social media.

CONCLUSION

Setting out a coordinated marketing plan at the beginning can at least improve the odds of delivering a successful event. Within this framework, creative ideas can begin to flow.

Fortunately, abundant advice and examples specific to all these aspects are readily available on the Internet. As such, this chapter focuses on a framework for prioritizing marketing activities and constructing an achievable plan. Concentrating limited resources into critical marketing activities is key to delivering a great event experience. Following this framework is one tool to improve the odds.

REFERENCES

Berry, L. L. (2000). Cultivating service brand equity. *Journal of the Academy of Marketing Science*, *28*(1), 128–137. doi:10.1177/0092070300281012

Dichter, E. (1985). What's in an image. *Journal of Consumer Marketing*, *2*(1), 75–81. doi:10.1108/eb038824

Fetchko, M., Roy, D. P., & Clow, K. E. (2018). *Sports marketing*. Routledge. doi:10.4324/9781315175614

Fotiadis, A., Xie, L., Li, Y., & Huan, T. C. T. (2016). Attracting athletes to small-scale sports events using motivational decision-making factors. *Journal of Business Research*, *69*(11), 5467–5472. doi:10.1016/j.jbusres.2016.04.157

Fotiadis, A. K., Vassiliadis, C. A., & Sotiriadis, M. D. (2016). The preferences of participants in small-scale sport events: A conjoint analysis case study from Taiwan. *Turizam: međunarodni znanstveno-stručni časopis, 64*(2), 175-187.

Gantz, W., & Lewis, N. (2014). Sports on traditional and newer digital media: Is there really a fight for fans? *Television & New Media*, *15*(8), 760–768. doi:10.1177/1527476414529463

Gibson, H. J., Kaplanidou, K., & Kang, S. J. (2012). Small-scale event sport tourism: A case study in sustainable tourism. *Sport Management Review*, *15*(2), 160–170. doi:10.1016/j.smr.2011.08.013

Keller, K. L. (2001). *Building customer-based brand equity: A blueprint for creating strong brands*. Marketing Science Institute.

Merrilees, B., Getz, D., & O'Brien, D. (2005). Marketing stakeholder analysis: Branding the Brisbane goodwill games. *European Journal of Marketing*, *39*(9/10), 1060–1077. doi:10.1108/03090560510610725

Montana, J., Guzman, F., & Moll, I. (2007). Branding and design management: A brand design management model. *Journal of Marketing Management*, *23*(9-10), 829–840. doi:10.1362/026725707X250340

Parent, M. M., & Foreman, P. O. (2007). Organizational image and identity management in large-scale sporting events. *Journal of Sport Management*, *21*(1), 15–40. doi:10.1123/jsm.21.1.15

Priporas, C. V., Vassiliadis, C. A., Stylos, N., & Fotiadis, A. K. (2018). The effect of sport tourists' travel style, destination and event choices, and motivation on their involvement in small-scale sports events. *Event Management*, *22*(5), 745–765. doi:10.3727/152599518X15299559637707

Robinson, S., & France, A. (2011). Comparing sports marketing of amateur team sports to professional team sports. *New Zealand Journal of Applied Business Research*, *9*(1), 47.

Santomier, J. (2008). New media, branding and global sports sponsorship. *International Journal of Sports Marketing & Sponsorship*, *10*(1), 9–22. doi:10.1108/IJSMS-10-01-2008-B005

Sherwood, M., Nicholson, M., & Marjoribanks, T. (2017). Controlling the Message and the Medium? The impact of sports organisations' digital and social channels on media access. *Digital Journalism*, *5*(5), 513–531. doi:10.1080/21670811.2016.1239546

Thompson, A. J., Martin, A. J., Gee, S., & Eagleman, A. N. (2014). Examining the Development of a Social Media Strategy for a National Sport Organisation. *Journal of Applied Sport Management*, *6*(2).

Vassiliadis, C. A., & Fotiadis, A. (2016). Managing Sport Tourism Experiences: Blueprinting Service Encounters. In The Handbook of Managing and Marketing Tourism Experiences (pp. 195-215). Emerald Group Publishing Limited.

Veltri, F. R., Miller, J. J., & Harris, A. (2009). Club sport national tournament: Economic impact of a small event on a mid-size community. *Recreational Sports Journal*, *33*(2), 119–128. doi:10.1123/rsj.33.2.119

Xu, R., & Pegg, S. (2007). Exploring the motivations for participant engagement in the Australian university games. *International Journal of Event Management Research*, *3*(2), 39–46.

Chapter 10
Small-Scale Sports Event Sponsorship

Chris A. Vassiliadis
https://orcid.org/0000-0001-8814-1518
University of Macedonia, Greece

Iason George Skoulas
University of Macedonia, Greece

Sofia Gkarane
https://orcid.org/0000-0002-6057-5477
University of Macedonia, Greece

ABSTRACT

The readers of this chapter are expected to understand, through the description of the basic sponsorship operation procedures, the importance of supporting sport event-based business operations. To this end, following a brief introduction including a description of the international situation in the sports sponsorship market, as well as the necessary concepts, types of sponsorships, and developments, the structure of the book chapter focuses on the key elements of the content of a sponsorship management plan for small-scale sporting events. Also important is the contribution of this chapter by presenting, at the end, three small-scale sport events in clarifying how sponsors of a sporting event can be attracted and how the sponsorship exchange system can be more effective.

DOI: 10.4018/978-1-7998-4757-1.ch010

INTRODUCTION

Small events and especially small sport events depend on their success to attract sponsors. According to the relevant event management literature, sponsorship is an asset management component that contributes to the improvement of the financial index ROI (Return Of Investment) of an Event and Event Management business. More specifically, sponsorships are a revenue item for an event and as such supports an event's budget, covering a significant portion of the event's necessary expenses (Schnitzer, 2014; Cafferata, 2004). The main reasons for sponsoring sporting events by interested investors are the following: a) television performance and coverage, b) brand promotion and c) consumer attraction through event watching (Abratt, Clayton & Pitt, 1987). According to the International Events Group (IEG), in 2017, sponsored mainly sporting events, which was the main emerging promotional activity worldwide, with particular emphasis on the use of Social Media i.e., using mostly Facebook and Twitter as communication tools for promoting and activating sponsorships. Sports events compared to other type of events e.g. festivals, exhibitions, entertainment, art etc., attract the largest share of investor sponsors, accounting for 70% of the total annual budgets available for sponsorships internationally (IEG LLC, 2017, p.12, 29).

There are various definitions given to the term sponsorship. One of the dominant definitions is that of the International Chamber of Commerce (ICC). According to the ICC and the European Sponsorship Association (ESA), "sponsorship" is defined as *any commercial agreement through which a sponsor seeks the mutual benefit of the sponsor and the other parties to the sponsorship, and provides contractual funding or other support to establish a link between the sponsor's image, trademarks or products, and a granted ownership, for rights to promote this relationship and / or for the grant of certain agreed direct or indirect benefits* (ICC, 2018, p.26). Another useful definition is the following one of McCarville and Copeland (1994, p.103), based on these authors; *sponsorship involves an exchange of resources with an independent partner in hope of gaining a corresponding return from the sponsor. The notion of mutual return distinguishes sponsorship from other forms of corporate support like philanthropy, charity and patronage, which do not involve the advancement of commercial objectives. Sponsorship is undertaken so that both partners can benefit.* This definition gives a good description of the differences between other related actions like patronage, charity and philanthropy. In this chapter we use also the term "sponsor" to *describe that party that provides funds to a sporting event organizer in exchange for the right to affiliate with the sporting organization or to own certain promotional activities and actions relating to the event of the sporting event* (Sport New Zealand, 2012). Sponsors are usually looking for opportunities to promote their brands, products and services through this collaboration with the event organizer. They can be paying or an in-kind sponsors. The last promotes their product and services without paying.

Improper sponsorship management causes problems with the performance and financial viability of an sport event, especially when it is considered as small-scaled event and is often affected by the limited resources available to private equity owners. Small-scaled sport events, because of the visitors, participants and public they attract e.g., local populations of spectators, participants, and clients, often they don't have the bargaining power of large-scale events to attract large multinational sponsors for their actions. But this is not a problem, as small-scaled sport event organizers often overcome this weakness by seeking support and partnerships with sponsors of the domestic, regional, and local investor market. This sponsoring and partnership relations can be developed and vice versa, i.a., from the local sponsor to the organizer. Thus, this chapter notes those necessary administrative considerations and the actions needed to plan the sponsorhip business activities of the small-scaled sports events in order to make the cooperation of the two basic parts i.e., sponsors and event organisors, most effective.

BACKGROUND

The Choragos was in the ancient times (i.e., Fourth, Fifth & Sixth centuries B.C.) related with ancient Greek theatrical sponsors. The sponsor was a wealthy Athenian citizen who undertook the expenses to support the: e.g., theater production i.e., paying for the dance and musicians (Cornwell, 1995), training the teens for the Panathenaic and other festivals, maintenance of a trireme ship, offering food to all members of the tribe on the day of the great feast of the Panathenians and Dionysians, and horse-breeding for the army or for the big feasts. In 1896 during the first Modern Olympic Games, Kodak contributed to the Olympic Organizing Committee and promoted her Kodak logo in the first modern official program. During the Olympic Games in Amsterdam in 1928, the begins the first collaboration with the sponsoring company Coca Cola, which continues to be one of the the leading Olympic Games sponsors, until today (IOC, 2006).

Developing collaborative event organizer relationships with suppliers and customers is a great opportunity that may be due to the previous successful relationship effort that was triggered by the sponsorship. Local consumer healthy products e.g. Foods, non-alcoholic beverages, parapharmaceuticals, appropriate clothing and apparel from the local market e.g., can be easily promoted to wider audience groups of small-scale sport events as visitors and customers who shows a particular interest in traditional and local health products. Mount & Niro (1995) found in their study that small-scale event organizers appear to be effective in attracting sponsors from regional and local SME's. They use often communication tactics like personal contact and proposals, to attract sponsorships from SMEs (Slack & Bentz, 1996). Local SMEs usually want to, create and build their image to the community, increase awareness for their cooperation; their services and products, boost their positioning strategy using the event media promotion and exposure channels, and bring more visitors and other investors to their destination (Gartner and Shuman, 1988; Gwinner and Eaton, 1999; Gkarane and Vassiliadis, 2016). Mainly the sport sponsors select to invest their money to sponsor, not their own sport events but third – party- owned sport events (Mintel, 2011). A commercial sponsorship can be triggered when an exchange relationship is put in action. More specifically, this relationship is based at least on two partners who are interested for developing a win-to-win situation. Each of them expects, in the near future, a returned value or else i.e., financial benefit or other benefits from their sponsorship-investment (Molm, 1990).

The process begins usually from the event management staff, with the identification of potential sponsors for their event. At next the management staff prepare the sponsorship proposals. After the contract the responsible for sponsorship management staff, have to build and sustain long-term win-to-win relations with their event sponsors. In this situation the system of event sponsorship exchanges include three basic parts namely, the sponsor, the owner or property and the audience (Bowdin, Allen, O'Tool, Harris & McDonnell, 2011). The destination and community planners seek economic and local community benefits from organizing events in their regions. In the same line, the event visitors seek to enjoy positive experiences from their trip and destination and event visit e.g., from viewing and participating. However, sponsors try to fit their marketing purposes with those of the event organizer (i.e., sponsee) and they seek benefits (e.g., cause related marketing) from their participation in the event program. We can say that in the same manner, the organizer expects to attract a large number of profitable market segments (i.e., event visitors) for his sport event (Getz, 2003). The tourism Demand is related with five sports-tourism activities namely the, Events, Attractions, Tours, Resorts and Cruises. The Small Scale Sport Events are a whole product category with specific regional/national/international sports-events subcategories (Kurtzman, 2005). All those types and subcategories of sports-events often need for their financial and organizational & functional sustainability to use different means to attract sponsors from the business market.

The Environment of the Event Management System

The environment in which we analyze the development of event sponsorship functions involves different parts, also expressed as stakeholders, but also factors and relationships, based on the expected benefits and objectives of each. In the modern financial reality, the organizers/ sponsees or else expressed the event managers, needs to know the benefit expectations and wants of the parties, in order to negotiate the value of their own offer more effectively with the other parties.

This system includes the following key stakeholders, namely Audiences / Visitors (eg spectators, participants, visitors), Sponsors (eg businesses, organizations, institutions, corporate, media, public authorities and bodies) and the responsible organizer and owner of the event. In the next section, we present the diversity of the goals and benefits of the different parts that make up the operating environment of the sponsorship management system. Based on Bowdin et *al.*, (2011, p. 443-44), the three parts are expressed as "trinity of sponsor, event and audience".

Beneficial Relations of the Three Exchange-System Sponsorship Parts

In this business market, visitors, investors, working staff, people of the community i.e., are usually interested about an event and they are also motivated from different benefits they seek (Bladen, Kennell, Abson & Wilde, 2018, p.165; Parent, 2008). Table 1 shows the main utilities that are related with those basic parts of benefit-seekers. Soteriades (2013) in his article focuses on event sponsorship management and proposes relevant efficient management strategies. He even notes that sponsorship management is one of the most interesting functions that an event manager should have the ability and skills to perform. Sponsorship is a type of communication action that enforces the organization-public relationship (Broom, Casey, & Ritchey, 2000). In this manner the three parts in a sponsorship exchange system, develop relationships that are distinguished at three levels of communication, namely, personal, professional/business and social/community relations (Bruning & Ledingham, 1999; Ledingham & Bruning, 1998).

The beneficial relationships emerging through the contact system of these three parties could hypothetically function as follows:

- The event manager tries to attract sponsors and then maintain the relationship with them
- The sponsoring company selects profitable event organizers (sponsees) for its business function in order to succeed in its communication strategy. This procedure results more effectively through targeting unique specific audiences for the sponsor and the sponsees
- Event visitors, residents, and viewers expect the satisfaction of their personal, psychological, and social needs

Table 1. Benefits for the three parts in a sponsorship exchange system

	Source	Benefits (How can the sponsoring of sport events leverage the expectations of the parts?)		
		Owner/Property: Event Organizer or Sponsee	**Sponsor: Business**	**Audience: Event Visitors, Community**
1	Bowdin, Allen, O'Tool, Harris & McDonnell, 2011, p.448; Crompton, 1994	*Financial investment *In-kind services *Marketing and media expertise *Event brand enhancement *Product and service offers for event goers	*Influencing consumer attitudes *Building & Increasing brand awareness for the corporation and the product(s)/services * Corporate & Product Brand image creation & enhancement *Product trial/ service exposure *Sales or hospitality opportunities *Market interactivity *Access to specific niche/target markets * Associating products and services with lifestyles *Improving product sales and merchandising opportunities *Demonstrating product/service attributes *Employee rewards and recognition *Crating goodwill and climate about the corporation/organization *Entertaining key clients with corporate hospitality	
2	Getz, 2005; Crompton, & McKay, 1997; Iso Ahola, 1983			Event visitors: *Escape the personal and/or the interpersonal world *Seeking personal and/or interpersonal rewards
3	Kim, 2013			Event visitors: *Friendly place (Feeling as a good resident) *The sport event (The game Itself) *Financial aspects and offers (Economical sport event tourism)
4	Bladen, Kennell, Abson & Wilde, 2018; Kahle, Kambara & Rose, 1996; Kim & Chalip, 2004 (+)			*Enjoy camaraderie of attending with like-minded people *Feel obligated to attend as a result of history of attending (+)Impact factors to attend an event: *Perceived risk of attending *Financial constraints
5	Crompton, 1996		*Increase awareness *Image enhancement *Product trial or sales opportunities *Hospitality opportunities	
6	Delpy, Grabijas, & Stefanovich, 1998		*Opportunities to introduce and promote new products to a marketplace *Differentiate and sell product *Reward sales staff *Entertain current and/or potential clients *Increase media and public exposure *Enhance or change an image *Improve employee morale *Reach new market segments and distribution channels *Lock out competitors	

continued on following page

Table 1. Continued

	Source	Benefits (How can the sponsoring of sport events leverage the expectations of the parts?)		
		Owner/Property: Event Organizer or Sponsee	**Sponsor: Business**	**Audience: Event Visitors, Community**
7	Mason, 2005; Meenaghan, 2001		*Influence in a more easy way, of the attitudes and behavior toward brand	*Consumer engagement by bestowing benefit on an activity which the consumer has an intense emotional response to *Visitors with the highest involvement and most awareness of a sponsor's investment and benefit are the ones that are most pleased (satisfied)
8	Schulenkorf & Schlenker, 2017; Schulenkorf & Edwards, 2012; Smith 2012; Lane, Murphy & Bauman, 2013; Eley & Kirk, 2002	*Small-scale events lack the large capital expenditure and financial risks and can use more profitable the money they attract from the business part *Utilizing local infrastructure *Can be a tool to reduce social inequality through accessibility for people with disabilities with financial and SCR-policy benefits also for the organizer *A path for increasing physical activities *Event organizers and host community can bring to the community through cooperation, social integration		*Small-scale events enforce social relationships of the local population with the event (i.e., build connections between investors, local authorities, destination managers, volunteers, residents) *Can bring greater concern for leveraging community sport events in the context of social disadvantage *Can change attitudes of the next generations about their place and social, cultural, political differences of the residents
9	Preuss, 2006	*International reputation *Urban (Rural) revival *Increased tourism and visitors *Quality of life, workplaces *Place promotion *Inter-regional planning and cooperation policy and strategies *Production of investment ideas and cultural values *Education	*Local business opportunities and activities (i.e., market targeting, product and brand management strategies, corporate promotional activities) *Opportunities for City Marketing strategies and actions	*Improved public welfare *Additional temporary employment and income for the residents *Renewed community spirit
10	Ross, 2001	*Attract tourists (e.g., high-yield and repeaters) *Can generate increased rate of tourism growth *Enforce economic sustainability & grow (lodgings, F&B, retailing) *Exposure and enhances positive image for the community *Helps the favorable image and brand - place building and the new product creation strategy for the event destination *Can maximize the facility use in the event community *Helps to secure a financial legacy for management of new sport facilities and events in the destination * Can increase community support for sport and sport-events	*Use the media to extend the normal communications reach	*Building community relationships and strengthens corporate support *Creates youth opportunity / entertainment *Helps to enforce the develop of new infrastructure for the residents and event visitors *Improve the organizational, marketing, and bidding capability of the community

continued on following page

Table 1. Continued

	Source	Benefits (How can the sponsoring of sport events leverage the expectations of the parts?)		
		Owner/Property: Event Organizer or Sponsee	**Sponsor: Business**	**Audience: Event Visitors, Community**
11	Soteriades, 2013	*Cash and or in-kind event support * The event is strengthened via revenue and resources	*The spread of the brand, products and services and the need for brand awareness *Effective methods and tools by communicating *The emphasis on customer relationship management *Imperative for efficiency *You can reduce the firm's promotional budget	*Leisure experience(s) *Enforce unique social environments *Be in accordance with the requirements of modern lifestyle (growing interest in sports and arts)
12	Malchrowicz-Mosko & Poczta, 2018	*Successfully impact tourist revival policy *Helps the improvement of regions' image *More simply (Do not have to compete for the rights to organize the event) *The hosts can use the existing sports infrastructure and already have experience in organizing the event	*Benefits from the participation of sport fans and athletes (amateurs & professionals) as key market targets	*Streat-style sporting events attract tourists and can build tourists; loyalty to the events
13	Bazzanella, Peters & Schnitzer, 2019		*Important leverage for brand strategy	*Extend the tourism season *Can be scheduled also in low tourism season

Note: Self-created table based on the selected sources of the literature review

The condition for effective cooperation between the parties in the sponsorship exchange system includes the following conditions for success (Bowdin, et al., 2011; Gwinner and Bennet, 2008):

- Reinforce the distinctiveness of the brand and its products / services due to its level of reputation and recognition
- Investigate the relevance, attractiveness and relation of the event to the interests and preferences of the audience (i.e., visitors, athletes)
- Identify the type and the profile of events and the relevance, attractiveness and relationship of the sponsor's products and services to the event
- Investigate the event's organizer and his audience attitudes, about sponsor's products and services
- Act as a sponsor-copartner or well wisher and support the event by serving and facilitating the event's visitors and also the event's audience market in the name of the event organizer
- Check if it's more useful to act as a sponsor-copartner or well wisher, and support the event by serving and facilitating the event's visitors and also the event's audience market in the name of the event organizer
- Check if the event can support the sponsor's purchase policy of products and services

Small-scale events due to their characteristics such as restricting available funds, staff resources, equipment and media influencing capabilities should carefully plan their management and organizational activities. In particular they should ensure that their presence on the E-Social Media is continuous and efficient, social media tools such, Facebook, You Tube, Twitter, are free and it's easy to use them for their users (Wankel, Marovich & Stanaityte, 2010, p.229). The increasingly common use of Social Media is a contemporary reality associated with the lifestyle and convenience of consumers who seem to prefer them more and more for their information and for completing their financial transactions (Thorpe, 2017). Social media brings new relationship experiences between the parts of a social e network and can change the interaction level between different geo-located groups, people and parts (Lim, Hwang, Kim & Biocca 2015; Hambrick, 2012). Important marketing aspects for the brand name strategy success of the organizer, local community and business parts are the psychological commitment of visitors and customers to a brand i.e., event's brand name, sponsor's corporate, product and services brands but also specific actions that are related with the investigation of the behavioral loyalty status and to investigate the status of behavioral loyalty of the visitors and customers e.g., visitor and customer behavior and intentions to buy and to suggest to others (Popp, & Woratschek, 2016; Bauer, Stokburger-Sauer, & Exler, 2008; Koo, Quartermann, & Flynn, 2006). In their research about social media and branded communities, Popp and Woratschek (2016) conclude, that sport-event sponsors, benefits from an increase in brand loyalty because of his loyal sport fans, but also that sport is a perfect tool for deploying branded communities and helps to increase the awareness level of corporate names and their product and services. A distinct and recognizable brand name reflects the profile of the event organizer as well as the sponsor's identity, while also supports the corporate identity and helps to distinguishing them from competitors (Koo, Quartermann, & Flynn, 2006). Success for recognizing small event products and services, depends on recognizing the event's sign and logo that can be communicated earlier through activities involving the presence of the brand name, logo and the aim of the event on Social Media platforms and related audiences and e-communities. Then the effort can be supported in the venue, for example by printing and using t-shirts with the event's brand name, decorating the venue with details of the event's brand name, selling souvenirs with the event's brand, and other more. Communicating the value proposition of the customer, as well as offering a brand of promise of unique experiences in the field, can be important aspects of a successful event (Parent, Eskerud & Hanstad, 2012).

Sponsorship promotion is an important point of reference for the organizer's Marketing Program. Indeed, a key question for managers is whether a particular sporting event i.e., his Values, Culture and attributes can capture the interest and attract the attention of the audience, the local community or visitors, that the sponsor wishes to reach (Lough and Irwin, 2001). Matching the expected benefits between the two parties, i.e., sponsors and organizers, is a pillar of success for both the organizer and the Sponsor's MKT Plan. This specificity can gradually lead to the development of joint projects and to the strengthening of professional relationships between them. An in-depth study and proposal for future research based on the results and conclusions of this chapter would be the process of identifying the factors that influence the performance of small-scale events e.g., for different categories of sports per sponsored product categories. Research shows that many studies in the knowledge field of sponshorship research are related with one or more of the three basic sponsorship effect dimensions, namely the "awareness", "image", and "Purchase intention and other effects" like financial value (Walliser, 2003).

The following figure 1 shows the major component criteria of cooperation between the two parts, with a unique view to a beneficial embodiment of a sponsorship. The process for the final sponsorship partnership can be analyzed based on three action phases (Douvis, Sarli, Kriemadis, & Vrondou, 2015, p.30-33), namely the: 1st., "Information collection", 2nd., "Proposal preparation or receipt of proposal and evaluation" and 3rd., "Negotiations and contact development and signing". The process can vary from three weeks to five months.

The end result of the effort to develop a sponsorship communication campaign is to attract appropriate visitors, participants and listeners to the event. The process of selecting a sporting event e.g. by visitors, users and listeners, it is supported by the degree of goodwill shown in the sponsor's branded products but also by the degree of their active involvement in the sporting event and its support (Meenaghan, 2001). According to Priporas, Vassiliadis, Stylos & Fotiadis (2018), athletes self view-perceptions and their fit with the values and the event brand and image are important aspects for the selection and of course for the attractiveness of small-sports events. Changes in the travel style of sport tourists positively affect the level of involvement in sport events but also their motivation to participate in sport events. The above authors also confirmed with their study that the motivation of sport tourists to participate in sports events positively affects their level of involvement. An important factor in the communication strategy to be followed by the organizer of a small-scale event for the success of the sponsorship program is the relationships it has developed with those who influence the public from viewers of sporting events and consumers i.e., opinion leaders, makers like famous VIP personas, Editors and Directors of local, regional and national media, social media Influentials. Sponsorships are an important part of the overall effort to bring a positive image and attitude to the sporting event and to the overall product that can satisfy the end user through particularly enjoyable and unique experiences. (Barez, Manion, Schoepfer, & Cherian, 2007; Anthony, 1981).

Sponsors react as investors and they recognize by organizer's sponsorship programs (sponsees), the opportunities for their businesses and their related products (Grohs and Reisinger, 2014). “Entertainment and festivities” can attract and motivate the group of sport event visitors to visit the area because they may feel that this place and the sponsored products and services during the event are related with their life style, their personal needs and expectations. Small-scaled sporting events visitors can experience different social situations i.e., storytelling nights, local business products, and unique activities, as well as they can participate in extraordinary or unusual activities that are not promised and implemented by competitors or other events e.g., with combining competitions, racing, music and cultural events and activities in their sport programs (Priporas et al., 2018, p. 259). Sport event organizers are important to design for their sponsors, customer oriented sponshorship proposals with the scope to leverage their promotional strategy (Miloch and Lambrecht, 2006).

Sponsors use specific criteria, also known as screening criteria, for selecting and ranking sporting events, in order to subsequently allocate invested funds dedicated to promoting the company and its products. Basic sponsor related selection criteria for selecting sponsorship can be the following one (Douvis, et al, 2015, p.24): Image enhancement, Revenue opportunities, Geographical coverage of its target market by sponsee, Financial health of potential partner, Prospective contract’s terms. “Image enhancement” seems to be important for event organizers (sponsees) and sponsors, and the “same brand characteristics,” “prior quality of relationship” and “revenue opportunities” also for some of them.

Crompton suggests in his article a mnemonic acronym namely the “CEDAR EEE” screening criteria construct (Crompton, 1993, p.105; Bowdin et al., 2011, p. 469). According to his proposal, the next eight criteria are important for business organisations to determine which sponsorship opportunities will be supported. The first identification in this checklist is related with the “Customer Audience”, the second with the “Exposure Reach”, the third with the “Distribution Channel Support”, the fourth with the “Competitive Advantage”, the fifth with the “Level of Resource Investment Required”, the sixth with the “Organization’s Reputation”, the seventh with the “Event Characteristics” and finally the eighth with the “Entertainment or Hospitality Opportunities”, (Crompton 1993; Bowdin et al., 2011, p. 470-471; Douvis, et al, 2015). Small-scale event organizers (sponsees) and business investors (sponsors) can support their day-to-day sponsorship management functions by adopting the evaluation tools outlined above. For example, both the organizer of the event and the potential sponsor need to clearly identify the recipients of the sponsorship actions in order to have a successful outcome in their communication and business marketing strategy. Recipients of sponsorship actions may be e.g. event visitors in the electronic and conventional environment, amateur and professional athletes, the general public or local community, local, regional and public authorities, business and other stakeholders.

Figure 1. Basic criteria that affect the sponsorship proposal of the organizer

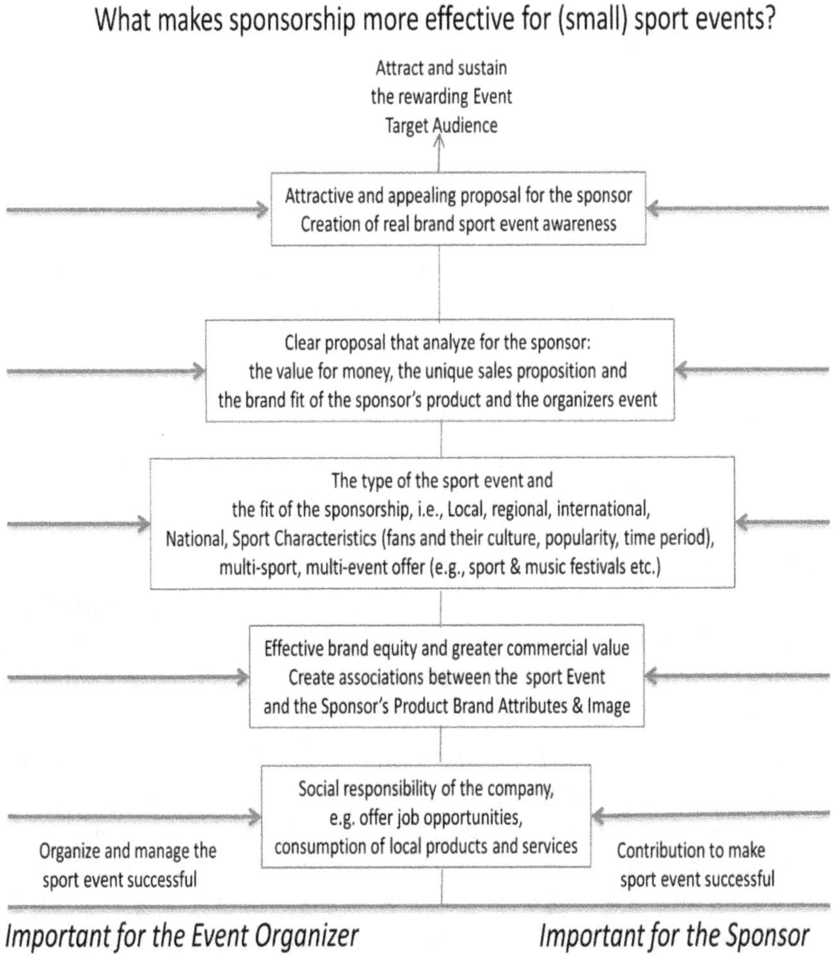

Sources: Own creation based on Kim J-W., (2010) The worth of sport event sponsorship: an event study *Journal of Management and Marketing Research* 5(1), 1-14. Sport New Zealand (2012) New Zealand Government, Sport Sponsorship; Securing and retaining commercial partners, Wellington: NZ. ISBN:1-977356-28-5.

The exposure reach is also an important aspect that has to be analyzed in a sponsorship partnership exchange. Sponsor's product brand recall but also sponsee's event brand recalls are affected from the type of exposure and the related type of international audience e.g., direct active visitors in the event venue or the indirect wider public target audience of the media users e.g., time line and broadcast platform for the presentation of the event on the social media (i.e., Facebook, Instagram, Twitter, YouTube, Snapchat, Pinterest, Weibo, WeChat) and electronic and non electronic media (i.e., TV, Radio broadcasting, transit advertising using transportation means, stable billboard advertising, outdoor and indoor mall advertising, newspapers, newsletters, periodicals, etc.). Exposure to the message may include a joint effort of both, e.g., the organizer and the sponsor, to promote the event and the sponsor's product and services, by sharing their available distribution channels as well as points of sale at which they can locally, regionally or even nationally, enhance their presence. For example, the organizer may participate with a team of athletes of his organization in a corresponding other sporting event. During his presence there, he can display in his organized exhibition stand both offers i.e., his planned sport event that concerns him and the products of his event-sponsors (Ko, Kim, Clausen & Kim, 2008; Levin, Joiner, Cameron, 2001). Similarly, sponsors can promote the sport event through e.g., electronic social media, point-of-sale information, sales promotion programs, advertising campaigns, public relations, or CSR (Corporate Social Responsibility) programs, combining their products and values with business culture and the philosophy of the event offering. Sponsors can be involved thru their presence in e.g., special small sport events with the hobbies and activities of the consumers who recognize and respect I their every day life this business interest. Adapting brand image positioning strategies to audience interests and beliefs is not an easy marketing function, e.g. by using other media means (Zarantonello and Schmitt, 2013). Sponsorship thru using small sport events can be more effective by fitting the Demand side needs, desires and wishes with those of the Supply side e.g., while contributing to the successful completion of the marketing and communication goals (Pappu and Cornwell, 2014; Dolphin, 2003; Scheinbaum, Finney, Lacey and Sneath, 2006; Miloch and Lambrecht, 2006). Advertising strategy and other communication tools i.e., the communication mix, can be activated in a parallel way, and they can contribute as a key synergetic supplement to the success of the sponsorship communication strategy (Pope and Voges, 2000; Tripodi, 2001).

Intermediaries or else the distribution channels (e.g., national, regional, local media platforms, local travel agents, media and communication providers) in this sponsorship system are another important factor for sponsoring's proposal success. Organizers of small-scale events can make synergies with the right intermediaries to ensure that the message connection between the business sponsor partners and their desired target audiences will be completed effectively. Travel agencies as interested members could promote the event and its sponsors, as well as local authorities, intermediaries in support of tourism activities e.g. Destination and event promotion websites, can distribute the brand value, the products and services of event sponsors as wholesalers, suppliers and retailers in this relationship sponsorship exchange system. (Tiew, Holmes, & De Bussy, 2015; Kriemadis and Kartakoulis, 2011; Crompton, 1993).

The event selection process from the business investor (sponsor) and specifically the small sport event selection procedure is important part of the management decision procedure for the sponsor's media promotion strategy program. It is also important at this stage to decide which other competitors support the event or event, or whether there may be a partnership sponsorship of the company with another sponsor, active in a sector other than its own product category sponsor. Because of the variety and the wide supply range of types and sports events this process cannot be described as easy, especially if we consider that there is a rational management decision limit to the selection of the most efficient events. Choosing the right sporting event depends on whether it can be linked to unique situations and experiences that will impress viewers and consumers of the event's products and sponsors. Experience based event customer management can leveraging the sponsor's marketing and brand equity communication strategy, because of the direct contact with the individuals and especially with people that are passionate about this or this kind of sports events. Positive experiences can then support donors' efforts for effective image-making and oral commentary activities in the conventional and electronic environment (e.g., positive Word of Mouth, e-WoM) (Reic, 2017; Donlan and Crowther, 2014; Breuer and Rumpf, 2012; Tynan and McKechnie, 2009; Nicholls and Roslow, 1999; Crompton, 1993).

Related with this event selection procedure is also the opportunity to be able to distinguish the company from the competition through the selection of the sporting event and to differentiate it from the competition in the eyes of consumers by building their own positive image in their minds. For the event organizers attracting appropriate sponsors means also attracting people for their events. The presence of other sponsors in the event sponsorship and the possible ambush marketing scenarios about the competition must be also taken in to account (Walker, Hall, Todd, & Kent, 2011; Crompton, 1993).

The investment of resources (e.g., money, time, human resources, in-kind investments) and funds is also a key factor for the sponsor's sponsorship administrative decisions. What will be the amount of investment? What is the amount of sponsorship costs overall and by type? For example, will the small-scale sporting event be sponsored by the sponsoring company with a sponsorship of handling time and space in the media? What are the Fees for the Rights? E.g., for sports-event organisor, music event rights? What are the sponsorhip activation costs and the costs for ancillary activities, like an experiential communication campaign? What is the amount of sponsorship costs per category for graphic design, printing, radio promotion, online banners, and social media? What category of event organisor sponsorship is to be invested and what is the amount of the final costs? e.g., Cost for Tera sponsor, Giga sponsor, Mega-sponsorship, Platinum sponsor, Golden sponsor, Silver sponsor, Main-Major Sponsor, Media sponsorship, Supporter, Travel-, Lodging/Venue-, Transportation-, Catering- sponsor etc. (Reic, 2017; Crompton, 1993).

Members of the sponsorship system often face the challenge of identifying capable partners who responsibly, diligently, and confidently support the issues of collaboration and coordination of the sponsorship. The previous history of each member's partnerships influences both the final decision and the successful evolution of the small sport event sponsorship activities. As can be seen, the reputation of the sponsorship partner can influence the evolution of any sponsorship proposal. Also event organisers have to seek the right Sponsor Business Managers (General, regional, local and Brand managers) and to negotiate with them about the win-to-win event situation. They have to describe and present the Value to the Sponsor e.g., higher level of repeat sales, up-selling opportunities, cross-selling opportunities and etc (Crompton, 2014; 1993).

Also in the sponsorship planning process, an important feature for the sponsorship success is the hosting alternatives and characteristics but also and the event's entertainment opportunities. The process of enriching the benefits for spectators and participants, in a sporting event, is a common concern both for the potential sponsor/investor and the organizer/ sponsee of the event. Event destinations are "Servicescapes" in other words places with "facility's exterior, for example, landscape design, weather conditions, outdoor emotional effects (smelling, hearing, etc.), signs, and interior characteristics, for, example, ambiance, interior design, look and type of other customers and staff", (Vassiliadis and Fotiadis, 2016, pp.199) where the service manager can be responsible for right type of the offer mix in this Servicescape. In small-scale sport events, athletes and visitors are aware with the social environment, they usually know each other from past, from the athletic web, and the social media applications (Line, Hanks, & McGinley, 2018). Vassiliadis and Fotiadis (2016, pp. 201-209) describe in their analysis a small-scale sport event blueprinting approach for the service design of sporting events with the scope to improve the quality of services they provide. In the Physical Evidence area of this Services Blueprint they define 13 basic activities that are related with customer actions. These services blueprints can act as small sport-event improvement-planning tools, with the emphasis to event offer problematic areas which negatively affect the whole customer and spectator experience. The above authors present the "SMF small scale-sport event 2013", which is a small-scale sports event where Servicescape venue places have been designated for the development of events and activities for athletes, attendants and children. Exhibition areas, dining areas, free camping sites, traditional small train transport (sponsored by EOT), parking and ancillary services, childcare playground spaces, party and entertainment venue spaces, and VIP hosting area, are some important Servicescape spaces in their analysis. These spaces should be refined through design processes in a long-term basis. Strategic long-term analysis based on services blueprints can enforce the creation, development, and maintenance of the event's sustainable competitive advantage. In the same time they leverage the opportunity to develop more attractive event offers for the sponsors and their product-service offer.

CONCLUSION

Despite the growing research approach to the sponsorship phenomenon, the process of evaluating the performance of a sponsorship program is still a concern for practitioners and management people in practice. This chapter presents the key components of a sponsorship system. Emphasis is placed on the expected benefits that key parts of the system expect and, concluding the chapter, analyzes the key issues to consider in developing a co-operative and sustainable sponsorship program.

Case Study: The Sponsorship Problematic - The Case of the Three Small-Scaled Sport Events

The following case study presents three small-scale sports events that are examples of the Greek sports reality. The reader of the case can acquire the ability to identify common and different elements related to the way of organizing and managing resources and the dynamics of each event in attracting sponsorships. Comparing the three sporting events between them we notice that their choice was made deliberately since the first (SMF) concerns an open-air rural area next to a village, the second (Almira-Man) concerns a coastal area next to a summer settlement and finally the third (Yedi Kule Conquest) concerns an urban area with a cultural heritage. Due to the different characteristics of the sports and programs that follow these three special events, the reader is expected to identify the differences and answer the following questions that enable him to perceive and discuss the relevant theory of sports sponsorship management.

Read the information of the following table about three small-scale sport events.

1. Visit the web addresses of the websites listed below and below the table. What kind of audience does each event address?
2. Identify the products promoted by the sponsor and determine if they are compatible with the target audience. For convenience, you can make assumptions and build on the theory of Ansoff (Ansoff, 1957; Ansoff Matrix; https://en.wikipedia.org/wiki/Ansoff_Matrix).
3. Consider sponsored communication support. Comment on whether it is appropriate for the audience that is attracted to each event, and express them by substantiating your arguments.

Table 2. Three Small Scaled Sport Event Cases from Greece

Small Scaled Sport Event	Start Year	Organizer(s)	Supporter(s) / Sponsor(s)
1.SMF (Sfendami Mountain Festival)- *Biathlon sport event* ~800 Athletes [300 Runners & 500 Bikers (mtb)]	2007 until today (**)	Investor and manager: Mr. Haralambos Tsanaktsidis and his Sfendamos team	• Supporters: -Municipality of Pidna Kolindros - Sub-Regional Administration Pieria - Municipal Environmental Civilization Culture & Family support body of Kolindros - Selected Group of Special Rescue Missions of Thessaloniki (EPOMEA) • Sponsors: -SHIMANO, bicycle components, fishing tackle and rowing equipment -Autovision, car quality control services -Amstel, Breweries -Pharmnet.gr, Health and Beauty, cosmetics -DIOS, mineral water -IDEAL, bikes -LOUX, soft drinks -SCOTT, bikes -OTE, Performance nutrition • Media sponsors: -Live Media, Live event broadcast production, encoding and distributing of video over the internet
2. *Almira Man-Triathlon sport event* ~415 Athletes ~2.500 Visitors	2014 until today	Investor and manager: Mr. Papadopoulos Iordanis and his team	• Supporters: -Municipality of Katerini, -Sub-Regional Administration Pieria -Police Department - TRIAS, Sport & Culture Association -University of Macedonia -Nautical club Katerini -Greek Red Cross -Life quad Patrol - Mountaineering club Vrontous - Greek Orthodox Metropolis of Kitros, Katerini & Platamon • Sponsors: -PowerBar, sports nutrition -Amstel, Breweries -Magia & Vini, Bier Club -SHIMANO, bicycle components, fishing tackle and rowing equipment -Dole, Bananas -OMNI, sounds & lights support -Carbonfix (gr), repair services -Konstantopoulos S.A., Food-Industry -Tsaousidis Vasilios, Bakery -DIOS, mineral water -CookLife, catering -Olymous Riviera Mediterranean Hotels, Lodgings -Orthopetalia, Bike services -KTEL Pierias, Bus services -PITSIAS Market -NewLife, sport nutrition -Almira Beach Bar -Pepsi, cola company -Top cycles, cycling retail shop -Bistro 49, café-restaurant - MAXI, paper industry -Aegean highway, road infrastructure management and services -Compres sport, sport accessories • Media sponsors: -O.B.gr, e-news -101.5 Olympus, radio station

continued on following page

Table 2. Continued

Small Scaled Sport Event	Start Year	Organizer(s)	Supporter(s) / Sponsor(s)
3. *Yedi Kule Conquest* - *Multi-purpose event* ~210 Athletes ~1.500 Visitors	2015 until today	Sfendamos – NPO, with co-organizer the Thessaloniki Tourism Organization	• Supporters: -SMF, Timing -University of Macedonia -Civil protection volunteers (ΕΠ.ΟΜ.Ε.Α.) -Traffic police -Ephorate of Antiquities of Thessaloniki City -UNESCO -International Trade of Thessaloniki (ΔΕΘ) -State Theater of Northern Greece (ΚΘΒΕ) -AKMH, College -Movement for Greek Monument Free Visit (KEME) • Sponsors: -Aithrio, café -Alba, WC solutions -KYANA, cosmetics -LOUX, soft drinks -SCOTT, bikes -Olympic Museum/Protergia, electricity -Kreonidis "The Balcony", Traditional Tavern -Camelbak, recreation equipment -ANALOGIA, Engineering and Consulting • Media sponsors: -ERT3, TV station -95,1 Kosmo-Radio, Radio station -Plus 102, 6 - Radio station - FM 100, TV station -Live Media, Live event broadcast production, encoding and distributing of video over the internet -102fm & 9,58fm ERT Radio station -103 MORE, radio station

The SMF (*), the Almira Man as well as the Jedi Kule Conquest, are some examples of successful sponsorship partnerships with business and non-business stakeholders.

Notes: Where (*) the corresponding formal website of the event organizer: http://www.sfendami.com/?lang=en, https://www.almiraman.gr/english/almiraman_en.html & https://www.yedikule.gr/

(**): Today = the year of promoting the next sport event of 2020.

4. What do you observe about working with other stakeholders? What organizational issues, what strengths and weaknesses can arise?
5. What kind of benefits would the members of the *sponsorship exchange system* expect?
6. How would you plan the sponsorship proposal of the event organizer to achieve its goals?

REFERENCES

Abratt, R., Clayton, B. C., & Pitt, L. F. (1987). Corporate Objectives in Sports Sponsorship. *International Journal of Advertising*, *6*(4), 299–311. doi:10.1080/02650487.1987.11107030

Ansoff, I. (1957). Strategies for Diversification. *Harvard Business Review*, *35*(5), 113–124.

Antony, M. (1981). *Handbook of Small Business Advertising*. Addison-Wesley Publishing Company, Inc.

Barez, A., Manion, M. T., Schoepfer, K. L., & Cherian, J. (2007). Global Cases of Effective Sports Sponsorship: An Exploration of a New Communications Model. *Innovative Marketing*, *3*(3), 69–77.

Bauer, H. H., Stokburger-Sauer, N. E., & Exler, S. (2008). Brand Image and Fan Loyalty in Professional Team Sport: A Refined Model and Empirical Assessment. *Journal of Sport Management*, *22*(2), 205–226. doi:10.1123/jsm.22.2.205

Bazzanella, F., Peters, M., & Schnitzer, M. (2019). The perceptions of stakeholders in small-scale sporting events. *Journal of Convention & Event Tourism*, *20*(4), 261–286. Advance online publication. doi:10.1080/15470148.2019.1640819

Bladen, C., Kennell, J., Abson, E., & Wilde, N. (2018). *Events management: an introduction* (2nd ed.). Routledge.

Bowdin, G. A. J., Allen, J., O'Toole, W., Harris, R., & McDonnell, I. (2011). *Events Management* (3rd ed.). Butterworth-Heinemann, Elsevier.

Breuer, C., & Rumpf, C. (2012). The viewer's reception and processing of sponsorship information in sport telecasts. *Journal of Sport Management*, *26*(6), 521–531. doi:10.1123/jsm.26.6.521

Broom, G. M., Casey, S., & Ritchey, J. (2000). Concepts and theory of organization-public relationships. In J. A. Ledingham & S. D. Bruning (Eds.), *Public relations as relationship management: A relational approach to the study and practice of public relations* (pp. 3–22). Lawrence Erlbaum Associates.

Bruning, S. D., & Ledingham, J. A. (1999). Relationships between organizations and publics: Development of a multi-dimensional organization-public relationship scale. *Public Relations Review*, *25*(2), 157–170. doi:10.1016/S0363-8111(99)80160-X

Cafferata, R. (2004). Governance and Management in the Business of Sport. *Symphonia-Emerging issues in Management, 2*, 5-25.

Cornwell, T. B. (1995). Sponsorship-linked marketing development. *Sport Marketing Quarterly*, *4*(4), 13–24.

Crompton, J. (1993). Understanding a business organization's approach to entering a sponsorship partnership. *Festival Management & Event Tourism*, *1*(3), 98–109. doi:10.3727/106527093792337565

Crompton, J. (1994). Benefits and risks associated with sponsorship of major events. *Festival Management & Event Tourism, 2*(2), 65–74. doi:10.3727/106527094792292050

Crompton, J. (1996). The potential contributions of sports sponsorship in impacting the product adoption process. *Managing Leisure, 1*(4), 199–212. doi:10.1080/136067196376302

Crompton, J. (2014). Potential negative outcomes from sponsorship for a sport property. *Managing Leisure, 19*(6), 420–441. doi:10.1080/13606719.2014.912050

Delpy, L., Grabijas, M., & Stefanovich, A. (1998). Sport tourism and corporate sponsorship: A winning combination. *Journal of Vacation Marketing, 4*(1), 91–101. doi:10.1177/135676679800400108

Dolphin, R. (2003). Sponsorship: Perspectives on its strategic role. *Corporate Communications, 8*(3), 173–186. doi:10.1108/13563280310487630

Donlan, L., & Crowther, P. (2014). Leveraging sponsorship to achieve consumer relationship objectives through the creation of 'marketing spaces': An exploratory study. *Journal of Marketing Communications, 20*(4), 291–306. doi:10.1080/13527266.2012.684068

Douvis, J., Sarli, E., Kriemadis, A., & Vrondou, O. (2015). An Analysis of Sponsorship Deals in Sport. *International Journal of Sport Management, Recreation and Tourism, 17*, 14–36. doi:10.5199/ijsmart-1791-874X-17b

Eley, D., & Kirk, D. (2002). Developing Citizenship through Sport: The Impact of a Sport-Based Volunteer Programme on Young Sport Leaders. *Sport Education and Society, 7*(2), 151–166. doi:10.1080/1357332022000018841

Fink, J. S., Trail, G. T., & Anderson, D. E. (2002). Environmental factors associated with spectator attendance and sport consumption behavior: Gender and team differences. *Sport Marketing Quarterly, 11*, 8–19.

Gartner, M. P., & Shuman, P. (1988). Sponsorships and small businesses. *Journal of Small Business Management, 26*(4), 44–52.

Getz, D. (2003). Sport Event Tourism: Planning, Development, and Marketing. In S. Hudson (Ed.), *Sport and Adventure Tourism*. Haworth Hospitality Press.

Getz, D. (2005). *Event Management and Event Tourism* (2nd ed.). Cognizant Communication Corporation.

Gkarane, S., & Vassiliadis, C. (2016). Blueprinting an Event & Customer Oriented Marketing Mix: The Case of the Sfendami Mountain Festival Small Scale Event. *International Journal of Strategic Innovative Marketing*, *3*, 13–28.

Grohs, R., & Reisinger, H. (2014). Sponsorship effects on brand image: The role of exposure and activity involvement. *Journal of Business Research*, *67*(5), 1018–1025. doi:10.1016/j.jbusres.2013.08.008

Gwinner, K. P., & Bennet, J. (2008). The Impact of Brand Cohesiveness and Sport Identification on Brand Fit in a Sponsorship Context. *Journal of Sport Management*, *22*(4), 410–426. doi:10.1123/jsm.22.4.410

Gwinner, K. P., & Eaton, J. (1999). Building Brand Image through Event Sponsorship: The Role of Image Transfer. *Journal of Advertising*, *28*(4), 47–57. doi:10.1080/00913367.1999.10673595

Hambrick, M. E. (2012). Six degrees of information: Using social network analysis to explore the spread of information within sport social networks. *International Journal of Sport Communication*, *5*(1), 16–34. doi:10.1123/ijsc.5.1.16

ICC. (2018). ICC Advertising and Marketing Communications Code; Building consumer trust through responsible marketing. Paris: International Chamber of Commerce (ICC).

IEG. LLC. (2017). IG'S Guide to Sponsorship. Chicago: IEG, LLC.

IOC. (2006). *International Olympic Committee- 2006 Marketing Fact File*. IOC.

Iso Ahola, S. E. (1983). Towards a social psychology of recreational travel. *Leisure Studies*, *1*(1), 45–56. doi:10.1080/02614368300390041

Kahle, L. R., Kambara, K. M., & Rose, G. M. (1996). A functional model of fun attendance motivations for college football. *Sport Marketing Quarterly*, *5*(4), 51–60.

Kim, J.-W. (2010). The worth of sport event sponsorship: An event study. *Journal of Management and Marketing Research*, *5*(1), 1–14.

Kim, N. S., & Chalip, L. (2004). Why travel to the FIFA World Cup? Effects of motives, background, interest, and constraints. *Tourism Management*, *25*(6), 695–707. doi:10.1016/j.tourman.2003.08.011

Ko, Y. J., Kim, K., Claussen, C. L., & Kim, T. H. (2008). The effects of sport involvement, sponsor awareness and corporate image on intention to purchase sponsors' products. *International Journal of Sports Marketing & Sponsorship*, *9*(2), 79–94. doi:10.1108/IJSMS-09-02-2008-B004

Koo, G.-Y., Quartermann, J., & Flynn, L. (2006). Effect of perceived sport event and sponsor image fit on consumers' cognition, affect, and behavioral intentions. *Sport Management Quarterly, 15*, 80–90.

Kriemadis, T., & Kartakoulis, N. L. (2011). *Management and marketing for marketing clubs-Good governance and marketing applications*. University of Nicosia Press.

Kurtzman, J. (2005). Sports tourism categories. *Journal of Sport & Tourism, 10*(1), 15–20. doi:10.1080/14775080500101502

Lane, A., Murphy, N., & Bauman, A. (2013). An effort to "leverage" the effect of participation in a mass event on physical activity. *Health Promotion International, 30*(3), 542–551. doi:10.1093/heapro/dat077 PMID:24226297

Ledingham, J. A., & Bruning, S. D. (1998). Relationship management in public relations: Dimensions of an organization-public relationship. *Public Relations Review, 24*(1), 55–65. doi:10.1016/S0363-8111(98)80020-9

Levin, A. M., Joiner, C., & Cameron, G. (2001). The Impact of Sports Sponsorship on Consumers' Brand Attitudes and Recall: The Case of Nascars Fans. *Journal of Current Issues and Research in Advertising, 23*(2), 23–31. doi:10.1080/10641734.2001.10505118

Lim, J. S., Hwang, Y. C., Kim, S. K., & Biocca, F. A. (2015). How social media engagement leads to sports channel loyalty: Mediating roles of social presence and channel commitment. *Computers in Human Behavior, 46*, 158–167. doi:10.1016/j.chb.2015.01.013

Line, N. D., Hanks, L., & McGinley, S. (2018). When birds flock together: An identification of the destination social servicescape. *Journal of Travel & Tourism Marketing, 35*(7), 882–894. doi:10.1080/10548408.2018.1445065

Lough, N. L., & Irwin, R. L. (2001). A comparative analysis of sponsorship objectives for U.S. women's sport and traditional sport sponsorship. *Sport Marketing Quarterly, 10*(4), 202–211.

Malchrowicz-Mosko, E., & Poczta, J. (2018). A Small-Scale Event and a Big Impact—Is This Relationship Possible in the World of Sport? The Meaning of Heritage Sporting Events for Sustainable Development of Tourism—Experiences from Poland. *Sustainability, 10*(11), 4289. doi:10.3390u10114289

Mason, K. (2005). How Corporate Sport Sponsorship Impacts Consumer Behavior. *The Journal of American Academy of Business, Cambridge, 7*(1), 32–35.

McCarville, R., & Copeland, R. (1994). Understanding sport sponsorship through exchange theory. *Journal of Sport Management*, *8*(2), 102–114. doi:10.1123/jsm.8.2.102

Meenaghan, T. (2001). Understanding sponsorship effects. *Psychology and Marketing*, *18*(2), 95–122. doi:10.1002/1520-6793(200102)18:2<95::AID-MAR1001>3.0.CO;2-H

Miloch, K. S., & Lambrecht, K. W. (2006). Consumer Awareness of Sponsorship at Grassroots Sport Events. *Sport Marketing Quarterly*, *15*, 147–154.

Mintel. (2011). *Sports Marketing and Sponsorship - UK - Trade Perspectives: Sports Marketing Activities*. London: Mintel Group.

Molm, L. (1990). Structure, action, and outcomes: The dynamics of power in social exchange. *American Sociological Review*, *55*(3), 427–447. doi:10.2307/2095767

Mount, J., & Niro, B. (1995). Sponsorship: An empirical study of its application to local business in a small town setting. *Festival Management & Event Tourism*, *2*(3/4), 167–175. doi:10.3727/106527095792315576

Nicholls, J. A. F., Roslow, S., & Dublish, S. (1999). Brand recall and brand preference at sponsored golf and tennis tournaments. *European Journal of Marketing*, *33*(3/4), 365–386. doi:10.1108/03090569910253198

Pappu, R., & Cornwell, T. B. (2014). Corporate sponsorship as an image platform: Understanding the roles of relationship fit and sponsor-sponsee similarity. *Academy of Marketing Science. Journal*, *42*(5), 490–510.

Parent, M. M. (2008). Evolution and issue patterns for major-sport-event organizing committees and their stakeholders. *Journal of Sport Management*, *22*(2), 135–164. doi:10.1123/jsm.22.2.135

Parent, M. M., Eskerud, L., & Hanstad, D. V. (2012). Brand creation in international recurring sports events. *Sport Management Review*, *15*(2), 145–159. doi:10.1016/j.smr.2011.08.005

Pope, N. K. L., & Voges, K. E. (2000). The impact of sport sponsorship activities, corporate image, and prior use on consumer purchase intention. *Sport Marketing Quarterly*, *9*(2), 96–102.

Popp, B., & Woratschek, H. (2016). Introducing branded communities in sport for building strong brand relations in social media. *Sport Management Review*, *19*(2), 183–197. doi:10.1016/j.smr.2015.06.001

Preuss, H. (2006). *Lasting effects of major sporting events*. Available in www.idrottsforum.org

Priporas, C.-V., Vassiliadis, C. A., Stylos, N., & Fotiadis, A. (2018). The effect of sport tourists' travel style, destination and event choices, and motivation on their involvement in small-scale sports events. *Event Management*, *22*(5), 745–765. doi:10.3727/152599518X15299559637707

Reic, I. (2017). *Events Marketing Management-A Consumer Perspective*. Routledge.

Ross, S. D. (2001). Developing Sport Tourism-An eGuide for Destination marketers and Sports Events Planners. University of Illinois at Urbana-Champaign.

Scheinbaum, A. C., Finney, R. Z., Lacey, R. Z., & Sneath, J. Z. (2006). Engaging the Consumer through Event Marketing: Linking Attendees with the Sponsor, Community, and Brand. *Journal of Advertising Research*, *46*(4), 420–433. doi:10.2501/S0021849906060430

Schnitzer, M. (2014). Financing events. In J. Beech, S. Kaiser, & R. Kaspar (Eds.), *The business of events management* (pp. 113–135). Pearson.

Schulenkorf, N., & Edwards, D. (2012). Maximizing positive social impacts: Strategies for sustaining and leveraging the benefits of intercommunity sport events in divided societies. *Journal of Sport Management*, *26*(5), 379–390. doi:10.1123/jsm.26.5.379

Schulenkorf, N., & Schlenker, K. (2017). Leveraging sport events to maximize community benefits in low-and middle-income countries. *Event Management*, *21*(2), 217–231. doi:10.3727/152599517X14878772869766

Slack, T., & Bentz, L. (1996). The involvement of small businesses in sport sponsorship. *Managing Leisure*, *1*(3), 175–184. doi:10.1080/136067196376410

Smith, A. (2012). *Events and urban regeneration: The strategic use of events to revitalise cities*. Routledge. doi:10.4324/9780203136997

Soteriades, M. (2013). Events Sponsorhip: A framework for efficient management. *Wulfenia*, *20*(10), 226–241.

Sport New Zealand. (2012). *New Zealand Government, Sport Sponsorship; Securing and retaining commercial partners*. Sport New Zealand.

Thorpe, H. (2017). Action Sports, Social Media, and New Technologies: Towards a Research Agenda. *Communication & Sport*, *5*(5), 554–578. doi:10.1177/2167479516638125

Tiew, F., Holmes, K., & De Bussy, N. (2015). Tourism Events and the Nature of Stakeholder Power. *Event Management*, *19*(4), 525–541. doi:10.3727/152599515X14465748512768

Tripodi, J. (2001). Sponsorship - A Confirmed Weapon in the Promotional Armoury. *International Journal of Sports Marketing & Sponsorship*, *3*(1), 82–103. doi:10.1108/IJSMS-03-01-2001-B007

Tynan, C., & McKechnie, S. (2009). Experience marketing: A review and reassessment. *Journal of Marketing Management*, *25*(5-6), 501–517. doi:10.1362/026725709X461821

Vassiliadis, C., & Fotiadis, A. (2016). Managing Sport Tourism Experiences: Blueprinting Service Encounters. In M. Sotiriadis & D. Gursoy (Eds.), *The Handbook of Managing and Marketing Tourism Experiences* (pp. 195–215). Emerald Group Publishing Limited. doi:10.1108/978-1-78635-290-320161008

Walker, M., Hall, T., Todd, S. Y., & Kent, A. (2011). Does your sponsor affect my perception of the event? The role of event sponsors as signals. *Sport Marketing Quarterly*, *20*(3), 138–147.

Walliser, B. (2003). An international review of sponsorship research: Extension and update. *International Journal of Advertising*, *22*(1), 5–40. doi:10.1080/02650487.2003.11072838

Wankel, C., Marovich, M., & Stanaityte, J. (2010). *Cutting-edge social media approaches to business education*. Information Age Pub.

Zarantonello, L., & Schmitt, B. (2013). The impact of Event Marketing on Brand Equity: The mediating roles of Brand Experience and Brand Attitude. *International Journal of Advertising*, *32*(2), 5–40, 255–280. doi:10.2501/IJA-32-2-255-280

Chapter 11
When Ethical Values Drive the Creation and Development of Sporting Events

Selena Aureli
https://orcid.org/0000-0002-2169-1694
Bologna University, Italy

Hermann Graziano
Bologna University, Italy

ABSTRACT

Based on the case study of ColleMarathon, this chapter aims to describe how local volunteers were able to transform a very small-scale sporting event into a successful occasion that merged sports with ethical values and generated positive outcomes for the local communities. Members of the local sports associations and volunteers are the inventors, managers and workers of the marathon that want to communicate the spirit of care and authentic values as its title suggests, "The Marathon of Values." Ongoing growth (from 350 to more than 1000 athletes) and the participation of new businesses and entities has not changed the governance and the aim of the race: after 17 years, ColleMarathon is still managed by an organising committee made up of representatives of the sports associations and volunteers, who are set in motion by the values they want to disseminate with the event. Values are the glue that binds all actors and still attract participants that run through villages, hills, and old castles, meeting the local people and learning their cultural traditions.

DOI: 10.4018/978-1-7998-4757-1.ch011

CHAPTER OBJECTIVES

- Understand the impacts of a small-scale sporting event on the local community
- Identify what favours the local community and volunteers' commitment to the event
- Contribute to devising the creation and consumption of social capital in sporting events
- Describe possible links between sporting events and tourism

INTRODUCTION

Literature on sporting events usually concentrates on large or mega-events such as the Olympic Games or Football World Cup, as they have significant economic and social impacts, from urban development to job creation, regeneration of peripheral areas, revitalisation of public life through community interactions and tourism (Essex and Chalkley, 1998; Gratton and Taylor, 2000; Chalip et al., 2003; Liu and Gratton, 2010). In other terms, these events generate legacies, i.e., the tangible and intangible structures created for and by a sporting event that remains longer than the event itself (Preuss, 2007, 2015). Nevertheless, recent research has highlighted that such large events may also have negative outcomes (Liu and Wilson, 2014), and their social sustainability is questionable (Smith, 2009). Mega sporting events may increase civic pride, but they are one-off occasions that have little to offer for the long-term sustainability of local communities.

On the contrary, small-scale sporting events recurring every year may bring about more long-term impacts distributed equitably (while the organisation of a large event usually benefits some elites or specific groups of actors). Small-scale sporting events may reinforce collective identity and a sense of connectedness in their own neighbourhoods better than large events that change spaces (new infrastructures are created) and often modify the image of a location (to make it a symbol for renovation and hope).

Literature on small-scale sporting events suggests that these events have an economic impact of negligible relevance compared to large events (Wilson, 2006), but they may have strong positive social effects on the local community and potentially contribute to encouraging tourism activities, especially in rural areas (Bertella, 2014; Duglio and Beltramo, 2017).

Small events have different dynamics that govern the stages of conceptualisation and realization (Bertella, 2014), heavily rely on local stakeholders and volunteers whose perceptions are of key relevance (Bazzanella et al., 2019) and face more difficulties compared to large events in attracting participants (Fotiadis et al., 2016). Their differences from large events have made several researchers call for additional investigation on small-scale sporting event organisation and the outcomes generated (Gibson et al., 2012; Malchrowicz-Mośko & Poczta, 2018).

In line with this call for research, the present chapter aims to investigate the impacts associated with small-scale sporting events, devoting particular attention to the positive social outcomes that they may bring to local communities. In addition, it investigates the factors that grant ongoing participation and support of local stakeholders and communities in the realization of the sporting event.

LITERATURE REVIEW

Hosting sporting events has become increasingly popular among cities and local governments aiming to enhance the visibility of a location (e.g., a city, province or mountain area) and attract capital and investments. A sporting event is capable of transforming participants and spectators into tourists and attracting investments for infrastructures, especially in the case of mega-events (Andranovich et al., 2001; Magdalinski, and Nauright, 2004; Gratton et al., 2005). Businesspersons and academic literature have long emphasised the significance of sporting events for economic development (Pennington-Gray and Holdnak, 2002).

At the same time, researchers have devised the importance of sporting events for community well-being and development. Some suggest that a renewed image of a city hosting an event may help citizens to feel better about their city and can create a community identity (Gratton and Taylor, 2000; Smith and Ingham, 2003). Others have addressed the inherent social value of sport, assuming that all sport-related activities might bring civic engagement and develop community networks and social relations (Jarvie, 2003).

Positive social impacts on host communities are mainly associated with the organisation of small-scale sporting events and social events (Rohe, 2004). While the decision of hosting mega-events such as the Olympic Games is made by certain elites (politicians and industrialists) based on economic motives, possibly even taking place without the endorsement of the local community within the host city (Jarvie, 2003), small sporting events engage many members of the local community.

Small events largely involve volunteers and dialogue with the local community because local support may compensate for the lack of funding that small events suffer from. Small events require a collective effort that relies on continuous personal interactions among community members. When these interactions create norms and trust, social capital is developed (Coleman, 1990), which means that relationships of mutual reciprocity embedded in social networks are created. As described by Larsen and Bærenholdt (2019), small-scale sporting events are tied in with social capital but also contribute to creating social capital. This type of capital is very important as it has the merit of encouraging new investments as well as making existing investments go further (Hibbitt et al., 2001).

However, as suggested by Misener and Mason (2006), not all sporting events help create and improve the social infrastructure of a community because not all events get broad community participation. They argue that obtaining inclusive community involvement in activities surrounding sporting events that build social capital requires the following:

1. the event should embrace and be built around the core values of residents, community groups, and neighbourhood associations;
2. the local community needs the opportunity to be involved in the overall event hosting process, opportunities that may take of the form of neighbourhood information meetings or forums organised by event developers, where community members can voice their opinions and exchanges of ideas and resources can take place;
3. collaborative actions should empower citizens to foster additional opportunities for involvement and engagement of the local community, so that citizens may learn the skills necessary to further participate in community building;
4. open communication toward all community members so that the event is not understood as the development of the initiative of a closed group of people but an occasion for removing barriers that separate people.

Although being supported by the authors' literature review, these propositions were not empirically verified.

A similar lack of evidence refers to the assessment of the economic impact that a small-scale sporting event may generate for the local community. Several studies have emphasised how these events can benefit destinations by attracting sport tourists (Gibson et al., 2012), but the capability of events to attract tourists with 'non-sporting motives' such as supporting participants is not easily measurable (Murphy et al., 2015). Hence, a direct global impact is difficult to demonstrate. Moreover, we have to consider that events are usually planned to attract participants (sportsmen) and not tourists. In other terms, event organisers focus on delivering challenging competitive experiences, rather than on stimulating tourism-related outcomes even when they use tourism elements (such as the attractive and unique location features) in their communication strategies (Kennelly, 2017). Therefore, synergies are not always researched and developed.

Considering the need for additional investigation of the impact of small-scale sporting events on local communities, this chapter aims to answer to the following research question: are the conditions cited by Misener and Mason (2006) necessary for a small-scale sporting event to create positive social impacts on the local community? Do small-scale sporting events attract tourists even if unplanned?

Using the case study of ColleMarathon (a race organised in a small city of Central Italy), this chapter analyses how the sporting event was developed and if it applied the four conditions or drivers that should improve social relations and community participation.

DATA AND METHOD

In order to achieve the research goal, case study analysis seems the most appropriate tool of investigation for understanding how a sporting event is developed and for appreciating the impacts it generates on the local community. As suggested by Yin (2014) and Cooper and Morgan (2008), a qualitative approach allows for the undertaking of an in-depth investigation of a phenomenon in its real-life context and answers "how" questions about contemporary events.

Access to historical data allowed researchers to perform a longitudinal case study analysis, which describes how a small-scale sporting event was launched, developed through time and generated outcomes for the community.

The use of one case study can be subject to some critiques deriving from a poor generalisation of results. A case study does not aim to provide statistical generalisation (Tsang, 2014) but may offer an analytical generalisation that derives from the observation of a specific phenomenon, aiming to determine theory understanding and explanations useful for other cases (Yin, 2014).

Data collected refer to the key statistics of the phenomenon (number of participants and volunteers), its objectives (including changes in objectives through time), deployment (how it is organised) and linkages with the local community (the degree of involvement of local stakeholders). Moreover, data were collected from different sources. Researchers had access to archival data on the number of participants and volunteers involved in all editions of the marathon; they also collected textual data and videos from several media (newspapers, blogs, sport magazines, websites) and did two structured interviews with key informants (one of the 'founders' of the event and one representative of a charity association who joined the event during the 2010 edition).

The triangulation of data stemming from the different interviewees and sources as well as the use of a variety of methods to collect data on the same topic shall assure the validity of the research (Lincoln and Guba 1985). Finally, results stemming from different sources were discussed among the authors to increase trustworthiness and achieve validation of the results (Yin 2014).

CASE STUDY

The case study selected refers to ColleMarathon, a long-distance race first organised in 2003 in Barchi: a small village located in a countryside area of Italy, situated in the north of the Marche Region, devoted to agricultural and craft activities (mainly the cultivation of wine, olive oil and wheat, which are sold in Italy and abroad). Today, the marathon path originates from the outback of Barchi, passes through 9 "Borgo"[1] or villages and ends at the seaside of Fano (see Figure 1). The geographical area crossed by the marathon has no strong vocation to tourism if compared to the famous nearby district of Rimini, nor does it heavily rely on the manufacturing industry. Therefore, hosting this race and other sporting events appears as a means for local governments to market the territory, creating city exposure and attracting the tourist market.

The goal of attracting people to the destination can be devised from the inception used by the organisers to present the marathon on the institutional website:

"From the lush hills of Barchi to the charming and sunny coast of Fano, through the winding, gentle ridges and ancient fortified villages such as Mondavio, Orciano, S.Giorgio, Piagge, Cerasa and S.Costanzo ... A unique race, an unmissable opportunity for marathon runners and companions, who will be able to have an unforgettable experience: a journey through the history and culture of our people, rich in traditions that date back to the Middle Ages. After an exciting start accompanied by the shots of medieval bombardments, the athletes will compete on a fun, scenic and suggestive route, enlivened by engaging musical, historical and folkloric animations, in a crescendo of emotions up to the final apotheosis".

Yet, the tourism vocation of this sporting event is quite recent. One of the primary organisers interviewed declared that their initial goal was "*to hold the local community together and that the marathon could be an event useful for raising money to buy sports equipment for local schools and associations*". The origins of ColleMarathon date back to some years before 2003, when four runners, linked by close friendship, launched a half marathon (about 20 km) to be held at night, connecting few villages of the outback (Barchi, Piagge, Orciano and San Giorgio di Pesaro). After a few years and some changes in the path of the race (like ending at the coast), that event became a famous sporting event known as ColleMarathon, which now attracts runners from all over Italy (not only from cities within the Marche Region) and some foreign countries (see Table 1).

This sporting event has witnessed great development throughout time. In 2003, the marathon had 340 runners that soon became 540 runners after three years (in 2006). Then, the marathon registered 738 people in 2008 and from 2009 onwards,

Figure 1. The route of ColleMarathon

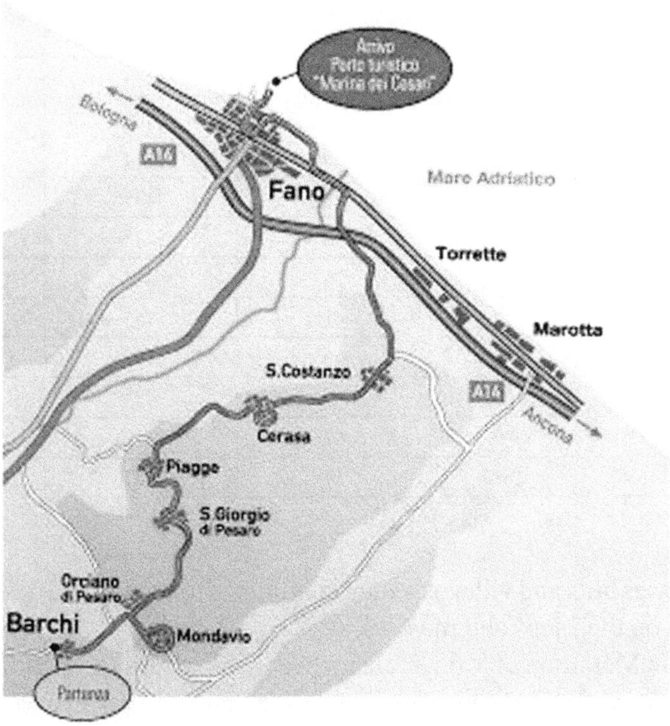

more than 1000 athletes participate in the event annually. Similarly, the number of volunteers (private citizens and members of local sports and charitable associations) grew, passing from 100 to 500 people throughout the years, and the number of public entities granting their patronage increased from the original four local municipalities to about 12 public subjects.

The ColleMarathon is a proper long-distance race, with an itinerary entirely closed to traffic. The athletes register and run with a GPS chip timer that detects the time of arrival. However, news and narratives reported in press releases, online blogs, newspapers and sportsmen forums describe the marathon more as a friendly, non-competitive event, and great emphasis is given to the territory and the attractions it offers. The natural landscape and historic villages are the key drivers for attracting tourists, but the animations organised by locals are also important. Along the route (every 3 km), there are groups of local citizens who organise choreographies, wear old-timey costume, play music or offer refreshments.

The official website of the marathon highlights two key characteristics that differentiate ColleMarathon from other races:

Table 1. Number of runners by geographical origin

Year	Runners	Italians	Foreigners	Runners From the Region	Other Italian Regions
2009	1008	966	42	373	593
2010	1061	1040	21	382	658
2011	999	970	29	414	556
2012	1117	1087	30	435	652
2013	1221	1179	42	423	756
2014	1171	1145	26	447	698
2015	1175	1134	41	455	679
2016	1191	1153	38	456	697
2017	1066	1022	44	432	590
2018	1013	976	37	298	678
2019	1466	1413	53	482	931

- its route crosses hills and villages, requiring runners to ascend and descend, putting a strain on their legs and muscles, and
- its motto "the Marathon of Values", launched in 2006, aiming to communicate the spirit of care and the importance of preserving authentic values linked to the culture of gifting and volunteering.

The decision to avoid a flat path, which winds through perfectly paved roads, is not casual. The organisers recalled during the interview that they did not want to replicate locally a classic marathon that attracts elite athletes and emphasises speed and competitive aspects. Running through villages and across hills slows down the speed of the race and allows participants to experience the location.

Both participants and local stakeholders perceive the values communicated by the marathon. When describing the event in online and paper reports, the value of welcoming emerges, which is demonstrated by volunteers who are devoted to making the whole journey pleasant and convivial. Volunteers donate their time to prepare the event, but they also actively support runners along the route, providing beverages and cheering the runners on. As one interviewee said, "*the soul of ColleMarathon are the people, they are the showpiece that take care of every runner in every village*". Also, the value of solidarity, expressed through specific charitable initiatives launched during the marathon, is relevant. For many years, these initiatives have regarded the local community. So, for example, a lottery was organised to support a local sports association dedicated to children. More recently, funds have been raised to create houses for disadvantaged people in Burundi, Africa and donations to Unicef have been collected. More important is the direct contribution of the marathon to charitable associations: all revenues coming from participants' fees and sponsorships are donated, after having deducted the operating expenses. Therefore, no ColleMarathon edition has ever recorded a profit. Lastly, great emphasis is attributed to the value of social inclusion, which is communicated at the start of the race or during collateral events. For example, on one occasion, a wheelchair athlete was invited as a spokesperson to prove how sport can give new opportunities to injured people. In another occasion, runners with Down's Syndrome joined the race to demonstrate how staying active can improve their lifestyle. Once an individual who had an organ transplant was invited as an example of how physical movement may improve quality of life and decrease the risk for cardiac events if done under medical supervision. That person and all the doctors that saved his life ran together along the marathon's route.

Although the event has gained national prominence through years, its increasing popularity has not changed the governance nor the aim of the race. In fact, after 17 years, ColleMarathon is still managed by the original Organising Committee made up of representatives of local sports associations and volunteers. Some people have changed, but not the associations they represent; this duration of membership is crucial for social trust (Elmose-Østerlund & van der Roest, 2017). As in the past, the race does not aim to make profits but tries to generate positive social outcomes. As one interviewee said, "*we did not let businesses or specialized event management companies enter the Committee because they put forward profit goals, while we want ColleMarathon to remain an inclusive sporting event that highlights the values of respect, team spirit and a healthy lifestyle*". This is demonstrated by the fact that for some disadvantaged categories, there is no participating fee; only a donation of five euros for Unicef is requested.

In line with the concept of inclusion, the Committee welcomes any new charitable association or a local company that wants to contribute (donating time, money, goods or services) to the marathon. For example, an increasing amount of local producers of organic products provide food and refreshments. On the one hand, producers improve their visibility. On the other hand, the Committee still preserves the local identity of the race (as reported: "*A run into the history, cultural and culinary traditions of our land*") and can better pursue the dissemination of sound principles including that of proper nutrition based on organic products and whole-wheat pasta. However, the participation of third entities has been limited to local or at least regional actors. The same applies to sponsors: ColleMarathon almost exclusively benefits from local private sponsors. Only recently has it opened up to one national supporter (i.e., a sportswear company) that provided them with some advice on how to increase the number of participants. Staying linked to local supporters and sponsors is important because they want to avoid commercialisation and "*keep the event small so that it can still be managed by locals, who perceive it as a community-based event*".

Absence of profit goals driving the organisation and deployment of the sporting event is also shown by the fact that the Organising Committee has no real marketing or communication strategy. They do not make advertising campaigns as they rely on runners' word of mouth who enjoyed the race. One interviewee said, "*We make efforts to make runners feel welcome, and this transforms them into loyal participants that come every year and bring some friends; the typical ColleMarathon participant visits us four times on average*". The growth in the number of participants was not planned. A professional approach to the event management (eventually brought through external partners) could increase the magnitude of ColleMarathon, but its organisers believe that recurring to professional experts could threaten the basis of relationships that currently support the deployment of the event. As one interviewee said, "*the engine of ColleMarathon is a friendship that binds all people involved, from organisers to volunteers and entrepreneurs providing time, money or other key resources that make the event happen*".

No formal structures or plans guide the design and deployment of the event. Spatial proximity makes it easy for local stakeholders to meet, have a dialogue and converge on the project. Direct knowledge allows for the creation of relationships, and subsequent, direct encounters increase reciprocal trust.

According to the interviewees, the spirit of the event has made it welcomed among all local inhabitants. No one has complained or fought against the event even though it limits citizens' movements on the day of the race (several streets are closed). Newspapers indicated that citizens appreciated the use of donations to restore two old paintings located in local churches and to support sport at the local level. Local accommodation businesses and restaurants appreciate the capability of the event to increase the number of tourists. As one interviewee said, "*In 2003, we decided to end the race in Fano, at the seaside, because participants and their families needed to find adequate accommodation facilities that were not available in the countryside. Considering the increasing number of participants, we have been questioning whether to end the race in one of the rural villages in the near future to favour more overnight stays in the countryside*". The capability of ColleMarathon to attract tourists has been recently understood also by the Marche Region, which has allocated some funds to support the race and enhance the accommodations of rural bed & breakfasts, farms and country houses.

DISCUSSION

The case study provides insight into a small-scale sporting event that is rich in social capital. The increasing involvement of local communities (citizens, volunteers, associations, businesses and municipalities) in this marathon is indicative of the number of social structures created over time. Active participation highlights high levels of trust and reciprocity. Similarly to what is described by Larsen and Bærenholdt (2019), social capital is both the engine for producing the event and the outcome generated. Moreover, the economic profit is also translated into social capital, as all the money raised through the competition is devoted to the local community and even social communities located beyond the local geographical area.

This was possible thanks to two key elements: 1. the event is built around core values shared by sport, charitable and volunteer associations and the community groups of the host territory, and 2. all members of the local community have the opportunity to be involved in the event's implementation process. This opportunity stems from existing neighbourhood relationships that facilitate the possibility to meet people and create friendships and is granted by the "spirit of openness and welcoming" given by the Organising Committee of the project.

Differently from what is suggested by Misener and Mason (2006), in this case, event developers do not organise formal/formalised encounters or neighbourhood meetings because community members voice their opinions and exchanges of ideas through direct interactions. Moreover, communication tools directed at community members seem unnecessary. The event was not created, nor it is understood as the initiative of a closed group and, therefore, not all tools proposed by the two authors are necessary in this case study; involvement and engagement of the local community is one building block of the event itself.

In the analysed case study, citizens make sustained efforts to assist the organisation of the sporting event, which translates into positive impacts for their own community. The event is designed to meet existing needs (e.g., contributing to local sports associations, helping disadvantaged people, assisting in the restoration of local art pieces and bringing some tourists to the area), and its incremental growth seems more sustainable compared to rapid changes usually brought on by large and mega-sport events.

Positive social outcomes strengthen local relationships and networks. Despite the limitation of not being able to survey local citizens and volunteers whether they feel better or obtained some tangible or intangible benefit as a result of the event, we believe that the increasing amount of volunteers and citizens contributing to the event is a good proxy for assessing their long-term appreciation of it.

From an economic point of view, the marathon is perceived to bring about tourism-related benefits. Since it attracts what Larsen (2019) has defined as "casual runners", the event's impact is not limited to the number of sportsmen enrolled in the race but is magnified by their families and friends who generate the demand for accommodation and restaurant services. While a one-day marathon addressed to professional athletes may have no impact in terms of an overnight stay, casual runners travel with their families, who want to visit the event location or its nearby resorts. Only recently have the event organisers understood that the event could be a driver to enhance tourism in rural areas.

In this case study, the attachment to the event, as demonstrated by the number of loyal runners who have joined the race several times, can be transformed into an attachment to the destination as suggested by the study of Halpenny et al. (2016). Yet, event leveraging (O'Brien, 2007), i.e., strategically incorporate actions that maximise benefits such as creating pre- and post-events, lengthening the duration of the event or organising tours that may increase visitors' spending, is still not a topic under evaluation. Neither short-term nor long-term benefits of sporting events as described by Chalip's (2004) model are actively researched in the analysed case study.

CONCLUSION

Using the case study of ColleMarathon, this chapter aims to contribute to the scientific literature on small-scale sporting events, which has traditionally focused on mega-events instead.

First, the analysed case confirms that a small-scale event can generate positive social outcomes, mainly related to the creation and reinforcement of social capital. The relevant and increasing participation of volunteers, single citizens and members of local associations in the co-creation of the event indicates that the marathon fulfils a socio-cultural function: the event is important for the community; it reinforces a community's sense of identity and enhances local networks. Economic-related impacts, such as tourism development, are less evident than social impacts, although they could be better exploited by event organisers.

Second, the case study confirms that local support (volunteers, citizens, sports associations and even local governments) is crucial, and this support can be achieved thanks to the centrality given to positive values and spatial proximity. Public resistance and opposition that characterises some mega-events are absent in this case thanks to the event's openness to all interested parties and efforts made by organisers to involve local inhabitants to work together for shared positive social values. Values are the glue and the driver of people's engagement. Moreover, the absence of commercial/ profit goals actively facilitates civic engagement.

While being aware of the limitations associated with the study of one single event, this case may inspire the organisation of other small-scale sporting events and push local governments to concern themselves with sporting events that are related to the cultural heritage of a given region.

REFERENCES

Adair, D. (Eds.). (n.d.). Sport Tourism: Interrelationships, Impacts and Issues. Channel View.

Andranovich, G., Burbank, M. J., & Heying, C. H. (2001). Olympic cities: Lessons learned from mega-event politics. *Journal of Urban Affairs*, *23*(2), 113–131. doi:10.1111/0735-2166.00079

Bazzanella, F., Peters, M., & Schnitzer, M. (2019). The perceptions of stakeholders in small-scale sporting events. *Journal of Convention & Event Tourism*, *20*(4), 261–286. doi:10.1080/15470148.2019.1640819

Bertella, G. (2014). Designing small-scale sport events in the countryside. *International Journal of Event and Festival Management*, *5*(2), 132–145. doi:10.1108/IJEFM-05-2013-0008

Chalip, L. (2004). Beyond impact: a general model for host community event leverage. Academic Press.

Chalip, L., Green, B. C., & Hill, B. (2003). Effects of sport event media on destination image and intention to visit. *Journal of Sport Management*, *17*(3), 214–234. doi:10.1123/jsm.17.3.214

Coleman, J. S. (1990). *Foundations of social theory*. Cambridge University Press.

Cooper, D. J., & Morgan, W. (2008). Case Study Research in Accounting. *Accounting Horizons*, *22*(2), 159–178. doi:10.2308/acch.2008.22.2.159

Duglio, S., & Beltramo, R. (2017). Estimating the economic impacts of a small-scale sport tourism event: The case of the Italo-Swiss Mountain Trail Collon Trek. *Sustainability*, *9*(3), 343. doi:10.3390u9030343

Elmose-Østerlund, K., & van der Roest, J. W. (2017). Understanding social capital in sports clubs: Participation, duration and social trust. *European Journal of Sport Science*, *14*(4), 366–386. doi:10.1080/16138171.2017.1378479

Essex, S., & Chalkley, B. (1998). Olympic Games: Catalyst of urban change. *Leisure Studies*, *17*(3), 187–206. doi:10.1080/026143698375123

Fotiadis, A., Xie, L., Li, Y., & Huan, T.-C. T. C. (2016). Attracting athletes to small-scale sports events using motivational decision-making factors. *Journal of Business Research, 69*(11), 5467–5472. doi:10.1016/j.jbusres.2016.04.157

Gibson, H., Kaplanidou, K., & Kang, S. J. (2012). Small-scale event sport tourism: A case study in sustainable tourism. *Sport Management Review, 15*(2), 160–170. doi:10.1016/j.smr.2011.08.013

Gratton, C., Shibli, S., & Coleman, R. (2005). Sport and economic regeneration in cities. *Urban Studies (Edinburgh, Scotland), 42*(5-6), 985–999. doi:10.1080/00420980500107045

Gratton, C., & Taylor, P. (2000). *Economics of Sports and Recreation*. Taylor&Francis.

Halpenny, E. A., Kulczycki, C., & Moghimehfar, F. (2016). Factors effecting destination and event loyalty: Examining the sustainability of a recurrent small-scale running event at Banff National Park. *Journal of Sport & Tourism, 20*(3-4), 3–4, 233–262. doi:10.1080/14775085.2016.1218787

Hibbitt, K., Jones, P., & Meegan, R. (2001). Tackling social exclusion: The role of social capital in urban regeneration on Merseyside—from mistrust to trust? *European Planning Studies, 9*, 141–161.

Jarvie, G. (2003). Communitarianism, sport and social Capital. 'Neighbourly insights into Scottish sport'. *International Review for the Sociology of Sport, 38*(2), 139–153. doi:10.1177/1012690203038002001

Kennelly, M. (2017). "We've never measured it, but it brings in a lot of business" Participatory sport events and tourism. *International Journal of Contemporary Hospitality Management, 29*(3), 883–899. doi:10.1108/IJCHM-10-2015-0541

Larsen, J. (2019). Running and tourism: A practice approach. In L. James, C. Ren, & H. Halkier (Eds.), *Theories and practice in tourism* (pp. 41–57). Routledge.

Larsen, J., & Bærenholdt, J. (2019). Running together: The social capitals of a tourism running event. *Annals of Tourism Research*, 79.

Liu, D., & Gratton, C. (2010). The impact of mega sporting events on live spectators' images of a host city: A case study of the Shanghai F1 Grand Prix. *Tourism Economics, 16*(3), 629–645. doi:10.5367/000000010792278347

Liu, D., & Wilson, R. (2014). The negative impacts of hosting mega-sporting events and intention to travel: A test of the crowding-out effect using the London 2012 Games as an example. *International Journal of Sports Marketing & Sponsorship, 15*(3), 12–26. doi:10.1108/IJSMS-15-03-2014-B003

Magdalinski, T., & Nauright, J. (2004). Commercialization of the modern Olympic Games. In T. Slack (Ed.), *The Commercialization of Sport* (pp. 185–204). Routledge.

Malchrowicz-Mośko, E., & Poczta, J. (2018, November 19). A Small-Scale Event and a Big Impact—Is This Relationship Possible in the World of Sport? The Meaning of Heritage Sporting Events for Sustainable Development of Tourism—Experiences from Poland. *Sustainability, 10*(11), 4289. doi:10.3390u10114289

Misener, L., & Mason, D. (2006). Creating community networks: Can sporting events offer meaningful sources of social capital? *Managing Leisure, 11*(1), 39–56. doi:10.1080/13606710500445676

Murphy, N., Lane, A., & Bauman, A. (2015). Leveraging mass participation events for sustainable health legacy. *Leisure Studies, 34*(6), 758–766. doi:10.1080/02614367.2015.1037787

O'Brien, D. (2007). Points of leverage: Maximising host community benefit from a regional surfing festival. *European Sport Management Quarterly, 7*(2), 141–165. doi:10.1080/16184740701353315

Pennington-Gray, L., & Holdnak, A. (2002). Out of the stands and into the community: Using sports events to promote destination. *Event Management, 7*(3), 177–186. doi:10.3727/152599502108751578

Preuss, H. (2007). The conceptualisation and measurement of mega sport tourism. *Journal of Sport & Tourism, 12*(3-4), 207–227. doi:10.1080/14775080701736957

Preuss, H. (2015). A framework for identifying the legacies of a mega sport event. *Leisure Studies, 34*(6), 643–664. doi:10.1080/02614367.2014.994552

Rohe, W. M. (2004). Building social capital through community development. *Journal of the American Planning Association, 70*, 143–144.

Smith, J. M., & Ingham, A. G. (2003). On the waterfront: Retrospectives on the relationship between sport and communities. *Sociology of Sport Journal, 20*(3), 252–274. doi:10.1123sj.20.3.252

Smith, S. (2009). Theorising the Relationship between Major Sport Events and Social Sustainability. *Journal of Sport & Tourism, 14*(2-3), 2–3, 109–120. doi:10.1080/14775080902965033

Tsang, E. W. K. (2014). Generalizing from Research Findings: The Merits of Case Studies. *International Journal of Management Reviews, 16*(4), 369–388. doi:10.1111/ijmr.12024

Wilson, R. (2006). The economic impact of local sport events: Significant, limited or otherwise? A case study of four swimming events. *Managing Leisure*, *11*(1), 57–70. doi:10.1080/13606710500445718

Yin, R. K. (2014). Case Study Research: Design and Methods. Sage Publications.

ENDNOTE

1 The literal translation of Borgo in English would be a village, but the term Borgo indicates a fascinating small town, generally fortified and dating back to the period from the Middle Ages to the Renaissance.

Chapter 12
Expenditure Behaviour and Satisfaction in Motor Sport Events:
Insights From the FIA World Rally Championship in Sardinia

Gianfranco Pischedda
University of Sassari, Italy

Ludovico Marinò
https://orcid.org/0000-0002-7064-0041
University of Sassari, Italy

Giacomo Del Chiappa
University of Sassari, Italy

ABSTRACT

This chapter examines the differences in expenditure and satisfaction among first-time and repeat spectators at a motor sports event. A structured questionnaire was developed, and data were collected on site via 318 interviews carried out during the 2019 Federation Internationale de l'Automobile World Rally Championship in Sardinia. Data were analysed by running a series of descriptive analyses, independent t-tests, and regression analyses. The results show that repeaters are more satisfied and spend more when compared to first timers. This study helps to extend the scientific debate related to the growing, and often still inconsistent, comparison of first-timers' and repeat visitors' behaviours by offering insights from a motor sports event, where little research exists so far. Based on the findings, managerial implications are discussed, and suggestions for further research are given.

DOI: 10.4018/978-1-7998-4757-1.ch012

INTRODUCTION

Events play a pivotal role in the marketing strategies of any tourism destination (Getz, 2008; Getz & Page, 2016; Leiper, 1990). Based on the existing literature (e.g., Getz, 2008), different types of events can be considered, namely: cultural (e.g., carnivals or festivals), business and trade (e.g., conventions, fair and expositions), educational and scientific (conferences, seminars etc.), entertainment and arts (concerts, festivals etc.), recreational (sports or games for fun), private (weddings, parties etc.) and sports (spectators, participants, sponsorships etc.). A vast amount of studies have been devoted to the analysis of the impacts generated by events, usually categorized into economic, environmental, sociocultural, political and touristic impacts (Beckman & Traynor, 2019; Bowdin, 2006; Herrero, Sanz, Devesa, Bedate & del Barrio, 2006; Warnick, Bojanic & Xu, 2015).

In this context, sports events are recognized for generating several benefits for the hosting destinations. For example, they can contribute to extending tourism seasonality (Bowdin, 2006), encourage spectators to spend, thus generating economic impacts for the hosting destination, and boost destination brand awareness and image (Morgan, Pritchard & Pride, 2004).

Thanks to the synergy between sports organizations and sports event organizers, which involve different stakeholders with different behaviours (Turco, Riley & Swart, 2002), motor sports are a major global industry producing significant economic, entertainment, cultural and marketing impacts. Considering the two main motor sports events worldwide - Formula 1 and MotoGP World Championships - in 2019, more than 20 events were held in Europe. Again, the 2019 F1 Monza Grand prix attracted 200,000 participants and generated an economic impact of 15 million euros (source: official website of Monza Municipality). The World Rally Championship (WRC), like many other motor sports events, contributes to destination awareness and image (Xing & Chalip, 2006), significantly boosting the visibility of the hosting destination, thanks to media exposure (TV, radio etc.) and social media coverage (comments, pictures and videos uploaded to peer-to-peer platforms) before, during and after the event. It is therefore unsurprising that, nowadays, sports events are playing a pivotal sub-industry role for many European regions and cities, thus explaining the reasons why policymakers, destination marketers and event managers are strongly and increasingly interested in deepening their understanding of the needs, expectations and behaviours of sports spectators (Del Chiappa & Atzeni, 2016).

As any type of sport events, motor sport events can be big or small. Based on existing literature, the distinction between small scale and big events is not simply related to the size of the event (Müller, 2015). On the contrary, it is also related to the fact that small scale events operate within existing infrastructures, require lower investments of public funds, are more manageable in terms of crowding and congestion compared to hallmark events and do not tax the resources of the destination hosting bigger events (Fotiadis, Xie, Li, & Huan, 2016; Higham 1999; Müller, 2015). Furthermore, small motor events usually take place in rural areas, as suggested by Zajc and Berzelak (2016).

As a matter of fact, previous studies which have investigated rally events (e.g., Mackellar & Reis, 2014) have mainly concentrated on analysing/estimating the total economic impacts of the event and interrogating spectators' spending behaviour, their satisfaction with the event/hosting destination, and their behavioural intentions (intention to return and intention to recommend it to others, both offline and online) (e.g., Kaplanidou & Gibson, 2012; Kemperman, Joh & Timmermans, 2004; Quick, 2000; Szwarc, 2005; Samra & Wos, 2014). Current tourism and event-related literature widely concurs that understanding the differences between first-timers and repeat visitors is a pivotal point from which to develop tourism marketing and management strategies (Lau & McKercher, 2004; Petrick, 2004; Silvestre, Santos & Ramalho, 2008; Yuan & Jang, 2008). Despite this, relatively few studies have investigated the consumer behaviours of ðrst-time and repeat sports event tourists (Scott & Turco, 2011), with existing research often reporting ðndings that are sometimes contradictory. For example, some scholars have suggested that first-time visitors spend more than repeat visitors (Jang, Bai, Hong & O'Leary, 2004), whereas others support the opposite view (Li, Cheng, Kim & Petrick, 2008; Wang, 2004) or even suggest that not significant differences exist between first-time and repeat visitors (So & Morrison, 2004).

By considering a sample of 318 completed questionnaire collected at the Federation Internationale de l'Automobile (FIA) WRC held in Sardinia, Italy (13-16 June 2019), this study was therefore carried out with the following objectives:

- To assess and compare satisfaction of ðrst-time and repeat sports event tourists;
- To assess and compare behavioural intentions (i.e. intention to return and to recommend) of ðrst-time and repeat sports event tourists;
- To ascertain which sociodemographic and travel-related characteristics are able to significantly influence spectators' spending behaviour;

The remaining part of the chapter is organized as follows. The next section reviews prior studies on sports events and first-time and repeat spectators. The third section will outline the methodology in detail. The following paragraph will consider the sociodemographic characteristics of the spectators, before determining whether any signiðcant differences exist between ðrst-timers and repeat spectators in terms of their spending behaviour, satisfaction with the event and behavioural intentions. Finally, solutions, recommendations, future research directions and a conclusion will be presented.

BACKGROUND

Since the 1960s, sports tourism has experienced an extraordinary growth and come to be recognized by both academia and industry as a relevant tool to boost the development of any area or region from an economic, cultural, environmental, marketing and political point of view (Coakley, 1986). Despite the growing interest in the field, a unique definition of sports tourism currently does not exist. Following Gibson (1998, 10), sports tourism can be defined as *leisure-based travel that takes individuals temporarily outside of their home communities to play, watch physical activities or venerate attractions associated with these activities.*

Three main causes/reasons leading to a growing interest in hosting a sports events can be identified: developments in technology, the opportunity to vastly increase television revenue (Whitson & Horne, 2006) and "city boosterism" (Black, 2007). Specifically, city boosterism includes several development opportunities for cities and nations such as the opportunity to rebuild infrastructure, to improve travel connections, to attract foreign investments and visitors, to increase accommodation availabilities, to enhance media coverage, to improve brand image and awareness on the global stage, and to extend tourism seasonality (Nauright, 2004; Toohey & Veal, 2007; Whitson & Horne, 2006). In addition, sports events can be used by policymakers to justify their projects of urban renewal and to advertise their status and personality to attract inward investment (Essex & Chalkley, 2004), especially in the tourism sector (Bohlin, 2000).

Given the wide array of benefits that events can bring to the hosting destination, a deep understanding of spectators' profile, spending behaviour, satisfaction with the event/destination and behavioural intentions is pivotal to any recognition of the nuances that need to be taken into account in order to develop successful tourism/ event marketing strategies. In this vein, comprehensive knowledge about whether differences in expectations, spending behaviour, satisfaction and behavioural intentions exist are based on the fact that spectators are either first-time or repeat spectators is particularly relevant for running effective marketing segmentation (Formica & Uysal, 1998), selectively planning and implementing loyalty programmes (Fakeye & Crompton, 1991), and contributing to destinations' position in its life cycle (Oppermann, 1998).

Based on the extant literature, several differences have been reported to exist between first-time and repeat spectators in term of their sociodemographic characteristics, expectations, perceptions and behaviours. For example, prior research has shown that ðrst-timers tend to be younger and single, compared to repeat visitors, whereas no significant differences have been reported to exist between first-time and repeat visitors based on gender, education and income (Gitelson & Crompton, 1984; Lau & McKercher, 2004). Furthermore, spectators at small or medium-sized events, such as marathon races (Wicker, Hallmann & Zhang, 2012), have been found to be aged around 40 years (Hallmann, Kaplanidou & Breuer, 2010), with a high educational attainment level (Funk, Toohey & Bruun, 2007), as well as being economically wealthy and willing to spend two or three nights in the hosting city (Daniels & Norman, 2003; Funk et al., 2007). Oppermann (1997, 1998) reported that ðrst-time visitors tend to have shorter stays at a destination when compared to their repeat counterparts, whereas Turco (2010) reported the opposite. Other differences can be found in the activities preferred by the two groups. In fact, first-timers seem to prefer iconic attractions, whereas repeat visitors tend to prefer social activities such as dining and shopping (Anwar & Sohail, 2004; Lau & McKercher, 2004). However, it should also be noted that other studies have found no significant differences between first-time and repeat spectators, such as Kaplanidou and Gibson's (2012) study on attendees of football events.

Other research has found differences between ðrst-timers and repeaters in their spending behaviour and post-experience evaluation. As far as spectators' spending behaviour is concerned, existing studies suggest that several factors can be considered as being inñuential. To this extent, economic constraints, sociodemographic characteristics, sport-related facets and travel-related characteristics are the most important (Sato et al., 2014). For example, some studies have found a positive effect between length of stay and per capita spending by tourists (Raya, 2012), while Saayman and Saayman (2008) observed the opposite. Li et al. (2008) reported that first-time visitors spent significantly more than repeaters on transportation, lodging and entertainment, whereas repeaters were reported as spending more on food, drink, shopping and gambling. On the other hand, Del Chiappa et al.'s (2014) study on spectators at a motor sports event found first-time spectators spent more on food and drink. Other studies (e.g., Kruger et al., 2010; Wang, 2004; Del Chiappa et al, 2017) reported that repeat visitors spend more than ðrst-time visitors. These contradictory findings suggest an inconsistent relationship between travel experience and travel expenditure (Cho, 2009). Other differences between ðrst-timers and repeat visitors are usually reported in their post-trip evaluations. In general, a deep knowledge of tourists' post-trip evaluations is considered to be of high importance to destination marketers, because such evaluations may directly influence tourists' repurchase behaviour (Petrick et al., 2001) and their intention to recommend to others, both offline (e.g., Reid & Reid, 1993) and online (e.g., Quick, 2000). There is also a lack of consensus about which group is more receptive to satisfaction and more likely to return and to recommend. Indeed, some studies have pointed out that repeaters express a higher level of satisfaction than first-time visitors (Li et al., 2008), while other studies suggest the opposite (Anwar & Sohail, 2004). In an attempt to explain why first-timers are usually less satisfied than repeaters, some studies have suggested that this circumstance could depend on the pre-trip expectations that are linked to quality of information (Assael, 2004). In other words, this outcome occur when policymakers, destination marketers and/or event organizers run marketing and promotional operations that overly exaggerate the experiences the destination can provide, thus creating an inconsistency between expectations generated by promotional operations and the actual experience that visitors might have when at the destination/event, thus rendering them dissatisfied and less prone to return and/or to recommend (Oliver, 1980).

There also remains a lack of consensus on first-time and repeat spectator spending behaviours and behavioural intentions. This study was therefore carried out to assess and compare the consumer behaviours of first-time and repeat visitors to the FIA WRC, held in Sardinia, Italy (13-16 June 2019), with the aim of investigating whether any significant differences exist between the two groups of spectators in terms of their spending behaviours, satisfaction with the event and behavioural intentions.

METHODOLOGY

Established in 1973, in 2019, the FIA WRC organized 14 rallies worldwide, including Sardinia, Italy. WRC events typically include 15-25 special stages (SSs) run on closed roads. Sardinia has been hosting Italy's FIA WRC since 2004. Thanks to its geology, coastlines, flora and Mediterranean scrub, Sardinia can offer an unforgettable experience to rally fans and drivers. That is why it is considered one of the most beautiful and challenging WRC races. This is somehow confirmed by data and figures related to the event. In 2019, 94 teams from 23 different countries participated in the race, of which 50 were from Italy; on the whole, the event registered more than 50,000 spectators in the service park, and about 60,000 unique spectators at the SSs. Furthermore, the event was watched on television by more than two million Italian viewers. For the purposes of the study, a survey instrument was developed, based on a review of the literature on sports events and motor sports assessments, especially in relation to first-time and repeat visitors' behaviour (Del Chiappa et al., 2014). The questionnaire was originally designed in Italian and then translated into English by a professional translator. Hence, back-translation was used for quality assurance purposes.

The questionnaire was divided into three sections. In the first, sociodemographic information (gender, age, marital status, level of education and occupation), as well as the travel-related characteristics of respondents (where to stay, length of stay, travel party, prior experience with the destination and the event etc.), was asked for. Consistent with existing studies, the second section assessed the level of agreement with a list of 10 items specifically used to measure spectators' satisfaction and behavioural intentions regarding the destination and the event. For this purpose, a five-point Likert scale (1=strongly disagree; 5=strongly agree) was used. The final section asked respondents to provide information about their immediate group's average daily expenditure on accommodation and other services used during their stay (e.g., hotel, bed and breakfast, rented apartment, local transportation, food and beverage, souvenirs and car rental service).

Data were collected on site during the period of the 2019 FIA WRC in Sardinia (13-16 June). Five interviewers first intercepted potential respondents (aged more than 16 years both at the service parking area and at the site of the SSs) then administered the questionnaire via face-to face encounters. At the end of the event, a sample of 318 completed surveys was obtained. Sports tourism survey data were coded and analysed using Stata (Version 2013), and a series of descriptive analyses, independent t-tests and regression analyses were performed in line with the purposes of the study.

FINDINGS AND DISCUSSION

Respondents were primarily male (69.2%), aged more than 51 years (21.1%) or belonged to the age group 31-35 years (17.3%), who reported themselves to be high school graduates (42.99%), employed (41.72%), and married or cohabiting (34.4%). Most of the respondents were foreign (68.5%), whereas only 13.6% were reported to be Sardinian residents. Furthermore, interviewees were mostly repeaters (58%). First-time visitors accounted for 42%, most of whom (53.3%) had decided to visit Sardinia just to attend the event. Around 60% of respondents had spent between three and seven days in Sardinia and were travelling with friends (42%), in groups comprising two to three people. Furthermore, they mostly relied on official programmes (42.5%), the event website (40%) or friends or relatives (33%) to gain information about the event. Overall, spectators were reported to be satisfied with both the event (M=4.61) and their holiday experience in Sardinia (M=4.63); this certainly helps to explain why respondents were reported as highly willing to revisit Sardinia (M=4.70) and to attend the event (M=4.57), as well as to sustain destination-related traditional word of mouth (Sardinia: M=4.68) as well as event-related traditional and electronic word of mouth (WOM: M=4.48, eWOM=4.41) (Table 1).

That said, repeaters were significantly more satisfied than first-time spectators both with the event (repeaters: M=4.71; first-time spectators: M=4.61; t=-2.78, $p<0.01$) and with the destination experience (repeaters: M=4.74; first-time spectators: M=4.54; t=-2.48, $p<0.05$). When compared to first-time spectators, repeaters are

Table 1. Comparisons of ðrst-time and repeat WRC spectators' satisfaction and behavioural intentions: mean scores and independent t-tests

Items (Five-Point Likert Scale)	Total	First-timers	Repeaters	*t*
	Mean	Mean	Mean	
I'm satisfied with my visit to this event	4.61	4.51	4.71	-2.78 ***
I'm satisfied with my visit to Sardinia	4.63	4.54	4.74	-2.48 **
I will encourage friends/relatives and neighbours to visit this event	4.48	4.33	4.65	-3.84 ***
I will encourage friends/relatives and neighbours to visit Sardinia	4.68	4.61	4.76	-2.13 **
Based on my experience while attending this event, I think I will write a positive comment/review on a social media platform (Facebook, Twitter etc.)	4.41	4.30	4.53	-2.62 ***
In the near future, I would like to attend to this event again	4.57	4.41	4.76	-4.27 ***
In the near future, I would like to come back to Sardinia	4.70	4.63	4.78	-2.2 **

(** $p<0.05$, *** $p<0.01$)

more prone to attend the event in the future (repeaters: M=4.76; first-time spectators: M=4.41; t=-4.27, $p<0.05$), and to recommend it to others, both offline (repeaters: M=4.65; first-time spectators: M=4.33; t=-3.84, $p<0.01$) and online (repeaters: M=4.53; first-time spectators: M=4.30; t=-2.62, $p<0.01$). The same can be noted regarding the likelihood to revisit the destination (repeaters: M=4.78; first-time spectators: M=4.63; t=-2.2, $p<0.05$) and to recommend it to others (repeaters: M=4.76; first-time spectators: M=4.61; t=-2.13, $p<0.05$).

In addition, Ordinary Least Squares (OLS) regression analysis was carried out to ascertain which sociodemographic and travel-related characteristics are able to significantly influence spectators' spending behaviour (Table 2).

When sociodemographic information is considered, findings reveal that marital status exerts a significant influence on total expenditure ($p<0.01$), as well as employment status, with employees ($p<0.01$) and retired individuals ($p<0.01$) spending the least. Residential status significantly shapes spending behaviour, with international spectators ($p<0.01$) spending more than Sardinian residents. Finally, expenditure was reported to be significantly influenced by prior experience ($p<0.05$), with first-time spectators spending less than repeaters, and length of stay ($p<0.05$), with those enjoying a shorter stay spending less than those individuals enjoying a

Table 2. Results of OLS analysis (standard errors in parentheses)

Variable		Coefficients (1)	
Gender	Male	-0.02	(0.05)
Age	18-20	-0.14	(0.19)
	21-25	0.054	(0.14)
	26-30	0.03	(0.10)
	31-35	-0.04	(0.08)
	41-45	-0.07	(0.08)
	46-50	0.03	(0.09)
	>50	0.01	(0.10)
Marital status	Single	1.29***	(0.09)
	Engaged	1.24***	(0.10)
	Married/cohabiting	1.32***	(0.09)
	Widow	1.35***	(0.16)
	Divorced	1.35***	(0.11)
Level of education	Primary school	-	
	(omitted for multicollinearity)	-	
	Secondary school	-0.03	(0.15)
	High school	0.03	(0.15)
	Bachelor's degree	0.04	(0.15)
	PhD/master's degree	0.01	(0.21)
Occupation	Employee	-0.17**	(0.07)
	Executive/manager		
	(omitted for multicollinearity)	-	
	Self-employed	-0.13	(0.08)
	Occasional worker	-0.11	(0.10)
	Unemployed	-0.20	(0.13)
	Retired	-0.25**	(0.13)
	Student	-0.12	(0.14)
	Other	-0.65	(0.52)
Residential status	Sardinian		
	(omitted for multicollinearity)	-	
	Italian	0.42	(0.22)
	Foreign	0.62***	(0.22)
Prior experience	First time at WRC Sardinia	-0.09**	(0.04)
Length of stay	Less than 3 days	-0.18**	(0.09)
	3-7 days	-0.08	(0.06)
	More than 7 days (omitted for multicollinearity)	-	
Constant		3.73***	(0.29)
N			246
Prob>F			0.000
R-squared			0.2585

** p<0.05, *** p<0.01

longer stay in Sardinia. Age and level of education were reported as not being able to significantly influence the level of expenditure.

On the whole, the findings highlight strong similarities with those reported in previous research carried out in different event settings. For example, the findings are in line with existing studies (e.g., Kruger et. al, 2010; Wang, 2004) which find that repeaters spend more than first-time visitors. Furthermore, these findings reveal that repeaters are significantly more willing to return to the event/destination and to recommend them to others when compared to first-time visitors, thus supporting Del Chiappa et al.'s (2014) study on motor sports events and Del Chiappa et al.'s (2017) study on cultural events.

SOLUTIONS AND RECOMMENDATIONS

From a managerial perspective, the results suggest that policymakers and destination marketers should run marketing operations aimed at attracting an effective visitor/spectator mix, in which the proportions of first-timers and repeaters are balanced, in turn enabling the hosting destination to obtain the highest level of economic and marketing benefits. For example, the lower average expenditure of first-time spectators might be explained with reference to their relatively poor knowledge and familiarity with the destination; hence, policymakers and destination marketers should plan and implement marketing and promotional operations aimed at effectively disseminating information related to their attractions, service providers and diverse entertainment opportunities (e.g., other local events, museums, excursions) to first-timers, so that they can be incentivized to experience more while at the event/destination, thus increasing their average level of expenditure. Furthermore, loyalty schemes could be offered to repeaters (who are "high spenders") to retain these types of visitors, for example, in the form of special discounts on the cost of experiencing certain shows, attractions and leisure activities.

FUTURE RESEARCH DIRECTIONS

Although this study helps to fill a gap in the existing literature and proposes some managerial implications, limitations still remain. First, a convenience sample from a single event in a specific hosting destination was used, thus rendering the results hardly generalizable. Future studies could be carried out at other motor sports events for wider generalizations. Second, the study focused on the actual expenditure reported by visitors, but did not consider the moderator effect that the economic budgets of spectators could exert on their spending behaviours; further, the career ladder of visitors/spectators could not be taken into account. These aspects could merit attention in future studies, given the relevance they might have in seeking to better understand why differences exist between the real expenditure of respondents and to improve event promotion and marketing communications.

CONCLUSION

By selecting the 2019 WRC rally in Sardinia, the purpose of this study was to better understand first-time and repeat spectators' spending behaviour, satisfaction and behavioural intentions, thus providing fresh and updated insights that might help to extend the scientific debate on motor sports event management and marketing, in turn providing policymakers, destination marketers and event organizers with useful information with which to effectively plan and implement their marketing strategies.

Specifically, from a theoretical point of view, the findings reveal that repeaters spend more than first-time spectators, as well as being more satisfied and prone to both return to the event/destination and recommend them to others. This is in line with some existing studies (e.g., Li et al., 2008; Oppermann, 1998), while contradicting others (Anwar & Sohail, 2004; Jang et al., 2004); this could be explained by arguing that these studies have been carried out in different event settings, all of which are obviously highly site-specific (in terms of the sociodemographic characteristics and personality of visitors, tourism offer, retail and commercial facilities etc.) and thus hardly generalizable. Meanwhile, the results show that all but two sociodemographic and travel related characteristics significantly influence the level of expenditure of spectators. Even though some inconsistencies exist in the findings, from a managerial point of view, this study provides useful information to policymakers, destination marketers and event organizers involved in planning and implementing effective and tailored marketing and promotional operations, as they will be able to recognize the sociodemographic and travel-related nuances of visitors/spectators, thus rendering the event (and the destination) in question attractive. Acknowledging its main limitations, this study also suggests future research directions.

REFERENCES

Anwar, S. A., & Sohail, M. S. (2004). Festival tourism in the United Arab Emirates: First-time versus repeat visitor perceptions. *Journal of Vacation Marketing, 10*(2), 161–170. doi:10.1177/135676670401000206

Assael, H. (2004). *Consumer behavior: A strategic approach.* Houghton Mifflin.

Beckman, E., & Traynor, M. (2019). Utilizing trade market analysis to identify the economic impact of a multiday special event in Miami Beach, Florida. *Tourism Economics, 25*(2), 253–273. doi:10.1177/1354816618800194

Black, D. (2007). The Symbolic Politics of Sport Mega-Events: 2010 in Comparative Perspective. *Politikon, 34*(3), 261–276. doi:10.1080/02589340801962536

Bohlin, M. (2000). Travelling to events. In L. L. Mossberg (Ed.), *Evaluation of Events: Scandinavian Experiences* (pp. 13–29). Cognizant Communication.

Bowdin, G. A. J. (2006). *Events management* (2nd ed.). doi:10.4324/9780080457154

Cho, V. (2009). A study of non-economic determinants in tourism demand. *International Journal of Tourism Research, 12*(4), 307–320. doi:10.1002/jtr.749

Coakley, J. (1986). *Sport in Society: Issues and Controversies.* Times Mirror/Mosby College Publishing.

Daniels, M. J., & Norman, W. C. (2003). Estimating the Economic Impacts of Seven Regular Sport Tourism Events. *Journal of Sport & Tourism, 8*(4), 214–222. doi:10.1080/1477508032000161528

Del Chiappa, G., & Atzeni, M. (2016). The role of emotions in a sport event experience. *Tourismos, 11*(5).

Del Chiappa, G., Melis, G., & Atzeni, M. (2017). Driving first-time and repeat spectators to cultural events. In A. Correia, M. Kozak, J. Gnoth, & A. Fyall (Eds.), *Co-creation and wellbeing in tourism* (pp. 47–59). Springer. doi:10.1007/978-3-319-44108-5_4

Del Chiappa, G., Tinaz, C., & Michele Turco, D. (2014). Driving first-time and repeat spectators to a motor sport event. *International Journal of Culture, Tourism and Hospitality Research, 8*(4), 388–400. doi:10.1108/IJCTHR-03-2014-0023

Essex, S., & Chalkley, B. (2004). Mega-sporting events in urban and regional policy: A history of the Winter Olympics. *Planning Perspectives, 19*(2), 201–204. doi:10.1080/0266543042000192475

Fakeye, P. C., & Crompton, J. L. (1991). Image Differences between Prospective, First-Time, and Repeat Visitors to the Lower Rio Grande Valley. *Journal of Travel Research, 30*(2), 10–16. doi:10.1177/004728759103000202

Formica, S., & Uysal, M. (1998). Market Segmentation of an International Cultural-Historical Event in Italy. *Journal of Travel Research, 36*(4), 16–24. doi:10.1177/004728759803600402

Fotiadis, A., Xie, L., Li, Y., & Huan, T. C. (2016). Attracting athletes to small-scale sports events using motivational decision-making factors. *Journal of Business Research, 69*(11), 5467–5472. doi:10.1016/j.jbusres.2016.04.157

Funk, D. C., Toohey, K., & Bruun, T. (2007). International Sport Event Participation: Prior Sport Involvement; Destination Image; and Travel Motives. *European Sport Management Quarterly, 7*(3), 227–248. doi:10.1080/16184740701511011

Getz, D. (2008). Event tourism: Definition, evolution, and research. *Tourism Management, 29*(3), 403–428. doi:10.1016/j.tourman.2007.07.017

Getz, D., & Page, S. J. (2016). Progress and prospects for event tourism research. *Tourism Management, 52*, 593–631. doi:10.1016/j.tourman.2015.03.007

Gibson, H. (1998). Sport Tourism: A Critical Analysis of Research. *Sport Management Review, 1*(1), 45–76. doi:10.1016/S1441-3523(98)70099-3

Gitelson, R. J., & Crompton, J. L. (1984). Insights into the repeat vacation phenomenon. *Annals of Tourism Research, 11*(2), 199–217. doi:10.1016/0160-7383(84)90070-7

Hallmann, K., Kaplanidou, K., & Breuer, C. (2010). Event image perceptions among active and passive sports tourists at marathon races. *International Journal of Sports Marketing & Sponsorship, 12*(1), 32–47. doi:10.1108/IJSMS-12-01-2010-B005

Herrero, L. C., Sanz, J. Á., Devesa, M., Bedate, A., & del Barrio, M. J. (2006). The Economic Impact of Cultural Events: A Case-Study of Salamanca 2002, European Capital of Culture. *European Urban and Regional Studies, 13*(1), 41–57. doi:10.1177/0969776406058946

Higham, J. (1999). Commentary—sport as an avenue of tourism development: An analysis of the positive and negative impacts of sport tourism. *Current Issues in Tourism, 2*(1), 82–90. doi:10.1080/13683509908667845

Jang, S., Bai, B., Hong, G.-S., & O'Leary, J. T. (2004). Understanding travel expenditure patterns: A study of Japanese pleasure travelers to the United States by income level. *Tourism Management, 25*(3), 331–341. doi:10.1016/S0261-5177(03)00141-9

Kaplanidou, K., & Gibson, H. (2012). Differences between first time and repeat spectator tourists of a youth soccer event: Intentions and image approaches. *Current Issues in Tourism, 15*(5), 477–487. doi:10.1080/13683500.2011.607924

Kemperman, A. D. A. M., Joh, C., & Timmermans, H. J. P. (2004). Comparing first-time and repeat visitors' activity patterns in a tourism environment. In G. I. Crouch, R. R. Perdue, H. J. P. Timmermans, & M. Uysal (Eds.), *Consumer psychology of tourism, hospitality and leisure* (pp. 103–119). doi:10.1079/9780851997490.0103

Kruger, M., Saayman, M., & Ellis, S. M. (2010). Does loyalty pay? First-time versus repeat visitors at a national arts festival. *Southern African Business Review, 14*(1), 79–104.

Lau, A. L. S., & McKercher, B. (2004). Exploration Versus Acquisition: A Comparison of First-Time and Repeat Visitors. *Journal of Travel Research, 42*(3), 279–285. doi:10.1177/0047287503257502

Leiper, N. (1990). Tourist attraction systems. *Annals of Tourism Research, 17*(3), 367–384. doi:10.1016/0160-7383(90)90004-B

Li, X. R., Cheng, C.-K., Kim, H., & Petrick, J. F. (2008). A systematic comparison of first-time and repeat visitors via a two-phase online survey. *Tourism Management, 29*(2), 278–293. doi:10.1016/j.tourman.2007.03.010

Mackellar, J., & Reis, A. C. (2014). World Rally Championships 2009 and 2011: Assessing the tourism value in Australia. *Journal of Vacation Marketing, 20*(1), 17–28. doi:10.1177/1356766713484728

Morgan, N. J., Pritchard, A., & Pride, R. (2004). *Destination Branding: Creating the unique destination proposition.* Academic Press.

Müller, M. (2015). What makes an event a mega-event? Definitions and sizes. *Leisure Studies, 34*(6), 627–642. doi:10.1080/02614367.2014.993333

Nauright, J. (2004). Global games: Culture, political economy and sport in the globalised world of the 21st century. *Third World Quarterly, 25*(7), 1325–1336. doi:10.1080/014365904200281302

Oliver, R. L. (1980). A Cognitive Model of the Antecedents and Consequences of Satisfaction Decisions. *JMR, Journal of Marketing Research, 17*(4), 460–469. doi:10.1177/002224378001700405

Oppermann, M. (1997). First-time and repeat visitors to New Zealand. *Tourism Management, 18*(3), 177–181. doi:10.1016/S0261-5177(96)00119-7

Oppermann, M. (1998). Destination Threshold Potential and the Law of Repeat Visitation. *Journal of Travel Research, 37*(2), 131–137. doi:10.1177/004728759803700204

Petrick, J. F. (2004). First Timers' and Repeaters' Perceived Value. *Journal of Travel Research, 43*(1), 29–38. doi:10.1177/0047287504265509

Petrick, J. F., Morais, D. D., & Norman, W. C. (2001). An examination of the determinants of entertainment vacationers' intentions to revisit. *Journal of Travel Research, 40*(1), 41–48. doi:10.1177/004728750104000106

Quick, S. (2000). Contemporary sport consumers: Some implications of linking fan typology with key spectator variables. *Sport Marketing Quarterly, 9*(3), 149–156.

Raya, M. J. (2012). Length of stay for triathlon participants in the challenge Maresme-Barcelona: A survival approach. *Journal of Sport and Social Issues, 36*(1), 86–105. doi:10.1177/0193723511433868

Reid, L. J., & Reid, S. D. (1993). Communicating tourism supplier services: Building repeat visitor relationships. *Journal of Travel & Tourism Marketing, 2*(2-3), 3–19. doi:10.1300/J073v02n02_02

Saayman, M., & Saayman, A. (2008). Socio-demographic and behavioural determinants of visitor spending at a national arts festival: A panel data analysis. *World Journal on Events, 1*(1), 28–33.

Samra, B., & Wos, A. (2014). Consumer in Sports: Fan typology analysis. *Journal of Intercultural Management, 6*(4–1), 263–288. doi:10.2478/joim-2014-0050

Sato, M., Jordan, J. S., Kaplanidou, K., & Funk, D. C. (2014). Determinants of tourists' expenditure at mass participant sport events: A ðve-year analysis. *Current Issues in Tourism, 17*(9), 763–771. doi:10.1080/13683500.2014.892918

Scott, A. K. S., & Turco, D. M. (2011). Spectator profiles and economic impact of the 2009 US Women's Open. *Thunderbird International Business Review, 53*(6), 701–708. doi:10.1002/tie.20446

Silvestre, A. L., Santos, C. M., & Ramalho, C. (2008). Satisfaction and Behavioural Intentions of Cruise Passengers Visiting the Azores. *Tourism Economics, 14*(1), 169–184. doi:10.5367/000000008783554802

Szwarc, P. (2005). *Researching customer satisfaction & loyalty: How to find out what people really think*. Kogan Page.

Toohey, K., & Veal, A. J. (2007). The Olympic Games: A social science perspective (2nd ed.). Wallingford, UK: CABI.

Turco, D. M. (2010), Understanding the sport mega-event tourist: 2010 World Cup South Africa and implications for 2014 World Cup Brasil. *XI National Congress of Sports Management APOGESD.*

Turco, D. M., Riley, R. S., & Swart, K. (2002). *Sport tourism*. Fitness Information Technology.

Wang, D. (2004). Tourist Behaviour and Repeat Visitation to Hong Kong. *Tourism Geographies*, *6*(1), 99–118. doi:10.1080/1461668032000172355

Warnick, R. B., Bojanic, D. C., & Xu, F. (2015). Using a Trade Market Analysis Technique to Refine Measurements for Economic Impact Analysis of Special Events. *Journal of Travel Research*, *54*(1), 52–65. doi:10.1177/0047287513513160

Whitson, D., & Horne, J. (2006). Underestimated Costs and Overestimated Benefits? Comparing the Outcomes of Sports Mega-Events in Canada and Japan. *The Sociological Review*, *54*(2_suppl), 73–89. doi:10.1111/j.1467-954X.2006.00654.x

Wicker, P., Hallmann, K., & Zhang, J. J. (2012). What is influencing consumer expenditure and intention to revisit? An investigation of marathon events. *Journal of Sport & Tourism*, *17*(3), 165–182. doi:10.1080/14775085.2012.734058

Xing, X., & Chalip, L. (2006). Effects of Hosting a Sport Event on Destination Brand: A Test of Co-branding and Match-up Models. *Sport Management Review*, *9*(1), 49–78. doi:10.1016/S1441-3523(06)70019-5

Yuan, J., & Jang, S. (2008). The Effects of Quality and Satisfaction on Awareness and Behavioral Intentions: Exploring the Role of a Wine Festival. *Journal of Travel Research*, *46*(3), 279–288. doi:10.1177/0047287507308322

Zajc, P., & Berzelak, N. (2016). Riding styles and characteristics of rides among Slovenian mountain bikers and management challenges. *Journal of Outdoor Recreation and Tourism*, *15*, 10–19. doi:10.1016/j.jort.2016.04.009

Compilation of References

Abratt, R., Clayton, B. C., & Pitt, L. F. (1987). Corporate Objectives in Sports Sponsorship. *International Journal of Advertising*, *6*(4), 299–311. doi:10.1080/02650487.1987.11107030

Adair, D. (Eds.). (n.d.). Sport Tourism: Interrelationships, Impacts and Issues. Channel View.

Aicher, T. J., Karadakis, K., & Eddosary, M. (2015). Comparison of sport tourists' and locals' motivation to participate in a running event. *International Journal of Event and Festival Management*, *3*(3), 215–234. doi:10.1108/IJEFM-03-2015-0011

Aitchison, C. (1999). New cultural geographies: The spatiality of leisure, gender and sexuality. *Leisure Studies*, *18*(1), 19–39. doi:10.1080/026143699375032

Alexandris, K., Theodorakis, N., Kaplanidou, K., & Papadimitriou, D. (2017). Event quality and loyalty among runners with different running involvement levels: The case of "The Alexander the Great" International Marathon. *International Journal of Event and Festival Management*, *8*(3), 292–307. doi:10.1108/IJEFM-08-2016-0057

Allen, J. (2009). *Event planning: The ultimate guide to successful meetings, corporate events, fundraising galas, conferences, conventions, incentives and other special events*. John Wiley & Sons.

Allen, J. B., & Bartle, M. (2014). Sport event volunteers' engagement: Management matters. *Managing Leisure*, *19*(1), 36–50. doi:10.1080/13606719.2013.849502

Allen, J., O'toole, W., Harris, R., & McDonnell, I. (2008). *Festival and special event management*. John Wiley & Sons Incorporated.

Almiraman.gr. (2020). *Almira Man - May 2020 Paralia, Katerini, Greece*. Available at: https://www.almiraman.gr/english/almiraman_en.html

Andranovich, G., Burbank, M. J., & Heying, C. H. (2001). Olympic cities: Lessons learned from mega-event politics. *Journal of Urban Affairs*, *23*(2), 113–131. doi:10.1111/0735-2166.00079

Ansoff, I. (1957). Strategies for Diversification. *Harvard Business Review*, *35*(5), 113–124.

Antony, M. (1981). *Handbook of Small Business Advertising*. Addison-Wesley Publishing Company, Inc.

Anwar, S. A., & Sohail, M. S. (2004). Festival tourism in the United Arab Emirates: First-time versus repeat visitor perceptions. *Journal of Vacation Marketing*, *10*(2), 161–170. doi:10.1177/135676670401000206

Assael, H. (2004). *Consumer behavior: A strategic approach*. Houghton Mifflin.

Azara, I., Wiltshier, P., & Greatorex, J. (2018). Against all odds: Embedding new knowledge for event continuity and community well-being. *Event Management*, *22*(1), 25–36. doi:10.3727/152599517X15111988553964

Bang, H., & Chelladurai, P. (2009). Development and validation of the volunteer motivations scale for international sporting events (VMS-ISE). *International Journal of Sport Management and Marketing*, *6*(4), 332–350. doi:10.1504/IJSMM.2009.030064

Bang, H., & Ross, S. D. (2009). Volunteer motivation and satisfaction. *Journal of Venue and Event Management*, *1*(1), 61–77.

Barez, A., Manion, M. T., Schoepfer, K. L., & Cherian, J. (2007). Global Cases of Effective Sports Sponsorship: An Exploration of a New Communications Model. *Innovative Marketing*, *3*(3), 69–77.

Bauer, H. H., Stokburger-Sauer, N. E., & Exler, S. (2008). Brand Image and Fan Loyalty in Professional Team Sport: A Refined Model and Empirical Assessment. *Journal of Sport Management*, *22*(2), 205–226. doi:10.1123/jsm.22.2.205

Baum, T., Deery, M., & Hanlon, C. (Eds.). (2009). *People and work in events and conventions: A research perspective*. Cabi. doi:10.1079/9781845934767.0000

Bazzanella, F., Peters, M., & Schnitzer, M. (2019). The perceptions of stakeholders in small-scale sporting events. *Journal of Convention & Event Tourism*, *20*(4), 261–286. Advance online publication. doi:10.1080/15470148.2019.1640819

Beckman, E., & Traynor, M. (2019). Utilizing trade market analysis to identify the economic impact of a multiday special event in Miami Beach, Florida. *Tourism Economics*, *25*(2), 253–273. doi:10.1177/1354816618800194

Berry, L. L. (2000). Cultivating service brand equity. *Journal of the Academy of Marketing Science*, *28*(1), 128–137. doi:10.1177/0092070300281012

Bertella, G. (2014). Designing small-scale sport events in the countryside. *International Journal of Event and Festival Management*, *5*(2), 132–145. doi:10.1108/IJEFM-05-2013-0008

Bichi, A., Wijlens, R., & Wallace, E. (2017). *Strategic research and Innovation Agenda 2016-2021*. EPSI.

Bitner, M. J. (1992). Servicescapes: The Impact of Physical Surroundings on Customers and Employees. *Journal of Marketing*, *56*(2), 57–71. doi:10.1177/002224299205600205

Bjerke, M. B., & Renger, R. (2017). Being smart about writing SMART objectives. *Evaluation and Program Planning*, *61*, 125–127. doi:10.1016/j.evalprogplan.2016.12.009 PMID:28056403

Black, D. (2007). The Symbolic Politics of Sport Mega-Events: 2010 in Comparative Perspective. *Politikon*, *34*(3), 261–276. doi:10.1080/02589340801962536

Bladen, C., Kennell, J., Abson, E., & Wilde, N. (2018). *Events management: an introduction* (2nd ed.). Routledge.

Boezeman, E. J., & Ellemers, N. (2007). Volunteering for charity: Pride, respect, and the commitment of volunteers. *The Journal of Applied Psychology*, *92*(3), 771–785. doi:10.1037/0021-9010.92.3.771 PMID:17484556

Bohlin, M. (2000). Travelling to events. In L. L. Mossberg (Ed.), *Evaluation of Events: Scandinavian Experiences* (pp. 13–29). Cognizant Communication.

Booms, B. H., & Bitner, M. J. (1981). Marketing strategies and organisation structures for service firms. In J. Donnelly & W. R. George (Eds.), *Marketing of Services*. American Marketing Association.

Bowdin, G. A. J., Allen, J., O'Toole, W., Harris, R., & McDonnell, I. (2012). *Events Management*. Taylor & Francis Group.

Bowdin, G. A. J. (2006). *Events management* (2nd ed.). doi:10.4324/9780080457154

Bowdin, G. A. J., Allen, J., O'Toole, W., Harris, R., & McDonnell, I. (2011). *Events Management* (3rd ed.). Butterworth-Heinemann, Elsevier.

Breuer, C., & Rumpf, C. (2012). The viewer's reception and processing of sponsorship information in sport telecasts. *Journal of Sport Management*, *26*(6), 521–531. doi:10.1123/jsm.26.6.521

Broom, G. M., Casey, S., & Ritchey, J. (2000). Concepts and theory of organization-public relationships. In J. A. Ledingham & S. D. Bruning (Eds.), *Public relations as relationship management: A relational approach to the study and practice of public relations* (pp. 3–22). Lawrence Erlbaum Associates.

Brown, A. L., Meer, J., & Williams, J. F. (2019). Why do people volunteer? An experimental analysis of preferences for time donations. *Management Science*, *65*(4), 1455–1468. doi:10.1287/mnsc.2017.2951

Brown, G. (2020). *Eventscapes-Transforming Place, Space and Experiences*. Routledge.

Bruning, S. D., & Ledingham, J. A. (1999). Relationships between organizations and publics: Development of a multi-dimensional organization-public relationship scale. *Public Relations Review*, *25*(2), 157–170. doi:10.1016/S0363-8111(99)80160-X

Burnett, C. (2006). Building social capital through an 'active community club'. *International Review for the Sociology of Sport*, *41*(3/4), 283–294. doi:10.1177/1012690207078381

Burrai, E., Buda, D.-M., & Stanford, D. (2019). Rethinking the ideology of responsible tourism. *Journal of Sustainable Tourism, 1*(16).

Bussell, H., & Forbes, D. (2002). Understanding the volunteer market: The what, where, who and why of volunteering. *International Journal of Nonprofit and Voluntary Sector Marketing, 7*(3), 244–257. doi:10.1002/nvsm.183

Buterfield, G. (2019). *Everything you need to know about Ashbourne Royal Festival 2019.* Retrieved February 28, 2019 from: https://www.derbytelegraph.co.uk/news/ashbourne-royal-shrovetide-2019-2570247

Butler, R. W. (1980). The concept of tourism area cycle of evolution: Implications for management of resources. *The Canadian Geographer. Geographe Canadien, 24*(1), 5–12. doi:10.1111/j.1541-0064.1980.tb00970.x

Byers, T. (Ed.). (2016). *Contemporary issues in sport management: A critical introduction.* Sage Publications. doi:10.4135/9781473919761

Cafferata, R. (2004). Governance and Management in the Business of Sport. *Symphonia-Emerging issues in Management, 2*, 5-25.

Carlisle, J. (2017). *U.S., Mexico and Canada officially launch bid to co-host 2026 World Cup.* Retrieved from https://www.espn.co.uk/football/fifa-world-cup/story/3100808/usmexico-and-canada-officially-launch-bid-to-co-host-2026-world-cup

Carmouche, R., Shukla, N., & Anthonisz, A. (2010). *Events marketing and communication strategy.* JUTA.

Cater, E. (1993). Ecotourism in the third world: Problems for sustainable tourism development. *Tourism Management, 14*(2), 85–90. doi:10.1016/0261-5177(93)90040-R

Chalip, L. (2001). Sport and tourism: Capitalising on the linkage. *The Business of Sport*, 77-89.

Chalip, L. (2004). Beyond impact: a general model for host community event leverage. Academic Press.

Chalip, L., & Costa, C. A. (2005). Sport Event Tourism and the Destination Brand: Towards a General Theory. *Sport in Society, 8*(2), 218–237. doi:10.1080/17430430500108579

Chalip, L., Green, B. C., & Hill, B. (2003). Effects of sport event media on destination image and intention to visit. *Journal of Sport Management, 17*(3), 214–234. doi:10.1123/jsm.17.3.214

Chalip, L., & Leyns, A. (2002). Local Business Leveraging of a Sport Event: Managing an Event for Economic Benefit. *Journal of Sport Management, 16*(2), 132–158. doi:10.1123/jsm.16.2.132

Cho, V. (2009). A study of non-economic determinants in tourism demand. *International Journal of Tourism Research, 12*(4), 307–320. doi:10.1002/jtr.749

Clary, E. G., Snyder, M., Ridge, R. D., Copeland, J., Stukas, A. A., Haugen, J., & Miene, P. (1998). Understanding and assessing the motivations of volunteers: A functional approach. *Journal of Personality and Social Psychology, 74*(6), 1516–1530. doi:10.1037/0022-3514.74.6.1516 PMID:9654757

Clement, E., & Demonque, C. (1995). *Philosophie*. Paris: Hatier. Available from: http://www.winchestercriterium.org/criterium/

Clifford, D. K. Jr. (1965). Managing the Product Life Cycle. *Management Review, 54*(6), 34–38.

Coakley, J. (1986). *Sport in Society: Issues and Controversies*. Times Mirror/Mosby College Publishing.

Coleman, J. S. (1990). *Foundations of social theory*. Cambridge University Press.

Collins, C. (2018). *Ireland's soccer team manager denies targeting Catholic players in Northern Ireland.* Retrieved Mar 3, 2018 from https://cruxnow.com/church-in-uk-and-ireland/2018/03/09/irelands-soccer-team-manager-denies-targeting-catholic-players-northern-ireland/

Cooper, D. J., & Morgan, W. (2008). Case Study Research in Accounting. *Accounting Horizons, 22*(2), 159–178. doi:10.2308/acch.2008.22.2.159

Cornwell, T. B. (1995). Sponsorship-linked marketing development. *Sport Marketing Quarterly, 4*(4), 13–24.

Costa, C. A., Chalip, L., Green, B. C., & Simes, C. (2006). Reconsidering the role of training in event volunteers' satisfaction. *Sport Management Review, 9*(2), 165–182. doi:10.1016/S1441-3523(06)70024-9

Council, K. C. (n.d.). *Sports Events Checklist*. Retrieved from https://www.kentsport.org/wp-content/uploads/2016/06/sports_sheet_sports_events_checklist.pdf

Crompton, J. (1993). Understanding a business organization's approach to entering a sponsorship partnership. *Festival Management & Event Tourism, 1*(3), 98–109. doi:10.3727/106527093792337565

Crompton, J. (1994). Benefits and risks associated with sponsorship of major events. *Festival Management & Event Tourism, 2*(2), 65–74. doi:10.3727/106527094792292050

Crompton, J. (1996). The potential contributions of sports sponsorship in impacting the product adoption process. *Managing Leisure, 1*(4), 199–212. doi:10.1080/136067196376302

Crompton, J. (2014). Potential negative outcomes from sponsorship for a sport property. *Managing Leisure, 19*(6), 420–441. doi:10.1080/13606719.2014.912050

Crompton, J. L., & McKay, S. L. (1994). Measuring the economic impact of festivals and events: Some myths, misapplications and ethical dilemmas. *Festival Management & Event Tourism, 2*(1), 33–43. doi:10.3727/106527094792335782

Csobán, K. V., & Serra, G. (2014). The role of small-scale sports events in developing sustainable sport tourism – a case study of fencing. *Applied Studies in Agribusiness and Commerce*, *8*(4), 17–22. doi:10.19041/Apstract/2014/4/3

Cullingford, C. (1995). Children's attitudes to holidays overseas. *Tourism Management*, *16*(2), 121–127. doi:10.1016/0261-5177(94)00022-3

Cunha, M. P., & Putnam, L. L. (2019). Paradox theory and the paradox of success. *Strategic Organization*, *17*(1), 95–106. doi:10.1177/1476127017739536

Cuskelly, G., Auld, C., Harrington, M., & Coleman, D. (2004). Predicting the behavioral dependability of sport event volunteers. *Event Management*, *9*(1-2), 73–89. doi:10.3727/1525995042781011

Cyclefest. (n.d.). Available from: http://www.winchestercriterium.org/cyclefest/

Daniels, M. J. (2007). Central place theory and sport tourism impacts. *Annals of Tourism Research*, *34*(2), 332–347. doi:10.1016/j.annals.2006.09.004

Daniels, M. J., & Norman, W. C. (2003). Estimating the Economic Impacts of Seven Regular Sport Tourism Events. *Journal of Sport & Tourism*, *8*(4), 214–222. doi:10.1080/1477508032000161528

Dayan, D., & Katz, E. (1994). *Media events*. Harvard University Press.

Del Chiappa, G., & Atzeni, M. (2016). The role of emotions in a sport event experience. *Tourismos*, *11*(5).

Del Chiappa, G., Melis, G., & Atzeni, M. (2017). Driving first-time and repeat spectators to cultural events. In A. Correia, M. Kozak, J. Gnoth, & A. Fyall (Eds.), *Co-creation and wellbeing in tourism* (pp. 47–59). Springer. doi:10.1007/978-3-319-44108-5_4

Del Chiappa, G., Tinaz, C., & Michele Turco, D. (2014). Driving first-time and repeat spectators to a motor sport event. *International Journal of Culture, Tourism and Hospitality Research*, *8*(4), 388–400. doi:10.1108/IJCTHR-03-2014-0023

Delpy, L., Grabijas, M., & Stefanovich, A. (1998). Sport tourism and corporate sponsorship: A winning combination. *Journal of Vacation Marketing*, *4*(1), 91–101. doi:10.1177/135676679800400108

Dichter, E. (1985). What's in an image. *Journal of Consumer Marketing*, *2*(1), 75–81. doi:10.1108/eb038824

Dimanche, F. (2003). The role of sport events in destination marketing. Aiest 53rd Congress in Sport and Tourism, Athens, Greece.

Doherty, A. (2005). A profile of community sport volunteers. Toronto: Parks and Recreation Ontario and Sport Alliance of Ontario.

Doherty, A. (2009). The volunteer legacy of a major sport event. *Journal of Policy Research in Tourism, Leisure & Events*, *1*(3), 185–207. doi:10.1080/19407960903204356

Dolles, H., & Söderman, S. (2008). Mega-Sporting Events in Asia — Impacts on Society, Business and Management: An Introduction. *Asian Business & Management*, *7*(2), 147–162. doi:10.1057/abm.2008.7

Dolphin, R. (2003). Sponsorship: Perspectives on its strategic role. *Corporate Communications*, *8*(3), 173–186. doi:10.1108/13563280310487630

Donlan, L., & Crowther, P. (2014). Leveraging sponsorship to achieve consumer relationship objectives through the creation of 'marketing spaces': An exploratory study. *Journal of Marketing Communications*, *20*(4), 291–306. doi:10.1080/13527266.2012.684068

Doshi, K., Schumacher, D., & Snyder, K. (2001). *Report on economic impact*. NASC.

DOSM. (2019). *Domestic Tourism Survey 2018*. Department of Statistics Malaysia.

Douvis, J., Sarli, E., Kriemadis, A., & Vrondou, O. (2015). An Analysis of Sponsorship Deals in Sport. *International Journal of Sport Management, Recreation and Tourism*, *17*, 14–36. doi:10.5199/ijsmart-1791-874X-17b

Dowse, S., Powell, S., & Weed, M. (2018). Mega-sporting events and children's rights and interests – towards a better future. *Leisure Studies*, *37*(1), 97–108. doi:10.1080/02614367.2017.1347698

Dowson, R., & Bassett, D. (2015). *Event planning and Management: A practical handbook for pr and events professionals*. Kogan Page Publishers.

Duglio, S., & Beltramo, R. (2017). Estimating the economic impacts of a small-scale sport tourism event: The case of the Italo-Swiss mountain trail CollonTrek. *Sustainability*, *9*(3), 1–17. doi:10.3390u9030343

Dunning, E., & Elias, N. (1986). *Quest for excitement: Sport and Leisure in the Civilizing Process*. Basil Blackwell.

Edgell, D. L., & Swanson, J. R. (2018). *Tourism policy and planning: Yesterday, today, and tomorrow* (3rd ed.). Routledge. doi:10.4324/9781351033541

Edwards, M. B. (2015). The role of sport in community capacity building: An examination of sport for development research and practice. *Sport Management Review*, *18*(1), 6–19. doi:10.1016/j.smr.2013.08.008

Eley, D., & Kirk, D. (2002). Developing Citizenship through Sport: The Impact of a Sport-Based Volunteer Programme on Young Sport Leaders. *Sport Education and Society*, *7*(2), 151–166. doi:10.1080/1357332022000018841

Elmose-Østerlund, K., & van der Roest, J. W. (2017). Understanding social capital in sports clubs: Participation, duration and social trust. *European Journal of Sport Science*, *14*(4), 366–386. do i:10.1080/16138171.2017.1378479

Emery, P. R. (2002). Bidding to host a major sports event: The local organising committee perspective. *International Journal of Public Sector Management, 15*(4), 316–335. doi:10.1108/09513550210430255

Essex, S., & Chalkley, B. (1998). Olympic Games: Catalyst of urban change. *Leisure Studies, 17*(3), 187–206. doi:10.1080/026143698375123

Essex, S., & Chalkley, B. (2004). Mega-sporting events in urban and regional policy: A history of the Winter Olympics. *Planning Perspectives, 19*(2), 201–204. doi:10.1080/0266543042000192475

Fairley, S., Green, B. C., O'Brien, D., & Chalip, L. (2014). Pioneer volunteers: The role identity of continuous volunteers at sport events. *Journal of Sport & Tourism, 19*(3-4), 233–255. doi:10.1080/14775085.2015.1111774

Fakeye, P. C., & Crompton, J. L. (1991). Image Differences between Prospective, First-Time, and Repeat Visitors to the Lower Rio Grande Valley. *Journal of Travel Research, 30*(2), 10–16. doi:10.1177/004728759103000202

Farny, S., Kibler, E., Hai, S., & Landoni, P. (2019). Volunteer retention in prosocial venturing: The role of emotional connectivity. *Entrepreneurship Theory and Practice, 43*(6), 1094–1123. doi:10.1177/1042258718769055

Farrell, J. M., Johnston, M. E., & Twynam, G. D. (1998). Volunteer motivation, satisfaction, and management at an elite sporting competition. *Journal of Sport Management, 12*(4), 288–300. doi:10.1123/jsm.12.4.288

Favre, C. (2017). The Small2Mighty tourism academy: Growing business to grow women as a transformative strategy for emerging destinations. *Worldwide Hospitality and Tourism Themes, 9*(5), 555–563. doi:10.1108/WHATT-07-2017-0034

Fetchko, M., Roy, D. P., & Clow, K. E. (2018). *Sports marketing*. Routledge. doi:10.4324/9781315175614

Finkelstien, M. A. (2009). Intrinsic vs. extrinsic motivational orientations and the volunteer process. *Personality and Individual Differences, 46*(5-6), 653–658. doi:10.1016/j.paid.2009.01.010

Fink, J. S., Trail, G. T., & Anderson, D. E. (2002). Environmental factors associated with spectator attendance and sport consumption behavior: Gender and team differences. *Sport Marketing Quarterly, 11*, 8–19.

Formica, S., & Uysal, M. (1998). Market Segmentation of an International Cultural-Historical Event in Italy. *Journal of Travel Research, 36*(4), 16–24. doi:10.1177/004728759803600402

Fotiadis, A. K., Vassiliadis, C. A., & Sotiriadis, M. D. (2016). The preferences of participants in small-scale sport events: A conjoint analysis case study from Taiwan. *Turizam: međunarodni znanstveno-stručni časopis, 64*(2), 175-187.

Fotiadis, A., Vassiliadis, C., & Yeh, S. P. (2016). Participant's preferences for small-scale sporting events: A comparative analysis of a Greek and a Taiwanese cycling event. *EuroMed Journal of Business, 11*(2), 232–247. doi:10.1108/EMJB-07-2015-0039

Fotiadis, A., Xie, L., Li, Y., & Huan, T.-C. T. C. (2016). Attracting athletes to small-scale sports events using motivational decision-making factors. *Journal of Business Research, 69*(11), 5467–5472. doi:10.1016/j.jbusres.2016.04.157

Fourie, J., & Santana-Gallego, M. (2011). The impact of mega-sport events on tourist arrivals. *Tourism Management, 32*(6), 1364–1370. doi:10.1016/j.tourman.2011.01.011

Fredline, E. (2005). Host and guest relations and sport tourism. *Sport in Society, 8*(2), 263–279. doi:10.1080/17430430500087328

Funk, D. C., Toohey, K., & Bruun, T. (2007). International sport event participation: Prior sport involvement; destination image; and travel motives. *European Sport Management Quarterly, 7*(3), 227–248. doi:10.1080/16184740701511011

Gammon, S. (2012). Sports events: Typologies, people and place. In S. J. Page & J. Connell (Eds.), *The Routledge handbook of events* (pp. 104–118). Routledge.

Gantz, W., & Lewis, N. (2014). Sports on traditional and newer digital media: Is there really a fight for fans? *Television & New Media, 15*(8), 760–768. doi:10.1177/1527476414529463

Gartner, M. P., & Shuman, P. (1988). Sponsorships and small businesses. *Journal of Small Business Management, 26*(4), 44–52.

Getz, D. (1984). Tourism, community organization and the social multiplier. *Leisure, Tourism and Social Change*, 85-100.

Getz, D. (2005). Event management & event tourism. Cognizant Communication Corporation.

Getz, D. (2007). *Event studies: theory, research and policy for planned events.* Elsevier. Retrieved from http://books.google.com/books

Getz, D. (2003). Sport Event Tourism: Planning, Development, and Marketing. In S. Hudson (Ed.), *Sport and Adventure Tourism.* Haworth Hospitality Press.

Getz, D. (2005). *Event Management and Event Tourism* (2nd ed.). Cognizant Communication Corporation.

Getz, D. (2007). *Event studies: Theory, research, and policy for planned events.* Elsevier.

Getz, D. (2008). Event tourism: Definition, evolution, and research. *Tourism Management, 29*(3), 403–428. doi:10.1016/j.tourman.2007.07.017

Getz, D. (2012). *Event studies: Theory, research and policy for planned events* (2nd ed.). Routledge.

Getz, D., & Frisby, W. (1988). Evaluating management effectiveness in community-run festivals. *Journal of Travel Research, 27*(1), 22–27. doi:10.1177/004728758802700105

Getz, D., & Page, S. J. (2016). Progress and prospects for event tourism research. *Tourism Management, 52*, 593–631. doi:10.1016/j.tourman.2015.03.007

Getz, D., Svensson, B., Peterssen, R., & Gunnervall, A. (2012). Hallmark events: Definition and planning process. *International Journal of Event Management Research, 7*(1/2), 47–67.

Giampiccoli, A., Lee, S., & Nauright, J. (2015). Destination South Africa: Comparing global sports mega-events and recurring localised sports events in South Africa for tourism and economic development. *Current Issues in Tourism, 18*(3), 229–248. doi:10.1080/13683500.2013.787050

Gibson, H. J. (1998). Sport Tourism: A Critical Analysis of Research. *Sport Management Review, 1*(1), 45–76. doi:10.1016/S1441-3523(98)70099-3

Gibson, H. J., Kaplanidou, K., & Kang, S. J. (2012). Small-scale event sport tourism: A case study in sustainable tourism. *Sport Management Review, 15*(2), 160–170. doi:10.1016/j.smr.2011.08.013

Gibson, H. J., Willming, C., & Holdnak, A. (2003). Small-scale event sport tourism: Fans as tourists. *Tourism Management, 24*(2), 181–190. doi:10.1016/S0261-5177(02)00058-4

Gitelson, R. J., & Crompton, J. L. (1984). Insights into the repeat vacation phenomenon. *Annals of Tourism Research, 11*(2), 199–217. doi:10.1016/0160-7383(84)90070-7

Gkarane, S., & Vassiliadis, C. (2016). Blueprinting an Event & Customer Oriented Marketing Mix: The Case of the Sfendami Mountain Festival Small Scale Event. *International Journal of Strategic Innovative Marketing, 3*, 13–28.

Goldblatt, J. (2005). *Special Events, Event Leadership for a new World*. John Wiley & Sons.

Gratton, C., Dobson, N., & Shibli, S. (2000). The economic importance of major sports events: a case-study of six events. *Managing leisure, 5*(1), 17-28.

Gratton, C., Shibili, S., & Dobson, N. (2000). The economic importance of major sports events. *Managing Leisure, 5*(1), 17–28. doi:10.1080/136067100375713

Gratton, C., Shibli, S., & Coleman, R. (2005). Sport and economic regeneration in cities. *Urban Studies (Edinburgh, Scotland), 42*(5-6), 985–999. doi:10.1080/00420980500107045

Gratton, C., & Taylor, P. (2000). *Economics of Sports and Recreation*. Taylor&Francis.

Green, B. C., & Chalip, L. (2004). Paths to volunteer commitment: Lessons from the Sydney Olympic Games. *Volunteering as leisure/leisure as volunteering: An international assessment*, 49-67.

Grohs, R., & Reisinger, H. (2014). Sponsorship effects on brand image: The role of exposure and activity involvement. *Journal of Business Research, 67*(5), 1018–1025. doi:10.1016/j.jbusres.2013.08.008

Gursoy, D., & Kendall, K. W. (2006). Hosting mega events: Modeling locals' support. *Annals of Tourism Research, 33*(3), 603–623. doi:10.1016/j.annals.2006.01.005

Guttentag, D. A. (2009). The possible negative impacts of volunteer tourism. *International Journal of Tourism Research, 11*(6), 537–551. doi:10.1002/jtr.727

Gwinner, K. P., & Bennet, J. (2008). The Impact of Brand Cohesiveness and Sport Identification on Brand Fit in a Sponsorship Context. *Journal of Sport Management, 22*(4), 410–426. doi:10.1123/jsm.22.4.410

Gwinner, K. P., & Eaton, J. (1999). Building Brand Image through Event Sponsorship: The Role of Image Transfer. *Journal of Advertising, 28*(4), 47–57. doi:10.1080/00913367.1999.10673595

Hall, C. M., & Selwood, H. J. (1987). Cup gained, paradise lost? A case study of the 1987 America's Cup as a hallmark event. Geography and Society in a Global Context, 267-274.

Hall, C. M. (2008). Servicescapes, designscapes, branding, and the creation of place-identity: South of Litchfield, Christchurch. *Journal of Travel & Tourism Marketing, 25*(3-4), 233–250. doi:10.1080/10548400802508101

Hallmann, K., & Harms, G. (2012). Determinants of volunteer motivation and their impact on future voluntary engagement: A comparison of volunteer's motivation at sport events in equestrian and handball. *International Journal of Event and Festival Management, 3*(3), 272-291.

Hallmann, K., Kaplanidou, K., & Breuer, C. (2010). Event image perceptions among active and passive sports tourists at marathon races. *International Journal of Sports Marketing & Sponsorship, 12*(1), 32–47. doi:10.1108/IJSMS-12-01-2010-B005

Hallmann, K., & Zehrer, A. (2017). Event and community involvement of sport event volunteers. *International Journal of Event and Festival Management, 8*(3), 308–323. doi:10.1108/IJEFM-08-2016-0058

Halpenny, E. A., Kulczycki, C., & Moghimehfar, F. (2016). Factors effecting destination and event loyalty: Examining the sustainability of a recurrent small-scale running event at Banff National Park. *Journal of Sport & Tourism, 20*(3-4), 3–4, 233–262. doi:10.1080/14775085.2016.1218787

Hambrick, M. E. (2012). Six degrees of information: Using social network analysis to explore the spread of information within sport social networks. *International Journal of Sport Communication, 5*(1), 16–34. doi:10.1123/ijsc.5.1.16

Hamm, S. M., MacLean, J. C., & Misener, K. E. (2008). Understanding the commitment and motivation of episodic volunteers for a large sporting event. *Int J Volunt Adm, 25*(3), 26–38.

Hanlon, C., & Jago, L. (2000). Pulsating sporting events: An organisational structure to optimise performance. *Events beyond 2000: Setting the agenda*, 93.

Harrison, S. (2017). The popularity paradox: issues of safeguarding mob football games in the East Midlands of England. In *Sharing Cultures 2017–Proceedings of the 5th International Conference on Intangible Heritage*. Green Line Institute for Sustainable Development.

Henderson, A. C., & Sowa, J. (2019). Volunteer satisfaction at the boundary of public and nonprofit: Organizational-and individual-level determinants. *Public Performance & Management Review*, *42*(1), 162–189. doi:10.1080/15309576.2018.1471405

Heracleous, L., & Wirtz, J. (2014). Singapore Airlines: Achieving sustainable advantage through mastering paradox. *The Journal of Applied Behavioral Science*, *50*(2), 150–170. doi:10.1177/0021886314522323

Herrero, L. C., Sanz, J. Á., Devesa, M., Bedate, A., & del Barrio, M. J. (2006). The Economic Impact of Cultural Events: A Case-Study of Salamanca 2002, European Capital of Culture. *European Urban and Regional Studies*, *13*(1), 41–57. doi:10.1177/0969776406058946

Hibbitt, K., Jones, P., & Meegan, R. (2001). Tackling social exclusion: The role of social capital in urban regeneration on Merseyside—from mistrust to trust? *European Planning Studies*, *9*, 141–161.

Higham, J. (1999). Commentary—sport as an avenue of tourism development: An analysis of the positive and negative impacts of sport tourism. *Current Issues in Tourism*, *2*(1), 82–90. doi:10.1080/13683509908667845

Hinch, T. D., & Higham, J. E. S. (2001). Sport Tourism : A framework for research. *International Journal of Tourism Research*, *3*(1), 45–58. doi:10.1002/1522-1970(200101/02)3:1<45::AID-JTR243>3.0.CO;2-A

Hopkins, C. D., Grove, S. J., Raymond, M. A., & LaForge, M. C. (2009). Designing the e-Servicescape: Implications for Online Retailers. *Journal of Internet Commerce*, *8*(1-2), 23–43. doi:10.1080/15332860903182487

Houlihan, B., & Green, M. (2011). *Routledge Handbook of Sports Development*. Routledge.

Hoyle, L. H. (2002). *Event Marketing: how to successfully promote events, fesiivals, convenions, and expositions*. John Wiley & Sons.

ICC. (2018). ICC Advertising and Marketing Communications Code; Building consumer trust through responsible marketing. Paris: International Chamber of Commerce (ICC).

IEG. LLC. (2017). IG'S Guide to Sponsorship. Chicago: IEG, LLC.

International Labour Organization. (2011). *Manual on the measurement of volunteer work*. Retrieved from https://www.ilo.org/wcmsp5/groups/public/---dgreports/---stat/documents/publication/wcms_162119.pdf

IOC. (2006). *International Olympic Committee- 2006 Marketing Fact File*. IOC.

Iso Ahola, S. E. (1983). Towards a social psychology of recreational travel. *Leisure Studies*, *1*(1), 45–56. doi:10.1080/02614368300390041

Ivanov, S., & Zhechev, V. (2012). Hotel revenue management - A critical literature review. *Tourism Review*, *60*(2), 175–197.

Jang, S., Bai, B., Hong, G.-S., & O'Leary, J. T. (2004). Understanding travel expenditure patterns: A study of Japanese pleasure travelers to the United States by income level. *Tourism Management*, *25*(3), 331–341. doi:10.1016/S0261-5177(03)00141-9

Jarvie, G. (2003). Communitarianism, sport and social Capital. 'Neighbourly insights into Scottish sport'. *International Review for the Sociology of Sport*, *38*(2), 139–153. doi:10.1177/1012690203038002001

Jules, C., & Good, D. (2014). Introduction to special issue on paradox in context: Advances in theory and practice. *The Journal of Applied Behavioral Science*, *50*(2), 123–126. doi:10.1177/0021886314524920

Kahle, L. R., Kambara, K. M., & Rose, G. M. (1996). A functional model of fun attendance motivations for college football. *Sport Marketing Quarterly*, *5*(4), 51–60.

Kang, Y. S., & Perdue, R. (1994). Long-term impact of a mega-event on international tourism to the host country: A conceptual model and the case of the 1988 Seoul Olympics. *Journal of International Consumer Marketing*, *6*(3-4), 205–225. doi:10.1300/J046v06n03_11

Kaplanidou, K., & Gibson, H. (2012). Differences between first time and repeat spectator tourists of a youth soccer event: Intentions and image approaches. *Current Issues in Tourism*, *15*(5), 477–487. doi:10.1080/13683500.2011.607924

Kaplanidou, K., & Gibson, H. J. (2010). Predicting behavioral intentions of active event sport tourists: The case of a small-scale recurring sports event. *Journal of Sport & Tourism*, *15*(2), 163–179. doi:10.1080/14775085.2010.498261

Kaplanidou, K., & Vogt, C. (2006). Studying sport tourism event and destination images on intend to travel: a conceptual theoretical model utilising the theory of planned behaviour. *14th EASM Congress*.

Kaplanidou, K., & Vogt, C. (2007). The interrelationship between sport event and destination image and sport tourists' behaviours. *Journal of Sport & Tourism*, *12*(3-4), 183–206. doi:10.1080/14775080701736932

Kaplanidou, K., & Vogt, C. (2010). The meaning and measurement of a sport event experience among active sport tourists. *Journal of Sport Management*, *24*(5), 544–566. doi:10.1123/jsm.24.5.544

Kay, T., & Bradbury, S. (2009). Youth sport volunteering: Developing social capital? *Sport Education and Society*, *14*(1), 121–140. doi:10.1080/13573320802615288

Keller, K. L. (2001). *Building customer-based brand equity: A blueprint for creating strong brands*. Marketing Science Institute.

Kemperman, A. D. A. M., Joh, C., & Timmermans, H. J. P. (2004). Comparing first-time and repeat visitors' activity patterns in a tourism environment. In G. I. Crouch, R. R. Perdue, H. J. P. Timmermans, & M. Uysal (Eds.), *Consumer psychology of tourism, hospitality and leisure* (pp. 103–119). doi:10.1079/9780851997490.0103

Kennelly, M. (2017). "We've never measured it, but it brings in a lot of business" Participatory sport events and tourism. *International Journal of Contemporary Hospitality Management*, *29*(3), 883–899. doi:10.1108/IJCHM-10-2015-0541

Kerwin, S., Warner, S., Walker, M., & Stevens, J. (2015). Exploring sense of community among small-scale sport event volunteers. *European Sport Management Quarterly*, *15*(1), 77–92. doi:10.1080/16184742.2014.996581

Kim, E. (2018). A systematic review of motivation of sport event volunteers. *World Leisure Journal*, *60*(4), 306–329. doi:10.1080/16078055.2017.1373696

Kim, E., & Cuskelly, G. (2017). A systematic quantitative review of volunteer management in events. *Event Management*, *21*(1), 83–100. doi:10.3727/152599517X14809630271195

Kim, E., Fredline, L., & Cuskelly, G. (2018). Heterogeneity of sport event volunteer motivations: A segmentation approach. *Tourism Management*, *68*, 375–386. doi:10.1016/j.tourman.2018.04.004

Kim, H., Borges, M. C., & Chon, J. (2006). Impacts of environmental values on tourism motivation: The case of FICA, Brazil. *Tourism Management*, *27*(5), 957–967. doi:10.1016/j.tourman.2005.09.007 PMID:32287716

Kim, J.-W. (2010). The worth of sport event sponsorship: An event study. *Journal of Management and Marketing Research*, *5*(1), 1–14.

Kim, M., Zhang, J. J., & Connaughton, D. (2010). Modification of the volunteer functions inventory for application in youth sports. *Sport Management Review*, *13*(1), 25–38. doi:10.1016/j.smr.2009.04.005

Kim, N. S., & Chalip, L. (2004). Why travel to the FIFA World Cup? Effects of motives, background, interest, and constraints. *Tourism Management*, *25*(6), 695–707. doi:10.1016/j.tourman.2003.08.011

Kim, W., Jun, H. M., Walker, M., & Drane, D. (2015). Evaluating the perceived social impacts of hosting large-scale sport tourism events: Scale development and validation. *Tourism Management*, *48*, 21–32. doi:10.1016/j.tourman.2014.10.015

Koo, G.-Y., Quartermann, J., & Flynn, L. (2006). Effect of perceived sport event and sponsor image fit on consumers' cognition, affect, and behavioral intentions. *Sport Management Quarterly*, *15*, 80–90.

Kotler, P. (1973). Atmospherics as a marketing tool. *Journal of Retailing*, *49*(4), 48–64.

Kotler, P. (2000). *Principles of Marketing, Product life cycle: characteristic, strategies and objectives*. Pearson Education.

Ko, Y. J., Kim, K., Claussen, C. L., & Kim, T. H. (2008). The effects of sport involvement, sponsor awareness and corporate image on intention to purchase sponsors' products. *International Journal of Sports Marketing & Sponsorship*, *9*(2), 79–94. doi:10.1108/IJSMS-09-02-2008-B004

Kriemadis, T., & Kartakoulis, N. L. (2011). *Management and marketing for marketing clubs-Good governance and marketing applications*. University of Nicosia Press.

Kristiansen, E., Skirstad, B., Parent, M. M., & Waddington, I. (2015). 'We can do it': Community, resistance, social solidarity, and long-term volunteering at a sport event. *Sport Management Review*, *18*(2), 256–267. doi:10.1016/j.smr.2014.06.002

Kruger, M., Saayman, M., & Ellis, S. M. (2010). Does loyalty pay? First-time versus repeat visitors at a national arts festival. *Southern African Business Review*, *14*(1), 79–104.

Kurtzman, J. (2005). Sports tourism categories. *Journal of Sport & Tourism*, *10*(1), 15–20. doi:10.1080/14775080500101502

Kwiatkowski, G., & Könecke, T. (2017). Tourism and recurring sport events: Event tourists' and regular tourists' profiles and expenditures at the Windsurf World Cup on Sylt. *Sport, Business and Management. International Journal (Toronto, Ont.)*, *7*(5), 464–482.

Lamb, D., & Ogle, A. (2016). The Motivations of Event Volunteers at Local Community Events. In *Managing and Developing Communities, Festivals and Events* (pp. 50–68). Palgrave Macmillan. doi:10.1057/9781137508553_4

Lane, A., Murphy, N., & Bauman, A. (2013). An effort to "leverage" the effect of participation in a mass event on physical activity. *Health Promotion International*, *30*(3), 542–551. doi:10.1093/heapro/dat077 PMID:24226297

Larsen, J. (2019). Running and tourism: A practice approach. In L. James, C. Ren, & H. Halkier (Eds.), *Theories and practice in tourism* (pp. 41–57). Routledge.

Larsen, J., & Bærenholdt, J. (2019). Running together: The social capitals of a tourism running event. *Annals of Tourism Research*, 79.

Lau, A. L. S., & McKercher, B. (2004). Exploration Versus Acquisition: A Comparison of First-Time and Repeat Visitors. *Journal of Travel Research*, *42*(3), 279–285. doi:10.1177/0047287503257502

Laverie, D. A., & McDonald, R. E. (2007). Volunteer dedication: Understanding the role of identity importance on participation frequency. *Journal of Macromarketing*, *27*(3), 274–288. doi:10.1177/0276146707302837

Ledingham, J. A., & Bruning, S. D. (1998). Relationship management in public relations: Dimensions of an organization-public relationship. *Public Relations Review*, *24*(1), 55–65. doi:10.1016/S0363-8111(98)80020-9

Lee, Y., Kim, M., & Koo, J. (2016). The impact of social interaction and team member exchange on sport event volunteer management. *Sport Management Review*, *19*(5), 550–562. doi:10.1016/j.smr.2016.04.005

Leigh, J., Lamont, M., & Cairncross, G. (2013). Towards a process model of induction and training for young event volunteers. *International Journal of Event Management Research*, *8*(1), 1–20.

Leiper, N. (1990). Tourist attraction systems. *Annals of Tourism Research*, *17*(3), 367–384. doi:10.1016/0160-7383(90)90004-B

Levin, A. M., Joiner, C., & Cameron, G. (2001). The Impact of Sports Sponsorship on Consumers' Brand Attitudes and Recall: The Case of Nascars Fans. *Journal of Current Issues and Research in Advertising*, *23*(2), 23–31. doi:10.1080/10641734.2001.10505118

Levitt, T. (1965). EXPLOIT the Product Life Cycle. *Harvard Business Review*, *43*(6), 81–94.

Lim, J. S., Hwang, Y. C., Kim, S. K., & Biocca, F. A. (2015). How social media engagement leads to sports channel loyalty: Mediating roles of social presence and channel commitment. *Computers in Human Behavior*, *46*, 158–167. doi:10.1016/j.chb.2015.01.013

Line, N. D., Hanks, L., & McGinley, S. (2018). When birds flock together: An identification of the destination social servicescape. *Journal of Travel & Tourism Marketing*, *35*(7), 882–894. doi:10.1080/10548408.2018.1445065

Liponski, W. (2003). World Sports Encyclopedia; Worldwide list of traditional games and sports. MIB Publishing Company LLC.

Liu, D., & Gratton, C. (2010). The impact of mega sporting events on live spectators' images of a host city: A case study of the Shanghai F1 Grand Prix. *Tourism Economics*, *16*(3), 629–645. doi:10.5367/000000010792278347

Liu, D., & Wilson, R. (2014). The negative impacts of hosting mega-sporting events and intention to travel: A test of the crowding-out effect using the London 2012 Games as an example. *International Journal of Sports Marketing & Sponsorship*, *15*(3), 12–26. doi:10.1108/IJSMS-15-03-2014-B003

Liu, Z. (2003). Sustainable tourism development: A critique. *Journal of Sustainable Tourism*, *11*(6), 459–475. doi:10.1080/09669580308667216

Li, X. R., Cheng, C.-K., Kim, H., & Petrick, J. F. (2008). A systematic comparison of first-time and repeat visitors via a two-phase online survey. *Tourism Management*, *29*(2), 278–293. doi:10.1016/j.tourman.2007.03.010

Li, X., & Vogelsong, H. (2006). Comparing Methods of Measuring Image Change: A Case Study of a Small-Scale Community Festival. *Tourism Analysis*, *10*(4), 349–360. doi:10.3727/108354206776162769

Lockstone-Binney, L., Holmes, K., Smith, K., Baum, T., & Storer, C. (2015). Are all my volunteers here to help out? Clustering event volunteers by their motivations. *Event Management*, *19*(4), 461–477. doi:10.3727/152599515X14465748512605

Loo, R. (2003). Assessing "Team Climate" in Project Teams. *International Journal of Project Management*, *21*(7), 511–517. doi:10.1016/S0263-7863(02)00058-3

Lough, N. L., & Irwin, R. L. (2001). A comparative analysis of sponsorship objectives for U.S. women's sport and traditional sport sponsorship. *Sport Marketing Quarterly*, *10*(4), 202–211.

Lugosi, P., Robinson, R. N. S., Golubovskaya, M., & Foley, L. (2016). The hospitality consumption experience of parents and carers with children: A qualitative study of foodservice settings. *International Journal of Hospitality Management*, *54*, 84–94. doi:10.1016/j.ijhm.2016.01.012

Lyras, A., & Peachey, J. W. (2011). Integrating sport-for-development theory and praxis. *Sport Management Review*, *14*(4), 311–326. doi:10.1016/j.smr.2011.05.006

Mackellar, J., & Reis, A. C. (2014). World Rally Championships 2009 and 2011: Assessing the tourism value in Australia. *Journal of Vacation Marketing*, *20*(1), 17–28. doi:10.1177/1356766713484728

Maennig, W., & Zimbalist, A. (2012). What is a mega sporting event. *International handbook on the economics of mega sporting events*, 9-14.

Magdalinski, T., & Nauright, J. (2004). Commercialization of the modern Olympic Games. In T. Slack (Ed.), *The Commercialization of Sport* (pp. 185–204). Routledge.

Malchrowicz-Mośko, E., & Poczta, J. (2018). A small-scale event and a big impact-Is this relationship possible in theworld of sport? The meaning of heritage sporting events for sustainable development of tourism-experiences from Poland. *Sustainability*, *10*(11), 1–19. doi:10.3390u10114289 PMID:30607262

Mansfeld, Y., & Pizam, A. (Eds.). (2006). *Tourism, security and safety*. Routledge.

Mason, K. (2005). How Corporate Sport Sponsorship Impacts Consumer Behavior. *The Journal of American Academy of Business, Cambridge*, *7*(1), 32–35.

Masterman, G. (2014). *Strategic sports event management* (3rd ed.). Routledge. doi:10.4324/9780203114674

Mata-Codesal, D., Peperkamp, E., & Tiesler, N. C. (2015). *Migration, migrants and leisure: meaningful leisure?* Academic Press.

McCabe, S. (2006). The making of community identity through historic festive practice: The case of Ashbourne Royal Shrovetide Football. *Festivals, tourism and social change*, 99-118.

McCabe, S., & Stokoe, E. H. (2004). Place and Identity in Tourists' Accounts. *Annals of Tourism Research*, *31*(3), 601–622. doi:10.1016/j.annals.2004.01.005

McCarville, R., & Copeland, R. (1994). Understanding sport sponsorship through exchange theory. *Journal of Sport Management*, *8*(2), 102–114. doi:10.1123/jsm.8.2.102

McCole, D., Jacobs, J., Lindley, B., & McAvoy, L. (2012). The relationship between seasonal employee retention and sense of community: The case of summer camp employment. *Journal of Park and Recreation Administration*, *30*(2).

McMillan, D. W., & Chavis, D. M. (1986). Sense of community: A definition and theory. *Journal of Community Psychology*, *14*(1), 6–23. doi:10.1002/1520-6629(198601)14:1<6::AID-JCOP2290140103>3.0.CO;2-I

Meenaghan, T. (2001). Understanding sponsorship effects. *Psychology and Marketing, 18*(2), 95–122. doi:10.1002/1520-6793(200102)18:2<95::AID-MAR1001>3.0.CO;2-H

Merrilees, B., Getz, D., & O'Brien, D. (2005). Marketing stakeholder analysis: Branding the Brisbane goodwill games. *European Journal of Marketing, 39*(9/10), 1060–1077. doi:10.1108/03090560510610725

Milano, C., Novelli, M., & Cheer, J. (2019). Overtourism and degrowth: A social movements perspective. *Journal of Sustainable Tourism, 27*(12), 1857–1875. Advance online publication. doi:10.1080/09669582.2019.1650054

Mill, R. M. (1985). *The Tourism System.* Prentice hall International.

Miloch, K. S., & Lambrecht, K. W. (2006). Consumer Awareness of Sponsorship at Grassroots Sport Events. *Sport Marketing Quarterly, 15*, 147–154.

Mintel. (2011). *Sports Marketing and Sponsorship - UK - Trade Perspectives: Sports Marketing Activities.* London: Mintel Group.

Misener, L., & Mason, D. (2006). Creating community networks: Can sporting events offer meaningful sources of social capital? *Managing Leisure, 11*(1), 39–56. doi:10.1080/13606710500445676

Molm, L. (1990). Structure, action, and outcomes: The dynamics of power in social exchange. *American Sociological Review, 55*(3), 427–447. doi:10.2307/2095767

Mombeuil, C. (2018). Interaction from tourism development in Port-au-Prince, Haiti. *Journal of Tourism. Heritage & Services Marketing, 4*(1), 8–14.

Monga, M. (2006). Measuring motivation to volunteer for special events. *Event Management, 10*(1), 47–61. doi:10.3727/152599506779364633

Montana, J., Guzman, F., & Moll, I. (2007). Branding and design management: A brand design management model. *Journal of Marketing Management, 23*(9-10), 829–840. doi:10.1362/026725707X250340

Morgan, N. J., Pritchard, A., & Pride, R. (2004). *Destination Branding: Creating the unique destination proposition.* Academic Press.

Morrison, A. M. (1995). *Hospitality and travel marketing*. Delmar.

Moscardo, G., Konovalov, E., Murphy, L., McGehee, N. G., & Schurmann, A. (2017). Linking tourism to social capital in destination communities. *Journal of Destination Marketing & Management, 6*(4), 286–295. doi:10.1016/j.jdmm.2017.10.001

Mount, J., & Niro, B. (1995). Sponsorship: An empirical study of its application to local business in a small town setting. *Festival Management & Event Tourism, 2*(3/4), 167–175. doi:10.3727/106527095792315576

Mowday, R. T., Porter, L. W., & Steers, R. (1982). *Organizational linkages: The psychology of commitment, absenteeism, and turnover.* Academic Press.

Müller, A., & Bíró, M. (2015). *Organizing sports events*. Retrieved from https://sporttudomany.uni-eszterhazy.hu/public/uploads/organising-sports-events_570f84971d1e4.pdf

Müller, M. (2015). What makes an event a mega-event? Definitions and sizes. *Leisure Studies*, *34*(6), 627–642. doi:10.1080/02614367.2014.993333

Murphy, N., Lane, A., & Bauman, A. (2015). Leveraging mass participation events for sustainable health legacy. *Leisure Studies*, *34*(6), 758–766. doi:10.1080/02614367.2015.1037787

Musa, R., & Kassim, R. M. (2013). Predictors and outcomes of sport event experiential value: Insight from Formula One Petronas Malaysia Grand Prix. *International Journal of Management and Marketing Research*, *6*(1), 107–121.

Nam, T., & Pardo, T. A. (2011). Conceptualizing Smart City with Dimensions of Technology, People, and Institutions. *12th Annual International Conference on Digital Government Research*. 10.1145/2037556.2037602

Nauright, J. (2004). Global games: Culture, political economy and sport in the globalised world of the 21st century. *Third World Quarterly*, *25*(7), 1325–1336. doi:10.1080/0143659042000281302

Nelson, K. B. (2009). Enhancing the Attendee's Experience through Creative Design of the Event Environment: Applying Goffman's Dramaturgical Perspective. *Journal of Convention & Event Tourism*, *10*(2), 120–133. doi:10.1080/15470140902922023

Nicholls, J. A. F., Roslow, S., & Dublish, S. (1999). Brand recall and brand preference at sponsored golf and tennis tournaments. *European Journal of Marketing*, *33*(3/4), 365–386. doi:10.1108/03090569910253198

Nichols, G. (2017). Volunteering in community sports associations: A literature review. *Voluntaristics Review*, *2*(1), 1–75. doi:10.1163/24054933-12340015

Nichols, G., & Ojala, E. (2009). Understanding the management of sports events volunteers through psychological contract theory. *Voluntas*, *20*(4), 369–387. doi:10.100711266-009-9097-9

Nicholson, M., Smith, A. C., Stewart, B., & Hoye, R. (2018). *Sport management: Principles and applications*. Routledge.

O'Brien, D., & Chalip, L. (2007). Sport events and strategic leveraging: pushing towards the triple bottom line. *Tourism management: Analysis, behaviour, and strategy*, 318.

O'Brien, D. (2007). Points of leverage: Maximising host community benefit from a regional surfing festival. *European Sport Management Quarterly*, *7*(2), 141–165. doi:10.1080/16184740701353315

O'Toole, W. (2011). *Events feasibility and development from strategy to operations*. Elsevier.

Oliver, R. L. (1980). A Cognitive Model of the Antecedents and Consequences of Satisfaction Decisions. *JMR, Journal of Marketing Research*, *17*(4), 460–469. doi:10.1177/002224378001700405

Omoto, A. M., & Packard, C. D. (2016). The power of connections: Psychological sense of community as a predictor of volunteerism. *The Journal of Social Psychology*, *156*(3), 272–290. doi:10.1080/00224545.2015.1105777 PMID:27064179

Oppermann, M. (1997). First-time and repeat visitors to New Zealand. *Tourism Management*, *18*(3), 177–181. doi:10.1016/S0261-5177(96)00119-7

Oppermann, M. (1998). Destination Threshold Potential and the Law of Repeat Visitation. *Journal of Travel Research*, *37*(2), 131–137. doi:10.1177/004728759803700204

Page, S. J. (2019). *Tourism management*. Routledge. doi:10.4324/9780429422898

Papachroni, A., Heracleous, L., & Paroutis, S. (2015). Organizational ambidexterity through the lens of paradox theory: Building a novel research agenda. *The Journal of Applied Behavioral Science*, *51*(1), 71–93. doi:10.1177/0021886314553101

Pappu, R., & Cornwell, T. B. (2014). Corporate sponsorship as an image platform: Understanding the roles of relationship fit and sponsor-sponsee similarity. *Academy of Marketing Science. Journal*, *42*(5), 490–510.

Parent, M. M. (2008). Evolution and issue patterns for major-sport-event organizing committees and their stakeholders. *Journal of Sport Management*, *22*(2), 135–164. doi:10.1123/jsm.22.2.135

Parent, M. M., Eskerud, L., & Hanstad, D. V. (2012). Brand creation in international recurring sports events. *Sport Management Review*, *15*(2), 145–159. doi:10.1016/j.smr.2011.08.005

Parent, M. M., & Foreman, P. O. (2007). Organizational image and identity management in large-scale sporting events. *Journal of Sport Management*, *21*(1), 15–40. doi:10.1123/jsm.21.1.15

Parent, M. M., & Smith-Swan, S. (2013). *Managing major sports events. Theory and practice*. Routledge. doi:10.4324/9780203132371

Park, Y. P. (2014). *Heritage Tourism*. Routledge.

Pauline, G. (2011). Volunteer satisfaction and intent to remain: An analysis of contributing factors among professional golf event volunteers. *International Journal of Event Management Research*, 10.

Pearce, J. L. (1993). *Volunteers: The organizational behavior of unpaid workers*. Routledge.

Pennington-Gray, L., & Holdnak, A. (2002). Out of the stands and into the community: Using sports events to promote destination. *Event Management*, *7*(3), 177–186. doi:10.3727/152599502108751578

Petrick, J. F. (2004). First Timers' and Repeaters' Perceived Value. *Journal of Travel Research*, *43*(1), 29–38. doi:10.1177/0047287504265509

Petrick, J. F., Morais, D. D., & Norman, W. C. (2001). An examination of the determinants of entertainment vacationers' intentions to revisit. *Journal of Travel Research*, *40*(1), 41–48. doi:10.1177/004728750104000106

Pizam, A. (2010). Creating memorable experiences. *International Journal of Hospitality Management*, *29*(3), 343. doi:10.1016/j.ijhm.2010.04.003

Pope, N. K. L., & Voges, K. E. (2000). The impact of sport sponsorship activities, corporate image, and prior use on consumer purchase intention. *Sport Marketing Quarterly*, *9*(2), 96–102.

Popp, B., & Woratschek, H. (2016). Introducing branded communities in sport for building strong brand relations in social media. *Sport Management Review*, *19*(2), 183–197. doi:10.1016/j.smr.2015.06.001

Poria, Y., & Timothy, D. J. (2014). Where are the children in tourism research? *Annals of Tourism Research*, *47*, 93–95. doi:10.1016/j.annals.2014.03.002

Poris, M. (2006). Understanding what fun means to today's kids. *Young Consumers*, *7*(1), 14–22. doi:10.1108/17473610610701358

Prayag, G. (2012). Senior travelers' motivations and future behavioral intentions: THE CASE OF NICE. *Journal of Travel & Tourism Marketing*, *29*(7), 665–681. doi:10.1080/10548408.2012.720153

Prayag, G., & Grivel, E. (2014). Motivation, satisfaction, and behavioral intentions: Segmenting youth participants at the Interamnia World Cup 2012. *Sport Marketing Quarterly*, *23*(3), 148–160.

Preuss, H. (2006). *Lasting effects of major sporting events*. Available in www.idrottsforum.org

Preuss, H. (2007). The conceptualisation and measurement of mega sport tourism. *Journal of Sport & Tourism*, *12*(3-4), 207–227. doi:10.1080/14775080701736957

Preuss, H. (2015). A framework for identifying the legacies of a mega sport event. *Leisure Studies*, *34*(6), 643–664. doi:10.1080/02614367.2014.994552

Priporas, C.-V., Vassiliadis, C. A., Stylos, N., & Fotiadis, A. K. (2018). The Effect of Sport Tourists' Travel Style, Destination and Event Choices, and Motivation on Their Involvement in Small-Scale Sports Events. *Event Management*, *22*(5), 745–765. doi:10.3727/152599518X15299559637707

Putnam, R. D. (2000). Bowling alone: America's declining social capital. In *Culture and politics* (pp. 223–234). Palgrave Macmillan.

QARA. (2019). *Sports Industry Insights*. Retrieved from https://medium.com/qara/sports-industry-report-3244bd253b8

Quick, S. (2000). Contemporary sport consumers: Some implications of linking fan typology with key spectator variables. *Sport Marketing Quarterly*, *9*(3), 149–156.

Radikonyana, P. S., Heath, E., Fairer-Wessels, F., Prinsloo, J., & Pelser, T. G. (2015). A Strategic E-Marketing Framework for sport mega event. *Journal of Applied Business Research*, *31*(2), 437–454. doi:10.19030/jabr.v31i2.9127

Raya, M. J. (2012). Length of stay for triathlon participants in the challenge Maresme-Barcelona: A survival approach. *Journal of Sport and Social Issues*, *36*(1), 86–105. doi:10.1177/0193723511433868

Reamon, S. (2016). Managing Volunteers: Recruitment, Retention, and Relationship Building. *SPNHA Review*, *12*(1), 74–95.

Reber, A. S. (1995). *The Penguin dictionary of psychology*. Penguin Press.

Reeves, M., Moose, S., & Venema, T. (2014). The Growth Share Matrix. BCG – The Boston Consulting Group.

Reic, I. (2017). *Events Marketing Management; A consumer perspective*. Routledge.

Reic, I. (2017). *Events Marketing Management-A Consumer Perspective*. Routledge.

Reid, L. J., & Reid, S. D. (1993). Communicating tourism supplier services: Building repeat visitor relationships. *Journal of Travel & Tourism Marketing*, *2*(2-3), 3–19. doi:10.1300/J073v02n02_02

Report, A. (2019). *Global sports tourism market 2019-2023*. Retrieved from https://www.absolutereports.com/global-sports-tourism-market-13792981

ReportP. (2016). Available from: www.eventbrite.co.uk/how-it-works/

ReportP. (2017). Available from: www.eventbrite.co.uk/how-it-works/

ReportP. (2018). Available from: www.eventbrite.co.uk/how-it-works/

Richards, G., Marques, L., & Mein, K. (2014). Event design: conclusions and future research directions. In G. Richards, L. Marques, & K. Mein (Eds.), *Event Design: Social perspectives and practices* (pp. 198–212). Routledge. doi:10.4324/9780203761908

Ringuet-Riot, C., Cuskelly, G., Auld, C., & Zakus, D. H. (2014). Volunteer roles, involvement and commitment in voluntary sport organizations: Evidence of core and peripheral volunteers. *Sport in Society*, *17*(1), 116–133. doi:10.1080/17430437.2013.828902

Ritchie, B. W. (2004). Exploring small-scale sport event tourism: The case of Rugby Union and the Super 12 competition. *Sport tourism: Interrelationships, impacts and issues*, 135-154.

Ritchie, B. W., & Adair, D. (Eds.). (2004). *Sport tourism: Interrelationships, impacts and issues* (Vol. 14). Channel View Publications. doi:10.21832/9781873150672

Robinson, S., & France, A. (2011). Comparing sports marketing of amateur team sports to professional team sports. *New Zealand Journal of Applied Business Research*, *9*(1), 47.

Roche, M. (1994). Mega-events and urban policy. *Annals of Tourism Research*, *21*(1), 1–19. doi:10.1016/0160-7383(94)90002-7

Rohe, W. M. (2004). Building social capital through community development. *Journal of the American Planning Association*, *70*, 143–144.

Roque, V., & Raposo, R. (2015). Social media as a communication and marketing tool in tourism: An analysis of online activities from international key player DMO. *Anatolia*, *2917*(October), 1–13.

Ross, S. D. (2001). Developing Sport Tourism-An eGuide for Destination marketers and Sports Events Planners. University of Illinois at Urbana-Champaign.

Rothenberg, A. (1971). The process of Janusian thinking in creativity. *Archives of General Psychiatry*, *24*(3), 195–205. doi:10.1001/archpsyc.1971.01750090001001 PMID:5542345

Rothenberg, A. (1996). The Janusian process in scientific creativity. *Creativity Research Journal*, *9*(2-3), 207–231. doi:10.1080/10400419.1996.9651173

Saayman, M., & Saayman, A. (2008). Socio-demographic and behavioural determinants of visitor spending at a national arts festival: A panel data analysis. *World Journal on Events*, *1*(1), 28–33.

Samra, B., & Wos, A. (2014). Consumer in Sports: Fan typology analysis. *Journal of Intercultural Management*, *6*(4–1), 263–288. doi:10.2478/joim-2014-0050

Santomier, J. (2008). New media, branding and global sports sponsorship. *International Journal of Sports Marketing & Sponsorship*, *10*(1), 9–22. doi:10.1108/IJSMS-10-01-2008-B005

Sarason, S. B. (1974). *The psychological sense of community: Prospects for a community psychology*. Jossey-Bass.

Sato, M., Jordan, J. S., Kaplanidou, K., & Funk, D. C. (2014). Determinants of tourists' expenditure at mass participant sport events: A ðve-year analysis. *Current Issues in Tourism*, *17*(9), 763–771. doi:10.1080/13683500.2014.892918

Save The Children. (2017). *The truth about voluntourism*. Retrieved September 20, 2017 from: https://www.savethechildren.org.au/Our-Stories/The-truth-about-voluntourism

Scheinbaum, A. C., Finney, R. Z., Lacey, R. Z., & Sneath, J. Z. (2006). Engaging the Consumer through Event Marketing: Linking Attendees with the Sponsor, Community, and Brand. *Journal of Advertising Research*, *46*(4), 420–433. doi:10.2501/S0021849906060430

Schlesinger, T., & Gubler, R. (2016). Motivational profiles of sporting event volunteers. *Sport in Society*, *19*(10), 1419–1439. doi:10.1080/17430437.2015.1133596

Schnitzer, M. (2014). Financing events. In J. Beech, S. Kaiser, & R. Kaspar (Eds.), *The business of events management* (pp. 113–135). Pearson.

Schulenkorf, N. (2012). Sustainable community development through sport and events: A conceptual framework for sport-for-development projects. *Sport Management Review*, *15*(1), 1–12.

Schulenkorf, N., & Edwards, D. (2012). Maximizing positive social impacts: Strategies for sustaining and leveraging the benefits of intercommunity sport events in divided societies. *Journal of Sport Management*, *26*(5), 379–390. doi:10.1123/jsm.26.5.379

Schulenkorf, N., & Schlenker, K. (2017). Leveraging sport events to maximize community benefits in low-and middle-income countries. *Event Management*, *21*(2), 217–231. doi:10.3727/152599517X14878772869766

Scott, A. K. S., & Turco, D. M. (2011). Spectator profiles and economic impact of the 2009 US Women's Open. *Thunderbird International Business Review*, *53*(6), 701–708. doi:10.1002/tie.20446

Seo, S., Yun, N., & Kim, O. Y. (2014). Destination food image and intention to eat destination foods: A view from Korea. *Current Issues in Tourism*, (December), 1–22.

Seraphin, H., Gowreesunkar, V., Zaman, M., & Bourliataux, S. (2019). Community Based Festivals as a tool to tackle tourismphobia and antitourism movements. *Journal of Hospitality and Tourism Management*, *39*, 219–223. Advance online publication. doi:10.1016/j.jhtm.2018.12.001

Seraphin, H., Platania, M., Spencer, P., & Modica, G. (2018). Event and tourism development within a local community: The case of Winchester (UK). *Sustainability*, *10*(10), 3728. doi:10.3390u10103728

Seraphin, H., & Yallop, A. (2019). Proposed Framework for the Management of Resorts Mini Clubs: An Ambidextrous Approach. *Leisure Studies*, *38*(4), 535–547. Advance online publication. doi:10.1080/02614367.2019.1581249

Sfendami.com. (2019). *Sfendami*. Available at: http://www.sfendami.com/?lang=en

Shanka, T., & Taylor, R. (2004). Discriminating factors of first-time and repeat visitors to wine festivals. *Current Issues in Tourism*, *7*(2), 134–145. doi:10.1080/13683500408667976

Sherwood, M., Nicholson, M., & Marjoribanks, T. (2017). Controlling the Message and the Medium? The impact of sports organisations' digital and social channels on media access. *Digital Journalism*, *5*(5), 513–531. doi:10.1080/21670811.2016.1239546

Shimp, T. A. (2010). Integrated Marketing Communication in Advertising and Promotion/por Terence A Shimp (No. 658.8 S45.). Academic Press.

Shone, A., & Parry, B. (2004). *Successful event management: a practical handbook*. Cengage Learning EMEA.

Shonk, D. J., Greenwell, T. C., Bravo, G., & Won, D. (2012). Site selection, satisfaction, and intent to return: An exploratory study of the perceptions of rights holders of small-scale sporting events. *Journal of Convention & Event Tourism*, *13*(1), 1–15. doi:10.1080/15470148.2012.649580

Shukla, N., & Nuntsu, N. (2005). Event Marketing. In D. Tassiopoulos (Ed.), *Event Management* (2nd ed.). Juta Academic.

Silvestre, A. L., Santos, C. M., & Ramalho, C. (2008). Satisfaction and Behavioural Intentions of Cruise Passengers Visiting the Azores. *Tourism Economics*, *14*(1), 169–184. doi:10.5367/000000008783554802

Skoll, G. R., & Korstanje, M. E. (2014). Terrorism, homeland safety and event management. *International Journal of Hospitality and Event Management, 1*(1), 95–110. doi:10.1504/IJHEM.2014.062869

Slack, T., & Bentz, L. (1996). The involvement of small businesses in sport sponsorship. *Managing Leisure, 1*(3), 175–184. doi:10.1080/136067196376410

Slak Valek, N., Shaw, M., & Bednarik, J. (2014). Socio-demographic characteristics affecting sport tourism choices: A structural model. *Acta Gymnica, 44*(1), 57–65. doi:10.5507/ag.2014.006

Smith, A. (2012). *Events and urban regeneration: The strategic use of events to revitalise cities*. Routledge. doi:10.4324/9780203136997

Smith, A., & Stewart, B. (2007). The travelling fan: Understanding the mechanisms of sport fan consumption in a sport tourism setting. *Journal of Sport & Tourism, 12*(3), 155–181. doi:10.1080/14775080701736924

Smith, J. M., & Ingham, A. G. (2003). On the waterfront: Retrospectives on the relationship between sport and communities. *Sociology of Sport Journal, 20*(3), 252–274. doi:10.1123sj.20.3.252

Smith, S. (2009). Theorising the Relationship between Major Sport Events and Social Sustainability. *Journal of Sport & Tourism, 14*(2-3), 2–3, 109–120. doi:10.1080/14775080902965033

Smith, S. M. (2017). Organisational ambidexterity: Welcome to paradox city. *Human Resource Management International Digest, 25*(1), 1–3. doi:10.1108/HRMID-06-2016-0087

Sofia, G., & Chris, V. (2017). Blueprinting an event and tourist service marketing strategy: the case of the SMF Greek tourism small-scale sport event. In *Strategic Innovative Marketing* (pp. 19–24). Springer. doi:10.1007/978-3-319-33865-1_3

Soteriades, M. (2013). Events Sponsorhip: A framework for efficient management. *Wulfenia, 20*(10), 226–241.

Spivey, N. (2005). *The Ancient Olympics*. Oxford University Press.

Sport New Zealand. (2012). *New Zealand Government, Sport Sponsorship; Securing and retaining commercial partners*. Sport New Zealand.

Sport, U. K. (2004). *Measuring success 2: Thee economic impact of Major Sport Events*. UK Sports.

Stebbins, R. A. (1996). Volunteering: A serious leisure perspective. *Nonprofit and Voluntary Sector Quarterly, 25*(2), 211–224. doi:10.1177/0899764096252005

Stebbins, R. A. (2009). Would you volunteer? *Society, 46*(2), 155–159. doi:10.100712115-008-9186-1

Stukas, A. A., Snyder, M., & Clary, E. G. (2016). *Understanding and encouraging volunteerism and community involvement*. Academic Press.

Sun, Y. Y., Rodriguez, A., Wu, J. H., & Chuang, S. T. (2013). Why hotel rooms were not full during a hallmark sporting event: The 2009 World Games experience. *Tourism Management, 36*(June), 469–479. doi:10.1016/j.tourman.2012.09.011 PMID:32287741

Swart, K., George, R., Cassar, J., & Sneyd, C. (2016). The 2014 FIFA World Cup: Tourists' satisfaction levels and likelihood of repeat visitation to Rio de Janeiro. *Journal of Destination Marketing & Management*, (January), 1–12.

Szwarc, P. (2005). *Researching customer satisfaction & loyalty: How to find out what people really think*. Kogan Page.

Tarlow, P. (2014). *Tourism security: strategies for effectively managing travel risk and safety*. Elsevier.

Thompson, A. J., Martin, A. J., Gee, S., & Eagleman, A. N. (2014). Examining the Development of a Social Media Strategy for a National Sport Organisation. *Journal of Applied Sport Management, 6*(2).

Thomson, A., Cuskelly, G., Toohey, K., Kennelly, M., Burton, P., & Fredline, L. (2019). Sport event legacy: A systematic quantitative review of literature. *Sport Management Review, 22*(3), 295–321. doi:10.1016/j.smr.2018.06.011

Thorpe, H. (2017). Action Sports, Social Media, and New Technologies: Towards a Research Agenda. *Communication & Sport, 5*(5), 554–578. doi:10.1177/2167479516638125

Tiew, F., Holmes, K., & De Bussy, N. (2015). Tourism Events and the Nature of Stakeholder Power. *Event Management, 19*(4), 525–541. doi:10.3727/152599515X14465748512768

Tinnish, S. M., & Mangal, S. M. (2012, October). Sustainable event marketing in the MICE industry: A theoretical framework. *Journal of Convention & Event Tourism, 13*(4), 227–249. doi:10.1080/15470148.2012.731850

Toohey, K., & Veal, A. J. (2007). The Olympic Games: A social science perspective (2nd ed.). Wallingford, UK: CABI.

Treuren, G. J. (2014). Enthusiasts, conscripts or instrumentalists? The motivational profiles of event volunteers. *Managing Leisure, 19*(1), 51–70. doi:10.1080/13606719.2013.849506

Tribe, J. (2016). *The economics of recreation, leisure and tourism* (5th ed.). Routledge.

Tripodi, J. (2001). Sponsorship - A Confirmed Weapon in the Promotional Armoury. *International Journal of Sports Marketing & Sponsorship, 3*(1), 82–103. doi:10.1108/IJSMS-03-01-2001-B007

Tsang, E. W. K. (2014). Generalizing from Research Findings: The Merits of Case Studies. *International Journal of Management Reviews, 16*(4), 369–388. doi:10.1111/ijmr.12024

Tum, J., Norton, P., & Wright, J. N. (2011). *Management of Events Operations*. Elsevier.

Turco, D. M. (2010), Understanding the sport mega-event tourist: 2010 World Cup South Africa and implications for 2014 World Cup Brasil. *XI National Congress of Sports Management APOGESD*.

Turco, D. M., Riley, R. S., & Swart, K. (2002). *Sport tourism*. Fitness Information Technology.

Twynam, G. D., Farrell, J. M., & Johnston, M. E. (2002). Leisure and volunteer motivation at a special sporting event. *Leisure/Loisir, 27*(3-4), 363-377.

Tynan, C., & McKechnie, S. (2009). Experience marketing: A review and reassessment. *Journal of Marketing Management, 25*(5-6), 501–517. doi:10.1362/026725709X461821

Tyrrell, T. (2017). Revenue management. In L. L. Lowry (Ed.), *The SAGE international encyclopedia of travel and tourism* (pp. 1030–1034). Sage Publications.

Tzetzis, G., Alexandris, K., & Kapsampeli, S. (2014). Predicting visitors' satisfaction and behavioral intentions from service quality in the context of a small-scale outdoor sport event. *International Journal of Event and Festival Management, 5*(1), 4–21. doi:10.1108/IJEFM-04-2013-0006

Van Niekerk, M. (2017). Contemporary issues in events, festivals and destination management. *International Journal of Contemporary Hospitality Management.*

Vassiliadis, C. A., & Fotiadis, A. (2016). Managing Sport Tourism Experiences: Blueprinting Service Encounters. In The Handbook of Managing and Marketing Tourism Experiences (pp. 195-215). Emerald Group Publishing Limited.

Vassiliadis, C., & Fotiadis, A. (2014). *Conjoint analysis of sporting events: the case of Taiwan.* Paper presented at the 2nd International Conference on Contemporary Marketing Issues, Athens, Greece.

Vassiliadis, C., & Fotiadis, A. (2016). Managing Sport Tourism Experiences: Blueprinting Service Encounters. In M. Sotiriadis & D. Gursoy (Eds.), *The Handbook of Managing and Marketing Tourism Experiences* (pp. 195–215). Emerald Group Publishing Limited. doi:10.1108/978-1-78635-290-320161008

Veltri, F. R., Miller, J. J., & Harris, A. (2009). Club sport national tournament: Economic impact of a small event on a mid-size community. *Recreational Sports Journal, 33*(2), 119–128. doi:10.1123/rsj.33.2.119

Visser, W. (2015). *Sustainable Frontiers. Unlocking Change through Business, Leadership and Innovation.* Greenleaf Publishing.

Vives, A., Jacob, M., & Aguiló, E. (2018). Online hotel demand model and own-price elasticities: An empirical application in a mature resort destination. *Tourism Economics.* Advance online publication. doi:10.1177/1354816618800643

Vives, A., Jacob, M., & Payeras, M. (2018). Revenue management and price optimization techniques in the hotel sector: A critical literature review. *Tourism Economics, 24*(6), 720–752. doi:10.1177/1354816618777590

Walker, M. (2018). *Is Northern Ireland a football team or an expression of identity? What does the Northern Ireland team mean to Protestant community?* Retrieved March 30, 2019 from:https://www.irishtimes.com/sport/soccer/international/is-northern-ireland-a-football-team-or-an-expression-of-identity-1.3843260

Walker, M., Hall, T., Todd, S. Y., & Kent, A. (2011). Does your sponsor affect my perception of the event? The role of event sponsors as signals. *Sport Marketing Quarterly, 20*(3), 138–147.

Walliser, B. (2003). An international review of sponsorship research: Extension and update. *International Journal of Advertising, 22*(1), 5–40. doi:10.1080/02650487.2003.11072838

Wang, P. Z. (2004, January). Assessing motivations for sports volunteerism. In Conference of the Association-for-Consumer-Research (ACR 2003). Assoc Consumer Research.

Wang, D. (2004). Tourist Behaviour and Repeat Visitation to Hong Kong. *Tourism Geographies, 6*(1), 99–118. doi:10.1080/1461668032000172235[5]

Wankel, C., Marovich, M., & Stanaityte, J. (2010). *Cutting-edge social media approaches to business education.* Information Age Pub.

Warner, S. (2012). Sport and community. *Sociology of sport and physical activity*, 237-254.

Warner, S., & Dixon, M. A. (2011). Understanding sense of community from the athlete's perspective. *Journal of Sport Management, 25*(3), 257–271. doi:10.1123/jsm.25.3.257

Warner, S., Newland, B. L., & Green, B. C. (2011). More than motivation: Reconsidering volunteer management tools. *Journal of Sport Management, 25*(5), 391–407. doi:10.1123/jsm.25.5.391

Warnick, R. B., Bojanic, D. C., & Xu, F. (2015). Using a Trade Market Analysis Technique to Refine Measurements for Economic Impact Analysis of Special Events. *Journal of Travel Research, 54*(1), 52–65. doi:10.1177/0047287513513160

Watt, D. C. (1998). *Event management in leisure and tourism.* Addison Wesley Longman Ltd.

Weed, M., & Bull, C. (2004). Sports Tourism: Participants, Policy and Providers. Elsevier Butterworth, Heinemann.

Weed, M. (Ed.). (2007). *Sport & tourism: A reader.* Routledge. doi:10.4324/9780203937686

Wendel, M. L., Burdine, J. N., McLeroy, K. R., Alaniz, A., Norton, B., & Felix, M. R. (2009). Community capacity: theory and application. *Emerging Theories in Health Promotion Practice and Research, 277*, 302.

Wertz, S. (1991). *Talking a good game: inquiries into the principle of sports.* Southern Methodist University Press.

Whitson, D., & Horne, J. (2006). Underestimated Costs and Overestimated Benefits? Comparing the Outcomes of Sports Mega-Events in Canada and Japan. *The Sociological Review, 54*(2_suppl), 73–89. doi:10.1111/j.1467-954X.2006.00654.x

Wicker, P., Hallmann, K., & Zhang, J. J. (2012). What is influencing consumer expenditure and intention to revisit? An investigation of marathon events. *Journal of Sport & Tourism, 17*(3), 165–182. doi:10.1080/14775085.2012.734058

Wilson, R. (2006). The economic impact of local sport events: significant, limited or otherwise? A case study of four swimming events. *Managing Leisure, 11*(1), 57-70.

Wilson, R. (2006). The economic impact of local sport events: Significant, limited or otherwise? A case study of four swimming events. *Managing Leisure, 11*(1), 57–70. doi:10.1080/13606710500445718

Wohlfeil, M., & Whelan, S. (2006). Consumer motivations to participate in marketing-events: The role of predispositional involvement. *ACR European Advances, 7*, 125–131.

Xing, X., & Chalip, L. (2006). Effects of Hosting a Sport Event on Destination Brand: A Test of Co-branding and Match-up Models. *Sport Management Review, 9*(1), 49–78. doi:10.1016/S1441-3523(06)70019-5

Xu, R., & Pegg, S. (2007). Exploring the motivations for participant engagement in the Australian university games. *International Journal of Event Management Research, 3*(2), 39–46.

Yedikule.gr. (2019). Available at: https://www.yedikule.gr/

Yeoman, I. (2013). A futurist's thoughts on consumer trends shaping future festivals and events. *International Journal of Event and Festival Management, 4*(3), 249–260. doi:10.1108/IJEFM-06-2013-0017

Yin, R. K. (2014). Case Study Research: Design and Methods. Sage Publications.

Yoshioka, C. F., Brown, W. A., & Ashcraft, R. F. (2007). A functional approach to senior volunteer and non-volunteer motivations. *The International Journal of Volunteer Administration, 24*(5), 31-43.

Yuan, J., & Jang, S. (2008). The Effects of Quality and Satisfaction on Awareness and Behavioral Intentions: Exploring the Role of a Wine Festival. *Journal of Travel Research, 46*(3), 279–288. doi:10.1177/0047287507308322

Yürük Kayapınar, P. (2018). Etkinlik pazarlaması. In N. Altuğ & Ş. Özhan (Eds.), *Pazarlamada güncel gelişmeler* (pp. 261–286). Nobel Akademik.

Yusof, A., & Shah, P. M. (2007). An examination of tourist profiles and travel motivations of sport tourist attending an event in lake Kenyir, Malaysia. *Malaysian Journal of Sport Science and Recreation*, 53–68.

Zajc, P., & Berzelak, N. (2016). Riding styles and characteristics of rides among Slovenian mountain bikers and management challenges. *Journal of Outdoor Recreation and Tourism, 15*, 10–19. doi:10.1016/j.jort.2016.04.009

Zarantonello, L., & Schmitt, B. (2013). The impact of Event Marketing on Brand Equity: The mediating roles of Brand Experience and Brand Attitude. *International Journal of Advertising*, *32*(2), 5–40, 255–280. doi:10.2501/IJA-32-2-255-280

Zarei, A., & Yusof, A. B. I. N. (2014). Informational sources of sport tourists attending ISTAF super series. *Journal of Physical Education and Sport*, *14*(4), 554–561.

Ziakas, V. (2010). Understanding an event portfolio: The uncovering of interrelationships, synergies, and leveraging opportunities. *Journal of Policy Research in Tourism, Leisure & Events*, *2*(2), 144–164. doi:10.1080/19407963.2010.482274

About the Contributors

Anestis Fotiadis is a Full Professor of Tourism in the College of Communication and Media Sciences, Zayed University, UAE. His research focuses on event management, rural tourism and sustainable development. He has published more than 40 research papers in international academic journals such as Tourism Management and Journal of Business Research along with several books and book chapters. Anestis K. Fotiadis can be contacted at: Anestis.Fotiadis@zu.ac.ae.

Chris Vassiliadis constitutes member of the academic teaching and research staff of the Department of Business Administration of the University Macedonia in Thessaloniki, Greece. His research interests focus in the marketing of services and the management of tourist destinations. His research has been published in various journals, as, Journal of Targeting; Measurement and Analysis for Marketing, Tourismos: an International Multidisciplinary Journal of Tourism, Tourism and Hospitality Management, Journal of Tourism Management, Journal of Vacational Marketing, Journal of International Tourism Research, Journal of Hospitality & Leisure Marketing and the Journal of Tourism Analysis.

* * *

Anisah Abdul Wafi is a PhD student in Universiti Utara Malaysia, School of Tourism, Hospitality and Event Management, Malaysia. Her research interests include sports events, sports tourism, and event management.

Selena Aureli, PhD, is an Assistant Professor at Bologna University, Department of Management. She teaches Financial Reporting and Analysis to master students, Cost analysis and Managerial accounting to bachelor students. Her research interests span from performance measurement to alliance and network management, tourism and service industries.

Park Beede, PhD is an experienced educator in advertising and marketing. Starting an academic career in his native United States, Park has worked internationally in faculty and administrative roles throughout New Zealand, Australia and currently the United Arab Emirates. Specializing in advertising, research activities span topics in advertising, branding, and consumer behavior. In addition to academic roles, Park has held senior corporate roles in leading advertising agencies and consumer companies.

Lim Khong Chiu is an Associate Professor in Universiti Utara Malaysia, School of Tourism, Hospitality and Event Management, Malaysia. His research interests include physical and sport education, recreation and sport management, event management and sports tourism.

Giacomo Del Chiappa (PhD) is Associate Professor of Marketing at the Department of Economics and Business, University of Sassari (Italy), where he teaches Tourism Marketing and Management, Destination Management and Retail Marketing. He is also Senior Research Fellow at the School of Tourism & Hospitality of University of Johannesburg (South Africa), and co-chair of the Tourism, Culture and Arts Marketing SIG of the Italian Marketing Association. His research is related to destination governance and branding, sustainable tourism, consumer/tourist behavior, digital marketing and airport marketing. He is Associate Editor of European Journal of Tourism Research and member of numerous editorial boards of national and international scientific journals. He is author and co-author of numerous national and international publications. Among others, he has published in: Annals of Tourism Research, Journal of Service Management, Journal of Services Marketing, International Journal of Hospitality Management, Tourism Management, Journal of Travel Research, International Journal of Tourism Research, International Journal of Contemporary and Hospitality Management, Current Issues in Tourism, Journal of Hospitality Marketing and Management, Tourism Management Perspectives, Journal of Destination Marketing and Management, Journal of Travel & Tourism Marketing, Journal of Airport Transport Management.

Giovanna Del Gaudio is a PhD in Business Administration at Federico II University of Naples. Her research focuses on tourism destinations, value creation and value capture with the applications of the resource-based view in interconnected tourism industry. Her research bridges the strategic management, corporate strategy and marketing literatures in studying the emerging phenomenon of firms in the tourism field. She is author of a book, of some book chapters and articles published on national and international journals and she has attended several national and international conferences.

Valentina Della Corte is Full Professor of Business Management at Federico II University of Naples. She teaches Tourism Business Management, Strategic Management and Marketing Policies and Management of Cultural Heritage. She is the academic coordinator of the hospitality management degree course and member of the industry 4.0 task force. Author of numerous publications in national and international academic journals such as Tourism Management, European Journal of Innovation Management, Corporate Ownership & Control, International Journal of Business and Management, Mercati e competitività, International Journal of Quality and Service Sciences, International Journal of Leisure and Tourism Marketing, International Journal of Marketing Studies, Journal of Management and Sustainability. Author of books published by Egea, CEDAM and Giappichelli as well as of chapters in books edited by Elgar and Mc Graw Hill. She has participated, also as chair and reviewer, to national and international conferences such as Strategic Management Society Annual Meeting, Academy of Management Annual Meeting, Italian Academy of Management Annual Meeting, International Forum of Knowledge Asset Dynamic, International Conference on Tourism (ICOT), International Marketing Trends Conference, Forum on Marketing and Markets, AIDEA Annual Meeting and Sinergie Annual Meeting. Her research is focused on strategic management and marketing and in particular resource-based theory, business networks and coopetition, dynamic capabilities, value creation and appropriation both intra-firm and inter-firm, innovative marketing in tourism and heritages.

Sofia Gkarane is a PhD Candidate in the Department of Business Administration at University of Macedonia. She holds a Master in Business Administration and a Bachelor Degree in International Economics from University of Macedonia. Her research interests include small-scale event management, seasonality, sports marketing and international marketing. She has presented her work at a number of international academic conferences. She is currently Export Director at KYANA Professional Hair Care Company, which exports its products in 20 countries around the world (including Asia, Balkan, Europe and Middle East).

Hermann Graziano is an Adjunct Professor of Corporate Strategy at the Department of Management of Bologna University. Teacher of Marketing at the Department for Life Quality Studies of Bologna University.

Johan Afendi Ibrahim is a Senior Lecturer in Universiti Utara Malaysia, School of Tourism, Hospitality and Event Management, Malaysia. His research interests include tourism planning and development, urban and regional planning and geographic tourism.

Maximiliano E. Korstanje is a leading global cultural theorist specializing in terrorism, mobilities and tourism. Korstanje serves as a Senior Researcher at the University of Palermo, Buenos Aires, Argentina, (economics department) and as an Editor in Chief of International Journal of Safety and Security in Tourism and Hospitality (University of Palermo, Argentina). He has acted as a visiting professor at CERS (Centre for Ethnicity and Racism Studies) at the University of Leeds (United Kingdom), TIDES in the University of Las Palmas de Gran Canarias (Spain) and the University of La Habana (Cuba). In 2016, he was included as Scientific Editor for Studies and Perspective in Tourism (CIET) and as an honorary member of the Scientific Council of Research and Investigation hosted by UDET (University of Tourist Specialities, Quito Ecuador). With more than 1200 publications and 30 books, Korstanje is an editor of the Book Series Advances in Hospitality, Tourism and Service Industries (IGI Global, US) and Tourism Security-Safety and Post Conflict Destinations (Emerald Group Publishing, UK). He is elected as a foreign faculty member of the Mexican Academy of Tourism Research (Mexico) as well as a foreign member of The Tourism Crisis Management Institute (University of Florida, US). In 2018, his biography was selected to be part of the roster of Alfred Nelson Marquis Lifetime Achievement Award (Marquis Who`s Who). Korstanje has been awarded as Editor in Chief Emeritus for the International Journal of Cyber-warfare and Terrorism. Currently he works as an active advisor and reviewer of different editorial projects at the leading academic publishers such as Elsevier, Routledge, Emerald Group Publishing, Palgrave Macmillan, Cambridge Scholar Publishing, Edward Elgar, CABI, Nova Science Publishers and IGI global among others. His latest book is The Challenges of Democracy in the War on Terror (Routledge UK).

Ludovico Marinò is full professor in Business Administration at the Department of Economics and Business of University of Sassari, Italy. He is currently the dean of the Department of Economics and Business of University of Sassari, Italy. His research interests include health care management, quasi-market competition in public sector, performance measurement and higher education.

Claudel Mombeuil is a former assistant professor at Université Quisqueya. He has several years of experience working for NGOs in Haiti as a project manager. He has also worked for Yunus Social Business and Centre d'Entrepreneuriat et d'Innovation of Université Quisqueya as Business Consultant. He received his bachelor's degree in Business Administration from Université d'Etat d'Haiti (Haiti) and his MBA degree from I-Shou University (Taiwan) and has completed the requirements of the Ph.D. degree in management at Beijing Institute of Technology (China). He is particularly interested in interdisciplinary in the field of management with the main focus on corporate social responsibility, sustainable entrepreneurship, and usage and adoption of information technologies. His publications appeared in the Journal of Cleaner Production, Social Responsibility Journal, Journal of Retailing and Consumer Services, and Journal of Tourism, Heritage & Services Marketing. His book chapter(s) appeared in Emerald Publishing Limited.

Giuliana Nevola is a Ph.D. student in Management at University of Naples Federico II. She has a Master of Science in Tourism Management and a Master n Development Economics and International Cooperation at University of Tor Vergata in Rome. During her academic years, her studies were focused on Ethical Finance and Welfare policies applied on Tourism Sector. Her research topic is focused on Strategic Tourism Management and Sustainability.

Gianfranco Pischedda obtained his PhD in Business Administration at the doctoral school of University of Cagliari in partnership with University of Sassari, Italy. He was a PhD visiting student at the Center for Higher Education Policy Studies – University of Twente, The Netherlands. Currently, he has a scholarship at the Department of Economics and Business of University of Sassari, Italy, and his research interests include public management, performance measurement, health care management, and higher education.

Hugues Séraphin is a Senior Lecturer in Event and Tourism Management Studies. He is also an associate research at La Rochelle Business School (France). Hugues Seraphin holds a PhD from the Université de Perpignan Via Domitia (France) and joined The University of Winchester Business School in 2012. He was the Programme Leader of the Event Management programme between 2015 and 2018. Dr Hugues Seraphin has expertise and interests in tourism development and management in post-colonial, post-conflict and post-disaster destinations. He has recently published in International Journal of Culture, Tourism, and Hospitality Research; Current Issues in Tourism; Journal of Policy Research in Tourism, Leisure and Events; Journal of Business Research; Worldwide Hospitality and Tourism Themes; Tourism Analysis; and Journal of Destination Marketing & Management.

Jason Skoulas is a PhD candidate at the Department of Organization and Business Administration of the University of Macedonia. Mr. Skoulas' research interests are the following: They focus on the study and examination of the social marketing, the welfare state, the social economy as well as the civil society, the historical development of the economy in general internationally and its relationship with other institutions regarding the course of the financial credit system. Particular emphasis is given on the ethics of the business operation and the contribution of social marketing to changing consumer behavior as well as the communication of citizens to collective social goals that benefit society as a whole. His interests are also on the function and role of the sports management and organization at both in the competitive and coaching fields as well as in the administration field.

Pınar Yürük-Kayapinar is working as Assistant Professor in the departman of Public Relations and Advertising, Uzunköprü School of Applied Sciences at Trakya University. Her research interests are consumer behavior at contemporary marketing approach, marketing research, event marketing.

Index

I

L

M

P

R

S

T

V

W

www.ingramcontent.com/pod-product-compliance
Lightning Source LLC
LaVergne TN
LVHW061541290926
849162LV00004B/867